BIBLICAL
THEOLOGY

Retrospect and Prospect

Edited by Scott J. Hafemann

InterVarsity Press
Downers Grove, Illinois

Apollos
Leicester, England

InterVarsity Press
P.O. Box 1400, Downers Grove, IL 60515-1426
World Wide Web: www.ivpress.com
E-mail: mail@ivpress.com

APOLLOS (an imprint of Inter-Varsity Press, England)
38 De Montfort Street, Leicester LE1 7GP, England
Website: www.ivpbooks.com
E-mail: ivp@uccf.org.uk

InterVarsity Press®, U.S.A., is the book-publishing division of InterVarsity Christian Fellowship/USA®, a student movement active on campus at hundreds of universities, colleges and schools of nursing in the United States of America, and a member movement of the International Fellowship of Evangelical Students. For information about local and regional activities, write Public Relations Dept., InterVarsity Christian Fellowship/USA, 6400 Schroeder Rd., P.O. Box 7895, Madison, WI 53707-7895, or visit the IVCF website at <www.ivcf.org>.

Cover illustration: Les Szurkowski/Graphistock

USA ISBN 0-8308-2684-X
UK ISBN 0-85111-279-X

Printed in the United States of America ∞

Library of Congress Cataloging-in-Publication Data

Biblical theology: retrospect and prospect/edited by Scott J. Hafemann.
   p. cm.
Includes bibliographical references and indexes.
  ISBN 0-8308-2684-X (pbk.: alk. paper)
  1. Bible—Theology. I. Hafemann, Scott J.
  BS543 .B524 2002
  230'.041—dc21

                      2002009247

British Library Cataloguing in Publication Data
A catalogue record for this book is available from the British Library.

P	20	19	18	17	16	15	14	13	12	11	10	9	8	7	6	5	4	3	2	1
Y	18	17	16	15	14	13	12	11	10	09	08	07	06	05	04	03	02			

TO PROF. DR. DANIEL P. FULLER

a biblical theologian who

taught his students to

"stare at the fish" and

to go where the

text leads

CONTENTS

List of Abbreviations

General

ET	English translation
Exod. Rab.	*Exodus Rabbah*
LXX	Septuagint
Midr. Ps.	*Midrash on Psalms*
n.s.	new series
NT	New Testament
OT	Old Testament
par.	parallel(s)
y. Kil.	Jerusalem Talmud *Kilʾayim*

Reference works, journals, series

AGJU	Arbeiten zur Geschichte des antiken Judentums und des Urchristentums
ANTJ	Arbeiten zum Neuen Testament und Judentum
BibSac	*Bibliotheca Sacra*
BJRL	*Bulletin of the John Rylands University Library*
BZ	*Biblische Zeitschrift*
BZAW	Beinefte zur Zeitschrift für die alttestamentliche Wissenschaft
BZNW	Beihefte zur Zeitschrift für die neutestamentliche Wissenschaft und die Kunde der älteren Kirche
CBQ	*Catholic Biblical Quarterly*
EvQ	*Evangelical Quarterly*
FAT	Forschungen zum Alten Testament
HorBT	*Horizons in Biblical Theology*
HSM	Harvard Semitic Monographs
ICC	International Critical Commentary
IEJ	*Israel Exploration Journal*
Interp	*Interpretation*
JBL	*Journal of Biblical Literature*
JETS	*Journal of the Evangelical Theological Society*

JJS	*Journal of Jewish Studies*
JSJSup	Journal for the Study of Judaism Supplement Series
JSNT	*Journal for the Study of the New Testament*
JSNTSup	Journal for the Study of the New Testament Supplement Series
JSOT	*Journal for the Study of the Old Testament*
JSOTSup	Journal for the Study of the Old Testament Supplement Series
JTS	*Journal of Theological Studies*
NICOT	New International Commentary on the Old Testament
NIDOTTE	*New International Dictionary of Old Testament Theology and Exegesis*
NSBT	New Studies in Biblical Theology
NTS	*New Testament Studies*
NTTS	New Testament Tools and Studies
OTL	Old Testament Library
SBL	Society for Biblical Literature
SBLDS	Society for Biblical Literature Dissertation Series
SBT	Studies in Biblical Theology
SEAD	Society for Ecumenical Anglican Doctrine
SJT	*Scottish Journal of Theology*
STDJ	Studies on the Texts of the Desert of Judah
ThB	*Theologishe Beiträge*
TRE	*Theologische Realenzyklopädie*
TynB	*Tyndale Bulletin*
WBC	Word Bible Commentary
WThJ	*Westminster Theological Journal*
WUNT	Wissenschaftliche Untersuchungen zum Neuen Testament
ZAW	*Zeitschrift für die alttestamentliche Wissenschaft*
ZNW	*Zeitschrift für die neutestamentliche Wissenschaft*
ZTK	*Zeitschrift für Theologie und Kirche*

Acknowledgments

This book is the result of the hard work of many people, for whom scholarship and its support is their ministry for Christ and his kingdom. I am indebted to Dennis Okholm and Tim Phillips, who graciously allowed me to dedicate the Wheaton Theology Conference of 2000 to the task of biblical theology, gave me a free hand in organizing it, and with their expertise and willingness to pitch in helped me through the logistics. The Wheaton Theology Conference was their vision, and it is with gratitude to God that we remember that the conference of 2000 was the last Tim attended before the Lord took him home. Of the many who worked to make the conference happen, three more deserve special mention. Richard Schultz lent a helpful hand in putting the program together. As she has done for years, Cindy Ingrum gave herself tirelessly and without complaint (!) to organizing the details of the conference. And Todd Wilson came along at the end to help with formatting and proofing the essays—his willingness to give of himself and his enthusiasm for and growing expertise in biblical theology are a great encouragement. The prospect of biblical theology is in the minds and hearts of gifted and faithful students like Todd.

As always, the donors who have established the Gerald F. Hawthorne Chair of New Testament Greek and Exegesis played a major role in making this conference and volume possible; I would not have had the time or resources to do it without them. Many thanks also to InterVarsity Press, especially Bob Fryling and Jim Hoover, for their ongoing cosponsorship of the conference and support for this project. It continues to mean so much to us. And to Debara: you have been there again; thanks for your support in the late nights and filled weekends. Your constant joy at learning something new is infectious.

The conference in 2000 allowed me to gather together teachers, colleagues and friends (thanks, Paul, for your advice!) from around the world. Having them at Wheaton to discuss these important matters was the fulfillment of a dream. And in many ways, this conference represents the ongoing fruit of the impetus, methodology and framework for the doing of biblical theology that I have gained through the years from one of my most formative teachers, Professor Daniel P. Fuller. Hardly a week goes by that I do not share with my students an insight I have learned from him. It is therefore a great honor and act of praise to God to dedicate this book to him. May his dedication to the Scriptures and commitment to Berean exegesis be replicated in the century to come.

1

Biblical Theology

Retrospect and Prospect

Scott J. Hafemann

O n April 6-8, 2000, the ninth annual Wheaton Theology Conference brought together a mix of younger and senior scholars from inside and outside of evangelicalism to think together about the history and future of biblical theology. This book represents some of the fruit of this labor.

In the essays that follow, there is a lively and serious discussion concerning the contours of biblical theology. Nevertheless, all are convinced that although the biblical theology movement of the mid-twentieth century ran its course, biblical theology as such is not a movement. Indeed, as James Smart observed, to call biblical theology a "movement" in the first place was "the kiss of death."[1] Movements are temporary answers to abiding issues. Thus, by definition, movements come and go.

In stark contrast, biblical theology is an abiding response demanded by the subject matter of the biblical text itself. At the descriptive level, biblical theology recognizes that the authors and editors of the biblical texts understood themselves to be preserving and interpreting the significance

---

[1]James D. Smart, *The Past, the Present and Future of Biblical Theology* (Philadelphia: Westminster Press, 1979), p. 10.

of God's redemptive acts in the history of Israel, Jesus and the church. At the prescriptive level, biblical theology will and must last as long as the Bible is held to be God's Word about himself and his relationship to his creation. The Bible is not merely a witness to revelatory events or theological ideas but is itself an expression of theological activity and affirmation. To do biblical theology is to go where the Bible leads us, since the Scriptures are a record of historical events interpreted in terms of their theological significance. Thus biblical theology "is an enlargement of the dimensions of biblical science to make its character and methodology commensurate with the contents of the documents which it is its task to interpret."[2] As a result, biblical theology attempts to ascertain the inner points of coherence and development within the biblical narrative and exposition. It does its work inductively from within the Bible in an attempt to bring out the Bible's own message.

It is well known, however, that students of biblical theology disagree over its methodology, not to mention its structure and content. In view of this diversity, the purpose of this collection of essays is to look at the way in which biblical theology has been done in the last century in order to think about how it ought to be done in the next. This retrospect and prospect have made it clear that several salient issues now confront all those who desire to follow the biblical text wherever it may lead them theologically.

BIBLICAL THEOLOGY AND THE QUESTION OF DIVERSITY
Several of the studies (and much of the discussion at the conference) are a response to the fact that the diversity of Scripture preserves within its pages unresolved tensions. In the past, biblical theologies have taken this tension to be the remains of competing ideological viewpoints that have been imperfectly combined in the historical development of Scripture. Hence, as Gerald Wilson points out, the tension was often neutralized by trying to ascertain the best among many voices or by allowing the diversity to stand "as unresolved heterodoxy."

Neither option, however, is acceptable. In what follows, we will be challenged to consider whether the unity of Scripture consists in living in the midst of its (apparent?) tensions as poles on a spectrum, as mutually interpretive lenses in a prism, or as the expression of an enlarging

---

[2]Ibid., p. 11.

history of redemption. We will also be called to think through whether Scripture presents a collage of theological loci or one overarching and integrated center. The fact that no consensus has been reached concerning the theological heart of the Bible makes these questions all the more pertinent, albeit daunting, especially when we take seriously the task of integrating every corner of the canon into our biblical theology, from the Wisdom literature to the Johannine literature and James. Readers will be spurred on in this task by the creative, integrative work presented in the essays that follow by those in the earlier stages of their scholarly careers and by the seasoned reflections of Professors Dumbrell, Sailhamer, Wilson and Stuhlmacher.

The volume before us makes clear that a compelling biblical theology must speak with a cohesive voice concerning God and his covenant relationship with his people in order to address God's people about their Creator, Sustainer, Redeemer and Judge. At the same time, the historical framework posited by the Scriptures must be taken into consideration, since God has revealed himself as King in the history of Israel and in the kingdom of the crucified Messiah. To that end, Daniel Fuller and James Scott remind us that we cannot avoid raising anew the age-old questions of the law-gospel contrast on the one hand and of the roles of Israel and the church in redemptive history on the other. When all is said and done, are there two or more fundamental messages and peoples of God in the Bible or one? How this question is answered determines one's understanding of the history of redemption, personal justification and eschatology, which together lie at the heart of biblical revelation.

BIBLICAL THEOLOGY AND THE QUESTION OF THE CANON

The essays in this book and the passionate disagreement during the conference also call attention to the fact that biblical theology cannot make substantial progress in the decades to come unless it takes up the questions being raised in biblical scholarship concerning the literary unity and structure of the canon. Does the fact of the canon bespeak its own perceived unity theologically, thereby offering essential clues to its structure and meaning? If so, which canon and how? The programmatic work of Brevard Childs on the one hand and the Tübingen school on the other makes it clear that the Bible's theology cannot be developed in the abstract as if the canon in its *various* forms (!) and the history of its traditions do not exist.[3] If context is king when it comes to theological exegesis, we cannot escape the fact that the context of Scripture also includes its developing canonical shape as the depository of tradition history. This becomes equally true for the NT, if in fact the NT writings did not come into existence in isolation from one another and if the NT canon is the product of an early editorial design rather than of a long, slow process of collection and evaluation.[4]

However, biblical theology is just now coming to grips with the complexity and intentionality of the formation of the canon(s). This is illustrated by the questions and proposals raised concerning the tripartite Hebrew/OT canon and its significance for the doing of biblical theology in a world dominated by the Septuagint's influence on the ordering of the Christian Bible. Does the Tanak in its final form exhibit an explicit, editorial canon consciousness that provides exegetical and theological clues to its meaning? Does the Hebrew canon help us solve the problem of the interrelationship among the Law, the Prophets and the Writings? In pursuing these questions, we must be clear regarding the historical reconstructions and exegetical methodology that we bring to bear in answering them, especially as they revolve around the so-called canonical seams and programmatic conclusions within the OT.

At the same time, the conference brought home to many the pivotal question of whether the OT canon was closed prior to the coming of the Christ, so that in the doing of biblical theology we are faced with two distinct Testaments (see especially the essay by Christopher Seitz). Or was the content of the canon still open in the first century A.D., with the formation of the NT as the literary and theological-historical continuation of Israel's ongoing heritage, so that biblical theology is the study of one "history of tradition"? And what is the significance of the fact that there is no one, unified ordering of the books within the Hebrew or Septuagint tradition, not to mention the differences between the Masoretic Text and the Septuagint themselves? At what stage in the formation of the biblical canon do we do

---

[3]See now the mature work of Brevard S. Childs, *Biblical Theology of the Old and New Testaments: Theological Reflection on the Christian Bible* (Minneapolis: Fortress, 1992), and Peter Stuhlmacher, *Biblische Theologie des Neuen Testaments*, 2 vols. (Göttingen: Vandenhoeck & Ruprecht, 1992, 1999).

[4]For the first point, now argued in regard to the Gospels, see Richard Bauckham, ed., *The Gospels for All Christians: Rethinking the Gospel Audiences* (Grand Rapids, Mich.: Eerdmans, 1998), and for the latter, see David Trobisch, *The First Edition of the New Testament* (Oxford: Oxford University Press, 2000).

our biblical theology? These are difficult and pressing questions that biblical theology cannot relegate to the province of historical studies.

BIBLICAL THEOLOGY AND THE QUESTION OF CONFLICT

The work in this volume on the unity of the canon and its theological trajectories reveals that there is a strong impetus to overcome the conflict theories that have dominated biblical theology in the past. In order to remain faithful to the message of the biblical text, this volume encourages us to rethink the dichotomies so often posited in the past between the Law and the Prophets, priest and prophet, Jesus and Paul, creation and redemption, the kingdom of God and the church, as well as the interrelated theological systems of covenant theology and dispensationalism that have grown out of them.[5] The attempt to forge a historical and theological unity out of two conflicting realities, in which one must be sublimated to the other, is seriously being called into question in view of a renewed emphasis on the material unity of the Bible's message. This growing concern for a "unity paradigm" in the doing of biblical theology is seen in John Sailhamer's emphasis on the eschatological drive behind the canon; in G. K. Beale's understanding of the new creation as central to biblical theology; in the work of Brian Toews, Richard Schultz, Stephen Dempster and William Dumbrell on the Genesis foundation for biblical theology; in Jay Wells's work on figuration throughout the Old and New Testaments; in Gerald Wilson's emphasis on the Davidic cast to the psalms, confirmed by Dempster's view of the Davidic lens to the canon as a whole; in James Scott's focus on the fulfillment of Israel's hopes for restoration as central to Jesus' ministry and therefore foundational for the NT; in Andreas Köstenberger's emphasis on the integrative motifs of the NT; in Ted Dorman's call to the centrality of the history of redemption as fundamental for understanding the development of biblical theology; and in Stephen Fowl's and Nicholas Perrin's treatments of the overarching hermeneutical issues that confront us in working toward the unity of the Scriptures.

Essential to the doing of biblical theology in the decades to come, therefore, will be a threefold project of (1) mapping out the content of the biblical witness; (2) working on the development of this content throughout

---

[5]On the interrelationship of covenant theology and dispensationalism, see Stephen R. Spencer, "Reformed Theology, Covenant Theology and Dispensationalism," in *Integrity of Heart, Skillfulness of Hands: Biblical and Leadership Studies in Honor of Donald K. Campbell,* ed. Charles H. Dyer and Roy B. Zuck (Grand Rapids, Mich.: Baker, 1994), pp. 238-54.

the biblical canon, especially as this comes to the surface in the OT's use of earlier OT traditions and in the NT's use of the OT; and (3) striving to describe in ever greater scope a pan-biblical theology that incorporates the OT and NT into an integrated whole in which the questions of the Bible's unity and center are pursued in tandem, without sacrificing one for the other. To this end, Paul House provides a program for future studies, while Graeme Goldsworthy holds us accountable to the fact that the focus of our scholarly endeavor is not merely a collection of religious documents from the ancient world but the Word of God, the life-source for God's people.[6] In all of this, the text must remain the focus of our attention, not reconstructions of a supposed "history" behind or in front of the text or abstract formulations of a supposed "essence" of the text that locates theology in the religious experience of humanity rather than in the self-revelation of God in time and space. In speaking about the unity of the Bible we should not resort to abstract themes but to concrete biblical statements about what God has done to reveal himself and to redeem his people. The experiences and example of my own doctor-father, Peter Stuhlmacher, outlined in the essay below, have been paradigmatic in this regard.

LOOKING FORWARD

In working toward a pan-biblical theology that is focused on the Scriptures, we must not assume, however, that the unity of the Bible means reducing the biblical witness to that general proposition that is found to some degree in every book of the Bible. This presupposes that every writing must be viewed independently, as if it were not part of an ongoing revelation in response to an ongoing history of redemption. For there to be unity within the Bible, every corner of the canon need not repeat the main theme of every other corner (e.g., Wisdom literature must not rehearse the exodus; the covenant need not be rehearsed explicitly for it to be fundamental to the Prophets; Paul must not quote Jesus extensively; and Hebrews need not mention the kingdom of God to be part of the NT witness concerning the Christ!). Unexpressed presuppositions are no less central for being unexpressed. For as Robert Yarbrough made clear during the conference, the predicted demise of "revelation in history" has been premature. Moreover, its rejection of liberalism's optimistic evolutionary the-

---

[6]For my own attempt to do biblical theology for the church, see Scott J. Hafemann, *The God of Promise and the Life of Faith: Understanding the Heart of the Bible* (Wheaton, Ill.: Crossway, 2001).

ories and its stress on revelation as propositional truths still stand as a needed corrective to the attempt to abstract biblical theology from its historical contexts.[7]

Furthermore, the focus of this pan-biblical theology must be on the first and second comings of the Christ as the midpoint and end point of redemptive history. The goal of this redemption is the consummation of the new creation as the expression of the kingdom of God already inaugurated in the life, death, resurrection and ascension of Christ and in the consequent pouring out of the Spirit as a down payment of the future. At the same time, this eschatologically driven history of redemption must be filled with the developing covenantal relationship between God and his people that Scripture testifies is initiated at creation, maintained throughout Israel's history, and fulfilled in the Messiah's establishment of the new covenant (Jer 31:31-34; Ezek 36:22-31; Lk 22:17-20; 1 Cor 11:23-26; 2 Cor 3:3-6; Heb 8:1-13; 9:15; 12:24).

The key question in theology is the relationship between theology and history. In making our contribution to the theology of the church, we must not divorce revelation from history or give biblical theology any other object to study apart from the Scriptures as the deposit of that revelation. To do so will transform biblical theology into an open category that, confronted with the seemingly irreconcilable diversity of the Bible, will be filled with the experience of the church, formulated in its creeds and confessions, or with the experience of the individual, formulated in psychological or sociological or ideological categories. The biblical theology movement of the mid-twentieth century imploded precisely because, in the end, it located revelation in the divine encounter and separated the final object of theology from the biblical text.[8] In presenting this volume, it is therefore my honor to invite you to think along with its contributors concerning the theological dimension of the Bible. Doing so will challenge us to ask again for our century what it means that, in accordance with the Scriptures and in the Scriptures, God has revealed himself in space and time, for all ages.

---

[7]Robert Yarbrough, "James Barr and the Future of Revelation in History in New Testament Theology," Wheaton Theology Conference, 2000.

[8]For an analysis of this attempt to steer a course between fundamentalism and liberalism, see Brevard S. Childs, *Biblical Theology in Crisis* (Philadelphia: Westminster Press, 1970).

PART ONE

THE QUESTION OF
THE "OLD TESTAMENT"

*The Foundation
of Biblical Theology*

2

Biblical Theology and the Composition of the Hebrew Bible

John H. Sailhamer

In recent years OT studies have seen many changes. Hardly an area is untouched by new approaches and new perspectives. If there is a common theme, it is the shift from a focus on the earliest stages of the biblical text to that of its final shape. Already a major work on the theology of the Tanak[1] has been published by a leading biblical scholar, Rolf Rendtorff.[2] The results, in my opinion, are impressive and exciting.

Amid the many aspects of a theology of the final shape of the Hebrew Bible, one important question stands out: What prospects remain for a biblical theology that includes the Tanak and the NT? Can a theology of the Tanak be written as part of a biblical theology? Is there an exegetically warranted unity between the Hebrew Bible and the NT?

A DEFINITION OF THE FINAL SHAPE OF THE OLD TESTAMENT

What I understand as the final shape of the OT is *the compositional and ca-*

---

[1]The Tanak is the rabbinical name given to the Hebrew OT, the Law (Ta = *Torah*), the Prophets (na = *Nebi'im*) and the Writings (k = *Ketubim*). It is the same OT as in the Christian Bible, but the order of the individual books is different. The term is used in this chapter to refer to the OT canon and the order of its books at the time of Christ.

[2]Rolf Rendtorff, *Theologie des Alten Testaments: Ein kanonischer Entwurf* (Neukirchen Vluyn: Neukirchener Verlag, 1999).

nonical state of the Hebrew Bible at the time it became part of an established com-munity. By "compositional and canonical" I mean how an author put a book together and how it was attached to a collection of books. The idea of its being a "part of a community" is what I would call consolidation. The notion of consolidation is an attempt to respond to recent observations about the nature of texts. Communities like Judaism and Christianity, for example, derive their essential identity from texts. Yet the biblical texts often receive their final shape from those same communities. Communities endorse and impose canonical restrictions on their foundational texts. However, the consolidation of OT texts includes elements of composition as well as canonization. Communities not only produce canonical texts; they also create new texts. They do so, I would suggest, by producing the real-life authors of those texts.

PROBLEMS OF BIBLICAL THEOLOGY

There are many well-known problems and issues associated with biblical theology. Since the focus in this essay is on a biblical theology of the final shape of the Hebrew Bible, two problems that directly relate to it must be raised.

The first problem is the need for a text model. A text model is a description of the formation of the Hebrew Bible that adequately explains its present shape. This is what Wolfgang Richter has called a "Theory of Literature."[3] If we are going to talk about the final shape of the Hebrew Bible, we had better have some idea of how it arrived at that shape and how that shape changed over time. All biblical studies work with such theories, whether consciously or not. Our aim is to develop such a model consciously and to do so along lines that are consistent with an evangelical view of Scripture.

The second problem is the need to relate that shape to the NT. We will return to that problem later. At the moment let us first turn to a description of a text model of the OT.

A TEXT MODEL OF THE OLD TESTAMENT

The text model, or general understanding of the text proposed here, is drawn directly from my understanding of the nature of the final shape of

---

[3]Wolfgang Richter, *Exegese als Literatur Wissenschaft, Entwurf einer Alttestamentlichen Literatur Theorie und Methodologie* (Göttingen: Vandenhoeck & Ruprecht, 1971).

the Hebrew Bible. In the definition of the final shape mentioned above, there are three central components:

1. the notion of the composition of a specific biblical text
2. the notion of the canonical shaping of biblical texts and its influence on communities
3. the notion of the consolidation of a text within a specific community

Our text model thus views the biblical text at the point of intersection of these three coordinates: its composition, its canonization and its consolidation within a community.

Composition. The model proposed here takes seriously the notion that biblical texts have authors and that the meaning of authors can be discovered by reading their texts. The notion of authorship also represents a decisive moment in the history of a text. In this way of thinking about the final shape, composition is viewed neither in terms of a dynamic process nor a rigid status quo. The composition of a biblical book, like any other book, represents a creative and decisive moment in the history of the text.

The phenomenon of the two texts of Jeremiah offers a helpful example. It is fairly clear from comparing the Masoretic Text and the Septuagint that the book of Jeremiah comes to us in two final shapes. Both shapes appear destined for quite different communities.[4]

In Jeremiah 27:16, for example, the prophet Jeremiah confronts the false prophets. The message of the false prophets was that Judah's troubles would not last much longer. Relief was in sight. The temple vessels that had been taken to Babylon would soon be returned.

Jeremiah, however, offered another word. The captivity would *not* soon be over. There would be seventy years of captivity before the vessels were returned. Jeremiah thus proclaimed, "Do not listen to the words of your prophets who are prophesying to you, saying, 'Behold, the vessels of the LORD's house will *now shortly* be brought back from Babylon,' for it is a lie which they are prophesying to you" (author's translation [throughout the essay]).

A glance in the apparatus of *Biblia Hebraica* shows that the words "now shortly" were not in the Septuagint and also probably not in the Hebrew manuscript used by the translator.[5] In that text the false prophets affirm that

---

[4]See Emanuel Tov, *Text Criticism in the Hebrew Bible* (Minneapolis: Fortress, 1992), pp. 320-21, and Eugene Ulrich, *The Dead Sea Scrolls and the Origins of the Bible* (Grand Rapids, Mich.: Eerdmans, 1999), p. 69.
[5]Tov, *Text Criticism*, p. 320.

the vessels of the Lord's house will be brought back from Babylon. There is no mention of "shortly." Since that eventually happened, the false prophets appear to speak the truth! How could they be false prophets if their words came true? In the Masoretic Text, the false prophets say that the temple vessels would be returned *shortly*—which, of course, did not happen.

This is not a serious exegetical problem. Within the context, the false prophets clearly meant the vessels would be returned shortly. They were not thinking of Jeremiah's seventy years. If this were a mere text-critical problem, we would and should say the Masoretic Text offers a longer and therefore secondary text. It is a gloss of a scribe who wanted to supply a helpful comment. Thus the Septuagint represents the more original text.

The larger question, however, is what we make of this gloss in light of the composition of the book of Jeremiah. Is this an isolated textual gloss, or is it the work of an author? To address that question, two additional observations are necessary. First, this gloss is part of many similar glosses in Jeremiah that seem to fill in for the reader numerous historical details. This has led some scholars to suggest that the two versions of Jeremiah represent a preexilic and a postexilic edition of the book. That in fact may be the case, but if it is, it is not the whole story. To see the whole story one must take a closer look at the interpretations of Jeremiah's words reflected in these two texts. That leads to the second observation. These two versions of the book of Jeremiah both survived the exile and were thus a part of the canon of two distinct postexilic communities.

When we take the other textual variants into consideration, it becomes apparent that the community represented by the Masoretic Text had focused Jeremiah's prophecies on the events of the return from Babylonian captivity. When, in some texts, Jeremiah merely speaks of a people "from the north," the Masoretic Text identifies them as Babylon and king Nebuchadnezzar.[6]

In the text of the Septuagint, however, Jeremiah's words are not tied to specific historical events, in spite of the fact that the edition continued for several hundred years as a part of the canon in its community. The implication appears obvious. Even after the exile, this community seemed little

---

[6]William McKane, *A Critical and Exegetical Commentary on Jeremiah*, ICC (Edinburgh: T & T Clark, 1986), p. xxi: "The intention of the exegetical expansions in MT is to identify Judah's enemy with Babylon and, more particularly, with Nebuchadrezzar, whereas in Sept[uagint] there is no further elucidation of the 'enemy from the north.'"

concerned about the relation of Jeremiah's words to the historical realities of his day. Their focus remained on Jeremiah's words about an invasion of the land by a people from the north. There was, at least in *their* Bible, still the possibility of a future referent for Jeremiah's words—a referent that looked beyond the seventy years of the Babylonian captivity. For this community, Jeremiah's words had not been exhausted in the events of Israel's past.[7]

What is remarkable about the Septuagint version of the book of Jeremiah is how well it fits with Daniel 9. In Daniel 9, we see a godly Israelite, still in exile, pondering the meaning of these chapters of Jeremiah. His question is not merely whether or how Jeremiah's words have been fulfilled, but also why his own words will not be fulfilled "for many days hence" (Dan 8:26). He is dismayed that he must now seal up the vision until a later time. In Daniel 9, Daniel tries to understand Jeremiah's prophecy of the seventy years in this new light. The answer he receives is that Jeremiah's vision of the future was to be fulfilled not in seventy years but in seventy *weeks* of years. In Daniel, Jeremiah's words point beyond the events of the return from exile. The author of Daniel 9 would have had no use for a book of Jeremiah with glosses about Nebuchadnezzar. For him there was still a future for Jeremiah's word.

These texts illustrate the nature of biblical composition. The kinds of differences that exist between these two editions of Jeremiah are compositional in nature. Daniel 9 shows the kind of situation that could possibly give rise to the two compositions. The simultaneous existence of both texts suggests multiple communities and diverse interpretations of the same OT book.

We should also note that the differences in the text of Jeremiah are accompanied by a rather large rearrangement of the contents of the book. For example, the oracles against foreign nations in the Masoretic Text, Jeremiah 46—51, are located in the Septuagint version of Jeremiah just after the prophecy of the seventy years (Jer 25:15-38).[8] Moreover, the Dead Sea

---

[7]Ibid., p. 627: "In Sept[uagint] . . . there is no further elucidation of the enemy from the north. According to Sept., Judah, because of its lack of trust in Yahweh and disobedience (v. 8), is about to be vanquished by an enemy from the north who will devastate both Judah and the countries surrounding her, and leave behind a scene of desolation which will evoke astonishment and terror (v. 9)."

[8]At this point in the book (Jer 25:13b-14a) somebody, presumably the narrator or the author, begins to speak directly to the readers about the book we are now reading. In text linguistics this is called a metacommunicational gloss. This comment is not in the LXX.

Scrolls show us that the Septuagint translators were following closely their own Hebrew texts of Jeremiah. These differences between the two texts of Jeremiah were likely already in some early Hebrew texts.[9]

Hence, these two versions of Jeremiah are not merely distinct editions. Both texts are unique books in their own right. Furthermore, both books were part of communities that in all likelihood accepted them as canonical in the late postexilic period. They show that the composition of a biblical book represented a distinct moment in time and a particular point of view.

Canonization. Canonization, the next coordinate in our text model, looks at the point where a book becomes part of a larger collection and contributes to its overall shape. In current biblical studies, composition has generally been taken to precede canonization. Books received their final shape before they became part of a canon. Composition is seen as a historical process, while canonization is a theological one. I would agree to some extent with those who separate canon from composition in this way. The final literary shape of the OT books is not always identical with the canonical shape. It does not follow, however, that the formation of the OT canon was the result of purely theological forces. The two versions of Jeremiah, for example, show that composition occurs even after canonization. The nature of harmonistic textual variants like the addition of "now shortly" in Jeremiah 27:16 shows that the earlier version was already considered canonical, since they are attempts to harmonize an authoritative text. To the extent that such glosses are compositional, we can say there are compositional elements in the final canonical shape of the Hebrew Bible. Composition continues after canonization. It is also clear that such compositional elements were theologically motivated. This means that in classical terms of authorship, the shape of the OT canon as a whole must be taken seriously and integrated into our text model. Not only do the books of the Hebrew Bible have authors, but also the Hebrew Bible as a whole and as a canon is the product of composition and authorship.

Thus, in our understanding of the final text, the concept of canon does not follow a single trail to each and every canonical shape. Rather than speaking of a process of canonization, I would like to borrow a term from the field of biology and speak of the OT canon as a "punctuated equilibrium." It is "punctuated" in that it is the result not of a continuous process of development but of creative moments of formation that arise within

---

[9]Tov, *Text Criticism*, p. 320.

multiple canonical contexts. It is an "equilibrium" in that once established, the canonical shape continued in a more or less steady state until something triggered a major shift.

One further observation about canonization needs to be made. What we have said and will say about the compositional formation of the OT canon suggest it was the work of an individual, not a community as such. Individuals are part of communities and speak for communities, but, in the last analysis, the work of composition and canonization was the work of individuals.

Consolidation. The third notion in our model of the final shape of the Hebrew Bible is consolidation. Here the issue is the further development of a canonical text within a community. An example would be the well-known adjustment of the Septuagint to NT quotations of the Old, or to Origen's fifth column in the Hexapla, as well as the adjustment of the Masoretic Text along the lines of the emerging rabbinical exegesis.

A good deal of the Masoretic activity in the Hebrew Bible seems to cluster around texts that form the exegetical basis for established beliefs. For example, the two *yods* in the account of the creation of man (Gen 2:7, *wyyṣr*) were likely preserved in the Masoretic Text because they reflected the rabbinical notion that man was created with two natures (*yṣrim;* cf. Rashi). In the same way, the single *yod* in the identical verb used for the creation of the animals (Gen 2:19, *wyṣr*) supports the rabbinical doctrine that the animals have only one nature *(yṣr).* I am not suggesting this was the intent of the author of Genesis. That would be a question of composition. The preservation of a form of the Masoretic Text that supports a specific element of rabbinical exegesis is a function of consolidation. The notion of consolidation means that once texts become a part of a community, they take on essential characteristics of the beliefs of that community.

Thus the final shape of the Hebrew Bible is best described in terms of three intersecting coordinates: composition, canonization and consolidation. Composition preceded canonization but did not stop there. Canonical books took on varying compositional shapes that reflected theological viewpoints. Moreover, once established within a specific community, OT texts began to take on essential characteristics of those communities in a way that stopped short of actual new composition. The result was the production of the Hebrew Tanak: the Law, the Prophets and the Writings.

If our text model is valid, it suggests that lying behind the varying shapes of the Hebrew Tanak were various text communities drawing their

theological identity from those shapes. Elsewhere I have suggested that
the Hebrew Tanak is shaped around two sets of seams, Deuteronomy 34
and Joshua 1, as well as Malachi 3 and Psalm 1.[10] Deuteronomy 34 and
Malachi 3 look forward to the return of an age of prophecy. Moses, the
prophet, is dead, and his place has been taken by Joshua. Joshua is characterized in these seams not as a prophet but as a wise man. The wise man
who meditates on written Scripture has taken over the role of the prophet
who speaks directly with God. Scripture is now the locus of divine revelation. Yet the hope for a return of prophecy in the future still exists. The
Scriptures themselves (e.g., Deut 18) point in that direction. In the mean-
time, however, one prospers and becomes wise by meditating on the written Scripture.

These canonical seams suggest a conscious composition of the whole.
Its ranking of a collection of written texts over the gift of prophecy strongly
suggests its threefold shape was the form in which it was first received as
canon. Finally, we know from the history of the Hebrew Bible within Judaism that it was in the shape of the Tanak that the Hebrew Bible was con-
solidated within medieval Judaism. Indeed, the whole of the Masorah that
accompanied the Hebrew Bible was oriented toward this threefold division.

THE TANAK AND BIBLICAL THEOLOGY

This leads now to the second problem raised by a biblical theology of the
final shape of the text. How does the theology reflected in the Tanak relate
to the NT?

Few would contest the notion that the Hebrew Bible existed in a threefold form at some place and time during the pre-Christian period. This
was not its only form or even its most durable or authoritative form. It did
exist in that form, however, for a considerable period of time and for a significantly large portion of Judaism. According to Luke 24:44, it appears the
Tanak was the final shape of the Bible Jesus read. Judging by the prologue
to Ben Sirach, it already had that shape a century earlier.[11]

---

[10]John H. Sailhamer, *Introduction to Old Testament Theology: A Canonical Approach* (Grand Rapids, Mich.: Zondervan, 1995), pp. 239-352.
[11]An important implication of the prologue is that even the OT in Greek was read in a threefold form. This still does not tell us anything about the specific makeup of the Tanak at these
various times. There continued to be considerable discussion about the details of which
books were in and how they were to be arranged.

The so-called history of salvation[12] approach to biblical theology has largely ignored the question of the shape of the Tanak. The primary reason, of course, is that the arrangement of the books in the Tanak does not always follow the history of salvation. Ruth, for example, is not listed with Judges but with Proverbs. Chronicles falls at the end or with Psalms. In contrast, the salvation-historical approach answered the question of the unity of the two-part Christian Bible by locating that unity in the historical events leading from Judaism to Christianity. In that historical development, the OT reached its final goal in the events of the life of Christ and the early church. The unity of the two Testaments thus lies not in the shape of the Hebrew Bible but in the revelatory progression of salvation history.

The second attempt to link the Tanak with the NT is represented by Rendtorff's recent theology of the OT. Rendtorff has pressed the point that the OT (as the Tanak) was already a distinct entity in its final shape before the formation of the NT.[13] There is thus an inherent diversity between a theology of the Hebrew OT and NT theology. Such diversity stems, Rendtorff suggests, from the fact that the Tanak is a product of pre-Christian Judaism. Nevertheless, Christian theologians are obligated to treat the Tanak as the OT component in a biblical theology together with the NT.[14] As a result, the Jewish Tanak exerts a kind of gravitational pull on the NT. Its effect is to reposition the center of gravity of biblical theology away from the purely Christian NT.

A third attempt to link the Tanak with the NT is that of Hartmut Gese.[15] Gese sees the Tanak as a past stage in the OT's revelatory tradition history. The OT that is to be linked to the NT in a biblical theology is a distinct entity only in the final shape given it by the early church. The OT that has been shaped and embraced by the NT is the final form of its tradition history. The inherent diversity of the tradition in the OT is resolved in the tradition-historical process that culminated in the reading of the OT by Jesus, the early church and ultimately the NT canon. Unity comes out of a com-

---

[12]I have in mind here those approaches to biblical theology that focus on the salvific events of Israel's history as revelatory in addition to the biblical text. See Sailhamer, *Introduction to Old Testament Theology*, pp. 54-85.
[13]Rendtorff, "Die Hebräische Bibel war aber bereits davor die jüdische Heilige Schrift," *Theologie*, p. 4.
[14]Rolf Rendtorff, "Toward a Common Jewish-Christian Reading of the Hebrew Bible," *Canon and Theology: Overtures to an Old Testament Theology* (Minneapolis: Fortress, 1993), pp. 31-45.
[15]Hartmut Gese, *Alttestamentliche Vorträge zur biblischen Theologie* (Munich: Chr. Kaiser Verlag, 1977), pp. 23-30.

plex but singular line of reinterpretation.

I would like to suggest a fourth response. First, Rendtorff is right that the "final (threefold) shape" of the Tanak is already fixed in the pre-Christian period and that it is the form of the OT we must unite with the NT. However, there was not one but at least two (or multiple) versions of the Tanak within ancient Judaism (see below). We thus should ask not simply how the Tanak relates to the NT, but which form of the Tanak we should read with the NT. While it may be correct to say the NT does not wholly conform to the Tanak of later Judaism, it may also be correct to say the NT does conform to a Tanak of a slightly different shape and texture—one that perhaps developed in a different community. I am thus in agreement to some extent with Gese in that I believe the OT, in the form we now have it as the (pre-Christian) Tanak, shows real similarity to and unity with the NT. But unlike Gese, I take the (pre-Christian) Tanak, not the OT of the early church (the Alexandrian LXX), to be the canonical form in which it was received by the first Christian communities.

DANIEL AND THE TANAK

Let me illustrate by returning to the example of Daniel's reading of Jeremiah. Canonically and compositionally, the book of Daniel raises a perplexing question. What is the appropriate location of Daniel within the Tanak?

David Noel Freedman has addressed this question in his study of the shape of the Tanak in the pre-Christian period.[16] Freedman finds a great deal of symmetry and order in the Tanak,[17] but he also shows that the symmetry is largely missing if Daniel is included. In effect, Freedman's observations suggest that within the history of the OT canon we must reckon with the possibility of both a "Tanak with Daniel" and a "Tanak without Daniel."

The book of Daniel is not one of those books whose omission or inclusion would make little difference. This is especially true if the larger question is the relationship of the Tanak to the NT. Freedman shows that the major fluctuations in the order of the Writings largely turn on the position assigned to Daniel.

In the earliest complete medieval manuscript (Codex B19a), Daniel falls

---

[16]David Noel Freedman, *The Unity of the Hebrew Bible* (New York: Vintage, 1993).

[17]Ibid., pp. 79-80: "The correspondences among the major segments are so close, and the symmetry so exact, that it is difficult to imagine that these are the result of happenstance, or that a single mind or group of individuals was not responsible for assembling and organizing this collection of sacred works."

nearly at the end of the Tanak. It is followed only by Ezra/Nehemiah, a single book in the Hebrew Bible. With that arrangement, the edict of Cyrus (Ezra 1:2-4), which was the decree to return and rebuild the temple and which plays a central role in the "messianic" schematic of Daniel 9, immediately follows the book of Daniel and provides the introduction to the last book, Ezra/Nehemiah. In that position, the edict of Cyrus identifies the historical return under Ezra and Nehemiah as the fulfillment of Jeremiah's vision of seventy years. It is as if Daniel 9, and its view of seventy weeks of years, were nowhere in sight.

In another arrangement of the last books of the Tanak (*Baba Bathra* 14b), the book of Chronicles comes last and closes with a repetition of the edict of Cyrus (2 Chron 36:23). As Freedman points out, this arrangement of Chronicles and Ezra/Nehemiah is noticeably out of chronological sequence. After the close of Nehemiah, the Chronicler begins his narrative with Adam![18] This suggests the book of Chronicles was deliberately placed at the end of the Tanak, after the books of Ezra/Nehemiah and after the book of Daniel. It also suggests a conscious effort to close the Tanak with a restatement of the edict of Cyrus at the end of Chronicles.

There thus appears to have been at least two contending final shapes of the Tanak. The one closes with the book of Ezra/Nehemiah. In that version, the edict of Cyrus finds its fulfillment in the historical return from exile. The other shape of the Tanak closes with Chronicles and a repetition of the edict of Cyrus. In this arrangement, the edict of Cyrus has been shortened from that in Ezra/Nehemiah (Ezra 1:2-4), so that it concludes with the clause "Let him go up" (2 Chron 36:23). In the book of Chronicles, the subject of that clause is identified as he "whose God is with him." For the Chronicler this is possibly also a messianic image (cf. 1 Chron 17:12). Cyrus says, in effect, "let him (whose God is with him) go up to Jerusalem." To arrive at that dramatic conclusion the Chronicler has had to omit nearly two verses from the original edict in Ezra/Nehemiah. It is those verses that link the edict to the historical events of the return from exile.[19] Without them, the fulfillment of the Tanak's final words is left open.

---

[18]The order of the OT books followed by the English translations has corrected this by placing Ezra at the end of Chronicles, with the consequence of a redundant and immediate repetition of Cyrus's edict (2 Chron 36:23 and Ezra 1:2-4).

[19]In contrast to 2 Chronicles 36:23, the subject of the verb "let him go up" in Ezra/Nehemiah is "the heads of fathers' households of Judah and Benjamin and the priests and the Levites . . . even everyone whose spirit God had stirred to go up and rebuild the house of the LORD which is in Jerusalem" (Ezra 1:5).

The central role of the edict of Cyrus at the conclusion of the Tanak appears to be motivated by the expectation injected into the end of the Tanak by Daniel 9. In Daniel 9, Jeremiah's expectation of a return to Jerusalem is projected beyond the immediate return from Babylonian captivity. Jeremiah's promise of a return after seventy years is extended to seven times seventy years, or 490 years.

Regardless of how one might interpret these events, it is clear that they all hinge on the timing of "the publication of the word to restore and build Jerusalem" (Dan 9:25). The fact that one version of the Tanak ends with just such a decree (the edict of Cyrus) can hardly be coincidental. Moreover, in the introduction to the edict, the Chronicler consciously links the edict to Jeremiah's prophecy of the seventy weeks, which is the passage Daniel is pondering in Daniel 9.

Two final shapes of the Tanak thus appear to emerge. One concludes with Ezra/Nehemiah and identifies the return from Babylonian exile as the fulfillment of Jeremiah's prophecy of seventy years. This is a historical fulfillment. The other Tanak features Daniel and closes with the book of Chronicles. In doing so, it extends Jeremiah's seventy years beyond the time of the return from Babylon—a future fulfillment. That shape fits well with what appears to be the Hebrew text (*Vorlage*) of the Septuagint of Jeremiah and the reading of these texts by the NT. Both are open to events that look beyond the return from Babylonian exile.

CONCLUSION

The points raised in this essay show that changing attitudes toward the OT have opened the door to a range of new possibilities for constructing a biblical theology of the Old and New Testaments. While there continue to be those who will seek the earliest forms of the OT texts, there is a growing number of others who have turned their attention to the final shape. This should not be construed as a turn away from an interest in history. It is rather a focus on a largely overlooked stage of Israel's history, namely, the history of Israel immediately prior to the coming of Christ and the writing of the NT. Along with an interest in the final shape of the OT has also come a renewed focus on composition. Rather than seeking to discover the literary strata behind the biblical text, attention has shifted to the literary strategy of the biblical text. The quest for strategy has replaced the quest for strata. The convergence of these two interests leads to a necessary recasting of the basic questions of a biblical theology of the Old and New Testaments. This is true in at least three important ways.

In the first place, a focus on the final shape of the Hebrew Bible and its link to the notion of canon leaves little doubt that the OT can and should be approached theologically. In the past, biblical theologies have devoted much attention to that question, with largely negative results. It has been negative because composition has been viewed apart from the stage in which Scripture was recognized as authoritative (canonization). By contrast, Rendtorff's recent OT theology has only one sentence devoted to this question. In that sentence, which is the first sentence in the book, Rendtorff says, "The OT is a theological book."[20] Had Rendtorff been seeking any level other than the final canonical shape, he would have been obliged to say much more.

A focus on the final shape of the Hebrew Bible considerably reduces the time gap between the OT and the NT. If the formation of the Tanak took place during the second century B.C. or later, the OT is virtually laid at the doorstep of the NT. In a real sense, the OT, as the Tanak, belongs to the intertestamental period. The Tanak does not conclude in the same way as the history of Israel, that is, with the Babylonian captivity. Nor does the OT first come into being with Judaism, that is, in the priestly circles of the Second Temple. Our discussion has shown that at the end of at least one version of the Tanak we find ourselves already in the world of ideas of the NT.

A focus on the final shape, or final shapes, of the Hebrew Bible raises the possibility of an early (pre-Christian) version of the OT that intentionally links the book of Daniel with the edict of Cyrus in 2 Chronicles 36:22-23. To be sure, there are surface disturbances in that shape, such as the variant Hebrew versions of Jeremiah and the canonical location of the books of Daniel and Chronicles. But these very disturbances reveal the deep-seated disagreements over the meaning of Scripture that existed in the postexilic period. If we follow closely the nature of those disagreements, a picture begins to emerge. The line that runs through and divides the early versions of the Tanak is the same line that separates John the Baptist from the religious leaders of his day. The Tanak closes with the expectation of a new work of God. This work includes the return of prophecy characterized by Moses and Elijah and extends beyond the events that immediately surround Jerusalem and the Second Temple. It is along that story line that the NT writers pick up the narrative thread and take us into the world of the NT canon.

---

[20]Rendtorff, "Das Alte Testament ist ein theologisches Buch," *Theologie,* p. 1.

3

Genesis 1—4

The Genesis of Old Testament Instruction

Brian G. Toews

According to Walter Brueggemann, "Old Testament theological interpretation in the twentieth century has been dominated by von Rad's essay,
'The Theological Problem of the Old Testament Doctrine of Creation,'
which he first published in 1936."[1] In that essay von Rad stated that Israel's
faith was focused primarily on salvation not creation. In recent years, however, the prominence of the role of creation theology in OT theology has
grown.[2] Indeed, the argument of this essay is that the first four chapters of
Genesis serve as the introduction to the Pentateuch as well as the OT as a
whole and thus serve as the place to look for the basic organization of OT
instruction. These chapters create the theological prototypes for the OT,
which are repeated and elaborated upon through the Law, Prophets and
Writings,[3] for a scriptural theology looks at the text of the OT in its present

---

[1]Walter Brueggemann, *Theology of the Old Testament* (Minneapolis: Fortress, 1997), p. 159.
[2]See Rolf Rendtorff, "Some Reflections on Creation as a Topic of Old Testament Theology," in
*Priests, Prophets and Scribes: Essays on Formation and Heritage of Second Temple Judaism in Honor
of Joseph Blenkinsopp*, ed. E. Ulrich et al., JSOTSup 149 (Sheffield: JSOT, 1992), pp. 204-12; B.
Och, "Creation and Redemption: Toward a Theology of Creation," *Judaism* 44 (1995): 226-43;
Rolf Knierim, "Cosmos and History in Israel's Theology,"in *The Task of Old Testament Theology* (Grand Rapids, Mich.: Eerdmans, 1995), pp. 171-224.
[3]For the argumentation in support of approaching the OT text in its threefold structure, see

shape and form as instructive in the theological enterprise. It works with the OT as a single, unified body of literature in its final form as handed down to us by the Jewish and Christian communities. Although such a discussion is beyond our present purposes, for a Christian, whose Scripture includes the NT, the trajectory of theological concepts must also be followed into the NT to complete the scriptural perspective.

GENESIS 1—4 AS INTRODUCTION TO THE THEOLOGY OF THE OLD TESTAMENT

If the OT is a single, unified text with theological coherence, and if the Pentateuch is the foundation for the other parts of the OT, with Genesis 1—4 as the introduction to the Pentateuch, then it would seem reasonable that Genesis 1—4 is also the introduction to the OT.[4] There are several reasons for considering the first four chapters of Genesis to be the introduction to the Bible instead of the first chapter, the first three chapters or the first eleven chapters.[5] First, the structure of these four chapters indicates that they belong together. The book of Genesis is divided into major sections by the phrase "these are the generations of." The first of these statements is found in Genesis 2:4. This makes Genesis 1:1—2:3 the introduction to the text, but it also separates it from the subsequent sections of Genesis. The world of Genesis 1:1—2:3 is not the world of the rest of the OT Scriptures, nor is it the world of the reader of the Scriptures. There has been a fundamental change in the world in light of the events of Genesis 2:4—4:26. These chapters shape the world of the OT. Although many interpreters might see Genesis 1—3 as the introductory unit, Genesis 2:4—4:26 makes up the next unit of thought, since the next occurrence of the

---

Roger T. Beckwith, *The Old Testament Canon of the Christian Church and Its Background in Early Judaism* (Grand Rapids, Mich.: Eerdmans, 1985), and L. MacDonald, *The Formation of the Christian Biblical Canon*, 2nd ed. (Peabody, Mass.: Hendrickson, 1995).

[4]So too James Barr, *Old and New in Interpretation* (London: SCM Press, 1966), p. 18, who, in answer to the question of whether there is any starting point for the understanding of the OT, states, "In so far as the question is a real one at all, the only answer must be the creation story, because it is from here onwards that the story is cumulative." More recently, in *The Concept of Biblical Theology: An Old Testament Perspective* (Minneapolis: Fortress, 1999), p. 445, he has affirmed the same.

[5]It is not uncommon to find scholars who understand Genesis 1—11 to be the theological foundation of the Pentateuch. See, e.g., G. Smith, "Structure and Purpose of Genesis 1—11," *JETS* 20 (1988): 307-19. However, the view that Genesis 1—4 also serves as the theological introduction to the OT canon as a whole is unique. Moreover, most scholars analyze Genesis 1—3 as a unit, not Genesis 1—4, even though structurally Genesis 2:4—4:26 is a structural unit.

textual marker "the generations of" is found in Genesis 5:1.

Therefore Genesis 1:1—2:3 presents the ideal world that God created. The world in which the rest of the OT takes place is the world of Genesis 2:4—4:26. This is the real world of the OT text and the real world in which the reader lives.[6] Thus there is a tension between the ideal world and real world. This tension drives the OT narrative. Genesis 4 presents the first generation(s) of humanity living outside the Garden of Eden under the consequences of sin. Genesis 4 serves as the prototype for humanity outside the garden. The generations of humankind outside the garden understand life only in light of what transpired in the garden. Thus all of the events in the OT take place outside the garden, but they are understood in light of Genesis 2:4—4:26. This tension is never resolved in the OT narrative, except in its prophetic vision. The tension is ultimately released only in humankind's entrance into the blessing and rest of God granted in the new creation portrayed in Revelation 21—22.

A second reason for establishing Genesis 1—4 as the introduction to the Pentateuch and the OT as a whole is that the narrative patterns established in these chapters begin to repeat themselves from Genesis 5 onward. For example, the next major narrative unit in the book of Genesis is the flood account, which presents Noah as a kind of second Adam (see Gen 9:1-3) and God as the one who re-creates the earth after the flood waters have covered the earth, as in Genesis 1:2.

A third argument for understanding Genesis 1—4 to be the introduction is related to Genesis 5:1, which we have seen introduces the next section of the book of Genesis. It does so, however, with the expanded phrase "This is the *book of* the generations of Adam" (author's translation [throughout the essay]). This is the only time in the book of Genesis where the phrase "generations of" is used with the word *book*, thereby indicating the start of the OT story.[7] Genesis 1:1—4:26 presents the prologue to the book, while the story or narrative of humankind on the earth outside the

---

[6]See Susan Niditch, *Chaos to Cosmos: Studies in Biblical Patterns of Creation* (Chico, Calif.: Scholars Press, 1985), chap. 2, "Tales of Emergence: The Passage from Ideal to Reality." She calls paradise "pre-reality," which she views as an image of an ideal time to which one hopes to return (p. 29).

[7]The LXX translates the Hebrew text as "this is the book of the genealogy of men." Compare this with Matthew 1:1: "the book of the genealogy of Jesus." Thus both canons have similar beginnings. See A. W. H. Moule, "The Pattern of the Synoptists," *EvQ* 4 (1971): 162-71. He connects Genesis 5:1 to Matthew 1:1, suggesting that the Pentateuch and the Gospel of Matthew correspond to the Torah. The association of Genesis 5:1 and Matthew 1:1 also suggests Jesus Christ as the second Adam.

garden begins in Genesis 5:1. The prologue serves to set the stage for all the persons and events that follow.[8] The "book of man," that is, the OT, should thus be read and understood through the perspective of the first four chapters of Genesis as its hermeneutical lens. These chapters lay the foundation for a biblical worldview that is shared by the other biblical authors. Moreover, if the OT is the book of humankind, then the specific focus on the nation of Israel serves to illustrate truths about humanity in general. The OT presents the instruction of God to all of humankind through the story of God's dealings with Israel.

Finally, 1 Chronicles begins with the genealogy of Genesis 5:1-32 (1 Chron 1:1-4) and ends with the decree of the Persian king Cyrus (2 Chron 36:22-23), in this way serving as a concluding summary of the "book of man" (Israel). The fact that Chronicles begins with Genesis 5 confirms the unique role that Genesis 1—4 has in the OT Scriptures.

THE SHAPE OF A SCRIPTURAL THEOLOGY

Therefore OT instruction/*torah* takes its clues from the narration in Genesis 1—4. In particular, Genesis 1—4 reveals four fundamental structures around which the various issues of these chapters are built: God, his Word, humanity and the earth.[9] The relationship among these four structures, which together form a unified and interrelated complex or web of ideas, can be illustrated in this way:

GOD

Word

(God) and humankind
_____
earth/garden

God creates the world and reveals his word to people on the earth. In the chart there is a parenthesis around God, since God reveals himself on

---

[8]See Gerhard von Rad, *Genesis: A Commentary*, OTL (Philadelphia: Westminster Press, 1972), p. 70: "The title, 'This is the genealogy of . . . ' occurs at the beginning of eleven sections that contain lists. . . . There can be no doubt that the statement: 'This is the book of the genealogies . . . ' designates the beginning of an actual book."

[9]See too Stephen G. Dempster, who has focused on these four features of the Hebrew Bible in "An 'Extraordinary Fact': *Torah and Temple* and the Contours of the Hebrew Canon," *TynB* 48 (1997): 23-54, 191-218, and in his essay in this volume.

earth in a veiled form. Humankind is then called to listen and respond to the word of the God who dwells with them in the Garden of Eden. This ends up in the people's exile from the garden because they do not listen. This becomes the fundamental structure for the rest of the OT:

LORD

word

(LORD) and Israel + nations
_____
land

As in the garden before the Fall, the Lord reveals his word/law to Israel so that in the land they might listen and respond in order to be a blessing to all the nations.[10] In this scheme, humankind now consists of Israel and the nations. The Lord who dwells with Israel in the land is veiled behind the tabernacle or temple. He chooses Israel from the midst of the nations to serve as the means of blessing the rest of humanity. Like Adam and Eve in the garden, this ends up in Israel's exile from the land, because Israel does not listen to the voice of the Lord.

If Genesis 1—4 presents the fundamental theological structure of the OT, and if the rest of the OT has a literary and theological unity, then a scriptural theology should reflect this. Moreover, a scriptural theology that follows the threefold structure of the canon should present its instruction in three parts: Law, Prophets, Writings.[11] In doing so it should demonstrate how each part repeats the basic archetypes of Genesis 1—4. Toward this

---

[10]N. T. Wright's analysis of the basic Jewish story is very similar to mine. See his summary in *The New Testament and the People of God* (Minneapolis: Fortress, 1992), p. 221. Wright too understands the basic scheme of the OT story in creation terms. In addition, he describes the worldview of the biblical story in four symbols: temple (God's dwelling place), land (the New Eden), Torah and ethnic Israel (the true Adam). These four symbols overlap nicely with the four fundamental structures around which I have arranged the biblical story.

[11]Although critical of canonical theories, James Barr too suggests that "the most obvious way in which a theology might be written on 'canonical' principles but differently from Childs' approaches would be to organize its *content* around the patterns of the canon. Thus such a theology might very naturally have three great sections, covering Torah, Prophets and Writings, or perhaps better four, accepting the later division of Prophets into historical books and prophetic books. . . . *One of its advantages would be that the starting point of the whole might be clear: the beginning of Genesis.* This would in any case be in accord with my concept of 'story' and is not peculiar to a canonical approach" (*The Concept of Biblical Theology*, p. 439, emphasis added).

goal, in what follows I have summarized each major section in the OT using the language of the fundamental structures from Genesis 1—4 and their subpoints. This is designed to demonstrate that the patterns of Genesis 1—4 are reflected throughout the OT. After each summary the theological contribution of each part or book is discussed in order to illustrate how the rest of Scripture gives definition and shape to the instruction introduced in Genesis 1—4. What follows therefore is the shape of my scriptural theology in outline.

THE LAW

Genesis. In the generations of Noah (Gen 6:9—9:29), Noah is given commandments, to which he listens and then does all that God says. His obedience leads to the preservation of life on the earth. God has been patient with human sin, but the day of reckoning arrives and God de-creates the earth, undoing all that he had done in the six days of creation. When God finally pulls back the waters and the dry land appears, he opens the door of the ark and Noah, as the second Adam, walks on the earth. He brings acceptable offerings to God. The Lord reiterates to Noah the blessing first given to Adam (apart from the blessing to subdue or rule the earth). God demonstrates his goodness and mercy in promising or covenanting not to destroy the earth again by a flood. Yet Noah "falls" by drinking of "the fruit of the tree" and uncovering his nakedness.

In the account of the generations of Terah (Gen 11:27—25:12), the Lord blesses Abraham, like Adam, in his word to him, promising him a land, an innumerable seed and the role of being a mediator of God's blessing to humankind. Abraham listens to the voice of the Lord and is characterized as believing the Lord, fearing God, walking with God and keeping the law. He demonstrates that he loves his neighbor in his actions taken on behalf of Lot. But he also lies and deceives. He listens to Sarah in the matter of Hagar instead of listening to the promise of God. Nevertheless the Lord is faithful to his word and animates Sarah's womb so that the promised seed might come. Abraham passes the test of his faith in offering the seed son as a burnt offering.

In the generations of Isaac (Gen 25:19—35:29), Jacob is the deceiver par excellence. Instead of listening to the promise given to Rebekah, he listens to voice of his mother and deceives his father for the blessing. Because of his brother's death threats, Jacob must go into exile. On the way, the Lord reiterates to Jacob the blessing of Abraham. While with Laban he is blessed by God but also afflicted by Laban. Jacob's trouble ends with the Lord's deliverance and Jacob's safe return to the land. Jacob demonstrates the faith of Abraham in his petition to the Lord and the building of an altar.

In the generations of Jacob (Gen 37:2—50:26), Joseph's dreams foreshadow Joseph's destiny. Though he is persecuted by his brothers and tempted by Potiphar's wife, he clings to God. In his affliction the Lord is with him and raises him out of his sufferings to reign over the whole earth. In the providence of God he becomes a savior, giving life to Israel, his seed, and to the Egyptians. Joseph's brothers are transformed and are reunited in love with Joseph. Jacob's prophetic blessing of his sons reveals that in the last days it will be Judah who will reign over his brothers and over all the peoples so that the blessing of humanity on the earth or land will come through Judah.

Theological contribution. Noah is the obedient seed who preserves life on the earth, since faith defines the essence of listening to the voice of the Lord. The narrative then centers on the Abrahamic covenant or seed as the plan of the One to bless humanity on the earth, through which God demonstrates his goodness, faithfulness, compassion and mercy. The focus, however, shifts from the earth to the Promised Land. In fulfillment of his covenant promises, God repeatedly intervenes in the birth of the seed (son). He also acts providentially, using evil to accomplish his good purposes for humankind. As a result, the Lord is faithful to Abraham, so that Israel is fruitful and multiplies. Yet, in fulfillment of Genesis 3:15, the seed of the serpent is constantly at enmity with the seed of Abraham, though Abraham's seed is ultimately delivered. In the end, although Joseph provides the most detailed glimpse of the "seed of the woman," he is only a type of the king to come from Judah.

Exodus-Leviticus-Numbers. The Lord works through Moses to fulfill his promise to Abraham. He reveals his name and creates Israel by delivering them from its enemy, Egypt (and at the same time de-creates Egypt for not listening to Moses, God's prophet). The people listen to the Passover commands and are saved. The Lord then pulls the waters of the Red Sea back so that his people might walk on dry land. In the wilderness, the Lord then gives his people his law or instructions and tabernacles among them in his holiness. Nevertheless Israel does not continue to listen but builds a golden calf. However, the Lord is compassionate and gracious, slow to anger and abounding in loving kindness and truth, keeping loving kindness for thousands, forgiving iniquity, transgression and sin (Ex 34:6-7). But he will by no means leave the guilty unpunished (Ex 34:7). The Lord thus continues to lead Israel to the good land he has prepared, albeit in a veiled form. Israel continues not to believe and rejects God's goodness, devising its own plan to return to Egypt. Israel will die outside the land as a result of God's punishment. Nevertheless Baalam reiterates the Abrahamic blessings, demonstrating the Lord's continuing faithfulness to bless Israel in the land. Hence the Lord raises up another generation to replace the one that died. Unfortunately this generation repeats Israel's foolish worship and plays the harlot with the women and gods at Baal Peor. Israel has reproduced after its kind.

Theological contribution. The focus is now on the Lord's creation and deliverance of Israel, his instruction to them, his holy presence among them and Israel's response. The most concise OT definition of the Lord, that is, his divine name and that which makes him unique, is given in Exodus 34:6-7. In view of Genesis 1—4, the crossing of the Red Sea is parallel to creation, the tabernacle is parallel to the garden, and the golden calf as the rebellious work of Israel is parallel to the Fall of humankind. The eschatological hope announced in Genesis 3:15 is carried on in Balaam's oracles about the coming king.

Deuteronomy. Moses explains the law for Israel as they prepare to enter the land. Israel is to love God, cling to him, listen to and keep the commandments in the land that they might live. If Israel listens, they will enjoy the goodness of the Lord; but if they do not listen, the Lord will de-create all he has done for them and they will die in exile from the land. Though Moses therefore calls Israel to choose life by listening to the Lord, in the end he predicts the people's departure from the Lord but promises that they will return to the Lord and to the land with a circumcised heart that loves the Lord. The Song of Moses (Deut 32:1-43) testifies to this judgment but also speaks of the Lord's mercy and compassion to vindicate them. Moses then dies outside the land. Since then there has not been a prophet like Moses.

Theological contribution. The focus is on the law as God's wisdom for Israel's existence in the land and the blessings (life) and curses (death) attendant to it, together with God's promise to redeem Israel from its continuing disobedience in a new covenant in which it will be given a "circumcised heart" (Deut 30:1-14).

THE FORMER PROPHETS

Joshua. God, who has postponed the judgment on the Canaanites for their refusal to worship him, finally executes that judgment through Joshua and Israel. Conversely he demonstrates himself to be a merciful Savior in the salvation of Rahab. He is also the master of the Promised Land and gives it to Israel by fighting for them and delivering the land into the hands of Joshua and the people. Hence, on the one hand, God is faithful to his covenant promises to Abraham. On the other hand, Joshua and Israel listen to the word of the Lord and enjoy his victories. Their obedience indicates that they are servants of the Lord who execute his will. Thus the good land is given to them, wherein they enjoy the presence of the Lord and his rest at Shiloh, while Joshua continues to exhort Israel to worship the Lord and listen to and meditate on his law.

Judges. Once settled in the land, however, Israel does not listen to the word or covenant but worships the gods of the land. The Lord consequently judges Israel by putting them into the hands of the nations of the land. Nevertheless he remains a merciful Savior who raises up Spirit-endowed judges to save Israel from destruction. This cycle of sin, judgment and restoration repeats itself, with each generation becoming more corrupt. Like Adam and Eve in the garden, Israel continues to determine "good and evil in their own eyes." For Genesis 3:15 to be fulfilled, Israel needs a king.

Samuel. The Lord is a merciful Savior in that he saves the lowly and afflicted from their enemies, while the proud and lofty are brought down. After Saul's rejection because he did not listen to the voice of the Lord, David is anointed ruler. David too is afflicted but delivered from all his enemies by the Lord and ultimately raised up to be king over Israel. Jerusalem is finally established as the city of David, where the sovereign Lord will be present, with David as his servant-ruler. Although David wants to build the Lord a house, the Lord promises or covenants to build David a house by establishing his seed upon his throne forever. In turn David's seed will build a house for the Lord. As for David, he executes vengeance on the enemies of God but does not listen to the Lord in committing adultery with Bathsheba and arranging for the death of her husband, thereby introducing the curse of death into his family.

Kings. David's seed, Solomon, sits upon his throne and seeks the wisdom of God. In response, the Lord, as his Father, grants him wisdom to rule his people. In Jerusalem Solomon builds the house where the Lord will dwell and have his rest. In turn, Solomon's kingdom enjoys the goodness of the Lord in every way. His kingdom extends from Egypt to the Euphrates. In time, however, Solomon stops listening to the word of the Lord and is disciplined by the Lord through the nations surrounding him. His sin splits the kingdom. After Solomon's fall, neither Israel nor Judah, with few exceptions, listens to the Lord. Hence, after enduring with great patience their idolatry and false worship, God judges both nations. The Lord de-creates the land: the people are exiled; the city of Jerusalem and the house of the Lord are destroyed. Israel is in the hands of the nations. However, in his faithfulness to David, the Lord maintains his promise and keeps David's seed alive in anticipation of Israel's coming redemption.

Theological contribution. As declared in Deuteronomy, Israel is planted in the land but does not listen to God and is ultimately exiled. The focus is thus first of all on the Lord's faithfulness to deliver or give the land to Israel in which he acts as Warrior and Savior on its behalf while at the same time bringing about judgment on the Gentiles. At the same time, Israel's failure to listen to the Lord establishes a pattern of sin-judgment-deliverance that points to the need for a king to mediate the blessing or rule of God. These two elements combine to focus attention on David (king), his kingdom (temple) and the Davidic covenant, in which those who oppose the anointed of God will be judged and those who are with him will be blessed.

THE LATTER PROPHETS

Isaiah. Israel has rebelled against God its Father, the Holy One of Israel. The nation has not listened to the word or law of the Lord, as demonstrated by a worship that satisfies the law externally, all the while having its hands covered with the blood of evil and with injustice to its neighbor. In response the Lord has executed judgment against Israel by desolating the land and leaving only a small remnant. Jerusalem too has played the harlot. But the Lord will restore and redeem those who return to him. Jerusalem will then become the city of righteousness in a new creation. However, those who do not worship the Lord will come to an end in a fiery judgment.

Jeremiah. Judah, like Israel, has refused to keep the covenant of the Lord. They have worshiped other gods and the works of their hands. As a result, the Lord will bring Babylon to desolate the land and take them into exile. Just prior to Judah's exile, Jeremiah, a prophet like Moses, is sent to the nations with a message of repentance, destruction and restoration. Although Jeremiah will be persecuted by his enemies, the Lord will be with him to deliver him. For its part, Babylon will rule in the earth but in the end will be judged. The nations too will be judged for their enmity against Israel. Jeremiah, like Moses, proclaims that the Lord will bring Israel back to the land and establish a new covenant with them that will not be broken, since their sins will be forgiven and they will be empowered to keep God's law (Jer 31:31-34). Hence the Lord is faithful to his word of judgment—Israel is exiled. At the same time, a son of David is alive, thus giving witness as well to God's continuing loving kindness and faithfulness.

Ezekiel. Experiencing the exile, Ezekiel has been called to the rebellious house of Israel. Israel is called to listen to the prophet, but they will not. The glory of the Lord has therefore departed from the temple due to the abominations taking place within it. The judgment of Jerusalem has finally taken place. Not only is Israel judged, but also the nations because of their pride. This is not God's last word, however. Ezekiel also prophesies that Israel will be renewed in the land. The people will be raised from the death of exile. Their enemies will be judged, and the glory of the Lord will once again dwell in a glorious temple.

Theological contribution. The Latter Prophets provide the canonical commentary on Israel's exile and return as the embodiment of the pattern of sin-judgment-restoration. While the wicked will be judged, the remnant will be saved and the nation restored. The focus therefore now becomes the Messiah, the seed of the woman, who will bring about Israel's restoration after the judgment of the exile. This restoration is tied to the establishment of a new covenant in fulfillment of the promises to Abraham and David, in which God as creator will remake his people, granting them a new heart for God's law and placing them in a newly created earth. The focus of this new covenant restoration of God's people in a new creation is on the presence of the glory of God in a new temple in Jerusalem.

THE TWELVE MINOR PROPHETS

As a whole, the Book of the Twelve recounts the same pattern of sin-judgment-restoration found in the major prophets. In regard to Israel's sin, Israel has broken the covenant of the Lord. It has not demonstrated love and justice for its neighbor. Its worship is unacceptable. It has rebelled and worshiped idols. It has not listened to the law or received instruction. It rejects the prophets who have been sent to call it to repentance. Indeed, not even the exile has brought the nation back to the Lord. As a result, Israel's punishment will be exile and a continued subjection to the nations in the postexilic period. At the same time, God will also judge the nations in acts of de-creation for hating and persecuting Israel, for their pride, for their lack of love to their neighbor and for their idolatry. Finally, when the nation returns to the Lord, it will be restored to the land under a Davidic king, the Spirit will be poured out on all the people, the Davidic kingdom will be rebuilt, the glory of Zion will be manifest, and Israel will be given rest from its enemies. For the nations who believe, they too will participate in the Davidic kingdom and enjoy the merciful salvation of the Lord. They will come to Zion and join Israel in worshiping the Lord.

Theological contribution. The minor prophets focus on the one-flesh love relationship between the Lord and Israel in which the Lord and Israel share a marriage bond. This bond is expressed in the Lord's faithfulness to restore Israel after its seventy-year exile. Moreover, despite Israel's continued affliction or distress under the nations, the people of the Lord remain the objects of the Lord's compassion, mercy and faithful love. Nevertheless, though God is patient in judgment, his wrath will be finally meted out in the day of the Lord against Israel's harlotry, thereby purifying Zion by the pouring out of his Spirit.

THE WRITINGS

Psalms. The book of Psalms instructs the reader concerning faith in God's person, works and word. God will deliver the king and all those who are blessed in him from their troubles and from their enemies, bringing them to Zion to praise his glory. Thus, though the wicked prosper in the present, the suffering righteous will be vindicated in the end.

Job. The final narrative of the book of Job (Job 42:10-17) presents Job as one who has been restored from his captivity to receive a double portion of blessing (Job 42:10) in his last days (Job 42:12). Job's life is extended 140 years, twice the length of the exile. Thus Job, as the model of the righteous person in exile, initially fears God in his afflictions and learns through his suffering to listen to the word of God as the answer to why the righteous suffer. In the end, he therefore receives the blessings of God.

Proverbs. The book of Proverbs contains instruction to the Son of David, king of Israel. The Woman of Wisdom is to be embraced and all her wisdom applied, since the king must become one with Wisdom to reign over the kingdom of God. In turn, all those in the kingdom must become children of Wisdom.

Ruth. In the narrative, Naomi returns from exile and is blessed by God through Ruth, the embodiment of wisdom, who provides for her a redeemer, Obed, to serve her. Naomi thus serves as a narrative type of Israel's return from exile and its blessing in the Servant-Messiah.

Song of Songs. The surface level of the book suggests a love affair between Solomon and the Shulamite (based on Gen 2:23). In view of the surrounding books, however, the Song of Songs illustrates Wisdom's pursuit after the love of the Davidic king and his response to her, that they might become one. The coming Davidic Messiah will be the embodiment of Wisdom. In contrast to the man in the garden, the Messiah will embrace and love the wise commands of God.

Ecclesiastes. In light of the fall of humankind and the certainty of death (Gen 3:17-19), the wise man must receive life as a good gift from God. In response, he should fear God, keep his commandments and wait for his judgment. Once again, wisdom is mediated through the son of David.

Lamentations. Jerusalem, the city of David, has played the fool and has consequently died or fallen. The exile is the fruit of its way of life. Yet the Lord's faithfulness and loyalty to his word of promise to David arouse hope for the future.

Esther. God is faithful and works providentially to preserve Israel in the exile in order to raise up a seed on the land when it returns. Esther is a woman whose wise planning works not because of the divine provenance of her wisdom but because of divine providence. It is the hidden God that makes Esther's plan turn out to be so wise.

Daniel. The main point of Daniel is the coming deliverance of God's people in the kingdom of God. Daniel is the quintessential wise man, along with his three friends, who are delivered from all their trials because they fear God and keep his word. The nations and their kings are judged for their pride, but the son of man will come to receive an everlasting kingdom along with the saints.

Ezra-Nehemiah. Here, at the end of the canon, we find the narrative of the promised return after the exile, the building of the temple and the restoration of Jerusalem. Ezra is the wisdom figure in the book. He is the priest or scribe in whose hand is the wisdom of God. It is his role to instruct the postexilic community in the ways of the Lord as they anticipate the filling of the temple with God's glory and the filling of Jerusalem with a Davidic king.

1-2 Chronicles. To close the canon, Chronicles provides the typological presentation of the hoped-for messianic kingdom that will reestablish the rule of God designed for humanity in the beginning. The Davidic Messiah will come as the second Adam and establish his rule on the earth for those who seek the Lord. Solomon, the first son of David, provides a narrative type of the son of David to come who will fulfill the Davidic promise (1 Chron 17). The wisdom element in the book is also seen in Solomon as the sage-king and in the theology of retribution, which parallels the presentation of the blessing of the righteous and the judgment on the wicked from Psalm 1.[12]

Theological contribution. Taken as a whole, the Writings focus on the instruction or wisdom that leads to sharing in the blessing to be granted to the messianic king whom God will establish in Zion. The Writings thus serve as an excellent bridge from the OT to the messianic theology of the New Testament. Moreover, ending the OT with the Writings raises the issue of the role of wisdom in the theology of the NT.

CONCLUSION

A canonical theology must go beyond just another way to arrange the books. If there is good evidence to look at the Law, Prophets and Writings as literary-theological units, then this should determine the shape of OT theology as well. Moreover, Genesis 1—4 serves as the introduction not only to the Law but also to the canon as a whole. These chapters set forth the fundamental theological issues for the rest of the OT. Thus the instruction of the OT should be presented in accordance with the three- or four-part structure of the OT, demonstrating how each part of the OT contributes to the theological themes and narrative structure introduced at its beginning.

POSTSCRIPT: TOWARD THE NEW TESTAMENT

Scriptural theology seeks to understand the teaching of the OT on its own terms. However, the Scripture does not end with Chronicles but continues in the Gospels, Acts, Epistles and book of Revelation. The completed text of Scripture concludes with humanity's entrance into the ideal state of the new creation. The tension between the ideal and the real is finally resolved when God creates a new heaven and new earth (Rev 21—22). The end mirrors the beginning. Thus the implication for NT theology is that Genesis

---

[12]Following Joseph Blenkinsopp, "Wisdom in the Chronicler's Work," in *In Search of Wisdom,* ed. Leo Perdue (Louisville, Ky.: Westminister/John Knox, 1993), pp. 19-30.

1—4 serves as the genesis of NT instruction as well.[13] Hence the NT may be understood using the same four fundamental structures around which the OT is built: God (in Christ and as the Spirit), his Word (become flesh), humankind (as Israel and the nations in the church) and the earth (as new creation).

---

[13]What I am trying to do with Genesis 1—4 and the OT Paul Sevier Minear has done with Genesis and the NT. See *Christians and the New Creation: Genesis Motifs in the New Testament* (Louisville, Ky.: Westminister John Knox, 1994).

4

Genesis 2:1-17

A Foreshadowing of the New Creation

William J. Dumbrell

Genesis 2:1-3 looks back to God's work during the previous six days with tremendous satisfaction. Genesis 2:4a then sums up the section, bringing the number of times the words *create* and *make* occur in Genesis 1:1—2:3 to seven times each, thereby indicating the wholeness and completion of creation and the interrelationship between Genesis 1 and Genesis 2:3. The statement in Genesis 2:1 (NIV) that in this fashion the heavens and the earth were "completed" thus operates as a bridge signifying the end of the creation account and the opening of the narrative of Genesis 2. Specifically the narrator informs us in Genesis 2:2-3 that God had "completed" his work and that he had brought "all" his work to completion. Umberto Cassuto observes that in Genesis and Exodus the verb *kalah* ("to be completed, finished"), when referring to completed acts, indicates that the action already stands terminated.[1] Hence, God is now in the condition

---

[1]Umberto Cassuto, *A Commentary on the Book of Genesis*, 2 vols. (Jerusalem: Magnes Press, 1989), 1:61-62.

of one who had completed all his work. The Septuagint, the Samaritan Pentateuch, Peshitta and Jubilees 2, all aware of the difficulty that the Genesis account consequently raises for a seven-day work of creation, therefore read Genesis 2:2 as referring to the work done on the previous six days. They correctly recognized that the divine acts of creation had ceased with the work of the sixth day. The tight interrelationship of the first six days, from which the seventh is excluded by form, content and subsequent chapter divisions, provides a contrast of activity and purpose between Genesis 1 and Genesis 2:1-3.

CREATION AND THE SABBATH

Genesis 2:1-3 presents a pattern of seven lines rising to a crescendo in the first part of Genesis 2:3, with the second part of the verse emphasizing by way of conclusion the matter of Genesis 2:2, namely, that God had ceased from his work. The seventh day is mentioned three times (Gen 2:2, twice; Gen 2:3), each time in a sequence of seven words. In this way, Genesis 2:2-3 combines the creation account of Genesis 1 with a sabbath in a seven-day scheme. It is clear that although the noun *sabbath* does not occur, the verb *shabat* is used twice as a primary verb in Genesis 2:1-3, making a major function of the account the provision of a basis for the later observance of the sabbath. The Hebrew verb *shabat* means "to stop" or "to cease." Sometimes it is translated as "to keep sabbath," which is its later, OT-derived meaning. The verb occurs seventy-three times in the OT and is generally used of persons.[2] In none of the basic usages is the idea of physical rest or desisting from work primary. In our present context, the note of completion or perfection in the sense of bringing a project to its designed goal is implicit in the meaning of the verb and explicit in terms of the prominence given to the seventh day as completing the creation sequence and giving point to it. Furthermore, Gordon J. Wenham notes that the idea of blessing and hallowing the seventh day, that is, of endowing the day with the potential to fulfill its purpose in the divine plan and especially of setting it apart as holy, is without parallel, since God's blessing is normally restricted to animate beings.[3]

The seventh day thus acquires special status as the day that belongs to God alone. The seventh day of creation is the day that recognizes the sig-

[2]Gnana Robinson, "The Idea of Rest in the Old Testament and the Search for the Basic Character of the Sabbath," *ZAW* 92 (1980): 32-42.
[3]Gordon J. Wenham, *Genesis 1—15*, WBC 1 (Waco, Tex.: Word, 1987), p. 36.

nificance of what has been completed. When God's act (Gen 1) and purpose (Gen 2) are put together, we get a complete sequence—the week of creation. As a result, the account of Genesis 2:1-3 clearly invites creation generally and humanity particularly to keep sabbath. Most remarkable of all, unlike the previous six days, the seventh day is without end. The narrative intention seems to be to underline the place of the seventh day as distinctly special and unending and thus as introducing the context in which the historical happenings to come will occur. The idea of a rest after creation for the deity is found in many of the creation texts of the ancient world.[4] The notion of this rest as that which gives meaning to the account of creation as a whole and explains the ongoing purpose for which creation exists is peculiar, however, to the OT.

Genesis 2:4a serves as the introduction to the first *toledoth*-narrative in Genesis 2:4b—4:26. Genesis 2:5-7 then introduces Genesis 2:8-17 by detailing the provision of rain and a cultivator before the Eden narrative, which requires both, is presented.[5] The unending sabbath day provides the context in which the ideal life of the garden is to take place and be perpetuated in human experience. Since this divine purpose for creation precedes the human Fall, it will clearly continue beyond it. This point is also made in Hebrews 4:9-11, which tells us that there still remains a sabbath rest (*sabbatismos*) for the people of God. What remains to be experienced is not the sabbath as such, whose character of life in communication with the divine is always a possibility for humanity, but the complete rest associated with the sabbath before the Fall. Thus Hebrews 4:9-11 endorses the idea of a continuing sabbath but indicates that there are dimensions of the sabbath day that have continued to elude human experience. God's rest is the divine endorsement of creation and of his intentions for it as they emerge from this beginning, including his willingness to enter into fellowship with humanity.

THE GARDEN AS SEPARATED FROM ITS WORLD

Genesis 2:8-25 indicates the context and the nature of the fellowship that God and humanity were to share. The Hebrew syntax of Genesis 2:8 makes the point that man was formed outside the garden, abstracted from the world at large, and then placed within the garden. In reporting this, the

---

[4]John J. Scullion, *Genesis 1—11* (London: SPCK, 1984), p. 16.
[5]Mark D. Futato, "Because It Had Not Rained: A Study of Genesis 2:5-7 with Implications for Genesis 2:4-25 and Genesis 1:1—2:3," *WThJ* 60 (1998): 1-21.

narrative makes the point that humankind was not native to the garden. Yahweh, who is also Elohim, puts man in the garden, so that man's tenure in the garden depends upon his relationship with Yahweh Elohim. In biblical terms we may describe this as a movement of grace. The occupation of Eden, whatever its description may be, will therefore depend upon this grace. Genesis 2:9-17 explicate the implications of Genesis 2:8, with Genesis 2:9-14 describing the nature of the garden (Gen 2:8a) and Genesis 2:15-17 specifying the placement of man within the garden under the mandate to work it and take care of it (Gen 2:8b).

We turn first to the question of the garden's characteristics. We may notice in this connection the inference contained in the Hebrew word *gan* ("garden"). This Hebrew word refers to a fenced-off enclosure, particularly to a garden protected by a wall or a hedge (cf. 2 Kings 25:4; Jer 39:4; 52:7; Neh 3:15).[6] Eden is also a valued, fertile, well-watered place that is constantly cared for. This note is reinforced by the Septuagint translation of *gan* by *pardes*, itself a loan word from Persian. *Pardes* has the basic sense of "what is walled, what is hedged about" and can thus refer to a pleasure garden surrounded by a stone or an earthen wall. The Latin Vulgate translated the phrase "garden of Eden" by *paradises voluptatis*, "a delightful paradise." The existence of parks and gardens as special places in the ancient Near East is abundantly clear from Mesopotamian literature. Kings planted and boasted of extravagant gardens. The notion of the monarch as a gardener for the deity is also found in the ancient Near East.[7] In view of the royal connotation contained in the notion of the image (Gen 1:26), this role of Adam as gardener is instructive. Finally, Egyptian literature and art describe gardens as places of love and happiness.[8]

All of this underscores that the garden in Genesis 2 is to be viewed as a special, localized place that is spatially separated from its outside world. This world is presumably very much like our present world, which needs to be brought under the dominion of the divine rule for which Eden is the model. The differentiation of Eden from its world is further advanced by Genesis 3:24, where the cherubim guard the way to the tree of life with flaming swords. At the end of the canon, however, when history has run

---

[6]Cf. the Hebrew word *ganan* ("cover," "protect," "enclose," "fence") in *Lexicon in Veteris Testament Libris*, ed. L. Koehler and W. Baumgarten (Leiden: E. J. Brill, 1958), p. 190.

[7]M. Hutter, "Adam als Gärtner und König," *BZ* 30 (1986): 258-62.

[8]J. B. Pritchard, ed., *Ancient Near Eastern Texts Relating to the Old Testament* (Princeton, N.J: Princeton University Press, 1969), pp. 37-41.

its course and a new universe superintervenes, the new creation is presented not only as a new Jerusalem, a new covenant whose benefits are now
fully accessible, a kingdom of God's rule that is now fully understood and
demonstrated, and a new temple in which the contours of the new creation
are presented as a holy of holies, but also, lastly and most significantly, as
a new and universalized Eden (Rev 22:1-5).

THE GARDEN AS A SANCTUARY

The description of the garden in Genesis 2:8a, 9-14 contains many of the
motifs used in describing divine habitations in the ancient Near East. The
creation accounts in the ancient world commonly connect creation and
temple building. In the mythical structures of the ancient world, the sacred
mountain, where the deity who presided over the national fortunes could
be contacted, stood at the center of the earth, thus controlling it.[9] At this sacred site the victory that brought creation into being was also won and cel-
ebrated. In the ancient Near East, particularly, the sacred mountain was
the meeting place of heaven and earth, where celestial and mundane reality came together. There the gods assembled in council, presided over by
the principal deity (Anu/El). From this palace, world decrees, by which
creation was to be regulated, were promulgated. A sacred stream is also
frequently thought to issue forth from the cosmic mountain, whose water
teems with supernatural significance.[10] It was at this point that the upper
and lower waters of the cosmos met, thereby connecting heaven and earth
with the nether world.[11]

Hence sanctuaries and temples were constructed at these places so that
communication between the human and the divine worlds might take
place. In Mesopotamia, the temple could represent the cosmic mountain.
The fashioning of just such a temple after Marduk's victory over the chaos
figure, Tiamat, and after Marduk's recognition by the lesser deities of the
pantheon, is narrated in Enuma Elish. A temple tower *(ziggurat)* was built
in the temple precinct, and on the top of such a tower, which was con-

---

[9]Cf. the name of the Sumerian temple at Nippur as Dur-an-ki ("the bond of heaven and
earth"), the point at which the god Enlil had separated the two. So, among others, Michael
Fishbane, "The Sacred Center: The Symbolic Structure of the Bible," in *Texts and Responses*,
ed. Michael Fishbane and P. A. Flohr (Leiden: E. J. Brill, 1975), pp. 24-43.

[10]Jon D. Levenson, *Sinai and Zion: An Entry into the Jewish Bible* (San Francisco: HarperSan-
Francisco, 1985).

[11]R. J. Clifford, *The Cosmic Mountain in Canaan and the Old Testament*, HSM 4 (Cambridge,
Mass: Harvard University Press, 1972).

ceived of as the cosmic mountain on which the deity descended, the deity was believed to reside on earth.[12] In Canaan, the home of the presiding deity, El, was at the point where the double deeps (the upper and lower waters) met.

Against this general background, the presence of God in Eden points to its sanctuary character as sacred space. As we might expect of this divine center, the garden is the source of world fertility, for the great rivers take issue from the stream that rises in the garden.[13] There are also hints perhaps of the ancient world council of heaven at Genesis 3:22 (a motif taken up strongly by later Israelite prophecy), from which decrees are issued that affect the course of human relationships. Eden is thus presented as the *axis mundi*, the point from which the primal stream radiates to the four quarters of the world (Gen 2:10-14). In its center stood the trees of life and of the knowledge of good and evil, that is, the source of life and the manner by which life was to be conducted. Moreover, the creation narrative contains the vestiges of other ancient creation accounts in that it recounts a threat to the deity (Gen 1:2), combat (Gen 1:2), victory and the building of a temple. The placement of humankind in the garden as God's image furthers the analogy to the temple, with its image of the deity,[14] drawing together the motifs of kingship and the temple at the beginning of the Bible. Finally, since Eden is considered a divine space, Canaan is not only paralleled to Eden (Is 51:3; Ezek 36:35) but also fulsomely presented as an Israelite correspondence to Eden (cf. Deut 8: 7-10; 11:8-17), inasmuch as it too in its totality is a divine space (cf. Ex 15:17; Ps 78:54).

Ezekiel 28:1-10 clearly bears upon Genesis 2. Ezekiel 28:1-10 portrays

---

[12]F. R. McCurley, *Ancient Myth and the Biblical Faith: Scriptural Transformation* (Philadelphia: Fortress, 1983), p. 131.

[13]The "mist" (Gen 2:6 KJV) of the garden of Eden (Hebrew 'ed) is cognate with the Akkadian *idu* ("river"), but in this context it must mean "rain"; cf. Futato, "Because It Had Not Rained," pp. 6-7.

[14]Recently Rikki E. Watts, in a yet unpublished paper, has suggested that the essential model for conceptualizing the cosmos is that of the palace-temple, which is the most natural way in view of its background that Israel would think about the emergence of order out of chaos. The great king undergirds the city and its laws and so provides the necessary stability for society and long-term agriculture to develop (hence perhaps Eden is viewed as a garden). The days of Genesis 1 are work days, and creation is described throughout the OT in architectural terms: foundations, gates, bars, pillars, windows, canopy (cf. Is 66:1). On this model it is no surprise that on the last creation day the image of the god is placed in the completed palace-temple and that for the NT the ultimate expression of our restoration is the indwelling of (the) Spirit of (the) God. Thus the tabernacle or temple stands as a representation of the cosmos, with God's plan eventually being that all of creation becomes precisely this.

the king of Tyre as saying, "I am El." He is described as being in the seat of the gods and in the heart of the seas, thus reinforcing the allusion to El, whose dwelling place was at the springs of two rivers, amid the channels of the two deeps. The thrust of the oracle describes how Yahweh reveals the fallacy of the king's pride. In the further allusion of Ezekiel 28:13-14, Eden is clearly conceived of as a mountain sanctuary (cf. "holy mount of God," Ezek 28:14; "mount of God," Ezek 38:16 NIV). As such, the mountain of God is associated with holiness as opposed to profanity. Thus, even if the king of Tyre were in Eden, he would be cast out. Even if he were full of beauty and wisdom he would still go. If he were a cherub in God's most holy place, his sin would cause him to be expelled. Fire would consume him, and he would be no more. For although Ezekiel seems to have drawn upon a creation tradition common with that of Genesis, but not upon Genesis directly, the feature common to Eden and the mountain of Ezekiel 28 is holiness.[15] Ezekiel's identification of Eden as a holy mountain of God is confirmed by Genesis 2, where Eden, clearly elevated, is the source of living water for the world. We may also point to Ezekiel 36:33-36, where the Garden of Eden, as the symbol of fertility, is a fitting analogy for the land of Palestine about to be restored. Palestine as a whole is conceived of as a divine garden in Ezekiel 47:1-12.

The connections between Eden and the later Jerusalem temple are particularly strong. Wenham points out that the verbs *cultivate* or *work, serve* (ʿabad) and *guard (shamar)* in Genesis 2:15 are translated elsewhere in the OT as serving and guarding and can refer to priestly service and guarding in the tabernacle (Num 3:7-8; 8:25-26; 18:5-6; 1 Chron 23:32; Ezek 44:14; see also Is 56:6). Indeed, the only other time the OT uses both verbs together is in connection with the levitical service and guarding of the sanctuary (Num 3:7-8; 8:25-26).[16] In the context of Genesis 2:15, the meaning of ʿabad is "till" or "cultivate," but the regular use of the verb as "worship" later in the OT imports into the Genesis 2 context the aspect of human response in what seems to be this sanctuary, where the presence of God is directly experienced. Since after man's expulsion from the garden he is described in relationship to the earth by the same verb (Gen 3:23), this verb depicts the

---

[15]Gordon J. Wenham, "Sanctuary Symbolism in the Garden of Eden Story," in *I Studied Inscriptions from Before the Flood, Ancient Near Eastern, Literary and Linguistic Approaches to Genesis 1—11*, ed. Richard S. Hess and David T. Tsumura (Winona Lake, Ind.: Eisenbrauns, 1994), pp. 399-404.
[16]Wenham, *Genesis 1—15*, p. 67.

fundamental character of human dominion over the earth. Divine service is thus his role, first in submission to the Creator and then to the world, paralleling again the way in which Israel will be presented in Canaan.

The note emphasized under *'abad* is sustained by the Hebrew *shamar* ("keep," "guard"). Other nuances of this verb include "watching," "obeying," "retaining" and "observing." In Genesis 2:15 this watchful role may be understood in a twofold sense. Human dominion over the world committed to them will be that of a concern for the well-being of what is to be supervised. Hence the world outside the garden will be best served by humankind's service at the center of the world in the presence of God. There may also be latent in the notion the watchfulness that needs to be exercised against the serpent, which will appear in Genesis 3. Genesis 2:15-17 thus describes the position of humankind before the Fall, in which they existed in that openness in the divine presence suggested by the presentation of the seventh day in Genesis 2:4a. Moreover, humankind is authorized to exercise dominion over the world as a king/priest who paradoxically exercises that dominion by worship and service in the divine presence.

Targum Neofiti of Genesis 3:15 underscores this cultic notion by saying that Adam was placed in the garden to do service according to the law and to keep its commandments, language strikingly similar to the passages cited from Numbers concerning priestly supervision.[17] Later, two cherubim took over the responsibility of guarding the garden temple (cf. the verb used in Gen 3:24). Their role became memorialized in Israel's temple, when God commanded Moses to make two statues of cherubim and station them on either side of the ark in the Holy of Holies. Moreover, in Ezekiel's new temple, the walls of the holy place are profusely engraved with garden emblems,[18] while the function of the cherubim as guardians of the divine sanctuary reappears in the Holy of Holies in the Jerusalem temple.

Eden was the garden of God, and God's presence was the central aspect of the garden. That Eden is customarily understood in the later biblical

---

[17]G. K. Beale, *The Book of the Revelation* (Grand Rapids, Mich.: Eerdmans, 1999), pp. 1110-12, quotes the extensive rabbinic evidence. Beale suggests (as plausible, as I have done) that Adam was to enlarge the geographical boundaries of the garden until Eden extended throughout and covered the whole earth. What Adam failed to do Christ finally does. The Edenic imagery in Revelation 22:1 reflects the intention to show that the building of the temple that began in Genesis 2 will be completed in Christ and his people and will encompass the whole new creation.

[18]See the evidence cited; ibid., pp. 1110-11.

narratives as the earthly center where God was to be found is clear from Isaiah 51:3, where Eden and the garden of Yahweh are paralleled. As such, Eden is the representation of what the world is to become, as indicated by the fact that the new Jerusalem is presented in terms of the Holy of Holies of the Jerusalem temple (Rev 21-22; see again Ezek 36:33-36). As part of this association of the garden with the sanctuary, the Jerusalem temple is pictured as the forthcoming source of life-giving streams for the world (Ezek 47:1-12; cf. Joel 3:18).

ADAM IN THE GARDEN

Genesis 2:9-17 depicts Eden as a garden sanctuary in which man as priest/king offers worship at the center of the world. Genesis 2:15-17 concludes the account by focusing on Adam. It is to be noted that the adornments of the king of Tyre, likened to the original cherub in the garden (Ezek 28:13), correspond closely (in the LXX reading) to the precious stones set in the breastplate of the Israelite high priest (Ex 28:17-20).[19] By implication, this gives to the original inhabitant of the garden, Adam, a pronounced priest-ly/kingly character. In Ezekiel 28:11-19, the king of Tyre is represented as an Adamic figure, as made clear by the location of the garden, the use of the verb *bara'*, the presence of the cherub, and the idea of sin leading to expulsion. And the phrase "mountain of God" is a standard OT description for the temple (cf. Ps 48:1-3). Carol Newsom argues cogently, therefore, that the king of Tyre is also presented as a priest in Yahweh's temple.[20] As a result, the king's actions in the political realm are seen as a defilement of what is holy, while the oracle in Ezekiel 28 asserts the correct relationship between the king and Yahweh. The king is created by and subservient to Yahweh. Accordingly, if Genesis 1 emphasizes humankind's kingship, Genesis 2 presents a person as functioning in a priestly role in the divine presence.

Adam's role in Eden also raises the question of the relationship of Israel to Adam. Indeed, the analogies between Adam and Israel are significant for the later understanding of Israel's vocation in Canaan and for the subsequent course of biblical eschatology and mission. Israel, like Adam, is created outside the divine space to be occupied (cf. Gen 2:8, where the

---

[19]Daniel I. Block, *The Book of Ezekiel, Chapters 25—48*, NICOT (Grand Rapids, Mich.: Eerdmans, 1997), pp. 110-11.

[20]Carol A. Newsom, "A Maker of Metaphors—Ezekiel's Oracles Against Tyre," *Interp* 38 (1984): 151-65.

force of the Hebrew tense is an English pluperfect, cf. NIV, "had planted"). And like Adam, Israel is put into a sacred space to exercise a kingly/priestly role (cf. Ex 19:4-6). The Exodus 19:5-6 presentation of national Israel in a corporate, royal priestly role continues the divine purpose for humanity expressed in the early Genesis narrative. Moreover, like Adam, Israel is given laws by which the divine space is to be retained. Finally, Israel, like Adam, transgresses the law and so too is expelled from the divine space.[21]

The point is that the continued existence of Adam and Israel in divine space was conditional upon their obedience to the divine mandate. Adam possessed an immortality that could lapse, just as Israel was granted a covenant that could be revoked for national disobedience. Thus the relationship of Israel to Adam is important for the development of the eschatology of the Bible in that the creation account indicates the nature and purpose of Israel's special status in its role of exercising dominion in its world, a status that Adam had once exercised. For beginning with the Cain narrative, the movement from Adam to Israel will be accomplished by a series of divine selections that are designed to bring Israel onto the world stage. This series of movements results in God's concluding the Sinai covenant, by which he establishes a special relationship with Israel. In turn the Sinai covenant is designed to bring the world of nations into the sphere of the universal kingdom of God. The final status of the saved will be as kings and priests unto God (Rev 1:5-6; 5:10; 20:4-6), with the fulfillment of this expectation met at Revelation 22:1-5. These texts make it clear that the function of the creation account is to indicate the nature and purpose of Israel's special status as the bearer of the role that Adam once occupied. Moreover, since the Eden of the eschatological consummation is again perfect, we may expect that the intervening flow of history will point to the way in which the glorious end of history will finally be reached.

As a paradigm of the end, Genesis 2 thus displays the harmony that humankind's dominion was to secure for the world at large. Adam's role in Eden was to extend the contours of the garden to the whole world, since this is the transition that finally occurs in Revelation 22. As such, the presence of Adam in the garden presages Israel's role in its world and then that of Christ as well. At the same time, Genesis 2 indicates what dominion is and how it is to be exercised. Dominion is the service that takes its motiva-

---

[21]N. Lohfink, *The Christian Meaning of the Old Testament* (London: Burns and Oates, 1969), pp. 59-60.

tion from one's ultimate human relationship with the Lord God, on whose behalf dominion is exercised.

But the possibility existed, even within the garden, for people to exercise their God-given authority independently (Gen 2:16-17). We know this will happen in Genesis 3 and that it will have disastrous results for humanity's mandate and role. Nevertheless, the ongoing seventh day points to the possibility of life in the divine presence beyond the Fall. The account implies that faith in God's purposes can still bring us into an Edenlike human experience of the personal presence of God in the midst of a fallen world. Yet the Fall will deny to humankind the possibility that Eden held out to them. No longer immortal by virtue of their perfect relationship with God, humankind will not be able to develop and deepen that relationship by which life in God's presence would be retained. For humanity was created with a lapsible immortality.

The biblical expectation, however, is for an inheritance "that can never perish, spoil or fade" (1 Pet 1:4). It is clear then that the immortality to which the Bible finally progresses will be an important advance for the people of God beyond the relationship held by the first pair in the garden at the dawn of creation. But this harmony will be achieved only when the revelation of Revelation 21—22 becomes a reality: when the tabernacle of God and the Lamb is with humankind, when the new Jerusalem as the new Eden descends, and when the end-time Holy of Holies and the kingdom of God, in which everything is most holy, are with us.

THE EFFECTS OF THE FALL: HUMANKIND IN THE OUTSIDE WORLD

The paradox of revelation is that humankind, which was created to enjoy the immediacy of the divine presence of which the sabbath speaks, forfeited this blessing. Genesis 2:4—3:24 recounts the sorry tale of paradise gained and lost. In particular, the consequences that ensue from humankind's disobedience are recorded in the successive curses that are laid upon the serpent, the woman and the man (Gen 3:14-19). These three are cursed in a manner that strikes at the essence of their basic relationship to each other and to their world. The serpent is to be humiliated. There will be the broken intimacy between man and woman and, for woman, the pangs of childbirth. Man is cursed in relationship to the ground. After the Fall, man will find that his effort to cultivate the ground will be painful and disappointing.

But has the change occurred in humanity or in the environment or in both? It is normally suggested that, in addition to humankind's fallen state, the Fall caused the ground itself to become unyielding. Thus a change occurred in humanity and in the environment. Nevertheless, in keeping with our argument, it seems preferable to suggest that what is impaired as a result of the Fall is human control of the ground, not the ground itself. In this connection, the Hebrew phrase "because of" in Genesis 3:17 is ambiguous, since it can mean "on account of" or "for the benefit of." The sense most suited to the context of Genesis 1—3 is the former, that is, the ground yields a curse because of what will be inappropriate control of the ground in the future, inasmuch as the problem after the Fall is human inability to use the ground rightly. The Fall had left people "like God" in that they had power to make decisions by which the course of their lives and their world was to be determined. But since they were unlike God as well, they did not have the ability to ensure that their decisions would be right in themselves or the assurance that such decisions would promote the right consequences. That is to say, because of the Fall, people are now unable to exercise proper dominion over nature, as we saw Adam doing in Genesis 2.

Hence, in environmental terms, human failure to serve the world and thus to exercise dominion has resulted in the present spate of global problems. Unable to administer their charge, humans' mismanagement, neglect and exploitation only served to accentuate, increase and sharpen the inherent problems of the natural world over which they were charged to expend their energies as stewards of creation. Conversely, since Paul makes it clear that whatever the nature of this disruption of nature was, the advent of the new creation will remove it (Rom 8:18-23), from the Fall onward this hoped-for restoration becomes an important ingredient in the biblical, postexilic expectation for the end of the age. Moreover, this hope for the removal of the curse upon the ground is to some degree removed symbolically in Israel's gift of the Promised Land.

Clearly, then, Genesis 2 sets the basic course of biblical eschatology. The biblical movement is from creation and the Fall to the creation of Israel and its fall, to Christ as representative Israel, to the new Israel in Christ putting into effect Israel's mission to the new creation, to the final, full complement of the redeemed people of God who are kings and priests in the new creation. Thus in Genesis 2 we find a preliminary picture of the end of the age, in which redeemed humanity experiences eternal and indefectible fellowship with the Creator. Temple theology, which attests to the sovereign presence of God with his people, takes its rise in Eden. The garden narrative foreshadows a world, as the new Jerusalem, that is totally endorsed as sacred space. Furthermore, if I have argued correctly that the Genesis 2 narrative is the substance of an implied creation covenant, then the series of divinely imposed covenants throughout the canon also finds its rationale in Eden. This being so, we must conclude that the foundational factor in biblical theology is a creation theology.

But then how is the material between the beginning and the end integrated into this creation theology, when the remainder of the Bible is taken up preeminently with material relating to salvation history, the history of divine redemptive activity? The difference between the two is that creation, its beginning and end, is unmotivated, while redemption is a redemption from something to a redemption for something. The key to the understanding of the nexus between the theologies of creation and redemption therefore appears to be that in both Testaments redemption presupposes creation theology. Hence the first reflection on the significance of redemption, found in Exodus 15, is presented in terms of standard, ancient Near Eastern creation mythology. Likewise, the redemptive theology of Isaiah 40—55 and the theology of Isaiah 56—66 focus redemptive activity on the goal of the appearance of the new Jerusalem, the new creation. In the NT presentation of redemption, the explicit christological connection between creation and redemption is clear in passages such as John 1:1-18 and Colossians 1:15-20.

A biblical theology based on Genesis 2 concurs with the big picture presented in the Bible. The task ahead is to ensure that the details that support the superstructure we have suggested all fit into this framework. Biblical theology in itself is a descriptive endeavor. Nevertheless, once we have evaluated whether our understanding of the biblical picture and its supporting details presents a coherent and consistent worldview (for in the final analysis the Bible is coherent and consistent), we are not finished. We must then make the personal evaluation of whether the picture so drawn and supported is consistent with the reality we encounter in our world and with the psychology of the self of which we are all too brutally aware. But such a movement beyond description is a subjective judgment as to which of the two possible worldviews, beginning with or without the God and Father of our Lord Jesus Christ, we accept. For ultimately the gospel of our Lord Jesus Christ is about a new way of looking at ourselves and at our world. For as Paul knew very well and put so succinctly, if anyone is in Christ Jesus, he is a new creation (2 Cor 5:17).

5

Geography and Genealogy, Dominion and Dynasty

A Theology of the Hebrew Bible

Stephen G. Dempster

One of the main problems in doing biblical theology is that the theo-logical framework read out of the text has frequently been read in by the eyes of the interpreter.[1] These eyes, of course, have been equipped with various lenses that determine the perspective of the interpreter. More-over, the same lens used by a different theologian does not guarantee the same conclusion. As is frequently noted, the number of thematic centers identified for the OT is virtually equivalent to the number of interpreters.[2] The goal of this essay, however, is to view the Tanak through the lens its canonical structure provides in order to receive the perspective of the

[1]I would like to thank Jay Wells for his reading of this essay and his helpful criticisms. I would also like to thank the participants at the Biblical Theology Conference at Wheaton College (April 2000) for their contribution in helping me with this essay, in particular, Peter Gentry, Craig Carter and Byron Wheaton.

[2]E. E. Lemcio, "Kerygmatic Centrality and Unity in the First Testament," in *The Quest for Context and Meaning: Studies in Biblical Textuality in Honor of James A. Sanders,* ed. C. Evans and S. Talmon (Leiden: E. J. Brill, 1997), p. 361.

text.[3] Indeed, as a matter of practice, Rolf Rendtorff observes that Christian theologians rarely treat the OT in its final Jewish form, even though this was very likely the Bible of Jesus and the early church.[4]

It is therefore not surprising that one of the first to address this concern for the literary integrity of the complete Tanak is a Jewish scholar, R. E. Friedman.[5] His main point is that the big picture is so often missed because scholars are trained in exegesis, which often for practical reasons limits the scope of inquiry to a few verses. The exegete looks through a zoom lens. But when the range of vision is broadened to include the larger horizon of the book, a different picture emerges. The more wide-angle lens of the literary scholar allows one to see the intention of the editors of the Bible in their activity of combining the many sources into one literary work. The Bible is consequently viewed not so much as a library or a large anthology but as one text, with a beginning and an end, commencing with Eve in the Torah and concluding with Esther in the Writings.[6]

David Noel Freedman develops this idea further, concluding that the final shape of the Hebrew Bible is the result of deliberate editorial design. Not only can it be divided into the three sections of the Torah, Prophets and Writings, but also it can be divided into two halves consisting of approximately 150,000 words each. The first half, the Torah and Former Prophets, describes the judgment that fell upon Israel for covenantal violation, and the second, the Latter Prophets and Writings, depicts the promised salvation for Israel.[7]

Once read as a whole, the larger structure of the Tanak, or the Hebrew Bible, therefore provides a sort of wide-angle lens through which its contents can be viewed. Whatever may be said about the mystery of canoni-

---

[3]For reasons that I cannot argue here I am accepting the list of the books of the Hebrew Bible provided by *Baba Bathra* 14b. See the work by Roger T. Beckwith, *The Old Testament Canon of the New Testament Church and Its Background in Early Judaism* (Grand Rapids, Mich.: Eerdmans, 1985).

[4]Rolf Rendtorff, *Canon and Theology: Overtures to an Old Testament Theology* (Minneapolis: Fortress, 1993), pp. 53-60.

[5]R. E. Friedman, "The Hiding of the Face: An Essay on the Literary Unity of Biblical Narrative," *Judaic Perspectives on Ancient Israel*, ed. Jacob Neusner et al. (Philadelphia: Fortress, 1987), pp. 207-24. See also his more popular presentation, *The Disappearance of God: A Divine Mystery* (Boston: Little, Brown and Company, 1995).

[6]Friedman, "Hiding of the Face," pp. 211-12, 219.

[7]David Noel Freedman, *The Unity of the Hebrew Bible* (New York: Vintage, 1993). Note that John Sailhamer calls such a person responsible for the literary design of the Bible a canonicler. See John H. Sailhamer, *Old Testament Theology: A Canonical Approach* (Grand Rapids, Mich.: Zondervan, 1995), pp. 239-52.

zation, it is indisputable that the fact of canonization creates a new literary context for all the individual texts involved, and this fact makes one text out of many. The many texts are placed in a new context, and the many are read in the light of the one.[8] Inasmuch as readers "seek to understand the parts in the light of the whole,"[9] the editorial arrangement of the wider biblical context will constrain this understanding. At the same time, the fact that the canon is structured in terms of a narrative sequence with commentary means that canonization does not flatten the text in a unidimensional way but provides for evolution and growth, stressing that some things are more significant than others. Thus, for the purpose of this study, I am going to adopt this Tanak perspective (narrative—commentary—narrative) for viewing the content of the Hebrew Bible.[10]

THE BEGINNING AND ENDING OF THE TANAK

The beginning and ending of a literary work often provide the large context crucial for understanding the content. It is certainly so in the Hebrew Bible. Genesis and Chronicles provide the visual field of focus for the Tanak. The canon moves from creation to creation, the command of God that creates the world from chaos and the command of God through Cyrus to end the chaos of Jewish exile by rebuilding the temple. Genesis begins with Adam and quickly moves through history using genealogies until Abraham arrives on the historical scene. Chronicles begins with Adam and rapidly advances through time largely using genealogies until David arrives. Abraham and Sarah are called out of Babylon to go to the Promised Land at the beginning of Israel's national history in Genesis 12, and their distant descendants hear the same call at their new beginning after the exile in 2 Chronicles 36:22-23. This sense of beginning and ending needs to be further explored.

At the beginning of the canon, two inextricably related themes emerge: the creation of the world and the creation of humanity as the apex of that

---

[8]Note the important comments by Harry Gamble, *The New Testament Canon: Its Making and Meaning* (Philadelphia: Fortress, 1985), p. 75: "In the nature of the case, canonization entails a recontextualization of the documents incorporated into the canon. They are abstracted from both their generative and traditional settings and redeployed as parts of a new literary whole; henceforth they are read in terms of this collection. In this way their historically secondary context becomes their hermeneutically primary context."
[9]Sailhamer, *An Introduction to Old Testament Theology*, p. 214.
[10]Note the dramatic use of this sequence for the depiction of God in the Tanak by J. Miles, *God: A Biography* (New York: Vintage, 1996).

creation. The first command given to humanity is to have children and have dominion over the creation (Gen 1:26-28). In the beginning there is not only geography and genealogy but also dominion and dynasty—a royal humanity ruling an earthly habitat. In the next chapter there is a narrower focus, with the geographical aspect limited to the Garden of Eden. This paradise planted by the Lord is brimming with life, with fruit trees, a tree of life and a river that flows down out of Eden and divides into four other rivers, thus giving life to the rest of the world. The presence of cherubim later in the narrative (Gen 3:24) and the description of the garden as the place where the Lord God walks (Gen 3:8) contribute to understanding this place as a type of cosmic mountain where heaven and earth are united, the throne room of the world (see, e.g., Ezek 28:12-17). Many scholars observe the similarities between Eden and the later tabernacle and temple on Mount Zion,[11] where the footstool of the heavenly throne, the ark of the covenant, was located.

The genealogical aspect focuses on the creation of the man and the woman. The man is formed from the earth, and the woman is built from the man. Humanity is regarded as complete with the building of the woman. This idea of building recurs later in the idea of a woman building up her house (i.e., family) through having children (Gen 16:2; 30:3; Deut 25:9; Ruth 4:11).

The terms of planting and building that occur in Genesis at the beginning of the canon carry a heavy theological payload throughout the rest of the Hebrew Bible. They occur at the beginning of the second half of the Bible and are used particularly of the planting of Israel as the Lord's garden in the land, which spreads to the ends of the earth, and of the building of a dynastic house, which provides authority and rule (see below).

Genesis 3 describes the expulsion of the couple from Eden for listening to the serpent. Geographically they are uprooted from their home, to live in exile east of Eden. At the same time, there is genealogical hope, a promise embedded in the curse on the serpent, the so-called protoevangelium (Gen 3:15): there will be enmity between the seed of the woman and the seed of the snake; the woman's seed will strike the serpent on the head while the latter will impart a blow to the former. The triumph of the woman's seed suggests a return to the Edenic state and a restoration of the lost

---

[11]See, e.g., Gordon J. Wenham, "Sanctuary Symbolism in the Garden of Eden Story," *Proceedings of the World Congress of Jewish Studies* 9 (1986): 19-25.

regal status of humanity. As the woman was built from the man to complete the old creation, a seed will be built from the woman to regain dominion over it.

The fact that many modern scholars see no theological significance to the genealogical and geographical dimensions of the text here shows that they limit the scope of exegesis myopically to the immediate context or that they are trying to escape the "blinders" of Christian exegesis.[12] But once the scope is widened not only to the book of Genesis, but also to the larger literary domain of the canon, these dual motifs become obvious.

The first narrative of life outside Eden focuses on birth and children. Later, the first son of Adam and Eve, a farmer, kills his brother, a shepherd, and as a result he is alienated from the land, condemned to be a nomad (Gen 4:1-16). He defiantly builds a city but it is really an anticity, since Cain's character is stained with blood. Thereafter follows the first genealogy of the Bible, which is an antigenealogy, as it begins with Cain, the brother-killer, and ends with the child-killer Lamech (Gen 4:17-24).[13] But immediately after the genealogy, Eve has another son who replaces his slain brother, Abel (Gen 4:25-26). Following this there are two ten-member linear genealogies, each concluding with a segmented genealogy of three descendants (Gen 5:1-32; 11:10-26). One occurs before the universal judgment of the flood and concludes with the birth of a son, the tenth from Adam, who becomes a deliverer from the deluge. In fact, Noah's father specifically associates his immediate descendant with relief from the curse imposed upon the ground (Gen 5:29). This passage is telling, since it clearly shows at the end of the genealogy a hope focused on the birth of a child to grant relief from the curse!

The second ten-member genealogy occurs after the universal judgment at Babel. The building of the tower by the human community in the postflood world is an attempt to reproduce a cosmic mountain and so to get back to the garden, but it results in humanity being uprooted again and being scattered over the land. It is clear that the last member of this genealogy, the tenth from Noah, Abram, is another deliverer who holds hope for the world (Gen 11:26).

The narrative strategy used in this text is obvious. The seed of the wom-

[12]See the typical attitude regarding Genesis 3:15 in Sigmund Mowinckel, *He That Cometh: The Messiah Concept in the Old Testament and Later Judaism* (Nashville: Abingdon, 1954), p. 11.
[13]For the term *antigenealogy,* see Robert B. Robinson, "Literary Functions of the Genealogies of Genesis," *CBQ* 48 (1986): 600 n. 8. I would like to thank Peter Gentry for this reference.

an is being traced genealogically, and this seed, whether Seth, Noah or Abram, is crucial for the salvation of the human race. M. D. Johnson has argued that there are a variety of purposes for linear genealogies, including the political legitimation of the last descendant on the list. But here it is clear that these texts fit another purpose, that is, to exhibit "a sense of movement within history toward a divine goal."[14]

This is made explicit in the narrative of the text. The previous thousands of years can be sketched in eleven chapters; the next twenty-five years are dealt with in ten chapters. In the narrative world, it is as if the world has been waiting for this moment, the arrival of the tenth descendant of Noah, Abram. His arrival is accompanied by key theological pronouncements involving geography and genealogy. Abraham is told to leave the world of Babel, so that he can have God's piece of geography. Moreover, he and his barren wife hold the key to the promise, as they will be shown *(ra'ah)* that land and become a great nation, through which all families of the previously cursed ground *('adamah)* will be blessed (Gen 3:17; 12:1-3). As far as the historical context is concerned, this wording contains royal terminology since the promise would be the normal ambition of oriental monarchs.[15] But in the canonical context this promise indicates that Abraham will remove the curse. As scholars note, the word *blessing* occurs five times in the three verses of the call narrative (Gen 12:1-3) in sharp contrast to the five-fold curse mentioned in Genesis 1—11 (Gen 3:14, 17; 4:11; 5:29; 9:25). Moreover, the text implies that there will be opposition to the plan of blessing but this attack will be defeated. This same text is echoed later when Israel's conquest march is threatened by the potential curses of Baalam (Gen 12:3; Num 24:9).

In the ensuing narrative the text stresses geography and genealogy. Abraham and Sarah wander through the land growing older and thus losing whatever remaining human potential they ever had for a child. But Abraham is nonetheless a regal figure who defeats enemies in Genesis 14 and is rewarded by being blessed by a regal figure from Jerusalem, Melchizedek. This singular blessing is bestowed by the Creator of heaven and earth, thus linking Abraham's life with the Creator's purposes in history (Gen 14:18-20). The fact that it is conferred by someone who comes

---

[14]M. D. Johnson, *The Purpose of Biblical Genealogies* (Cambridge: Cambridge University Press, 1969), p. 80, cited in R. Braun, *1 Chronicles*, WBC (Waco, Tex.: Word, 1986), p. 3.

[15]Byron Wheaton develops this idea to some extent in "Abraham, Land and Stewardship" (unpublished Ph.D. dissertation, Westminster Theological Seminary, 2001).

from what is later known to be the holiest site in the Bible cannot be a co-incidence. This same holy site reemerges at the climax of the narrative (Gen 22:1-19). The long-anticipated descendant has now arrived, and Abraham is told to take him to this site and sacrifice him. There on the holy mountain, God provides *(ra'ah)* a sacrifice. He has shown *(ra'ah)* Abraham the land and has provided *(ra'ah)* him with a sacrifice. He has blessed him from Jerusalem twice. For the first time in the narrative God promises Abraham that in addition to blessing the world through Isaac, his descendants will possess the gates of their enemies, that is, they will decisively defeat the enemy by taking him at his most vulnerable point (Gen 22:17). Thus this text is an echo of Genesis 3:15, and for the sensitive reader there is an echo of the Day of Atonement ceremony in Leviticus 16, which describes Israel's most solemn sacrificial rite.[16]

The rest of Genesis must be briefly surveyed. The blessing of Abraham is transferred to Isaac, and almost immediately the text deals with the birth of Esau and Jacob and the transmission of the blessing to an individual, Jacob (Gen 25:11, 19-26). Jacob, who becomes the father of the Israelite nation, has a name that means "heel." And his name is later changed to Israel, God's fighter, for at all costs he fights for the blessing (Gen 32:28-29). Nonetheless, the attainment of the blessing means that his heel has been wounded; his leg has been crippled in the fight. Jacob's earlier vision at Bethel shows that God is building his own tower, which reaches the sky not in Babylon but in Canaan, uniting heaven to earth on a piece of rock in a field, upon which Jacob's head rests (Gen 28:10-15). Thus geography and genealogy coalesce.

The focus of Jacob's life dramatically shifts from Canaan to Mesopotamia where he, his wives and concubines produce virtually all of the family of Israel, and toward the end of his life he is engaged in blessing that same family before he dies (Gen 29:31—30:24; 49:2-27). The birth of Judah, which evokes thanks from his mother, Leah, in the following words, "This time I will praise the LORD" (Gen 29:35 NRSV [throughout the essay]), is echoed in the key blessing of Israel at the end of his life, "Judah, your brothers shall praise you" (Gen 49:8). Significantly, from this particular tribe will emerge a lionlike ruler, whom no one will be able to oppose. His

---

[16]Brevard S. Childs, *Biblical Theology of the Old and New Testaments: Theological Reflection on the Christian Bible* (Minneapolis: Fortress, 1992), pp. 327-35. It is therefore no coincidence that in Genesis 22 there is the first explicit sacrificial act of an Israelite and that it is done at what later becomes the holiest site.

scepter will hold sway, and the peoples will obey him. Moreover, the geography will be renewed, as vineyards will be so plentiful that they can be used for the tethering of animals (Gen 49:9-11).

Genesis closes on a note of hope. Israel is living in Egypt, but Joseph promises that God will visit them and bring them up out of the land to Canaan. At the end of Genesis there is a strong expectation of a royal warrior who will emerge from the tribe of Judah, crush his enemies, rule over the world and renew nature. The ending of Genesis points to the future to "a movement toward a divine goal within history."[17]

Chronicles, the last book of the Tanak, focuses on these same themes. It begins with the genealogy of Adam and moves through the genealogies of the tribes of Israel. In particular, the genealogy of Judah is placed at the front of the list, and David's ancestors and royal descendants are prominently featured. After the remainder of the genealogies, history begins in 1 Chronicles 10 with Saul's demise and David's rise.[18] The capture of Jerusalem and the reign of David become the focus of the next nineteen chapters. Again, it is as if all history has been waiting, in this case not for Abraham, but for David from the tribe of Judah. Or in the words of Walter Brueggemann, all history is regarded as a footnote to David.[19] As Gerhard von Rad remarks, "The Chronicler's account starts with David. This at the same time gives the keynote of the most important theme in the whole work, for what does it contain apart from David?"[20]

The covenant with David in which he is promised an heir forever becomes a critical component in this royal ideology. Indeed, this covenant with David provides the answer to von Rad's question. Apart from David, the Chronicler's work contains Jerusalem and the temple. To be fair to von Rad, though, these geographical elements were seen as inseparable from David. In Chronicles, after the genealogies concluding with David, the geographical focus thus quickly shifts to Jerusalem and to David's desire to build a temple for the Lord. This focus on the temple, the place of God's presence to which all people can come, then dominates the narrative from David's procurement of the site and provisions for the temple, to Sol-

---

[17]Johnson, *The Purpose of Biblical Genealogies*, p. 80.

[18]Note W. Rudolph's comment about the description of Saul's demise in 1 Chronicles 10: "Aus dem Dunkel, in dem Saul versinkt, geht strahlend der Stern David," cited in Braun, *1 Chronicles*, p. 149.

[19]Walter Brueggemann, *David's Truth in Israel's Imagination and Memory* (Philadelphia: Fortress, 1985), p. 100.

[20]Gerhard von Rad, *Old Testament Theology*, 2 vols. (New York: Harper & Row, 1962), 1:350.

omon's building and dedication of the structure (1 Chron 17—2 Chron 7). The evidence is clear: the hope for the world is found in genealogy and geography, dynasty and dominion, scion and Zion. David has arrived. The temple has been built. The process of world restoration is well on its way!

Nevertheless, the sin of the people leads to the destruction of Jerusalem and the temple, as well as to the exile of the people to Babylon—of all places. It seems as if Babylon has the last word at the end of the canon. But just as at the beginning of the canon God goes down to judge Babylon and so bring to nothing the human pretensions to unite heaven to earth, so at the end of the canon he commands through a foreign king an exiled Judah to go up and build the temple from which heavenly blessing will flow. God is not finished with Abraham. There has been a setback, but the blessing will come through the Davidic house. Hope remains.

THE TANAK: BETWEEN THE BEGINNING AND THE END

The Torah. Once the wide-angle lens of the canon has shown the larger picture of the Bible, a zoom lens can be used to see some of the finer detail. Exodus through to the end of the Torah describes the journey of Israel from Egyptian oppression to Sinai, the wilderness wanderings and finally the march to Canaan. It is the journey of a people, delivered by God to be subject to his rule, from one geographical location to another, namely, from Egypt to Canaan. The clear reason for their deliverance from Egypt is God's fulfillment of the Abrahamic covenant so that, in the words of the song of Miriam and Moses, "You brought them in and planted them on the mountain of your own possession, the place, O LORD, that you made your abode, the sanctuary, O LORD, that your hands have established" (Ex 15:16-17).

Thus the goal of exodus is the building of the Edenlike sanctuary so that the Lord can dwell with his people. A large part of the law at Sinai is the preparation and building of this sanctuary, which is placed at the center of the encampment (Ex 25—31; 35—40). Later, when Israel is on the verge of entering the land where the sanctuary will be permanently fixed, Balaam is hired by Balak, king of Moab, an archenemy, to curse Israel. But instead of cursing, he blesses Israel and envisions the nascent nation like gardens and trees planted by the Lord beside the waters. In his speech a king emerges, exalted in majesty, in order to destroy the enemies of Israel. In language identical to the blessing of Judah in Genesis 49, this royal figure is like a lion that can withstand any opposition (Num

24:5-9). Similarly, in the next oracle of Balaam, a star rises out of Jacob and a scepter from Israel to smash the heads of the Moabites, who are envisioned in this context as representing the enemy of Israel (Num 24:16-24). The royal, genealogical notes struck earlier in Genesis echo powerfully here (cf. Gen 3:15; 12:3; 49:10).[21]

The Torah concludes with Israel at the borders of the land of promise, hearing the law again and being told to worship at a central sanctuary. Before Moses dies outside the land of promise, the genealogical and geographical connections are strongly made. He blesses the tribes of Israel, with Judah being promoted to second position on the tribal list (Deut 33:7). The tribes are envisioned as treading on the backs of their enemies (Deut 33:29). Then, before he dies, Moses is granted a vision of the borders of the entire land of Israel (Deut 34:1-5).

The Prophets. The next section, the Prophets, has two subdivisions. The Former Prophets consist of Joshua, Judges, Samuel and Kings, which continue the Torah narrative from the conquest to the exile in Babylon. This completes the first half of the Hebrew Bible.[22] The Latter Prophets, which begin the second half, comprise Jeremiah, Ezekiel, Isaiah and the Twelve, which are largely anthologies of prophetic speeches delivered mainly during the time described in the latter part of the book of Kings.

As the Prophets begin, the geographical theme is salient. The land that Moses sees with his eyes Israel marches upon with its feet. It is this land that has been promised to Abraham and is linked to Eden. The angelic wielder of the sword in Joshua does not bar Israel from the land as the cherubim did Adam and Eve from the garden in Genesis (Gen 3:24; Josh 5:13-15).

Geographical considerations are extremely important; the first tribe allotted its land in Joshua is Judah (Josh 15:1-63), just as Judah is the first tribe mentioned in Judges (Judg 1:1-21). In the historical books the focus of concern quickly moves from Shiloh to Gibeah to Jerusalem, the place of Melchizedek's blessing and God's provision of a sacrifice. Moreover, Samuel concludes with the purchase of the temple site and an angel with

---

[21]As Sailhamer astutely points out (*Introduction to Old Testament Theology*, p. 212), "So striking is the final eschatological victory of this king envisioned in Numbers 24 and so closely are these images paralleled in the later visions of Daniel (e.g. Dan 11:30), that classical literary criticism was unanimous in assigning these verses to a later, postexilic, apocalyptic redactor."

[22]See Freedman, *Unity of the Hebrew Bible*, pp. 4-5.

drawn sword pointed at Jerusalem. The sword's thrust is averted not by a command from an angel but by one from a prophet, when David is ordered to purchase the temple site and offer sacrifices on an altar (2 Sam 24:18; cf. Gen 22:11-12). The angel in Genesis 22 intervenes to stop Abraham from sacrificing his child of promise. The prophet intervenes in 2 Samuel 24 only when David asks God to strike him and his house and spare the people as a whole. On this cosmic mountain, sacrifice will provide the stability for the creation, and the temple that is built later by Solomon will become the spiritual center for all nations.

Once again, however, tragedy ensues as idolatry causes the disintegration of the kingdom. As a result, the northern and southern kingdoms are respectively conquered and exiled by their enemies. At the end of the historical narrative of the Former Prophets, nothing but ruins remain of the nation of Judah and its capital, Jerusalem. The remnant of the population is scattered in exile. Zion is an ash heap.

If the movement from the possession of the land to exile is the geographical trajectory of the Former Prophets, what about the genealogical aspect? Joshua, the successor of Moses, embodies some of the regal and conquering features of primal humanity in Genesis 1 and predicted in the promises to Judah and Israel (Gen 49:8-10; Num 24:17-19). Viewed atomistically or politically, Joshua seems inhumane when he instructs the leaders of Israel to place their feet on the necks of the prostrate Canaanite kings before he does them in with a sword (Josh 10:24-26). Viewed through the lens of the canon, however, it is clear that theologically this act declares that the defeat of the serpent is being worked out in history (cf. Gen 3:15; 49:8).[23] The conquest is much more than a simple military victory.

As the narrative develops in the Former Prophets, everything leads up to a figure who is anointed by Samuel. Almost immediately, this person demonstrates his ability as a leader by effectively slaying a gigantic anti-God symbol with a stone before decapitating him (1 Sam 17). For the next fifteen chapters, even before David is recognized as king, the narrator considers him to be one, just as he and his house will be the essential focus of the rest of the Former Prophets. The Davidic covenant, in which God grants David an enduring heir and a perpetual royal house because of David's desire to build a house or temple for God, is its climax (2 Sam 7).

---

[23]See O. P. Robertson, *The Christ of the Covenants* (Phillipsburg, N.J.: Presbyterian & Reformed, 1980), p. 101.

In light of this promise, one of the most ominous events throughout the tumultuous history that follows is Athaliah's near elimination of the Davidic seed (2 Kings 11:1-3). But more ominous is the vacant throne at the end of the Former Prophets, when Jerusalem has been destroyed and Jehoiachin, the king from the Davidic line, is in exile.

And so at the end of the Former Prophets, just before the last four verses (2 Kings 25:27-30), midway through the Hebrew Bible, the land has been lost—geography—and genealogy seems lost. The land of Israel is *tohu wabohu* (Jer 4:23; cf. Gen 1:2). The Davidic throne is vacant. The serpent has apparently won.

But then appear the next four verses, which state the incredible news that Jehoiachin has been released from prison and exalted to a position among the other kings in Babylon. He is given a place at the king's table and given new clothes. The news is absolutely stunning when read in the wider context of the canon,[24] where a seed of the woman will conquer the serpent, the seed of Abraham will lead to blessing for the world, the tribe of Judah will provide a ruler for the nations, and the Davidic covenant guarantees this triumph. Here at the midpoint of the canon it is clear that the seed of the woman may be down but not out. Everything is pinned on genealogy.

The next four books, the Latter Prophets, confirm this. These books provide virtually a running commentary on the events of the narrative to this point, a commentary continued in the Writings until the narrative line is resumed with the book of Daniel. There is a symmetrical balance between the Prophets and the Writings, with narrative followed by commentary in the former and commentary preceding the narrative in the latter.

Viewed with a zoom lens, these Latter Prophets seem more like preachers of doom; they announced the judgment for the nation for violating the Sinai covenant. But viewed with the wide-angle lens of the canon, they are preachers of radical hope beyond the doom.

The first chapter in the second half of the Hebrew Bible describes Jeremi-

---

[24]When read more atomistically, 2 Kings 25:27-30 may be seen as the last historical source the historian had at his disposal (Noth), or it may offer a modest hope based on the Davidic covenant (Levenson). Still others have argued from a larger canonical perspective encompassing the Writings that this last representative of the Davidic dynasty is "lampooned and compromised in exile," a "puppet monarch" who eats defiled food from a pagan king's table. As such, he is pointedly contrasted with Daniel's firm resolve not to eat the king's food (Dumbrell). See Martin Noth, *Überlieferungsgeschichtliche Studien*, 2nd ed. (Tübingen: Max Niemeyer Verlag, 1957), p. 87; Jon D. Levenson, "The Last Four Verses in Kings," *JBL* 103 (1984): 353-61; William J. Dumbrell, *The Search for Order: Biblical Eschatology in Focus* (Grand Rapids, Mich.: Baker, 1994), p. 138.

ah's role in terms that are probably true of all the prophets to follow: to up-
root, to demolish, to destroy, to pull down, to build and to plant (Jer 1:10).
The initial four verbs show that the main brunt of their work is demolition,
but the concluding two verbs show that there is hope for construction after
the demolition. In fact, the two verbs of building and planting in the land
resonate in the four prophetic books: they predominate in Jeremiah, but are
also found in Ezekiel, Isaiah and the Twelve.[25] The last close coincidence of
these two verbs in the Former Prophets was in Nathan's oracle to David,
when the Lord said that he would plant Israel in the land and that David's
son would build a house for Yahweh and that Yahweh would build a house
for David (2 Sam 7:10, 16). The last coincidence of these two verbs in the
Latter Prophets is in the Twelve, where it is stated that the Lord will build
David's fallen house, raising its ruins from the dust. As a result, the people
will again build the desolate cities, and Israel will again be planted in the
land, never to be uprooted again (Amos 9:11-15).

Thus, when the wider literary context of Jeremiah's call is considered,
geography and genealogy become prominent. The exile is not the last
word. The people are going to be planted again, and the Davidic house,
both temple and dynasty, will be built. These words, which begin the second half of the Bible, echo God's planting and building at the beginning of
the first half of the Bible (Gen 2:8, 22). As their corollary, the first positive
oracle in Jeremiah points to a return from exile to Zion. In that day there
will be no mention of the ark, for the entire city will be the throne of Yahweh
and the focal point for the world's worship (Jer 3:14-18). A similar oracle occurs later, followed by another that promises the provision to David of a
righteous branch who will save Judah and Israel (Jer 23:3-6). The last chapter of Jeremiah, which follows the prediction of the final destruction of
Babylon, is virtually identical to the last chapter of Kings and therefore un-
derlines the Davidic hope with Jehoiachin's release. By placing this chapter
at the end of Jeremiah, it is clear that the building and planting have begun
with Jehoiachin. Babylon does not have the last word; David does.

In Ezekiel, the first positive oracle is a prediction of God's being a little
sanctuary for the people in exile, followed by the promise to return them
to the land (Ezek 11:14-21). In later prophecies this land is regarded as
nothing less than a return to Eden, ruled by God's servant, Prince David

---

[25]Jer 1:10; 18:9; 24:6; 29:5, 28; 31:5, 28; 35:7; 42:10; 45:4; Ezek 28:26; 36:36; Is 5:2; 65:21, 22; Amos
9:14-15.

(Ezek 36:35). But dominating Ezekiel's prophecy is the vision of the temple mount in the midst of the land, from which a stream descends (Ezek 47:1-12). This time, when it leaves the temple of Eden, it does not divide into four tributaries but grows into a mighty river changing the landscape and giving life everywhere it goes, even making the Dead Sea live. On both sides of the river, trees flourish and their fruit is used for food and their leaves for healing.

No sooner is this vision over than appears Isaiah's first positive oracle, in which the temple mountain dominates the landscape of the universe (Is 2:1-5). Zion has become Everest. Instead of the river flowing out of the temple, however, the rivers of the nations now defy gravity by flowing up to Jerusalem.[26] If Ezekiel renews Eden, Isaiah reverses Babel. Isaiah's depiction also continues the theme of the restoration of Eden, with this mountain dominating the landscape: "They will not hurt or destroy on all my holy mountain; for the earth will be full of the knowledge of the LORD as the waters cover the sea" (Is 11:9). What is said about Zion is thus said about the world. And ruling over this new world order is the shoot from the stump of Jesse's tree (Is 11:1), which destroys the enemies in such a way that even little children can play with snakes (Is 11:8). The battle is over.

In the first three chapters of the Twelve, Hosea 1—3, the people are envisioned coming back from exile after the judgment, seeking the Lord their God and David their king (Hos 2:1-3; 3:4-5). Nature will be renewed in a new covenant that God will make with his people, in which he will wed them forever (Hos 2:16-23).

There is no doubt that these themes resounding again and again in the Latter Prophets provide the hermeneutical lens for the ending of the first half of the Bible. Jehoiachin's release means life from the dead! The prophetic commentary ensures this reading.

The Writings. The third section of the Hebrew Bible develops this commentary further by providing an introduction to the Psalter with a genealogy of David (Ruth 4:18-22). Although generically Ruth is narrative, it is a narrative flashback that helps provide needed perspective. It does so by linking the child of Ruth and Boaz to the distant past, the first mothers of Israel with the promises given to them, and then linking the child to David in the future (from the point of view of the book). It is no accident that this

---

[26]See the significant statement by Dumbrell, who notes that this passage "subordinates geographical reality to biblical eschatology" (*Search for Order,* p. 83).

book concludes with a ten-member, linear genealogy whose last member is David. The focus has shifted from Noah (Gen 5) to Abraham (Gen 11) to David. David and building have become the main theme. Thus all the people of Bethlehem wish Ruth the best when Boaz marries her: "May the LORD make the woman who is coming into your house like Rachel and Leah, who together built up the house of Israel" (Ruth 4:11). The birth of Obed and the ensuing genealogy of David show not only the explicit "movement toward a divine goal within history,"[27] but also in some measure the attainment of that goal. Jehoiachin's release means that the hope is still alive.

In the Psalter, an introductory psalm combines genealogy with geography as Nathan's oracle is given explicit eschatological significance: a Davidic ruler is installed on Mount Zion with a mandate to rule the world and smash his enemies with an iron scepter (Ps 2:6-9). The royal psalms at the seams of the Psalter echo this theme (cf. Ps 72; 89).[28] Psalm 89 begins by stressing the Lord's destruction of the forces of chaos in creation and proceeds to emphasize that it is the Davidic dynasty that will destroy those forces in history (Ps 89:10-19, 20-26). Zion and the temple are regarded as the center of the earth, a new Eden where humans and animals can take refuge under the wings of the cherubim and be replenished by the river of the Lord's pleasures (Ps 36:8-10).

In the book of Job, which follows, the enemy of not only Israel but also humanity emerges. Coming as it does after the Psalms, the enemy's doom is certain, as is Job's hope for a redeemer. In much of the rest of the commentary in the third section, there is a Davidic emphasis, with the wisdom of God emanating from the royal house in Jerusalem. The grasping of this wisdom is related to grasping the tree of life in the Garden of Eden (Prov 3:18).

The commentary then comes to an abrupt end in the book of Lamentations, with the pouring out of grief over the destruction of Jerusalem bringing the reader back to the ending of the narrative thread in Kings. Here too geography is crucially involved inasmuch as Zion is destroyed, the place of the Lord's abode. Genealogy may be involved as well, since the center of the book singles out the man who has experienced the rod of God's wrath (Lam 3:1-18). Perhaps, as N. Porteous argues, this is none oth-

---

[27]Johnson, *The Purpose of Biblical Genealogies*, p. 80.
[28]On the editorial function of psalms such as these, see G. Wilson, *The Editing of the Hebrew Psalter*, SBLDS 76 (Chico, Calif.: Scholars Press, 1985), pp. 200-228.

er than Jehoiachin,[29] so that this text functions literarily to signal the return to the situation described at the end of the narrative in Kings. The city and king are in ruins. The narrative can resume.

And resume it does. To a Judah languishing in Babylon, Daniel sees a stone destroying a gigantic image, an anti-God symbol, and then becoming a great mountain filling the whole earth (Dan 2:27-45).[30] The Davidic hope is alive![31] What is more, a specific time scheme of seventy weeks is laid out before all this will be accomplished (Dan 9:24-27).[32] In a similar way, Esther, which follows, holds out hope for those exiles who are being persecuted at a later time. If the Babylonian beast is no longer a threat, neither is the Persian one.

The next two books are chronologically out of order, with Ezra/Nehemiah placed before Chronicles. Dumbrell may be right that the modest reforms of the former are thereby put in perspective.[33] The point is that these reforms are not simply little actions being done in the Persian province of Judah; they are being undertaken in the context of a great plan for the world, something which began, as the final book in the canon, Chronicles, indicates, in Eden with Adam at the beginning of history. Even more pertinent, however, is the fact that by concluding with Chronicles a powerful theological comment is made: "Israel is still in exile even though it has returned" (see, e.g., 1 Chron 3:17-23).[34] This makes perfect sense since the final perspective of Chronicles indicates that the return has already

---

[29]N. Porteous, "Jerusalem-Zion: The Growth of a Symbol," in *Verbannung und Heimkehr*, ed. A. Kuschke (Tübingen: Mohr Siebeck, 1961), pp. 244-45, cited in D. R. Hillers, *Lamentations* (Garden City, N.Y.: Doubleday, 1972), p. 63.

[30]See Dumbrell, *Search for Order*, p. 140: "The mountain symbolism, probably an allusion to the world mountain as the point of contact between heaven and earth, has overtones from the prophetic eschatology of Zion. Zion, whose glory and splendour will dominate the world, will be the world mountain of the new age."

[31]See too, independently of my work, the recognition of the Davidic symbolism in Daniel by A. Rofe, "The Battle of David and Goliath: Folklore, Theology, Eschatology," in *Judaic Perspectives on Ancient Israel*, ed. Jacob Neusner et al. (Philadelphia: Fortress, 1987), p. 144.

[32]This is extremely significant from the point of view of the canon, since there is reference to the seventy years of exile at the end of the canon (2 Chron 36:20-21).

[33]Dumbrell, *Search for Order*, p. 152.

[34]I would like to thank my colleague Craig Carter for this way of putting the matter. Thus in a very real sense all three sections of the Hebrew canon end on a note of exile. This is clear for Deuteronomy as the people are on the outside of the land looking in; it is less clear for Haggai—Malachi. Nevertheless, there too the fact that the people are in need of radical reform and that the return has had extremely modest gains shows that the people are still awaiting redemption. This too is the point of view of the community at Qumran and of other groups within Judaism. See C. M. Pate, *Communities of the Last Days* (Downers Grove, Ill.: InterVarsity Press, 2000), pp. 26-27.

happened (1 Chron 3:17-24). Hence Chronicles concludes with an exiled Judah being urged to return home and build the temple that will some day stand at the center of world geography, that temple which is inextricably tied to the dynasty of David.

CONCLUSION: DAVID AS THE WIDE-ANGLE LENS OF THE CANON

In the Davidic covenant, which represents the culmination of the promises of blessing to Abraham, David desires to build a house for Yahweh (i.e., a temple). Nevertheless, Yahweh tells him that his son will build it instead. Moreover, Yahweh will build a house for David (i.e., a dynasty; 2 Sam 7). Building a temple on Mount Zion at the center of the world stresses the element of geography, while building a dynasty stresses the element of genealogy. So it is no accident that both of these themes are found in the middle of the Hebrew Bible and at the end. Jehoiachin is released from prison—the Davidic dynasty is resurrected; Cyrus gives the command to build the temple in Jerusalem—the temple is resurrected. The Talmud is therefore not far wrong, as far as the message of the Tanak is concerned, when one of the rabbis is recorded as remarking that the world was created on David's account (*Sanhedrin* 98b).[35] And if not the world, then surely the Tanak. At the very least, its final form helps us to see the vast array of biblical material through a wide-angle, Davidic lens.[36]

---

[35]I would like to thank one of my students, Angelique Ross, for pointing out this reference to me.

[36]Much has been written about the putative alien ideology of kingship that supposedly stands in tension with an indigenous Mosaic faith within Israelite religion. For a needed corrective see, J. J. M. Roberts, "In Defense of the Monarchy: The Contribution of Israelite Kingship to Biblical Theology," in *Ancient Israelite Religion: Essays in Honor of Frank Moore Cross*, ed. P. D. Miller et al. (Philadelphia: Fortress, 1987), pp. 377-96.

6

What Is "Canonical" About a Canonical Biblical Theology?

Genesis as a Case Study of Recent Old Testament Proposals

Richard Schultz

In his programmatic 1970 monograph, *Biblical Theology in Crisis,* Brevard Childs described "the shape of a new biblical theology," which would offer a "disciplined theological reflection on the Bible in the context of canon,"[1] in short, a "canonical biblical theology." Such an approach would focus on the unique nature of Scripture as an inspired vehicle for divine communication and thus normative within the community of faith. During the past two decades a number of exegetical big guns have been lining up to fire their can(n)onical volleys across the bow of biblical studies, seeking to clear the deck for a new approach to the Bible that is more holistic, less theologically arid and thus capable of restoring the prophetic voice of the earlier testament to the contemporary church. In the process, several proposals and OT theologies have been published that claim to be or can be characterized as being canonical in their basic approach. Even a super-

---

[1]Brevard S. Childs, *Biblical Theology in Crisis* (Philadelphia: Westminster Press, 1970), p. 122.

ficial perusal of these volumes, however, reveals surprising diversity. This raises the fundamental question of what it is methodologically that makes a canonical theology canonical and what difference that makes, whether one is synthesizing the theology of one or both Testaments.

The purpose of this essay is to examine (in the chronological order of their publication) the recent canonical approaches to OT theology by Ronald Clements, Brevard Childs, Frank-Lothar Hossfeld, William Dumbrell, John Sailhamer, Paul House, Rolf Rendtorff, and Bruce Birch and his coauthors, in order to determine how each of these OT scholars understands and implements this method, especially in the light of Childs's original suggestions. In order to facilitate comparison, we will examine each author's canonical treatment of the book of Genesis or individual texts and themes derived from Genesis. What emerges from this survey is the observation that a canonical methodology has been understood in a wide variety of ways, although a common core of concerns and approaches nevertheless can be discerned.

RONALD CLEMENTS

Ronald Clements's *Old Testament Theology*[2] can be viewed as a significant precursor of the canonical approach. According to Clements, the concept of canon should play a central role in the presentation of an OT theology:

> At a very basic level we can see that it is because the OT forms a canon, and is not simply a collection of ancient Near Eastern documents, that we can expect to find in it a 'theology', and not just a report of ancient religious ideas. There is a real connection between the ideas of 'canon' and 'theology', for it is the status of these writings as a canon of sacred scripture that marks them out as containing a word of God that is still believed to be authoritative. (p. 15)

Though Clements is interested in literary and historical issues related to the formation and acceptance of the canon, he emphasizes the fact that a canonical approach seeks to understand the whole rather than just clarifying the individual parts. According to Clements, the most important feature of (the Palestinian) canon is its threefold division into Pentateuch, Prophets and Writings, which "correspond to three levels of authority" in which "there is evidently some design and system about the shape that has been accorded to the material" (pp. 16, 17). In expounding this canon-

---

[2]Ronald E. Clements, *Old Testament Theology: A Fresh Approach* (Atlanta: John Knox Press, 1978). Throughout the essay, where possible, references will be given in the body of the text.

ical theology, therefore, Clements clearly takes a canon-within-a-canon approach, emphasizing the Law and the Prophets (or promise), devoting separate chapters to each (chaps. 5-6; see Mt 11:13), while almost completely neglecting the Writings.

Although not offering a separate treatment of the book of Genesis, Clements's treatment of individual passages is suggestive. Referring to the promise to Abraham in Genesis 12:1-3 and Genesis 15:1-6, he emphasizes that this becomes a major OT motif whose development within "a wide biblical context" must be appreciated (p. 13). This motif synthesizes the "tradition about Israel's ancestors that has been preserved in the book of Genesis" as a "theology of election" (p. 88) that ultimately will impact other nations as well (p. 152), the land becoming the basic promise binding these traditions together (p. 92). Separate episodes in Genesis (i.e., independent traditions) have been "woven together" so that "a religious message of a larger and more enduring kind" begins to emerge (p. 34), without a reductionistic elimination of the rich variety of ways in which God's involvement in human affairs is presented.

BREVARD CHILDS

Already in his *Old Testament Theology in a Canonical Context*[3] it becomes clear that for Childs "canonical" means that the final form of the text is theologically binding and that the unfolding of theological themes within the OT canon is to be traced. Since Childs's approach has been the subject of much analysis, we will summarize only its key features for the sake of comparison. The goal of Childs's theology is to achieve "a theologically normative appraisal of the biblical literature for the life of the church," appropriately handling a literature marked by "enormous variety and multi-layered growth" (p. 5), though his theological construals seldom give much importance to this multilayeredness. The canonical approach to the OT may focus on only one portion of the Christian canon (i.e., the Hebrew canon), but reads it as Christian Scripture, that is, "as a witness to Jesus Christ precisely in its pre-Christian form . . . hearing its own theological testimony to the God of Israel whom the church confesses also to worship" (p. 9). Childs "reflects theologically on the text as it has been received and shaped" in its final canonical form. At the same time, he acknowledges

---

[3]Brevard S. Childs, *Old Testament Theology in a Canonical Context* (London: SCM Press, 1985; Philadephia: Fortress, 1986).

"the significance of the canonical process which formed the text" (p. 11),
shaping the tradition into independent books and larger canonical units,
building in "a dimension of flexibility which encourages constantly fresh
ways of actualizing the material" (p. 13).

Childs resists organizing his materials either systematically or (tradi-
tion-)historically, asserting that the ancient faith community's continuous
interpretative activity suggests that there are innumerable other options
for illuminating the text. As such, in his OT theology, he nowhere synthesizes the theology of Genesis as a whole. His most extensive treatment of
the book is a five-page discussion of Genesis 1—11 under the rubric "life
under threat" (pp. 222-26). Childs interprets the "final canonical positioning" of the creation and the primeval history as indicating its importance
for an understanding of reality. Childs notes the presence of chaos as a
threat from the beginning and the abrupt introduction of the serpent, ultimately leading to sin, shame and distorted human sexuality. On the basis
of his canonical perspective, Childs criticizes Gerhard von Rad's theological subordination of creation to redemption, as well as Claus Westermann's ontological interpretation of Genesis 1—11. In Childs's view, the
primeval narrative and the larger canonical witness (e.g., Is 11:6-16) know
of both a pre-Fall innocence and an eschatological restoration. Childs also
emphasizes the contribution of Genesis in developing a theology of the
self-revelation of God through creation (pp. 30-34).

Childs's canonical synthesis of Genesis is much clearer in his *Biblical
Theology of the Old and New Testaments*.[4] In part 3, "The Discrete Witness of
the Old Testament," he devotes twenty-two pages to a three-part discussion of the book (pp. 107-29). In this section the approach is largely nontheological; historical-critical issues and the viewpoints of various
scholars dominate his discussion. After tracing the debate concerning creation for several pages, he offers this conclusion, which echoes von Rad's
analysis, which he had earlier criticized theologically (see above): "Israel's
faith developed historically from its initial encounter with God as redeemer from Egypt, and only secondarily from this centre was a theology of creation incorporated into its faith" (p. 110). He then treats the priestly and
Yahwist creation accounts separately before tracing the creation tradition
within the rest of the OT. He follows a similar procedure in discussing the

---

[4]Brevard S. Childs, *Biblical Theology of the Old and New Testaments: Theological Reflection on the
Christian Bible* (Minneapolis: Fortress, 1992).

primeval history and the patriarchal traditions.

However, in part 6, "Theological Reflections on the Christian Bible," Childs takes an approach that is more reminiscent of his *Old Testament Theology in a Canonical Context.* In synthesizing the OT witness regarding God, the Creator (pp. 384-90), Childs begins with the Genesis account. He notes that, within the final form of the tradition, God's initial activity in creating the heavens and the earth is given precedence over Yahweh's historical acts of redemption from Egypt. Furthermore, the earlier creation tradition (Gen 2:4b-25) has been subordinated to the later (Gen 1:1-2:4a), so that it now functions as a detailed rehearsal of creation that prepared the way for the subsequent history of human alienation. He asserts that the terminology and structure of Genesis 1 serve to praise God and that, by culminating in the sabbath day, a potentially eschatological element is introduced. Childs gives special attention to creation themes that are developed further in the psalms (especially Ps 8), prophets and wisdom literature. In treating the theme of "Covenant, Election, People of God," Childs devotes more than half his space to a rehearsal of historical-critical disputes, such as whether early covenantal references are retrojections from a much later period (pp. 413-21). Ultimately, however, he asserts that if such is the case this redactional reworking simply "provides a more precise theological formulation of a relationship already described in different language" (p. 417). He makes only brief mention of several Genesis texts but argues intriguingly that the "shapers of scripture" have redacted the entire OT tradition in such a way as to understand God's dealings with Israel uniformly in terms of covenant. Thus Israel's primeval history is "construed as a series of covenants, starting with Noah (Gen 9:8ff.), and continuing with the promise of land and posterity sealed in a covenant to Abraham and his descendants (Gen 15:1ff.; 26:1ff.; 50:24)" (p. 419).

The impact of Childs's canonical approach on contemporary biblical studies cannot be overestimated. Most handbooks and dictionaries on biblical criticism offer thorough analyses of this approach, some of them even elevating canonical criticism to a new historical-critical method.[5] However, Childs's approach is not welcomed by all. For example, Manfred Oeming concedes that the canonical approach takes the text more seriously, is more objective, better suited for the church, more aware of the history that

---

[5]Susan Gillingham, *One Bible, Many Voices: Different Approaches to Biblical Studies* (Grand Rapids, Mich.: Eerdmans, 1998), pp. 168-69; John Hayes and Carl Holladay, *Biblical Exegesis,* rev. ed. (Atlanta: John Knox, 1987), chap. 10.

formed the text, and more theological.[6] However, he does not appreciate
the way in which Childs's "intertextual" studies relativize, level and harmonize distinctive, even disturbing, voices in the OT. He criticizes Childs
for neglecting historical-critical study, the ancient Near Eastern context of
the OT, individual texts, the situations of the actual editors of Scripture,
the complex compositional processes and the NT (pp. 248-41). In sum, according to Oeming, *"The so-called canonical approach is not a canonical approach at all!"* (p. 250).[7] In any case, since Oeming denies Childs's right
even to use the term "canonical approach" to describe his *Old Testament
Theology*, the question that is motivating our analysis of recent OT theologies—What is canonical about a canonical theology?—is clearly warranted.

FRANK-LOTHAR HOSSFELD

In a relatively unknown volume edited by Eugen Sitarz, its authors set forth
the "building blocks" for a theology (note the intentional use of the singular)
of the OT that can be quarried from the fuller Catholic canonical collection.[8]
Frank-Lothar Hossfeld's introductory pages regarding the Pentateuch
sound promising. After discussing the plurality and richness, as well as the
growth of OT literature, he claims that one can only dare to "conceive of the
diversity as a *whole*" because the individual books belong to the canon within which the Pentateuch has been assigned a foundational role (p. 14, emphasis added). He characterizes the Pentateuch as an ellipse with two focal
points: history and law. Disappointingly, in the remaining fifty pages Hossfeld simply traces the growth of the Pentateuch, summarizing the theologies
of the individual pentateuchal sources while basically leaving the work of
synthesizing *the* theology of the Pentateuch to his readers. His analysis of
the basic text (*Grundschrift*) of the Pentateuch contains the following sub-
units: Genesis 1:1—5:32, created rhythm and order, blessing; Genesis 6:9—
11:26, violence, judgment and renewed stability; Genesis 11:27—25:10, the
Abrahamic call and covenant with the successive realization of its promises;

[6]Manfred Oeming, "Text—Kontext—Kanon: Ein neuer Weg alttestamentlicher Theologie?"
in *Jahrbuch für Biblische Theologie*, Band 3, *Zum Problem des biblischen Kanons* (Neukirchen-
Vluyn: Neukirchener Verlag, 1988), p. 242. Oeming's descriptive terms for Childs's works
are *textgemässer, objektiver, gemeindegemässer, geschichtsgemässer, theologischer*.
[7]James Barr, *The Concept of Biblical Theology: An Old Testament Perspective* (Minneapolis: Fortress, 1999), chaps. 23-24, is even harsher in his criticism.
[8]Eugen Sitarz, ed., *Höre, Israel! Jahwe ist einzig: Bausteine für eine Theologie des Alten Testaments*
(Stuttgart: Verlag Katholisches Bibelwerk, 1987).

Genesis 25:21—Exodus 1:7, covenantal renewal with Jacob.

In sum, Hossfeld offers little canonical synthesis of pentateuchal theology; what is new in the Sitarz volume is that it summarizes the theological themes of individual OT books in their approximate canonical order. This approach is not uncommon in NT theology but, when first published, was virtually unparalleled in the OT, where systematic or religiohistorical ordering principles have dominated.

WILLIAM DUMBRELL

William Dumbrell similarly synthesizes the message of individual books in their Hebrew canonical order.[9] Due to the brevity of his methodological remarks, his approach must be derived largely from his treatment of specific books. His goal is to "bring the theological purpose of the respective OT books into clear focus" (p. 9), assuming that their authors had defined objectives in mind. Dumbrell views the OT as a whole (along with the NT) as offering a record of "how Israel's thinking advanced from creation to covenant at Sinai to a new covenant calculated to lead to a new creation" (p. 11). On the basis of his canonical approach, Dumbrell dismisses the search for a center as well as the claim that the OT contains inconsistent, differing theologies.

In developing the message of Genesis, Dumbrell points out the tenfold recurrence of the "these are the generations of" formula as "structuring" the book of Genesis but then basically disregards that structure (pp. 15-27). Instead, he divides the book into five sections: Genesis 1—2, creation and its implications; Genesis 3, the Fall; Genesis 4—11, the effects of the Fall; Genesis 12—36, the patriarchs; and Genesis 37—50, Joseph. The basis for this seems to be historical-thematic rather than literary-theological, since he explains how each of these subsections leads to the next. According to Dumbrell, Genesis 1:1—2:4a emphasizes the sovereignty and power of God, climaxing in the activity of the seventh, or sabbath day, which leaves it open-ended toward the future. Genesis 2:4b-25 expands on material from Genesis 1 (an approach similar to Childs's interpretation), drawing out the particular implications of creation for humanity and establishing an order that is directly reversed in the Fall narrative of Genesis 3, the further effects of which are traced in Genesis 4—11. As previously noted by

---

[9]William J. Dumbrell, *The Faith of Israel: Its Expression in the Books of the Old Testament* (Grand Rapids, Mich.: Baker, 1988).

others, Dumbrell points out that several of the narratives in Genesis 4—11
contain the following elements: sin, a divine confrontation that announces
an appropriate punishment, some amelioration and the imposition of
punishment, with the flood narrative constituting the midpoint in this section. However, Dumbrell disagrees with those who see a new beginning in
Genesis 8—9, arguing rather that an initial creation covenant is being reestablished, confirming the enduring relationship between God and the
world. Thus Genesis 4—11 offers "a perceptive analysis of the human predicament," to which Genesis 12:1-3 presents "the divine counter," with the
Abrahamic covenant's promise of land and progeny being the primary
emphasis of the ensuing patriarchal narratives (p. 23). According to
Dumbrell, God is portrayed as the only one who can fulfill these promises,
while the details of the events "foreshadow the later history of Israel" (p.
26). The Joseph narrative highlights Israel's preservation outside of the
Promised Land, functioning also as a bridge between the patriarchal narratives and the book of Exodus. Dumbrell concludes with a summary of
the book of Genesis, tracing the movement from God's grand design for
the world and the alienation of society through sin to the divine attack
upon this problem, so that the scattered nations of the world henceforth
find their center in Abraham. In the end, the "situation of Eden will potentially be realized in and through Israel" (p. 27).

JOHN SAILHAMER

John Sailhamer's *Introduction to Old Testament Theology* explicitly refers to
itself as a "canonical" approach, the first volume to do so since Childs.[10]
Although the monograph's primary focus is to set forth the basic methodological options for constructing an OT theology, he leaves no uncertainty
regarding the options that he chooses: text-based, canonical, prescriptive
and either diachronic or synchronic in presentation. For Sailhamer, "canonical" means that the biblical theologian views the texts or events of the
OT just as we have them in the OT canon rather than critically reconstruct-
ing them. In defining "criticism" Sailhamer explains that a critical approach is one that incorporates historical-critical methods such as literary,
source, form and tradition criticism, as well as what he terms "phenome-
nology," that is, the effective history of the text.

---

[10]John H. Sailhamer, *An Introduction to Old Testament Theology: A Canonical Approach* (Grand
Rapids, Mich.: Zondervan, 1995).

Nevertheless, since his canonical approach focuses on understanding "the peculiar shape and special function of the books that comprise the Hebrew canon" (p. 97), Sailhamer advocates the use of composition and redaction criticism, as well as text linguistics. In fact, the purpose of his introduction is "to demonstrate the nature of an OT theology based on the approach of compositional criticism" (p. 98). Sailhamer defines compositional criticism as the attempt "to trace the ways the biblical writers organized and fashioned literary units into unified texts and whole books as well as to understand the theological characteristics of their finished works" (p. 206). "Canonical" for Sailhamer means not only taking biblical claims regarding authorship and history at face value (which clearly distinguishes his understanding of "canonical" from Childs's), but also seeking to demonstrate the unity of the OT and NT Scriptures. The latter goal is warranted since many of the key theological themes of the NT already are anticipated "in the last stages of the composition of the OT" (p. 216).

Several examples will help to illustrate Sailhamer's understanding of the theological impact of the redactional shaping of the major sections and transitions within the OT canonical collection. Sailhamer views the Pentateuch as a single literary unit in which key poetic texts are deliberately placed after major narrative segments as a part of a discernible strategy to give that segment an "eschatological and messianic interpretation" (p. 99). Thus the poetic text Genesis 49, in speaking of the last days and the leading role of the tribe of Judah (Gen 49:1, 9), concludes the Joseph (or patriarchal) narrative in this manner.[11] Furthermore, the Pentateuch intends to demonstrate the failure of the Sinai covenant as a whole and of the law in particular to produce obedience in order to "engender a hope in the coming of a New Covenant" (p. 99). The function of Genesis 1—11 is to stress that the context for the narratives to follow is "all humanity," while Genesis 12—50 serves to present the "patriarchal biographies" over against the Mosaic biography. Genesis 26:5 affirms that Abraham "kept the law" through faith before the law was given, while according to Numbers 20:12 Moses failed to keep the law through a lack of faith after the law was given.[12]

---

[11]Sailhamer also identifies poetic conclusions in Genesis 2:23; 3:14-19; 4:23; 48:15-16, 20.

[12]Cf. the narrative typologies within the Pentateuch that he identifies in his earlier volume, *The Pentateuch as Narrative* (Grand Rapids, Mich.: Zondervan, 1992), pp. 37-44, which for Sailhamer give evidence of a theologically significant redactional shaping of the narratives. See also John H. Sailhamer, "The Mosaic Law and the Theology of the Pentateuch," *WThJ* 53 (1991): 241-61; "The Canonical Approach to the Old Testament: Its Effect on Understanding Prophecy," *JETS* 30 (1987): 307-15; "The Messiah and the Hebrew Bible," *JETS* 44 (2001): 5-23.

PAUL HOUSE

Paul House offers an exposition of the theology of the final form of individual books in their canonical order, focusing on God's characteristic actions as his canonical center and summarizing, where possible, the further development within the biblical canon of themes which are introduced in a given book.[13] Consequently, he is less interested in compositional strategy and in the relationship between individual books and blocks of books than in the development of specific themes within the canon. House clearly sets forth his method in an introductory chapter: an OT theology should analyze the Hebrew canon in its three-part scheme, also noting intertextual connections between books, while also keeping the OT's historical context before the reader. In sum, according to House, a "canonical" theology is "God-centered, intertexuality oriented, authority-conscious, historically sensitive and devoted to the pursuit of the wholeness of the Old Testament message" (p. 57).

As House expounds the theological message of Genesis in its relationship to the larger OT canon, it is immediately apparent that his outline of the book is thematically rather than structurally determined:

1—2: the God who creates
3:1—6:4: the God who judges and protects
6:5—11:9: the God who punishes and renews
11:10—25:18: the God who calls and promises
25:19—28:9: the God who provides continuity
28:10—36:43: the God who elects and protects
37—50: the God who preserves the covenant people

Thus Genesis 1—2 are grouped together presumably because they both describe creation, even though Genesis 2:4-25 is connected to the unfolding story of the rise of a covenant people. Unlike Childs, House sees no tension between Genesis 1 and Genesis 2. In his view, "Genesis 2:4-25 deals specifically with concepts introduced in the previous thirty-four verses," focusing on "God's initial relationship to the newly created human race" (p. 62). House subdivides Genesis 11—50 on the basis of the appearance of its major characters. In Genesis 11—25 his emphasis is on divine election and Abraham's faith-filled response of obedience. In the case of Joseph, he highlights the themes of forgiveness, redemptive suffering, blessing and faith.

---

[13]Paul R. House, *Old Testament Theology* (Downers Grove, Ill.: InterVarsity Press, 1998), pp. 56-57.

House's approach to canonical syntheses likewise varies. On the one hand, in his synthesis of creation he goes beyond simply summarizing the theological theme to tracing the intercanonical (or intertextual) development of aspects of Genesis 1—2 within the OT, discussing texts in Isaiah, Amos, Psalms, Job and Proverbs but not mentioning its consummation in Revelation. On the other hand, his canonical synthesis of the Abraham narrative focuses exclusively on its further development within the NT, while his theological reflections on the Jacob narrative (Gen 28—36) draw on Hosea 12, Malachi 1 and Romans 9 as key texts. In sum, for House the term *canonical* primarily seems to involve taking the historical narratives at face value as teaching normative truths about God and, by way of example, seeking to trace how some of the theological themes first introduced in Genesis or other OT books are developed further elsewhere in the biblical canon.

ROLF RENDTORFF

On the surface, the first volume of Rolf Rendtorff's two-volume work appears to utilize the same approach as House, offering a canonical retelling *(Nacherzählung)* of the OT from beginning to end, emphasizing the interrelationships between the various books.[14] According to Rendtorff, if one takes the OT canon seriously, "it becomes necessary to see the whole of the OT in the light of its final canonical form as an expression of the self-understanding of post-exilic Judaism," accepting that form as "having its own stature and dignity."[15] Thus one can maintain the integrity of the OT witness and recognize its later Jewish and Christian influence. Rendtorff's emphasis is on the theology in, not of, the OT as contained in the individual books, working out their "particular character and theological profile" while being "fitted" as far as possible into the canonical historical scheme (p. 11). For him, "final form" refers not simply to a literary or theological phenomenon but rather to the final stage in the history of an editorial or composition process, since, in his view, "theology is historically speaking a relatively late product" (p. 12, quoting R. Smend). Hence Rendtorff's first volume follows the Hebrew order of the OT books or collections; the sec-

---

[14]Rolf Rendtorff, *Theologie des Alten Testaments: Ein kanonischer Entwurf,* Band 1, *Kanonische Grundlegung* (Neukirchen-Vluyn: Neukirchener, 1999); Band 2, *Thematische Entfaltung* (2001). Rendtorff traces this approach back to Gerhard von Rad.

[15]Rolf Rendtorff, *Canon and Theology: Overtures to an Old Testament Theology* (Minneapolis: Fortress, 1993), p. 55.

ond considers individual themes and concepts, as far as possible in the order in which they are introduced in the canonical historical narrative. For in his view, the final form of the text alone serves as the basis for the faith, doctrine and life of the Jewish and Christian communities of faith.

Rendtorff expressly calls his OT theology "a canonical sketch." The significance of the threefold structure of the Hebrew canon is emphasized: in the first division God acts, in the second God speaks, in the third humans speak to and *about* God. Following a brief affirmation of the foundational nature of the Pentateuch within the OT, twenty pages are devoted to a theology of Genesis. Rendtorff notes no theological conflict between Genesis 1—2; Genesis 2 views the creation from another perspective, offering a more detailed and concrete description of the role and fate of the first couple, as well as portraying their creation as a direct act of God. In Genesis 1—11, Rendtorff gives special attention to the developing relationship between God and humans, especially following the flood. The greatness and beauty of creation as well as its distortion and endangerment by humanity are depicted. Rendtorff concludes this section by noting the striking parallels between the creation of the cosmos (1:31) and the completion of the tabernacle (Ex 39:43), one of many intertextual links that he highlights. Then, in the patriarchal narratives, the election of Abraham and the promise of the land and progeny are emphasized. Rendtorff displays considerable literary sensitivity in discussing how one derives theological conclusions from the explicit and implicit statements in the narratives, giving special attention to the divine speeches in the Abraham narrative and the divine encounters in the Jacob narrative. According to Rendtorff, Genesis concludes by looking ahead to the Exodus and return to the Promised Land, the Joseph narrative serving as a bridge to the Egyptian sojourn, which emphasizes God's sovereign leading and provision.

BRUCE BIRCH ET AL.

Bruce Birch, Walter Brueggemann, Terence Fretheim and David Petersen emphasize how biblical texts and books were shaped by the community of faith, a canonical emphasis that clearly is derived from Childs.[16] Though emphasizing the final form of the text, they also affirm the need for critical study of the processes that ultimately produced the final form. However, the canonical "narrative story" rather than the reconstructed

---

[16]Bruce Birch et al., *A Theological Introduction to the Old Testament* (Nashville: Abingdon, 1999).

compositional history must form the basis for faith reflection. The claim of the text "that it is speaking about encounter and relationship with God" is to be taken seriously and its authority for the ongoing life of the religious community is to be acknowledged (p. 17). A canonical approach, according to these authors, seeks to recover "the polyphonic voices of the OT with their unsettled diversity of witness" from the artificial unity of externally imposed systematic categories (p. 25). A canonical theology recognizes "the ongoing traditions as they live and receive interpretation in later Jewish and Christian contexts" but is careful to preserve the integrity of Israel's witness (p. 27).

These authors' treatment of the theology of Genesis remarkably encompasses more than sixty pages, in which they divide the book into the two traditional subsections: Genesis 1—11 (the created order and the re-creation of broken order) and Genesis 12—50 (promises made, threatened and fulfilled). Genesis 1—11 offers "a universal frame of reference" regarding God as one who is active in the world in general, not just in Israel, and who is highly relational, regarding the world as originally beautiful under the divinely appointed stewardship of humans who all too soon are devastated by sin (p. 41). As such, God's creative work is prior to his redemptive work. Genesis 1—2 have been "brought together in a theologically sophisticated fashion to function *together* as a canonical picture of creation," revealing key points of "complementarity" (p. 46). Unlike Childs, they view the initial "chaos" as posing no potential threat. In Genesis 3:1—6:4, sin intrudes, with social and cosmic effects. The literary links between Genesis 2—3 and Genesis 3—4 are noted and theologically exploited. Following the "great divide" caused by the flood (Gen 6:5—8:22), a "new world order" is established with a new "Adam" (i.e., Noah, Gen 9:1—11:26), preparing for God's choice of Abraham. Following the flood, "God rejects annihilation as the means to accomplish this reformation and graciously chooses a more vulnerable, long-term engagement, working from within the very life of the world itself" (p. 65).

In discussing the patriarchal narratives, the authors employ the repeated *toledoth* formulae as their structural orientation, noting how the Abraham narrative focuses on securing and then preserving progeny. Genesis 15 and Genesis 17, taken together, "refine and make specific the more general promises of Genesis 12:1-3," thereby depicting an "obligating"—and "dialogic"—God (p. 80). In discussing the Jacob narrative, they emphasize the significant role that Bethel plays in the course of Ja-

cob's conflict and struggle over the blessing. With regard to Genesis 37—
50, they note the emphasis on Jacob's descendants as a whole (plural),
without diminishing Joseph's central role in developing the theological
dimensions of alienation and reconciliation as well as divine providence.
In sum, the authors of this most recent OT theology, though not explicitly
calling theirs a "canonical theology," are more sensitive to the final canonical form (i.e., structure and shaping) of the book of Genesis than any
of their predecessors.

CONCLUSIONS

Having completed our survey of canonical approaches to OT theology, we
are in a position to draw some conclusions. (1) Despite considerable diversity, canonical approaches to OT theology generally focus on the final form
of the individual books, often in their Hebrew canonical order, regardless
of how their compositional histories might be reconstructed. (2) As a correlate, the proponents of this approach base their theological reflections on
the canonical presentation of Israel's history, regardless of the degree to
which they view it as conforming to historical reality. (3) Even more important, canonical theologies treat the OT and its derived theology as normative for us today, regardless of whether or not their author affirms the
divine origin of Scripture. (4) As such, perceived theological discrepancies
and tensions within the biblical accounts are downplayed and unifying
features are emphasized. (5) Although a Christian undertaking, these theologies seek to respect and preserve the unique voice and perspective of
the OT witness to faith, regardless of their author's attitude toward the ex-
clusivity of Christianity's claims.

It is surprising, then, to discover that these common emphases do not
translate into a common approach to synthesizing the theology of Genesis.
Beyond their common starting points, canonical approaches diverge
greatly. There is a sharp disjunction between a canonical approach and a
canonical method. Moreover, in opting for the final form as the basis for
one's theological reflection, it is not enough simply to emphasize its canonical finality rather than its complex compositional history. Rather, one
should emphasize the significance of its final form in view of its development, since there is clearly a relationship between the form, that is, structure, and the purpose or function of a biblical book or an individual text.
Despite the fact that many of the structural outlines that have been suggested look more like a table of contents or yet another outbreak of chias-

mania, there is great value in conceiving of a book's structure as a theological outline to be expounded.[17]

By way of example, it is therefore important to note that the book of Genesis begins (Gen 1:1—2:3) with a precisely ordered description of cosmic creation in which the regal commands of the transcendent God are immediately executed. These include the divine charge to his image bearers to rule as viceroys over the rest of creation, anticipating various models of leadership that will be instituted in the course of Israel's history (as well as, in particular, their failure to realize this divine ideal within the book of Genesis).

Then, with Genesis 2:4, the ten-part narrative structure begins with the first occurrence of the *toledoth* (or: "this is the account, or family history, of") formula.[18] Thus, theologically, Genesis 2—50 does not offer separate primeval and patriarchal histories but rather one continuous account of the origin of the covenant people through whom God will work to overcome the devastating effects of the Fall (as well as the genealogies of the nonelect line). The postflood narrative parallels the preflood, with the repeated sequence of blessing, family sin and curse, genealogy, sin's spread, judgment and covenant making, issuing in the call of Abraham through whom all of the scattered families of humankind can be unified in receiving the divine blessing.[19] The tower builders sought in vain to make a name for themselves (Gen 11:4); divine grace will make Abram's name

---

[17]For further discussion and illustration of the relationship between a book's structure and its theology, see Richard Schultz, "Integrating Old Testament Theology and Exegesis: Literary, Thematic and Canonical Issues," in *A Guide to Old Testament Theology and Exegesis*, ed. Willem VanGemeren (Grand Rapids, Mich.: Zondervan: 1999), pp. 185-88.

[18]The following hermeneutical implications can be derived from the *toledoth* structure of Genesis:

1. It divides the book into two unequal parts: Genesis 1:1—2:3 (creation) and Genesis 2:4—50:26 (covenant).
2. It indicates an unbroken sequence of divine activity from the creation to the elect family's settlement in Egypt.
3. It affirms the historical though compressed nature of Genesis 2—11.
4. It distinguishes between the chosen and nonelect line of descendants (the *toledoth*s of Shem/Ham/Japheth, Ishmael and Esau).
5. It emphasizes the prominent roles of Abraham and Jacob while indicating the subordinate, transitional role of Isaac.
6. It identifies the final section as the story of Jacob's family, thus highlighting Judah's ultimate role among the tribes of Israel.

[19]For a detailed exposition of this parallel structure, see Gary Rendsburg, *The Redaction of Genesis* (Winona Lake, Ind.: Eisenbrauns, 1986), pp. 6-25. Rendsburg (p. 8 n. 2) credits Jack Sasson, "The 'Tower of Babel' as a Clue to the Redactional Structuring of the Primeval History (Gen. 1—11:9)," in *The Bible World: Essays in Honor of Cyrus H. Gordon*, ed. Gary Rendsburg (New York: KTAV, 1980), pp. 211-19, with being the first to make this structural observation.

great (Gen 12:2). The narrative account of Terah's family (Gen 11:27—25:11) focuses on Abraham's attempt to fulfill the progeny promise through self-effort; the account of Isaac's family (Gen 25:19—35:29) focuses on Jacob's initial efforts to grab for himself the divine blessing, ultimately coming to rely instead on God as he departs from and later returns to Bethel.

The closing section (Gen 37:2—50:26) traces the movement of Jacob's family southward to Egypt, where it ultimately will grow into a great nation, giving special attention to Judah's personal development (Gen 37:26; 38; 43:3, 8; 44:14, 16, 18; 46:12, 28; 49:8-10). Although within the temporary horizon of the famine the brothers bow down to Joseph in fulfillment of his earlier dream (Gen 37:5-11; cf. 42:6-9), within the long-term horizon of Jacob's (possibly even eschatological) blessings, the brothers will bow before Judah (Gen 49:8).

In my opinion, such a canonical theology is derived by reading the book holistically, focusing "on the distinctive way in which the Bible's message is mediated by its literary forms,"[20] rather than reading it more atomistically, focusing on various themes from systematic theology that can be identified in the book.

After spending more than seventy pages reviewing and rather harshly critiquing various canonical OT theologies, James Barr offers some "afterthoughts about the canon."[21] He questions whether the so-called canonical approach, as proposed by Childs and others, really restores anything that was ever in the tradition of the Christian church. What is characteristic of the church's daily practice today, according to Barr, is an oracular rather than a canonical use of the Bible. In such an approach, a brief snippet of text—we might call it a prooftext—is presented as the Word of God containing the spiritual message that the congregation needs to hear.

However, rather than taking Barr's observation as an argument against a canonical approach, it offers the strongest possible incentive for adopting such an approach.[22] It is time for biblical theologians to intensify their efforts to equip church members to nourish themselves with meaty but

---

[20]Kevin Vanhoozer, "Language, Literature, Hermeneutics and Biblical Theology," in *A Guide to Old Testament Theology and Exegesis*, p. 35.

[21]Barr, *The Concept of Biblical Theology*, pp. 448-51.

[22]See Richard Schultz, "Responsible Hermeneutics for Wisdom Literature," in *Care for the Soul: Exploring the Intersection of Psychology and Theology*, ed. Mark McMinn and Timothy R. Phillips (Downers Grove, Ill.: InterVarsity Press, 2001), pp. 254-75.

succulent chunks of canonical text rather than snacking on tidbits. Biblical theologians need to help them attain a strategic understanding of the theological teaching and contemporary message of biblical books as a whole rather than the mere chronology of events and moral lessons that can be derived from individual texts. A canonical approach that takes the literary contours of the Bible seriously as the vehicle through which God has communicated his authoritative Word will better arm the church for the theological and moral conflicts that confront it in an increasingly pluralistic and relativistic society. Slinging about Bible slogans is not enough; the individual church members must be trained to handle the word of truth correctly (2 Tim 2:15), and the canonical approach to biblical theology is the best way to learn this strategic skill.[23]

---

[23]For a foundational text in this regard, see Graeme Goldsworthy, *Preaching the Whole Bible as Christian Scripture: The Application of Biblical Theology to Expository Preaching* (Grand Rapids, Mich.: Eerdmans, 2000).

7

Psalms and Psalter

Paradigm for Biblical Theology

Gerald H. Wilson

The peculiar character of the psalms and Psalter allow both together to provide a suggestive paradigm for a biblical theology. This should not surprise us since the riches of the psalms have informed the heart of Jewish and Christian worship, meditation, prayer and praxis for millennia. In part the psalms have been so influential because they bracket and thus give human flesh to the whole OT experience. On the one hand, they contain some of the earliest and yet some of the latest compositions in the OT canon, integrating as no other segment of the canon the diverse literary, historical and thematic streams that make up the Old Testament. In them royal ideology and prophetic critique, cultic theology and wisdom reflection, law and liturgy all collide and intertwine to create a complex yet piquant stew of biblical proportions. In their verses all the formative themes of promise and fulfillment, salvation and judgment, election and mission, creation and restoration, commandment and obedience coexist without embarrassment, so that in these few compositions of poetic beauty we encounter a microcosm of the OT traditions.

On the other hand, the psalms embody in their texts the deepest and most formative character of canonical Scripture. The psalms bring together in one literary moment the complex interaction between human and divine that is at the heart of canon and theology. They are manifestly human words directed to God that have—as acknowledged Scripture—come back at us as God's commanding words of truth. It is, above all, in the shape and shaping of the biblical Psalter that we are allowed to see biblical theology at work in the psalms: selecting, arranging, preserving, adapting, reshaping, contextualizing and reinterpreting ancient traditions so that they speak and continue to speak to ever new circumstances of the community of faith.

THE NATURE OF THE PSALMS

Diversity of form, function and expression. One of the chief characteristics of the psalms is diversity. This has been particularly well documented by the form-critical analysis of the psalms. Although the major psalm types are usually limited to three—praise, lament and thanksgiving—the subsidiary types are numerous and radically distinctive (torah, wisdom, royal, confidence, liturgical, historical, acrostic, etc.). Even among the major psalms of the same type, however, diversity of form is characteristic, as any student who has ever attempted to observe the regularities of form said to distinguish a particular *Gattung* will be only too willing to attest.

The functional nature of the psalms is equally varied. Despite the attempts of Sigmund Mowinckel and his followers, it is generally accepted today that it is impossible to press all of the 150 psalms into the liturgical confines of a hypothetical enthronement festival. The whole of life is encompassed in the psalms: private and public spheres, individual and communal prayers and personal and national concerns stand shoulder to shoulder with no attempt to group all of a type or of similar interest together.

The same breadth of diversity is discovered in the range of experience and emotion expressed in the psalms. Although we may be uncomfortable admitting it, the texts of the psalms range from great flashing rage to tender love, from deepest despair to utterly imperishable confidence. The psalms are a comprehensive exposé of human experience and emotion. And nowhere in the Psalter are these human emotions whitewashed or critiqued. Although we tend to run the biblical psalms through our filter of what is appropriate and inappropriate, omitting in worship those sentiments deemed less than Christian, the Psalter has no such qualms but is satisfied to let this riot of human emotions stand unexpurgated together as God's Word to us! The psalmists don't even try to dissemble, but they let raw emotion speak directly in honest pain, confusion, doubt and accusation to balance their moments of exalted joy and thanksgiving.

This is not to say, however, that the psalms and Psalter endorse all the very human attitudes and emotions expressed by the psalmists, including the vicious vengeance anticipated in the imprecatory psalms,[1] but they do endorse bringing all those attitudes and emotions to God in submission. The human dynamic of the psalms is movement toward God. In these poems the full range of life is brought before God as an act of worship—a sacrifice, so to speak, of submission to God.

Together the psalms lead us on the path of real life, not the pallid substitutes for life we sometimes construct for ourselves where everything is hermetically sealed and sterile. The life of the psalms is a messy life where pain and joy, self-knowledge and self-doubt, love and hatred, trust and suspicion break in upon one another, overlapping and competing for our attention. It is a life in which we have real choices on a daily basis between life and death. In these psalms this messy life—this real life—is constantly brought before God as our messiness ought to be, before it is cleaned up and sanitized. How else can God's healing, revealing, confronting, forgiving love penetrate to the darkest corners of our secret places unless we open the door to let in the light? Diversity is therefore one of the hallmarks of psalms and Psalter that must find its way into any biblical theology worthy of the name.

Unresolved tension. One important consequence of the messiness of the psalms—its diversity—is that the canonical Psalter, like the rest of Scripture, preserves within its pages an incredible amount of tension. Often biblical theologies have misunderstood this tension as the negative results of diachronic development or the remains of competing ideological viewpoints rather imperfectly combined in Scripture. As a result, such tension is often neutralized either by accepting the latest or best voice, or by allowing diversity to stand as unresolved heterodoxy. In the first instance, important voices have been eliminated as passé or less than orthodox, while the second path offers little help in defining the boundaries of normative faith.

In the Psalter, a variety of tensions remain: the chronological tension between monarchical and exilic perspectives; the ideological tension be-

---

[1]See the recent treatment of the psalms of violence in Erich Zenger, *A God of Vengeance?* (Louisville, Ky.: Westminster John Knox, 1996).

tween royal-Zionist hopes and sapiential criticism; the experiential tensions between praise/thanksgiving and lament/despair, confidence and questioning, just to name a few. These tensions are allowed to stand not as competing views but as limit posts at the perimeters of faith. Orthodoxy is to be lived out in the space between these extremes. Rather than a tether fastened to a mooring stake that inhibits freedom by drawing all back to a center, orthodox faith is defined at the periphery like the skin of a balloon that marks the outer boundaries of faith. If pressed too far, the balloon can explode, but the principle is expansive and inclusive rather than retrenchant and exclusive.

Like the balloon analogy, the Psalter does provide limits to orthodox faith. These limits are found in the canonical shape or final form of the Psalter that limits the contents, offers a theologically informed arrangement, and provides key insights into the appropriate understanding of the individual psalms and the whole collection.

THE SHAPE OF THE PSALTER

The limitation of the collection. It is precisely in the shaping of the canonical collection that the decisive step toward biblical theology is taken by creating a theologically motivated framework for the psalms that provides an enduring interpretive context through which to understand the individual psalms and indeed the whole ensemble. It is in the shaping of the whole collection that these individual human psalms make the transition to become the Word of God to us.

The first and most obvious element of shaping is the limitation of the Psalter text to this particular collection of 150 psalms, no more and no less. The limitation of the Psalter is recognized in the Septuagint, even though the Greek text offers an alternative tradition of combining or dividing certain compositions[2] and even includes an additional psalm (151) at the end. The radical difference that can be achieved by the addition of new compositions and the rearrangement of the contents of the Psalter is clearly demonstrated by the Qumran Psalm Scroll (11QPs[a]). There we find among the psalms of the final third of the canonical Psalter a large number of apocry-

---

[2]In the LXX, canonical Psalms 9 and 10 are joined to become a single composition, while Psalm 147 is divided into two independent psalms. The result is a Psalter that still includes 150 compositions. The appearance of an additional Psalm 151 at the end of the collection is offset by the recognition expressed in the heading of this psalm that it is "outside the number" of the accepted Psalter collection.

phal psalms in an arrangement that is completely different than that of the canonical Psalter.[3]

The fixation of the contents of the text has the effect of providing a fixed witness to the Word of God spoken in the psalms. It is in this collection, in this arrangement that the authorizing community of faith claimed to hear the voice of God. And it is particularly important in the psalms—such manifestly human compositions addressed to God—that we acknowledge that the boundaries of the Psalter provide a way of checking and critiquing our distorted human perceptions. As with the canon as a whole, we must deal with the collection we have received rather than picking and choosing what fits with our ideas of what is true or correct. Just as John the Baptist was tempted to question Jesus' messiahship (Mt 11:3; Lk 7:19-20), we may be tempted to look for another (psalter), but the canon demands that we take ever new looks at the one that has already come. The limitation of the collection to these 150 psalms means that not all human expressions of lament, thanksgiving and praise communicate God's will and purpose for us, but these do! As a result, we must do as Psalm 1 enjoins us and meditate on them day and night to find the way that God knows.

The two segments of the collection. It is generally recognized today that the canonical Psalter exhibits two distinct segments (Pss 2—89; 90—145) that employ different methods of editorial arrangement. These two segments appear to be chronologically related, with the first (Pss 2—89) having reached a fixed form at an earlier date than the latter.[4] For the first segment it is evident that the placement of royal psalms at strategic junctures (Pss 2, 72, 89) has produced a collection focused on the Davidic kingship that particularly questions the demise of that monarchy in the exile (Ps 89). The addition of the latter segment responds to the lamenting question generated by the first and points the reader to the kingship of YHWH that dominates the *YHWH malak* ("YHWH reigns/has become king") psalms of the fourth book (Pss 90—106). The result is a complete Psalter that seeks to move beyond the exilic experience of Israel and to provide future grounding for faith in YHWH.

The collection's introduction and conclusion. The two distinctive segments

---

[3]See Gerald H. Wilson, "11QPs[a] and the Canonical Psalter: Comparison of Editorial Technique and Shaping," *CBQ* 59 (1997): 448-64.

[4]Gerald H. Wilson, "The Shape of the Book of Psalms," *Interp* 46 (1992): 129-42; cf. the conclusions of Peter W. Flint, *The Dead Sea Psalms Scrolls and the Book of Psalms* (Boston: Brill Academic Publishers, 1997), pp. 237-40.

of the Psalter outlined above are sandwiched together between an introduction (Ps 1) and a conclusion (Pss 146—150). The former calls the reader
to meditate seriously on the *torah* of God in order to find blessing (Ps 1:1)
on the way that YHWH knows (Ps 1:6). Brevard S. Childs and others have
persuasively suggested that Psalm 1 intends the reader to take the *torah* of
Psalm 1:2 broadly as "instruction/guidelines" and thus to encourage the
reading of the psalms as the Word of God.[5]

The concluding *hallel* psalms (Pss 146—150) provide a conclusion to the
whole Psalter in response to the final verse of Psalm 145:21: "My mouth
will speak the praise of YHWH, and let all flesh bless his holy name forever and ever" (author's translation [throughout the essay, except as noted]).
The effect of this concluding praise is to affirm that the final word of the
Psalter is one of praise. This does not undermine the diversity of lament,
thanksgiving and praise that are preserved throughout the Psalter, but it
does provide the concluding commentary that despite the reality of pain
and suffering, despite the real hiddenness of God that often characterizes
human experience, God's final purpose is restoration and universal blessing. Thus it is appropriate that the final Hebrew title for the Book of Psalms
is *tehillim*, "praises," not as a way of denying the reality and validity of lament but as a way of affirming the ultimate end of the "way YHWH
knows" (Ps 1:6). Thus Psalms 146—150 offer a fitting conclusion to the
"blessed one" of Psalm 1:1.

The shifting thematic emphases of the collection. Between introduction and
conclusion, a number of commentators have observed a shifting of thematic emphases that roughly coincide with the two segments of the
Psalter mentioned above. Let me mention only three of these to make the
point clear.

1. Lament to praise. Drawing on the observations of others that the first
   half of the Psalter is dominated by lament before giving way to praise
   in the latter half, Walter Brueggemann posits that Israel is called to
   move by obedience through the painful hiddenness of God addressed
   by lament to a direct apprehension of God that moves beyond obedience to exalted and unmotivated praise of the Creator.[6]

---

[5]Brevard S. Childs, *Introduction to the Old Testament as Scripture* (Philadelphia: Fortress, 1979),
pp. 513-14.
[6]Walter Brueggemann, "Bounded by Obedience and Praise: The Psalms as Canon," *JSOT* 50
(1991): 63-92. See my comments on Brueggemann's ideas in "The Shape of the Book of
Psalms," *Interp* 46 (1992): 134-37.

2. Human to divine kingship. I have on numerous occasions advanced the contention that a shift takes place between the first three books of the Psalter and the last two in the kind of expectations directed to the Davidic kings. The first three books are shaped by the positioning of royal psalms that stress the authorization of the Davidic kings (Ps 2), the transmission of the Davidic covenant promises to subsequent generations of rulers (Ps 72) and the agonized questioning that results from the demise of the monarchy in exile (Ps 89). The last two books by contrast focus on the kingship of YHWH as introduced in the *YHWH malak* psalms (Pss 93—99). The effect of combining these two larger segments is to shift expectations away from the restoration of the human Davidic kings to the direct rulership of YHWH.[7]

3. Adjusting messianic hopes. In response to my suggestion of a shift in emphasis from Davidic kingship to the rulership of YHWH, a number of scholars have countered with the likelihood of a messianic rather than a historical reading of these psalms and by pointing out the continuing presence of strongly messianic psalms with references to the Davidic covenant promises in the last two books, in particular Psalm 132.[8] Others draw on the work of Gerald T. Sheppard, who seeks to show that Psalms 1 and 2 are intended together to provide an introduction to the whole Psalter that emphasizes the reinterpretation of the royal psalms in light of messianic expectations of restoration.

First, it is clear that at some point in the history of the Psalter the royal psalms began to be interpreted messianically. By associating that move with the use of Psalm 1 and Psalm 2 as an introduction to the whole Psalter, Sheppard and his followers assume such a reading is part of the final shaping of the Psalter collection. The recent work of Christoph Rösel, however, strongly suggests that Psalm 2 was already part of a consistent "messianic redaction" of Psalms 2—89 before Psalm 1 and the last two books were added to complete the Psalter.[9] There are then, in my opinion, two stages in the messianic reinterpretation of the royal psalms. The first, associated with Psalms 2—89, anticipates the restoration of a human Da-

---

[7]Gerald H. Wilson, "Shaping the Psalter: A Consideration of Editorial Linkage in the Book of Psalms," in *The Shape and Shaping of the Psalter*, ed. J. C. McCann, JSOTSup 159 (Sheffield: JSOT, 1993), pp. 72-82.

[8]My friend Bernhard Anderson has pointed this out to me on a number of occasions.

[9]Christoph Rösel, *Die messianische Redaktion des Psalters: Studien zu Entstehung und Theologie der Sammlung Psalm 2—89* (Stuttgart: Calwer Verlag, 1999).

vidic kingship, and the second, associated with the final form of the Psalter, focuses on the kingship of YHWH.

A study of the distribution in the Psalter of the Hebrew term *melek* ("king") brings a new perspective into the discussion. In the first three books this word is used in four ways: (1) to refer in the most general sense to "kings" or "kingship" (e.g., Ps 33:16); (2) to describe foreign human kings of nations other than Israel/Judah (e.g., Ps 2:2, 10; 45:9; 76:12); (3) in reference to the human kings of Israel/Judah (e.g., Ps 2:6; 21:1, 7; 45:11; 89:18); and (4) to describe the divine kingship of YHWH (Ps 5:2; 10:16; 24:7, 8, 9, 10; 29:10; 44:4; 47:2, 6, 7; 48:2; 68:24; 74:12; 84:3). When, however, we cross the boundary of the earlier segment of the Psalter (Pss 2—89) and enter the final two books (Pss 90—150) we discover an interesting change. While the word *melek* is still employed as before to describe kings in general (e.g., Ps 140:10), the human kings of the foreign nations (e.g., Ps 102:15; 105:14, 20, 30; 110:5; 119:46), and YHWH as king (Ps 95:1; 98:6; 99:4; 145:1; 149:2), references to the kings of Israel and Judah employing this term are entirely lacking from these books.

The effect of this change is to highlight the growing emphasis on the kingship of YHWH established early in the fourth book through the introduction of the *YHWH malak* psalms,[10] while deflecting attention away from human kingship in Israel.

By way of contrast, two other important words applied in the earlier segment of the Psalter to describe the kings of Israel/Judah in general and David in particular—"servant" (*'ebed*) and "anointed one" (*mašiah*)—continue unabated into the second segment as well.[11] The effect of this shift is to refocus attention on the roles of the anticipated Davidic kings as anointed servants while distancing them from the rulership normally associated with the term *melek*.

Indeed, this understanding of the Davidic messiah is consistent with the role of humans in Genesis 1—2. As I have attempted to show in a small article in *Quaker Religious Thought*, to "exercise dominion" and "subdue the earth" are to bring it under God's rule. Humans are "ser-

---

[10]The *YHWH malak* psalms include the collected Psalms 93, 95, 96, 97, 98, 99, and the two separated Psalms 47 and 146.

[11]After appearing seven times in six psalms in the first three books (Ps 2:2; 18:50; 20:7; 28:8; 84:10; 89:39, 52), the term *mašiah* occurs only three times in two psalms in the last two books (Ps 105:15; 132:10, 17), a slight reduction in emphasis. The term *servant* (*'ebed*) also occurs in reference to kings seven times in four psalms in the earlier segment (Ps 18:1; 36:1; 78:70; 89:4, 21, 40, 51) and only two times in two psalms (Ps 132:10; 144:10) in the latter.

vants" who exercise protective care over the creation.[12] So at the beginning of the canon we find the same tension between rulership (Gen 1:26-
28) and servanthood (Gen 2) embodied in the Psalter's understanding of
the Davidic kings.[13]

This change implies a shift in the way these royal psalms and references
to the Davidic kings were interpreted. While it is clear that the anointed servants of Israel continue to play an important role in the future plans of
YHWH for his people, that role is increasingly distanced from the kind of
rulership associated with an earthly *melek*. YHWH is the eternal king (*melek*)
who rules over his people. Even with the decidedly militant picture of
David in Psalm 132 and the reference there to the promise of an enduring
throne for David and his descendants based on the Davidic covenant (cf.
Ps 132:10-12), it is also clear that it is YHWH who sits enthroned in Zion
forever and ever as king (Ps 132:13-14). It must have been immensely difficult among the diaspora community to disassociate David and his descendants from kingship entirely. Nevertheless, the role of the Davidic
melek recedes in the final form of the Psalter while David's role as the eschatological messiah (*masiah*) and servant (*'ebed*) who ushers in the kingdom and reign of YHWH is emphasized.[14] Thus the Psalter admits a
militant messianic view of the David kingship (particularly in Pss 2—89),
and yet the same Psalter offers a subtle alternative that emphasizes ser-
vant-hood subordinated to the rulership of YHWH.

The final form of the Psalter would ultimately affect the way the royal
psalms and earlier references to Davidic kingship were interpreted. In
light of the distancing that takes place in the later books, these references
would have been increasingly understood eschatologically as hopeful
anticipation of the Davidic descendant who would—as YHWH's anointed servant—establish God's direct rule over all humanity in the kingdom

---

[12]Gerald H. Wilson, "Restoring the Image: Prespectives on a Biblical View of Creation," *Quaker Religious Thought* 24 (1990): 11-21.

[13]Deuteronomy 17:14-20 exhibits the same tension. Israel may have a king, only one who will
not exercise the normal modes of kingly power, military, political or financial.

[14]The attempt to describe a consistent and thoroughgoing "eschatological programme" that
enfuses the whole Psalter is the goal of David C. Mitchell, *The Message of the Psalter: An Eschatological Programme in the Book of Psalms*, JSOTSup 252 (Sheffield: Sheffield Academic
Press, 1997). His work is ultimately unpersuasive since it (like earlier attempts to recon-
struct an enthronement festival) is based largely on tenuous connections between particular
psalms and a supposed eschatological program discovered in Zechariah 9—14. While
Mitchell's attempt at least takes the Psalter arrangement seriously, it ultimately fails by
seeking to say too much—or at least more than the psalms themselves clearly say.

of God.[15] Ultimately this shift prepares the way for Jesus' peculiar understanding of his role as the suffering, dying kind of messiah who inaugurates an eternal kingdom of God that is "not of this world" but of the Spirit.[16]

PARADIGM FOR BIBLICAL THEOLOGY

It is now time to conclude with a few comments regarding how the psalms and Psalter together offer a paradigm for doing biblical theology.

Diversity. The diversity of human perspective allowed to stand alongside one another in the psalms suggests that a biblical theology must represent an inclusive rather than an exclusive orthodoxy. Like the Psalter, a biblical theology must remain flexible enough to permit contrasting views of the human experience of life before God, while still marking out the parameters of the faith. The image of the expansive balloon—which maintains its unique shape by limiting outward expansion at the periphery—is a more apt model than a tethered rope that inhibits expansion by pulling all back to a preordained center. There is no clear center of the Psalter, but an outer limit that provides shape and contour.

Tension. The coexistence of tension is another feature of the Psalter that should inform the paradigm of biblical theology. Too often biblical theology has been unable to handle conflicting voices that offer alternative visions. The insights of the wisdom tradition and their tension with the revealed faith of covenant, obedience to law and ritual temple worship are a case in point. Neither Gerhard von Rad nor Walther Eichrodt was able to find a comfortable place in his theology for the wisdom teachings. Indeed, von Rad had to return to the subject in a separate volume to attempt to rectify the earlier omission.[17] The pessimistic insights of Qohelet suffer much the same fate when some authors ostracize the Preacher's words as negative examples of life lived without God,[18] even in the face of the epilogue's positive evaluation of Qohelet as sage and of the verity of his insights (Ec-

---

[15]This may even offer a partial solution for the apparent confusion between king and YHWH in such passages as Psalm 45:2-7, where the king appears in Psalm 45:5 to be called "God."

[16]Whether the continued use of the terms "anointed one" (*mašiah*) and "servant" (*'ebed*) in the last two books of the Psalter has any relationship to the suffering servant songs in Isaiah is not clear. But it is interesting that these two concepts are brought together by the heavenly voice at Jesus' baptism and transfiguration when it quotes portions of Psalm 2:7 ("son" = *mašiah*) and the servant song of Isaiah 42:1-2 ("in whom I delight" = *'ebed*). Cf. Jesus' reply to Pilate: "My kingdom is not of this world" (Jn 18:36 NIV).

[17]Gerhard von Rad, *Wisdom in Israel* (Nashville: Abingdon, 1972).

[18]Tremper Longman III, *The Book of Ecclesiastes* (Grand Rapids, Mich.: Eerdmans, 1998).

cles 12:9-14). By contrast, biblical theology that follows the paradigm of the psalms and Psalter will make room for tense dialogue and conflicting viewpoints as necessary windows onto the complexity of life in a fallen world that is moving onward toward resurrection.

A heart and not a center. The search for a center for biblical theology has thus far led to no consensus. Instead, a plethora of centers have been suggested, calling into question whether such a search is feasible or even desirable. For the most part, such a search for a center has the effect of emphasizing a critical minimum core that supplies structures for organizing theological expression. This has the effect of at least devaluing the peripheral voices of the canon, or at the worst eliminating them, since they do not easily fit with the central structures.

The Psalter offers a heart and not a center. Situated in the core of the fourth book of the Psalter, the *YHWH malak* psalms form a beating heart that pumps enlivening blood outward to serve even the peripheral limbs. The kingship of YHWH provides a new understanding of the royal psalms as well as the torah psalms.[19] The painful laments of exile, the questioning wisdom observations on the prosperity of the wicked and the exalted choruses of "halleluyah" offer necessary counterpoints to the rather strained and militant Zionist ideology, and yet all must yield ultimately to the vision of YHWH enthroned forever as king and judge of the world.

A compelling biblical theology would give voice to peripheral as well as central concerns, drawing hints of cohesive structures from the shape and shaping of the final form of text and canon. It would understand diversity and tension as necessary explorations of the realities of a broken world on its way to restoration, rather than as interim signposts to be left behind for a more exclusive orthodoxy. Finally, it would find at its heart the living God who is characterized by the themes of the *YHWH malak* psalms: God is Creator and Sustainer, Judge and Redeemer and eternal King over all that he has made.

---

[19]See the discussion of the torah psalms in James L. Mays, *The Lord Reigns! A Theological Handbook to the Psalms* (Louisville, Ky.: Westminster John Knox, 1994).

8

Figural Representation and Canonical Unity

M. Jay Wells

Biblical theology views the biblical canon as a unity. Hence, for a theology to be a biblical theology there must be an intrinsic unity between the Testaments. Nevertheless, since J. P. Gabler's 1787 address "On the Proper Distinction Between Biblical and Dogmatic Theology and the Specific Objectives of Each,"[1] in which he attempted to reclaim the Bible from the dogmatic-theological method of Protestant scholasticism, there have been two major detours along the way to recovering this unity.

DETOURS

The first significant (and long!) detour on this road to recovery began in the eighteenth- and nineteenth-century apologetic response to negative historical-critical scholarship. One abiding consequence of this apologetic has been an inadvertent shift in conservative theological method in which the "events" depicted in the text become the "material" for theology.[2] Fol-

---

[1]Translated into English and analyzed by John Sandys-Wunsch and Laurence Eldredge, "J. P. Gabler and the Distinction Between Biblical and Dogmatic Theology: Translation, Commentary and Discussion of His Originality," *SJT* 33 (1980): 133-58.
[2]On this apologetic and resultant tacit shift in biblical-theological method, see Hans Frei, *The*

lowing this detour, biblical theology has been transformed into a quest for ascertaining and understanding God's past revelatory acts and the human response they elicited as seen through the window of the biblical text. That is, the source material for the biblical theologian has become the events of the past behind the text, not the biblical text.

In this model, the interpreter qua historiographer—with all of its attendant epistemological concerns—must devise a special (i.e., usually Christian) historiography enabling him or her to discover, record, sift, evaluate and interpret the revelatory facts and events of the salvation history found in the Bible. In this model, biblical theology is not based solely upon what the particular biblical author says about certain events but is rather a combination of the author's and the interpreter's evaluations and interpretations of those events. The material for biblical theology consequently becomes what the biblical author says about the events and what the interpreter says about them.

In contrast, the approach advocated here is based on the premise that the biblical authors have already provided the material needed for a biblical theology in that they make theological claims about Israel's history and God's acts. Thus the interpreter's task is not to find and interpret the events behind the text but rather to find what the author is telling the reader by means of the text. As R. W. L. Moberly has put it, "the important thing is to grasp what is being said."[3]

The second significant detour concerns the NT use of the OT and is related to the salvation-history hermeneutical construct. Indeed, the first detour occasions the second. If the OT is merely a record of salvation-historical events, then it is reasonable to expect the NT authors to have transformed whatever meaning there was in the ancient, localized records of past history and to have reread them in light of their new experience—to have furnished a fuller meaning to the OT record of Israel's history. The result has been a variety of *sensus plenior*, "transformation and extension" or "charismatic rereading" views purporting to account for the NT authors' uses of the OT.[4]

Eclipse of Biblical Narrative: A Study in Eighteenth- and Nineteenth-Century Hermeneutics (New Haven, Conn.: Yale University Press, 1974), and John H. Sailhamer, *An Introduction to Old Testament Theology: A Canonical Approach* (Grand Rapids, Mich.: Zondervan, 1995).

[3]Cited in Scott J. Hafemann, *Paul, Moses and the History of Israel: The Letter/Spirit Contrast and the Argument from Scripture in 2 Corinthians 3* (Peabody, Mass.: Hendrickson, 1995), p. 194.

[4]For just two examples of this approach, see W. Janzen, "Land," in *Anchor Bible Dictionary*, ed. David Noel Freedman, 6 vols. (New York: Doubleday, 1992), 4:150-52, and Richard Hays, *Echoes of Scripture in the Letters of Paul* (New Haven, Conn.: Yale University Press, 1989).

This approach too, however, has taken us off the biblical theology course by failing to recognize the essential unity of the biblical canon.

FIGURAL REPRESENTATION

> What goals does the biblical narrator set himself? What is it that he wants to communicate in this or that story, cycle or book? What kind of text is the Bible, and what role does it perform in context? These are all variations on a fundamental question that students of the Bible would do well to pose loudly and sharply: the question of the narrative as a functional structure, a means to a communicative end, a transaction between the narrator and the audience on whom he wishes to produce a certain effect by way of certain strategies. Like all social discourse, biblical narrative is oriented to an addressee and regulated by a purpose or a set of purposes involving the addressee. Hence our primary business as readers is to make purposive sense of it, so as to explain the *what's* and the *how's* in terms of the *why's* of communication.[5]

In contrast to the approach of salvation history and its corollary, a *sensus plenior* reading of the text, and with Meir Sternberg's observations in mind, the compositional component of figural representation provides an important hermeneutical step back on the road to a unified biblical theology that encompasses the whole canon. Figural representation is a simple concept. It is the basic recognition that the biblical authors employ images or figures familiar to their readers (animals, objects, people, institutions, events from the past, etc.) to present their eschatological messages. One example of such a figural representation is found in the prophetic words of Zechariah 5:5-11. There the author depicts the time in the future when wickedness will be removed from the land of Israel. Wickedness is depicted as a woman sitting inside an ephah with a lead weight as its lid. The removal of wickedness from the land is then pictured as tantamount to two women carrying this woman in the ephah to the land of Shinar. The prophet thus writes of restoration using familiar and highly symbolic imagery; in other words, he represents the time of restoration figurally.

Of course, figural representation is not limited to the employment of familiar objects and institutions. An author often employs real historical events familiar to the reader as figures representing past, present or future realities. This kind of historical figuration is a way of seeing one event by

---

[5]Meir Sternberg, *The Poetics of Biblical Narrative: Ideological Literature and the Drama of Reading* (Bloomington: Indiana University Press, 1985), p. 1.

looking at another. That is, an author articulates a correlation or nexus between two real events for the purpose of illuminating one by means of the other. Hence the exodus from slavery in Egypt (a real historical event familiar to every Jew) is commonly employed as a figure to represent past, present or future acts of redemption (see e.g., Is 11:11-16). Figural representation is therefore not to be confused with typological interpretations, which approach the matter of figuration from a variety of reader-oriented perspectives that aim at finding meaning in texts or events. Over against these approaches, intertextual figural representation is not a method of interpretation brought to the text but a method of composition within the text. In short, figural representation is not something that a reader of a text does; it is what an author does.

To focus on figural representation, therefore, is to recognize that the authors of biblical texts are not merely recording the events and people about which they write but are reflecting upon them. As a matter of literary strategy, they employ them for particular thematic purposes. For example, an author might recount a past act of God in order to comfort his readers during a time of trouble by assuring them that just as God has acted faithfully in the past, in like manner he will remain faithful to his covenant and act again (see e.g., Is 51:10-11). An author might also use a past event in order to warn against disobedience or to anticipate judgment, as in Hosea 9:3 and Hosea 11:5, where Israel's past Egyptian slavery figurally represents the coming judgment and exile under the Assyrians.

Thus by means of such prospective figuration an author contemplates a future time in terms of the past or present. The prospect of a future event, hope or expectation is cast in the imagery of something antecedent. The author's purpose in drawing on past or present events is to look at the future, to instruct the reader in the way the future will be. The future is figurally represented in terms of past or present events. That is, the past heuristically configures the reader's conceptualization of the future.

Likewise, retrospective figuration is a heuristic device whereby past events are represented in terms and imagery of later events—for example, an author's circumstances and experience. That is, the author draws upon his life situation and experience to instruct the reader concerning the past. For example, in the Pentateuch Israel's experiences of redemption, sin and wandering in the wilderness are used figurally to frame the creation, fall and promise of redemption in Genesis 1—3.

But whether the figuration is retrospective or prospective, the point to emphasize here is that it is not the reader who has found the correspondence between two events. The reader is not the one who is responsible to connect thematically the future deliverance or coming judgment with the past event or vice versa. This remains the work of the author. Figural representation is not something that a reader of a text does; it is what an author has done. It is a compositional technique, not an interpretive one.

FIGURATION AND THE SHAPING OF THE PENTATEUCH

In turning our attention to the Pentateuch, our interest is in its shape, that is, in its theological configuration, the web of themes comprising the book. Our focus is on the book as a complete literary composition, an intentional arrangement of materials designed to convey a particular theological intent. In particular, the author has composed his book to address the plight of humanity, the presence of sin and death and God's plan to deal with this human predicament.

Theological introduction to the Pentateuch. In the introductory chapters (Gen 1—3) the author provides the theological underpinnings for the whole of the book, a theme complex that permeates not only the Pentateuch but also the subsequent canon. Herein is described the creation of a people, the preparation of a blessed dwelling place for that people and the subsequent entrance of sin and death. There is a distinctive literary purpose in recounting these events—to enlighten the reader to God's plan to redeem and restore that which is his. There is a distinctive literary form in the account—the imagery employed is in language drawn from the author's and readers' life experiences. The creation and plight of humanity are cast retrospectively in the imagery of God's gracious acts toward Israel and of Israel's experience at Sinai. At the beginning of his creative work God prepared out of an uninhabitable desert wasteland (reminiscent of the wilderness in which the disobedient people had been wandering) a fruitful land in which his people might dwell and fellowship with him in perfect blessing (reminiscent of the Promised Land). Having prepared a "very good" land (Gen 1:29-31 NIV [throughout the essay]), God made man and placed him in the garden in Eden to enjoy it and be fruitful and multiply (Gen 1:28). The idea of "good" entails "life," "land" and "posterity," encompassing that which the divine covenant brings. These central covenant themes figure in the conclusion to the Pentateuch (Deut 30:15), where "good" is synonymous with "life" and where "life" and "good" have as their antitheses "death" and "evil." The antithesis of "being good" and "being many" is to be exiled from the land of inheritance (Deut 28:63), that is, to lose the covenant blessings. God made a covenant with his people that they should obey what he commanded and thus enjoy his blessing (as in the covenant received at Mount Sinai). But Adam and Eve were disobedient to this covenant and as a consequence the warning of God—"you will die" (Gen 3:3)—became a reality. The disobedient couple were cast out from the land of blessing wherein they were originally to have life. They were exiled and barred from it, alienated and homeless.

Before expelling them from this land, however, God made a promise that what had occurred in the garden would be undone in the "seed" of the woman (Gen 3:15). With this promise the thematic stage is set for the rest of the book inasmuch as the plight of humanity has been retrospectively represented, cast in the familiar figures drawn from their experience (exodus, wilderness wandering, covenant, land promise). Thus, having set the thematic stage, the author will cultivate this web of themes—possession of land, disobedience, exile from land and restoration in a "seed"—in the narrative that follows. In fact, here we see the biblical-theological footing for the "Deuteronomic" conceptual framework of sin-exile-restoration that permeates the canon (see below). As the matter has been aptly stated:

> There remains in this verse [Gen. 3:15] a puzzling yet important ambiguity: Who is the "seed" of the woman? It seems obvious that the purpose of verse 15 has not been to answer that question, but rather to raise it. The remainder of the book is, in fact, the author's answer.[6]

The theological presentation of the Pentateuch. In the ensuing chapters the author lays out God's blueprint for bringing about the undoing of Adam's disobedience, further defining who the seed of the woman is and is not. In doing so, he moves from retrospective to prospective figuration. For the Pentateuch author, this divine program of final and ultimate undoing in the future looks like God's covenant acts in the past. The Noah story is employed as a portrait of the new humanity who is to be delivered from God's judgment; yet it is clear that the Noah story is not that redemption and restoration in all its fullness, for Noah and his seed continued in disobedience. The ultimate fulfillment still lies in the future.

The author then presents Abraham as the central figure in God's divine plan: God's purpose is to make obedient Abraham's name great and

---

[6]John H. Sailhamer, *The Pentateuch as Narrative: A Biblical-Theological Commentary* (Grand Rapids, Mich.: Zondervan, 1992), p. 108.

make of him a great nation so that he will be a blessing to all the families of the earth (Gen 12:1-3). It is to Abraham's "seed" that God will give the land to inherit for an everlasting covenant where God will make him exceedingly fruitful (Gen 13:14-17; 17:2-8). Here the author depicts the restoration of what was lost in the garden because of Adam's disobedience: in Abraham's seed is to be the fulfillment of the promise to the woman, a seed in whom would be the undoing of Adam's disobedience. The author has now provided a more vivid picture of the seed of the woman in the seed of Abraham. The character of this Abrahamic seed is embodied in the figure Abraham, the exemplar of faithful obedience to the covenant not seen in Adam.

The Abrahamic story is foundational to the Pentateuch, with an ensuing interplay between the Abrahamic ("obedience") and the Sinaitic ("disobedience") themes. In the remainder of the book the author contrasts this picture of future deliverance (Abrahamic faith) with Sinaitic Israel's continued unfaithfulness to the covenant. What the Sinaitic covenant people had thus far failed to do Abraham had done. What emerges in the book therefore is Sinaitic Israel as a theological reality, with a thematic discord between the Abrahamic and the Sinaitic.[7] Hence, the narrative of Sinaitic Israel, like that of the garden, is a story of blessing, stipulation, failure, judgment and future promise. The Sinaitic order is a part of the divine plan, but is not the ultimate fulfillment of that plan. Rather, the Moses-Sinaitic story, comprising the greater part of the Pentateuch, figurally represents God's ultimate redemption and restoration.

The theological conclusion to the Pentateuch. The author's summation of the book's theological intent is a note of stark reality: the people of Sinaitic Israel are "no longer his children . . . a warped and crooked generation . . . a perverse generation, children who are unfaithful" (Deut 32:5, 20). The covenant stipulation is obedience; Sinaitic Israel is continually disobedient.[8] In this conclusion we see the Deuteronomic view of Israel's history

---

[7]See the author's characterization of Sinaitic Israel as stiff-necked (e.g., Ex 32—34). Cf. Hafemann, *Paul,* pp. 189-254, for this central literary unit within the Pentateuch. As Hafemann concludes, pp. 229-30, "As such, like Adam and Eve, Israel's sin with the golden calf becomes both determinative and paradigmatic for Israel's future history as God's people."

[8]Sinaitic Israel is continually disobedient because they are without the Spirit of God. Again the comments of Hafemann are relevant; ibid., pp. 441-42: "In God's sovereignty, Moses was called to declare the saving will of God to the people without the accompanying life-giving work of the Spirit. As a result, the necessity of the veil in Exod. 34:29-35 announced the need for the ultimate replacement of the Sinaitic covenant. What Jeremiah and Ezekiel declared

taking shape. Sinaitic Israel has become a concrete theological concept that will influence subsequent theological presentations, canonical and noncanonical.[9] According to the author, Sinaitic Israel as a whole is clearly not the promised seed of the woman, for to that day the Lord had yet to give his people "a mind that understands or eyes that see or ears that hear" (Deut 29:4).

Yet, although Sinaitic Israel is an ensconced failure in the author's view, he does not leave the story there. He concludes his book on the ultimate note of promise: the Lord's plan is to give his people a new heart to obey. At that time, he will finally undo the disobedience of Adam, redeeming and restoring the humanity that is his. It is not until the people return to the Lord and obey him with all their heart that the Lord will restore them, gathering them from all the peoples among whom the Lord had scattered them. *Then* he will bring them back into the land to possess it. In this covenantal order the Lord will circumcise their heart. He will make them more prosperous and numerous than their fathers. He will do all of this in order that they may live, the ultimate reversal of the consequence of the Adamic disobedience. According to the author, in that day the exiles will be restored to the land from which they had been exiled because of disobedience (Deut 30:1-10). The Pentateuch thus closes with a stern negative assessment of the Sinaitic order, looking to the future and awaiting the promised seed of the woman, namely, the seed of Abraham, the prophet like Moses (Deut 31:14-32:47; 34:9-12). It is in this figure, not Sinaitic Israel, that God's people will be restored to their land when the Adamic disobedience is decisively undone.

Sinaitic Israel is continually disobedient because they are without the Spirit of God. Again the comments of Hafemann are relevant; ibid., pp. 441-42: "In God's sovereignty, Moses was called to declare the saving will of God to the people without the accompanying life-giving work of the Spirit. As a result, the necessity of the veil in Exod. 34:29-35 announced the need for the ultimate replacement of the Sinaitic covenant. What Jeremiah and Ezekiel declared concerning the 'problem' of the old covenant . . . Exod. 34:29ff. already demonstrates. . . . From its very beginning, therefore, the old covenant of the Law without the Spirit implicitly looked forward to the time when the Law would encounter a people whose hearts had been changed and empowered to keep God's covenant."

[9]For a valuable treatment of the Deuteronomic view of Israel's history, see James M. Scott, "Paul's Use of Deuteronomic Tradition," *JBL* 112 (1993): 645-65. Hence the NT writers' view of God's wrath upon Sinaitic Israel is not derived from their reflections on Israel's history per se but from the theology of the OT texts—a subtle yet exegetically important distinction. The OT writers have already theologically characterized the history of Israel. That is, the canon's theological idea of Israel's history is established—the very notion of Sinaitic Israel is a fixed conceptual structure, a perspective from which later OT authors and the NT authors directly draw.

FIGURATION AND THE SHAPING OF THE
OLD TESTAMENT CANON

Just as the author of the Pentateuch accomplished his literary purposes by recounting many of God's past acts as figural representations of God's future acts, the Deuteronomic historian, the prophets, the Chronicler and the Canonicler construct their literary works in like manner. They too look back in order to look forward. Yet they do so within the pentateuchal theme structure that permeated their thought world. That is, the very mode of their thought has been formed by a life saturated in the image world of the Pentateuch. In this sense, the Pentateuch is thematically paradigmatic for the subsequent canon.

Deuteronomic History. Like the Pentateuch, the Deuteronomic History (Joshua—Kings) is a book with a thematic unity and purpose. Composed in its final form in the midst of the Babylonian exile, it looks back through the history of Israel since the conquest from the perspective of the exile and destruction of Jerusalem and the temple. The portrait painted by the author is simple: persistent disobedience to the covenant, especially by most of Israel's kings, has brought these times of troubles. Reminiscent of the disobedient couple who had been banished from the good land provided by their covenant God, Israel has been exiled from their good land and the dwelling place of their God, the temple, has been destroyed (cf. Josh 23:16). All around is desolation and the people are again landless wanderers (cf. 2 Kings 17:14).

But the author does not stop here, for his purpose is larger than this word of judgment. The land may be gone, but the Lord's word remains. He is faithful, even when his people are not, and his promise endures, enduring even the exile. Thus the Deuteronomic history, like the Pentateuch, is ultimately a book looking toward the future. Though Sinai was a failure, there is coming a time when God will again bring his people into the land that he promised and redeem humanity from their rebellion. Indeed, the Deuteronomic historian's purpose is not only to clarify the reason for the exile but also to disclose in greater detail the nature of the promised restoration (undoing of Adamic disobedience).

David is the author's primary portrait of that promise as set forth in the Pentateuch. The figure of King David, whom the Lord had given rest from his enemies (2 Sam 7:1; cf. Deut 3:20; 25:19), is representative of that day when the Lord will restore his people and reestablish his kingdom. For in that day the Lord will appoint a place of their own for his people, where

evildoers will no longer afflict them. The Lord will therefore establish his
eternal kingdom in the seed of David, for David's throne will be established forever (2 Sam 7). Josiah is a figure representative of this Davidic
king to come. According to the author, there was no king like him in the
past nor had there been since (2 Kings 23:25). But, again, neither David's
reign nor Josiah's reform were the promised redemption and restoration.
Nor was their city the Jerusalem of promise—it had only been like it (2
Kings 23:26-27). The evidence was before the people: this Jerusalem lay in
ruins and its temple desolate. For the Deuteronomic historian, Sinaitic Israel was a failure and the promised kingdom was still in the future.

The Latter Prophets. Prospective figural representation abounds in the
prophets. These authors too were keenly aware of the pentateuchal theme
structure. They did not co-opt the imagery—Adam, Eden, land, exodus—
merely to reassure ethnic Israel that they would be restored from Babylonian exile. The books of the Prophets took the originally localized prophecies, oracles and visions of judgment and hope—formerly associated with
specific historical particularities—and arranged them into new eschatological messages of judgment and hope. That is, the authors thematically related the previous localized oracles to God's redemptive plan for all of history.

For example, Judah's preservation in 701 B.C. is employed in Isaiah as a
figure representative of God's final deliverance, a theme detected in the arrangement of the book's collections of material. For Christopher Seitz observes that

> by prefacing the narratives that tell of Zion's deliverance of 701 B.C. with chap-
> ters 34—35, the specific historical instance of Zion's protection in the days of
> Sennacherib has been placed within a much broader framework of God's on-
> going attention and care for the vineyard amidst the nations at large. The won-
> drous deliverance of 701 B.C. foreshadows Zion's final triumph as God's
> chosen place of exaltation and return. . . . What remains of paramount concern
> to those who have shaped the present tradition is . . . God's fundamental, abid-
> ing concern for Zion's final triumph and permanent fortification against the
> nations. Chapters 34—35 speak of that triumph; chapters 36—39 give a con-
> crete example of God's care at one moment in Zion's history.[10]

So too, in addressing a message of future hope to a people in exile, the
author can depict the time of restoration in the pentateuchal imagery of
the creation and exodus, thereby portraying the restoration to come as a

---

[10]Christopher R. Seitz, *Isaiah 1—39* (Louisville, Ky.: John Knox Press, 1993), pp. 240, 242.

second exodus act of deliverance that brings about a new creation (see Is 43:1-2; 51:3).

In the same way, Jeremiah's message of judgment against disobedient Judah is likewise cast in Deuteronomic language (Jer 25:1-14). Because the people remained in disobedience the Lord was going to send judgment on Judah, making the land and its inhabitants an "everlasting ruin [or, disgrace]" (Jer 25:9). This period of everlasting disgrace is further defined as a time when "this whole land shall become a desolate wasteland, and these nations will serve the king of Babylon seventy years" (Jer 25:11). In the language of Deuteronomic eschatology, Sinaitic Israel will be in ruin forever in the coming judgment. Judah had become no different from Babylon (cf. Jer 25:15-29). But the book's message is more than judgment. At the end of the apocalyptic period of seventy years Judah will be restored, again pictured in Deuteronomic language (Jer 29:10-14; cf. Deut 4:29-31; 30:1-10).

We know however from subsequent books in the OT canon that the seventy years and the return were not considered the ultimate fulfillment of the prophet's promises of restoration (cf. Dan 9:24-27). In Zechariah we find the confirmation that Zerubbabel was not the fulfillment of the prophesied rebuilding of the temple; he was only a picture of that future reality. According to Zechariah, that time was to arrive only when the people kept the covenant. The seventy years of judgment and captivity were not complete, for the people remained disobedient even after the seventy years (Zech 7:5).

The latter half of Ezekiel arranges a series of oracles that depict the time yet to come when God will finally redeem and restore his people and his creation (Ezek 34—48). Ezekiel 34 depicts the restoration of the Davidic house, with David shepherding his people. Because of the unfaithfulness and failure of the shepherds of Israel, the sheep "were scattered because there was no shepherd" (Ezek 34:5). Therefore the Lord was "against the shepherds" and was to "rescue [his] flock from their mouths" (Ezek 34:10-12). He will save his flock himself and set up over them one shepherd, his servant David, thus reconstituting Israel. In Ezekiel 36 the author represents this restoration of the house of David in language reminiscent of the web of themes found in the Pentateuch (cf. Gen 1—3; Deut 30:1-10): the Lord will take them from the nations, gather them from all the countries, and bring them into their own land and put a new spirit within them. By his Spirit he will make them follow his statutes and observe his ordinances as Abraham did (Ezek 36:24-27). "You will dwell in the land I gave your forefathers; you will be my peo-

ple, and I will be your God. . . . On the day I cleanse you from all your sins,
I will resettle your towns, and the ruins will be rebuilt. The desolate land
will be cultivated instead of lying desolate in the sight of all who pass
through it. They will say, 'This land that was laid waste has become like the
garden of Eden; the cities that were lying in ruins, desolate and destroyed,
are now fortified and inhabited'" (Ezek 36:28, 33-35).

Moreover, juxtaposed to the themes of the restoration of the Davidic
house and the renewal of Eden is the imagery of the resurrection of the dry
bones. These resurrected bones are "the whole house of Israel"—the new
revived Adam—into whom God has breathed the breath of life. This resurrection pictures the time when God will put his Spirit within Israel as a
people and place them on their own land (Ezek 37:1-14).

Ezra-Nehemiah-Chronicles. The author of Ezra-Nehemiah recounts the
return of the exiles from Babylon that "the word of the LORD spoken by Jeremiah" might be fulfilled (Ezra 1:1). With the temple complete under
Zerubbabel, Ezra returned under the decree of King Artaxerxes in order to
administer the affairs of the people. It has been suggested that Ezra's return from captivity to Jerusalem is cast in the pentateuchal imagery of a
new exodus and conquest.[11] Yet the author did not see Ezra's act as Israel's
final restoration, nor were Jeremiah's seventy years complete in the author's view. The complete reestablishment of the Davidic house had not
yet occurred—there was no Davidic king; David's dynasty had not been
reestablished, and the land of Israel remained under the rule of the nations. At the conclusion of Ezra-Nehemiah the reader finds Israel as it had
always been, disobedient (Neh 13:23-27; cf. Ezra 9:6-15; Neh 9:5-37). The
seventy-year period continued. The situation is summed up in the prayer
of Nehemiah: "We have acted very wickedly toward you. We have not
obeyed the commandments, decrees and laws you gave your servant
Moses" (Neh 1:7).

Chronicles recounts the past with a view to the future as well. By recounting the history of the Davidic line the author portrays what the everlasting covenant will look like and what it will not look like. Obedience to
God's law characterized covenant life under the rule of the Davidic king.
In contrast, Chronicles concludes its history of the Davidic line rather
abruptly by characterizing the last few kings with these somber words:

---

[11]K. Koch, cited in Michael Fishbane, *Biblical Interpretation in Ancient Israel* (Oxford: Clarendon, 1985), p. 363: "Ezra's march from Babylon to Jerusalem was a cultic procession which
Ezra understood as a second Exodus."

"He did evil in the eyes of the LORD his God" (2 Chron 36:5, 9, 12). The author then sketches briefly the underlying cause of the temple's ruin in Deuteronomic language (see 2 Chron 36:15-16). Sinaitic Israel was an abysmal failure, but the author's purpose is not only to tell a story of failure. He concludes with the edict of Cyrus to rebuild the temple, a figural sketch of hope (2 Chron 36:23).

The Canonicler. Finally, there is a discernible theological configuration of the canon as a whole—a unity of theological presentation by an intentional author (compiler). Throughout, the reader is directed to look to the future, an intent seen in this Canonicler's thematic arrangement of the books and in the "editorial joins," "contextualizing redactions" and "end redaction" of the canon as a whole.[12] Deuteronomy 34:10-12 and Malachi 4:4-6 appear to be redactional seams by which the Canonicler thematically connects the three books comprising the Tanak. From the Canonicler's postexilic perspective, "no prophet has risen in Israel like Moses" (Deut 34:10). He instructs the reader to be faithful to the covenant as commanded and steadfast in anticipation of the future when the Lord would send Elijah, the prophet who would announce the arrival of the "great and dreadful day of the LORD" (Mal 4:5-6). And so the OT canon speaks with a singular voice—the reader is to look forward obediently to the day when God will accomplish his promise of a new exodus redemption and restoration in the seed of the woman, the seed of Abraham, the seed of David.

TOWARD A BIBLICAL THEOLOGY OF THE WHOLE CANON

On the basis of the foregoing, the NT writers recognized that in Jesus they have witnessed the fulfillment of the OT promises as intended by the OT authors—the restoration of Israel in the seed of the woman, the seed of Abraham, the seed of David.

Indeed, Paul's gospel is the announcement of the fulfillment of the Abrahamic promise, just as the Scriptures preached beforehand with respect to Abraham (Gal 3:6-14). The dispute with Paul's opponents was not whether Israel is the recipient of the promised Abrahamic inheritance but rather the identity of that Israel to whom the Abrahamic promise had been made. The promise to Abraham was not voided by the Sinaitic order, insti-

---

[12]See Stephen G. Dempster, "The Formation of the Hebrew Bible: From Many Texts to One," in *The World of the Arameans: Biblical, Historical and Cultural Studies in Honor of Paul-E. Dion,* ed. P. M. Michele Daviau and M. Weigl (Sheffield: Sheffield Press, forthcoming), and Sailhamer, *Introduction to Old Testament Theology,* pp. 239-52.

tuted because of persistent disobedience until the arrival of the promised seed who would undo the Adamic situation in eschatological restoration (Gal 3:15-19). This promised inheritance was always inclusive of ethnic Jew and Gentile (Gen 12:3). Those who belong to Christ, who have been clothed with him (cf. Gen 3:21), are Abraham's true descendants, restored in the seed of the woman. These true descendants constitute God's eschatological Israel, his restored humanity. That is, in him who was seed of the woman is redemption from slavery, a new exodus, in order that the redeemed might receive adoption into the new Adamic family. Thus those who believe are no longer in slavery but are children, and if children then heirs to the Abrahamic promise with the seed of Abraham, seed of the woman (Gal 3:26-4:7), just as the Scriptures preached beforehand.

Paul, like the rest of the NT authors, thus proclaims the arrival of that which he understands the OT authors to have been figurally representing—a new creation redeemed and predestined for adoption in the last Adam. In Christ is the fulfillment of the inheritance promised to Abraham's seed, the seed of the woman. It was, in fact, concerning deliverance from the human predicament delineated in Genesis 1—3 that the prophets prophesied (see 1 Pet 1:10-12). It was revealed to them that they were not serving themselves but the recipients of this promised deliverance—the restored humanity in Messiah. The NT message is the explication of the eschatological gospel already proclaimed in the Scriptures. As Luke emphasized, Paul was "saying nothing beyond what the prophets and Moses said would happen" (Acts 26:22).[13]

The OT is far more than a record of salvation history that must be reconstructed, interpreted and reread by the NT authors and today's biblical theologian. The OT is a revelatory text that conveys an intentional eschatological-prophetic theology clearly seen in its use of figuration. In the same way, the NT is a revelatory text that announces the arrival and fulfillment of that prophecy without having to furnish it with its own prophetic meaning.

The theological universe of the NT authors is unquestionably imbued by a life immersed in the canonical image world—they live with texts in

---

[13]David P. Moessner, *Lord of the Banquet: The Literary and Theological Significance of the Lukan Travel Narrative* (Harrisburg, Penn.: Trinity Press International, 1989), has discerned in the compositional structure of the central section of Luke's Gospel (Lk 9:1—19:44) an intentional presentation of Jesus in the Deuteronomic imagery of the "prophet like Moses" who is leading the "new exodus" of his people.

their mind. Moreover, the use of figuration is one demonstration that the canon as a whole is a theological unity, for it speaks with one voice to one biblical-theological complex and does so without in the end banishing the respective authors from their own texts. The canon first proclaims (by figurally representative events, persons and institutions) the coming eschatological redemption and restoration of humanity—the decisive reversal of the Adamic disobedience and its consequences. The canon then announces the arrival of that promised redemption and restoration to which all of the figures, types, shadows and copies pointed: the restoration of Israel in the Davidic seed, the Abrahamic seed, the seed of the woman—a new, re-created humanity in the obedient last Adam. It is to this resolution that the one canon speaks with a singular voice.

PART TWO

THE WITNESS OF
THE "NEW TESTAMENT"

The Culmination
of Biblical Theology

9

Jesus' Vision for the Restoration of Israel as the Basis for a Biblical Theology of the New Testament

James M. Scott

B y any measure, constructing a comprehensive biblical theology is a tall order. It presupposes the fundamental, organic unity not only between the disparate writings of the NT but also ultimately between the two Testaments! Moreover, practically speaking, a comprehensive biblical theology must start with the NT as the Archimedean point toward which the whole project is oriented. It is inevitable that a comprehensive biblical theology will read the so-called OT in light of the NT, since the latter exemplifies how the OT—the Bible of Jesus and the early church—was understood by the nascent Jesus movement.[1]

In view of this watershed decision as to where to begin the project, I would like to suggest the following definition of a biblical theology of the NT: It is a historical-critical reconstruction and germane description of the OT/Jewish matrix, organic growth and structural interrelationship of the

---

[1]Cf. Morgens Müller, "Neutestamentliche Theologie als Biblische Theologie: Einige grundsätzliche Überlegungen," *NTS* 43 (1997): 475-90.

body of early Christian thought represented in the NT canon.[2] The best metaphor to illustrate this process is connective tissue, for this captures the living, dynamic character of the NT without losing sight of the structures that support and connect the whole. Our tissue metaphor would lead us to expect unity in diversity, as the living tradition that supports and connects the whole body of early Christian thought grows out from the center and responds or adapts to ever new situations. The character of this living tradition is largely determined by OT/Jewish tradition as the ground substance that gives the tissue its consistency (the matrix).

Even if we could agree on this definition, however, we are still faced with the exceedingly difficult problem of where to begin in the NT. Almost any starting point we choose within the NT will inevitably be reductionistic in some way, for it is impossible to begin with everything at once. Yet the way forward is not simply to take one or more of the recurrent themes in the NT and to trace it across the various corpora. Although that might indicate some of the basic coherence of the NT, it would ultimately fail to show more than longitudinal sections of NT thinking. Rather, the most logical place to commence is with Jesus. As is well known, Rudolf Bultmann held that "the proclamation of Jesus belongs to the presuppositions of the Theology of the NT and is itself not part of this Theology."[3] However, without Jesus and his influence, the NT writers would not have written what they did. Therefore, contra Bultmann, we ought to start with Jesus, the dynamo who set the whole early Christian movement in motion. Indeed, Jesus is the sine qua non of the NT, so that Jesus is the actual basis of NT theology.[4]

Having said this, we stand before yet another watershed issue: What is it about Jesus that allegedly forms the basis of NT theology? His teachings? His works? His death? His resurrection? His second coming? Some combination of these? And, of course, the lingering question will always be, How do we know for sure who Jesus was, what he taught, what he did, why he died? Fortunately, in the past few years a consensus has been emerging in at least one wing of historical Jesus research—the wing that

[2]On the notion of canon and its probable early (second century!) formation, see David Trobisch, *The First Edition of the New Testament* (Oxford: Oxford University Press, 2000).
[3]Rudolf Bultmann, *Theologie des Neuen Testaments*, 9th ed., Uni-Taschenbücher 630 (Tübingen: Mohr Siebeck, 1984), p. 1.
[4]Cf. Peter Stuhlmacher, *Biblische Theologie des Neuen Testaments*, 2 vols. (Göttingen: Vandenhoeck & Ruprecht, 1992, 1999), 1:18, 19, 24.

sees Jesus as an eschatological prophet of Israel.[5] According to scholars such as Ben F. Meyer,[6] E. P. Sanders,[7] John P. Meier,[8] N. T. Wright,[9] Dale C. Allison[10] and Scot McKnight,[11] among others, Jesus of Nazareth lived (and even died) for one thing: his vision for the restoration of Israel. In view of this consensus, the question for a biblical theology of the NT then becomes: How did Jesus acquire his vision for the restoration of Israel? How did Jesus articulate his vision? How did Jesus' death and resurrection relate to his vision for the restoration of Israel? And, most important, How did the followers of Jesus receive his vision for the restoration of Israel so that it became the vision of the early church? Does Jesus' vision for the restoration of Israel come to expression in the rest of the NT?

THE TERM *RESTORATION* AND THE OLD TESTAMENT / JEWISH MATRIX OF JESUS' VISION OF RESTORATION

The English word *restoration*, from the Latin *restaurare*, means "to renew," "to restore" or "to reestablish." In the most general sense, restoration denotes the attempt of individuals or groups in a society to reestablish in whole or in part earlier conditions (the *status quo ante*) that prevailed before a major change took place, such as an overthrow or a revolution.[12] The proponents of restoration movements are convinced that the earlier conditions to be recovered, whether political, legal, social, economic, cultural or religious, are more desirable than the currently prevailing situation. Restoration movements are also characterized by the religious belief in the temporal transcendence of certain norms and values. Restoration need not mean the negation of progress and hence fossilization. A restoration move-

---

[5]This emerging consensus does not exclude the possibility that Jesus was more than an eschatological prophet of Israel. Ultimately Martin Hengel ("E. P. Sanders' 'Common Judaism,' Jesus, and the Pharisees," *JTS* 46 [1995]: 5) is almost certainly correct: "As Isa. 61:1 and the new texts from 4Q demonstrate, 'eschatological prophet' and 'Messiah' stand closer to one another than Sanders allows."

[6]Ben F. Meyer, *The Aims of Jesus* (London: SCM Press, 1979); "Jesus' Ministry and Self-Understanding," in *Studying the Historical Jesus: Evaluations of the State of Current Research*, ed. Bruce Chilton and Craig A. Evans, NTTS 19 (Leiden: E. J. Brill, 1994), pp. 337-52.

[7]E. P. Sanders, *Jesus and Judaism* (Philadelphia: Fortress, 1985); *The Historical Figure of Jesus* (London: Penguin, 1993).

[8]John P. Meier, *A Marginal Jew: Rethinking the Historical Jesus*, vol. 2, *Mentor, Message and Miracles* (New York: Doubleday, 1994).

[9]N. T. Wright, *Jesus and the Victory of God* (Minneapolis: Fortress, 1996).

[10]Dale C. Allison, *Jesus of Nazareth: Millenarian Prophet* (Minneapolis: Fortress, 1998).

[11]Scot McKnight, *A New Vision for Israel: The Teachings of Jesus in National Context* (Grand Rapids, Mich.: Eerdmans, 1999).

[12]Cf. Joachim Mehlhausen, "Restauration," *TRE* 29 (1998): 87-88.

ment can understand itself as a reform movement that seeks continuity in the midst of historical change and the decay of traditions and authorities.

These general characteristics of restoration movements also apply in large part to the OT conceptions of Israel's restoration.[13] The northern kingdom of Israel and the southern kingdom of Judah had been sent into their respective exiles. This was the major catastrophe that evoked the hopes of reestablishing earlier conditions that had prevailed before the exiles took place. Traditions vary as to the exact components of restoration hope. Generally speaking, however, it was the hope that the nation—all twelve tribes of Jacob—would be returned to the land and reunited, as it had been in the golden age under a Davidic monarch who is enthroned with God in Jerusalem (see, e.g., Is 11:1, 11-12, 16). In other words, God will establish a son of David's house as the eschatological king. And this Davidic king will rule over not only the twelve tribes of restored Israel but also over the nations: "In that day the root of Jesse shall stand as an ensign to the peoples; him shall the nations seek" (Is 11:10; author's translation [throughout the essay, unless otherwise noted]). Indeed, Isaiah foresees that the mountain of God's house will be raised as the highest mountain and will draw all the nations to it, to the worship of the God of Jacob (Is 2:2-4), and it is on Zion that God will make a lavish feast for all peoples (Is 25:6).

Needless to say, such grand and glorious expectations, and many more besides, failed to materialize. Judean exiles did return from Babylon in the sixth century, although most did not go back, and the northern tribes never returned (see 1 Chron 5:26). The temple was rebuilt, although not to the former glory of the Solomonic temple. And, most telling of all, the land remained under foreign domination throughout the whole Second Temple period, except for a brief period of independence under the Hasmoneans. As a result, the hopes of restoration were continually pushed to the future.[14] By the time of Jesus there had already been several restoration movements headed by would-be kings,[15] but all of them had fizzled. Nevertheless, Jewish literature of the period lends cre-

---

[13]On the restoration of Israel, see James M. Scott, ed., *Restoration: Old Testament, Jewish and Christian Conceptions*, JSJSup 72 (Leiden: E. J. Brill, 2002).

[14]The most famous example of this phenomenon is Daniel 9:24, where the seventy years of Jeremiah 25:11-12; 29:10 are reinterpreted to mean seventy weeks of years. On this point and its canonical implications, see John H. Sailhamer's essay in this volume.

[15]Cf. Craig A. Evans, "Messianic Claimants of the First and Second Centuries," in *Jesus and His Contemporaries: Comparative Studies*, AGJU 25 (Leiden: E. J. Brill, 1995), pp. 53-81.

dence to the fact that hopes of restoration, however varied, were widely held and continued unabated.[16]

JESUS' VISION FOR THE RESTORATION OF ISRAEL

As mentioned above, the most important development in historical Jesus studies is the recent attempt to understand the ministry of Jesus in terms of the national restoration of Israel. Although many details remain unclear or disputed, one of the fundamental data from which this perspective proceeds is the fact that Jesus gathered around himself a group of precisely twelve disciples who symbolized the eschatological regathering of the twelve tribes of Israel. Using all available criteria for assessing the authenticity of Jesus materials, John P. Meier has convincingly demonstrated the existence of the circle of the twelve during Jesus' public ministry.[17] If, in continuity with the preaching of John the Baptist, Jesus was calling the nation of Israel to repentance, if Jesus was otherwise doing and saying the things that a prophet of Israel would say and do, then gathering twelve disciples would amount to a symbolic prophetic demonstration that Jesus was inaugurating the ingathering of the twelve tribes in anticipation of the coming kingdom of God. In Sanders's words, "Jesus intended to show that he had in view the full restoration of the people of Israel."[18] Moreover, Jesus is quoted in Matthew's Gospel as saying that his disciples will judge or rule the twelve tribes of Israel (Mt 19:28; cf. Lk 22:30). In support of this consensus, Meier summarizes the preliminary findings of his monumental work as follows: Jesus is "a 1st-century Jewish eschatological prophet who proclaims an imminent-future coming of God's kingdom, practices baptism as a ritual of preparation for that kingdom, teaches his disciples to pray to God as *abba* for the kingdom's arrival, prophesies the regathering of all Israel (symbolized by the inner circle of his twelve disciples) and the inclusion of the Gentiles when the kingdom comes—but who at the same time makes the kingdom already present for at least some Israelites by his exorcisms and miracles of healing."[19] Indeed, McKnight states, "Contemporary scholarship is nearly united in the view that Jesus' vision con-

---

[16]See E. P. Sanders, *Judaism: Practice and Belief 63 B.C.E.-66 C.E.* (London: SCM Press; Philadelphia: Trinity Press International, 1992), pp. 279-98.

[17]John P. Meier, "The Circle of the Twelve: Did It Exist During Jesus' Public Ministry?" *JBL* 116 (1997): 635-72.

[18]Sanders, *Historical Figure of Jesus*, p. 120.

[19]Meier, *A Marginal Jew*, 2:454. See also "The Circle of the Twelve," p. 648.

cerned Israel as a nation and not a new religion. He wanted to consummate God's promises to Israel, and he saw this taking place in the land of Israel."[20]

How did Jesus acquire his vision for the restoration of Israel? This question admits of several answers. First, Jesus may have acquired the initial impetus for his vision from his family background. As several scholars point out, the very fact that Joseph and Mary named their sons after patriarchs—James (Jacob), Joses (Joseph), Judas (Judah) and Simon (Simeon)—may indicate that Jesus' hope for the restoration of Israel was inherited from his parents.[21]

Second, Jesus probably acquired his vision for the restoration of Israel in part from his association with John the Baptist. In the beginning, Jesus was very likely a disciple of John, although the exact nature of that discipleship is unclear. According to Mark, our earliest Gospel, Jesus was baptized by John in the Jordan (Mk 1:9-11), and Jesus began his Galilean ministry only after John was imprisoned, clearly continuing John's emphasis on repentance and judgment (Mk 1:14-15). This suggests that the origins of Jesus' call and ministry lie in the ministry of the Baptist and in his desire to carry on and to build on some of John's main emphases. Jesus began his own work within the circle of John's prophetic and restorationist movement, a movement anchored in the vision of renewing Israel. John called the nation to repent before the coming judgment. "To have watched, heard, and participated in John's prophetic movement would have awakened the hopes of the nation for the end of its exile and the dawn of its restoration. John surely stirred the eschatological fires of the expectant among Israel."[22] "Both John and Jesus had a single vision: the restoration of Israel."[23]

Third, and perhaps most importantly, Jesus acquired his vision for the restoration of Israel from Scripture. In the process of reading the OT and hearing it expounded, Jesus came to understand the restoration texts as applying to himself and to his ministry to contemporary Israel. For instance, Jesus preached a message of good news to his people, announcing the imminent arrival of the kingdom of God (Mk 1:14-15), which was most likely based on the prophetic expectation for national restoration in Isaiah

---

[20]McKnight, *New Vision for Israel*, 6.
[21]Ibid., pp. 1-2 with n. 3; John P. Meier, *A Marginal Jew*, vol. 1, *The Roots of the Problem and the Person* (New York: Doubleday, 1991), p. 208.
[22]McKnight, *New Vision for Israel*, p. 4.
[23]Ibid., pp. 5-6.

52:7-9. Yet in applying Scripture to himself, Jesus did not regard the kingdom of God as merely a future hope; he also announced that, in some sense, the kingdom of God had already dawned through his ministry. Hence, when Jesus preached in the synagogue at Nazareth, he appealed to another prophetic text about the restoration of Israel (Is 61:1-2) and declared to the people that that passage was fulfilled in their hearing (Lk 4:16-21; cf. Mk 6:1-6; Mt 13:54-58). Here again, Jesus applies an OT restoration text to himself and to his ministry. This shows that Jesus' miracles and preaching were not simply acts of mercy; they were part of an agenda whose goal was the restoration of Israel. Jesus heralded that the works signaling the end of exile and the beginning of the restoration were being accomplished in and through his ministry to Israel.

How do Jesus' death and resurrection relate to his vision for the restoration of Israel? The Gospels make it clear that Jesus came to Jerusalem in order to die. This is attested in so many different texts and in so many different ways that its historicity seems beyond serious question. Hence Jesus deliberately provoked his death in Jerusalem. He was under no illusion that the kingdom would come immediately upon his arrival in Jerusalem, and his so-called cry of dereliction on the cross—"My God, my God, why hast thou forsaken me?" (Mk 15:34)—should not be interpreted as the protestation of a person whose hopes had been utterly dashed.[24] To be sure, Jesus' triumphal entry into Jerusalem on a donkey, in the style of Solomon's coronation ceremony (1 Kings 1:32-40) and of the triumphant king in Zechariah 9:9-10,[25] amid jubilant cries of fellow pilgrims, awakened the expectation that "the kingdom of our father David . . . is coming" (Mk 11:9-10). This expectation coheres with Jesus' promise to his disciples that they will "sit on thrones judging the twelve tribes of Israel" (Lk 22:30//Mt 19:28). However, unlike Solomon, Jesus was not officially acknowledged by the priesthood, even though upon entering Jerusalem he went directly to the temple and looked around, perhaps seeking official sanction (Mk 11:11).[26] Later, Jesus deliberately provoked the religious leaders to seek his life by staging a pro-

---

[24]Cf. Sanders, *Historical Figure of Jesus*, pp. 274-75.

[25]Cf. Craig A. Evans, "From Public Ministry to the Passion: Can a Link Be Found Between the (Galilean) Life and the (Judean) Death of Jesus?" in *Jesus and His Contemporaries: Comparative Studies*, AGJU 25 (Leiden: E. J. Brill, 1995), p. 310.

[26]See also Craig A. Evans, "'The Two Sons of Oil': Early Evidence of Messianic Interpretation of Zechariah 4:14 in 4Q254 4 2," in *The Provo International Conference on the Dead Sea Scrolls: Technological Innovations, New Texts and Reformulated Issues*, ed. Donald W. Parry and Eugene Ulrich, STDJ 30 (Leiden: E. J. Brill, 1999), p. 575.

phetic demonstration in the temple. Undaunted, Jesus continued to expect the coming of the kingdom in direct connection with Jerusalem. Looking beyond his imminent violent death symbolized in the bread and the cup, Jesus tells his disciples during the Last Supper: "I shall not drink again of the fruit of the vine until that day when I drink it new in the kingdom of God" (Mk 14:25 NIV). This statement shows that even after his death, Jesus expects to participate in the coming kingdom, including the aforementioned eschatological banquet on Zion promised in Isaiah 25:6.

If Jesus came to Jerusalem in order to die, how did he reconcile his death with his vision for the restoration of Israel? The Gospels lead us to believe that Jesus understood his death in terms of the Fourth Servant Song of Isaiah (Is 52:13—53:12; cf. Mk 14:24 with Is 53:12). For instance, Jesus explains that he came to give his life as a ransom "for the many" (Mk 10:45), which is best understood in light of Isaiah 53:11-12 (cf. Is 43:3-5).[27] Here we must recall that the Fourth Servant Song is set within the context of Isaiah 40—55, where the new exodus—the redemption from exile—is announced. When the people refuse to take advantage of this opportunity to return from exile, God uses the substitutionary death of the Suffering Servant—the just for the unjust—to effect national redemption and restoration.[28] Against this backdrop, Jesus' death "for the many" (Mk 10:45) coheres fully with his vision for the restoration of Israel.

What about Jesus' resurrection? Does this also cohere with his vision for the restoration of Israel? Without getting into a discussion of the historicity of the Easter event, we may observe that in many and sundry ways, the Gospels attest to the fact that Jesus expected not only to die in Jerusalem but also to rise from the dead. If, as we have seen, Jesus understood his death in terms of the Suffering Servant of Isaiah, then he may well have regarded his resurrection as a certainty, for the Fourth Servant Song clearly foresees the exaltation of the one who dies for the many (Is 52:13; 53:10-12). Whether or not the Fourth Servant Song originally implies the Suffering

---

[27]Rikki E. Watts, "Jesus' Death, Isaiah 53 and Mark 10:45: A Crux Revisited," in *Jesus and the Suffering Servant: Isaiah 53 and Christian Origins*, ed. William H. Bellinger Jr. and William R. Farmer (Harrisburg, Penn.: Trinity Press International, 1998), pp. 125-51.

[28]Cf. Hans-Jürgen Hermisson, "Das vierte Gottesknechtslied im deuterojesajanischen Kontext," in *Der leidende Gottesknecht. Jesaja 53 und seine Wirkungsgeschichte*, ed. Bernd Janowski and Peter Stuhlmacher, FAT 14 (Tübingen: Mohr Siebeck, 1996), pp. 1-25; Ronald E. Clements, "Isaiah 53 and the Restoration of Israel," in *Jesus and the Suffering Servant: Isaiah 53 and Christian Origins*, ed. William H. Bellinger Jr. and William R. Farmer (Harrisburg, Penn.: Trinity Press International, 1998), pp. 39-54.

Servant's resurrection from the dead, it is easy to see how the text could be interpreted in this way.

Moreover, given the national purpose of the Suffering Servant's death, his exaltation/resurrection is a harbinger of Israel's resurrection/restoration as a nation. As Ezekiel 37 makes clear, Israel was "dead" in exile.[29] Hence the resurrection of Israel from the death of exile is immediately associated with restoration: "Behold, I will open your graves, and raise you from your graves, O my people; and I will bring you home into the land of Israel. And you shall know that I am the Lord, when I open your graves, and raise you from your graves, O my people. And I will put my Spirit within you, and you shall live, and I will place you in your own land" (Ezek 37:12-14). For Israel to live, according to this text, is to return to the land.[30]

Against this backdrop, Jesus must see his resurrection as part and parcel of his vision for the restoration of Israel, and that for two reasons. First, he sees his resurrection in light of the Suffering Servant of Isaiah, whose death and exaltation is efficacious for the restoration of the nation. Second, Jesus' resurrection anticipates the resurrection/restoration of the nation as a whole.

THE RECEPTION OF JESUS' VISION FOR THE RESTORATION OF ISRAEL IN THE NEW TESTAMENT

If, as seems probable, the emerging consensus of historical Jesus research is substantially correct, then Jesus had a national agenda that aimed at the restoration of all Israel. With this working hypothesis, we turn now to our next question: How did the followers of Jesus receive his vision for the restoration of Israel? How, if at all, did Jesus' vision become the vision of the early church? Does Jesus' vision for the restoration of Israel come to expression in the rest of the NT?

The Pauline letters. The burden for our case rests primarily, though not exclusively, on the Pauline letters. If we cannot make the case there, it probably cannot be made in the rest of the NT. For Paul's letters afford us the largest and earliest corpus of writings in the NT, by an author whom

---

[29]For other passages expressing the idea that Israel in exile is dead, see Is 26:19; 59:10; Lam 3:6; Baruch 3:10-11; 4Q385 2.5-9 (alluding to Ezek 37:4-5, 6, 9); *Midr. Ps.* 71:4; *y. Kil.* 9.32c.

[30]Cf. Donald E. Gowan, *Theology of the Prophetic Books: The Death and Resurrection of Israel* (Louisville, Ky.: Westminster John Knox, 1998), pp. 121-37.

we know better than any other, and one who obviously knew at least some Jesus traditions.[31]

In Paul's letters we encounter the Jew from Asia Minor who was first a persecutor of the early Christian movement in Jerusalem and beyond and later a convert to that movement. From that point onward, Paul understood himself as one who had been sent by Jesus Christ—an "apostle of Christ Jesus" (e.g., 1 Cor 1:1) and an "ambassador for Christ" (2 Cor 5:20). Hence, to a significant extent, we would expect the apostle to share Jesus' vision for Israel. On the other hand, Paul also describes himself as the "apostle to the nations" (Rom 11:13). How can Paul be expected to continue Jesus' vision for the restoration of Israel when he characterizes himself an apostle to the nations? After all, Jesus' ministry was first and foremost to the lost sheep of the house of Israel, rather than to the nations. Is it possible for the apostle to be faithful to his Lord's vision and yet concentrate his own energies on a mission to the nations?

Listen to Paul's words in Romans 11:13-14: "Inasmuch then as I am an apostle to the Gentiles, I magnify my ministry in order to make my fellow Jews jealous, and thus save some of them." In his conception, therefore, Paul is the apostle to the nations for the sake of Israel. Indeed, Paul's ultimate goal in advancing the mission to the nations was so that, in accordance with the promise of God in Isaiah 59:20-21 and Isaiah 27:9, "all Israel"—that is, all twelve tribes of Jacob—would be saved, including the so-called ten lost tribes (Rom 11:26-27).[32] As an Israelite from the tribe of Benjamin (Rom 11:1), Paul is proof positive that God has not rejected his people irrevocably.

It important to see that Paul remained faithful to Jesus' vision and ministry, even as he focused his attention on a mission to the nations. Paul emphasizes that his gospel was "to the Jew first and also to the Greek" (Rom 1:16), and that the gifts and calling of God with respect to Israel, including the list of Israel's gifts from God presented in Romans 9:4-5, were irrevocable (Rom 11:29). Paul never denounced his heritage as an Israelite, and he never lost sight of Jerusalem—the natural headquarters of the nascent

---

[31]On Jesus tradition in Paul, see, e.g., David Wenham, *Paul: Follower of Jesus or Founder of Christianity?* (Grand Rapids, Mich.: Eerdmans, 1995); James D. G. Dunn, *The Theology of Paul the Apostle* (Grand Rapids, Mich.: Eerdmans, 1998), pp. 16-17, 185-95, 300-301, 650-53; Peter Stuhlmacher, "Jesustradition im Römerbrief?" *ThB* 14 (1983): 240-50; Nikolaus Walter, "Paulus und die urchristliche Jesustradition," *NTS* 31 (1985): 498-522.

[32]Cf. James M. Scott, "'And Then All Israel Will Be Saved' (Rom 11:26)," in *Restoration: Old Testament, Jewish and Christian Conceptions*, JSJSup 72 (Leiden: E. J. Brill, 2002), pp. 489-527.

movement—as central to his whole endeavor. Paul explicitly takes his gospel to the nations "from Jerusalem" (Rom 15:19). Thus Paul set his career within a framework that is common in Jewish sources of the Second Temple period. At the end of the ages, or the climax of history, the tribes of Israel will be gathered, and the nations will come to Jerusalem, bearing gifts and worshiping the God of Israel (cf. Rom 11:25-26; 15:8-9, 12 [quoting Is 11:10]; 15:16). But whereas Jesus' vision emphasized the particularistic aspect of the OT and Jewish hope of the restoration of Israel (albeit not to the exclusion of the nations), Paul's mission emphasized the universalistic aspect of the same OT and Jewish hope (albeit without losing sight of Israel).

The connection between Jesus and Paul is further strengthened by the gospel that both preach. The OT matrix of the gospel message leads us to Isaiah 51:17–52:12, which announces the restoration of Israel: the end of God's wrath on his people; the placement of God's wrath on Israel's tormentors; the freedom of Zion from subjugation; the return of God to reign in Zion as king; the redemption of Israel; the return home of people and priests in peace. In this complex of hopes for Israel's future is nestled the origins of the term *gospel*. As we have seen, Jesus appropriates the message of Isaiah 52:7 in his preaching of the good news of the imminent kingdom of God (Mk 1:14-15). Before his death, Jesus commissioned his disciples to preach his gospel message to Israel (Lk 9:1-6). After his resurrection, Jesus commissioned the same disciples to become apostles until the parousia. Their message is no longer merely Jesus' gospel of the kingdom, but rather the gospel of the kingdom of God that is inaugurated through Jesus' sending, death and resurrection. Finally, as a result of his encounter with the risen Lord on the way to Damascus, Paul sees himself among the apostolic "preachers of the good news," as the citation of Isaiah 52:7 in Romans 10:15 shows. Thus Jesus' vision for the restoration of Israel continues in the early church through the proclamation of the gospel message based on Isaiah 52:7. As the gospel that Paul preached and passed on to the Corinthians, 1 Corinthians 15:3-4 may contain an early creed from the Jerusalem church that reflects this modified gospel of the kingdom, in which the preacher becomes the preached.

Let's examine 1 Corinthians 15:3-4 in more detail. The expressly scriptural basis for Jesus' death, burial and resurrection suggests that Paul's tradition alludes to the Fourth Servant Song. Thus Jesus' death "for our sins" recalls the Suffering Servant's death "for their sins" (Is 53:11-12; cf. Rom 4:25, alluding to Is 53:12; Phil 2:9); Jesus' burial recalls the ignominious burial of the Suffering Servant (Is 53:9); and Jesus' resurrection recalls the exaltation/resurrection of the Suffering Servant (Is 53:11-12). The fact that the resurrection takes place "on the third day" alludes to Hosea 6:2 (LXX), a passage that likewise speaks of the nation's hope for restoration after exile. The application of this passage, together with the Fourth Servant Song, to Jesus' resurrection shows that Paul (and the tradition on which he relies here) sees Jesus' resurrection as the harbinger of Israel's national resurrection/restoration.

This interpretation is borne out by the subsequent context of 1 Corinthians 15: the resurrected Christ is "the first fruits of those who have died" (1 Cor 15:20). In other words, his resurrection anticipates a general resurrection to come. The national significance of this resurrection becomes clear in the immediately following verses. For according to 1 Corinthians 15:23-28, the resurrection takes place at Christ's parousia, which is simultaneously the time when his messianic reign over the kingdom of God begins, lasting until Christ, the messianic Son of God, has subjugated all his enemies (1 Cor 15:23-28). Paul's reference to the kingdom of God in this context alludes to Jesus' kingdom preaching. Indeed, as we learn from the parallel passage in Romans 11, the parousia entails, in accordance with several OT restoration promises, the coming of the Deliverer from Zion, the salvation of "all Israel," and the forgiveness of sins for Israel (Rom 11:26-27). If, as seems possible, Paul envisioned the establishment of Jesus' kingdom on earth before the Son definitively hands it over to the Father (1 Cor 15:28), then Paul's hope comes very close to Jesus' expectation of Israel's restoration in the land.[33]

The rest of the New Testament. Do other writings of the NT also display an influence of Jesus' vision for the restoration of Israel? One brief example must suffice to illustrate how the subject could be pursued. The letter of James presents some difficult challenges, particularly with respect to Paul's view of justification by faith without works of the law. If ever there was a case for contradictory perspectives in the NT, surely it

---

[33]On the notion of a messianic interregnum, see E. P. Sanders, "Review of Paula Fredriksen, *From Jesus to Christ," JJS* 41 (1990): 124; L. Joseph Kreitzer, *Jesus and God in Paul's Eschatology,* JSNTSup 19 (Sheffield: JSOT, 1987), pp. 131-64; David E. Aune, *Revelation 17—22,* WBC (Nashville: Thomas Nelson, 1998), pp. 1104-8; Otto Betz, *Jesus und das Danielbuch,* Band 2, *Die Menschensohnworte Jesu und die Zukunftserwartung des Paulus (Daniel 7,13-14),* ANTJ 6.2 (Frankfurt: Lang, 1985), pp. 138, 142-43; M. C. de Boer, "Paul and Apocalyptic Eschatology," *Encyclopedia of Apocalypticism,* vol. 1, *The Origins of Apocalypticism in Judaism and Christianity,* ed. John J. Collins (New York: Continuum, 2000), pp. 345-83 (377-78).

is here.[34] However, the obvious and frequent presence of Jesus tradition in the letter of James[35] prompts us to ask whether James may have also appropriated Jesus' vision for the restoration of Israel in some way. After all, James identifies himself as a "servant of the Lord Jesus Christ" (Jas 1:1a). Surely the one who refers to his master as "our Lord Jesus Christ, the Lord of glory" (Jas 2:1) would somehow promulgate Jesus' fundamental vision for the restoration of Israel.

At first glance, James appears to be little more than a compilation of wisdom sayings in letter form—that is, until one realizes what kind of letter this is. The key to interpretation occurs in the first verse, which addresses the letter "to the twelve tribes in the diaspora" (Jas 1:1b). This shows that we are dealing here with a particular kind of letter, a covenantal diaspora letter written to the scattered people of God who suffer in their exile this side of the expected redemption.[36] Normally the reference to "the twelve tribes in the diaspora" has been interpreted metaphorically, as if the letter were addressed to a Gentile Christian readership as the true Israel for whom heaven was their proper home and earth was only a foreign country. If, however, the adscription is taken literally, as addressing people who maintain a Jewish identity,[37] then a new interpretation of James begins to unfold in light of the diaspora letter tradition. We find examples of this type of letter in Jeremiah 29:1-23, the *Epistle of Jeremiah*, 2 Maccabees 1:1-9; 1:10—2:18 and *2 Baruch* 78-86. In these texts, an authoritative center (typically Jerusalem) consoles the assembled diaspora communities in the midst of their tribulation and admonishes them regarding their covenantal responsibilities in hope of the expected restoration. The specific content of the instruction varies, but the tone of consolation in tribulation and the appeal to the motivational power of the future hope remain constant.

The relevance of this epistolary type to the reading of James' letter is obvious. For James, as for the other writers of covenantal diaspora letters, the

---

[34]Cf. Stuhlmacher, *Biblische Theologie*, 2:59-69.

[35]James 2:8 (cf. Mt 22:39-40); 4:3 (cf. Mt 7:7); 4:13—5:6 (cf. Lk 6:20-21, 24-25; 16:19-31); 5:7-8 (cf. Mk 4:26-29); 5:12 (cf. Mt 5:34-37).

[36]Cf. Donald J. Verseput, "Genre and Story: The Community Setting of the Epistle of James," *CBQ* 62 (2000): 96-110. On the issue of the genre of James, see also Karl-Wilhelm Niebuhr, "Der Jakobusbrief im Licht frühjüdischer Diasporabriefe," *NTS* 44 (1998): 420-443; Manabu Tsuji, *Glaube zwischen Vollkommenheit und Verweltlichung*, WUNT 93 (Tübingen: Mohr Siebeck, 1997), pp. 5-50.

[37]See especially Richard Bauckham, *James: Wisdom of James, Disciple of Jesus the Sage*, New Testament Readings (London: Routledge, 1999), pp. 14-16.

exilic existence of Israel was a painful experience requiring perseverance
in hope of God's ultimate triumph on behalf of his people. Thus, directly
after the address "to the twelve tribes of the diaspora," James challenges
his readers to rejoice in the face of tribulation (Jas 1:2-8) and to endure
temptation, with the promise of receiving the crown of life that the Lord
has promised to those who love him (Jas 1:12). The exhortations of the
body of the letter can be seen as admonitions to diaspora communities to
fulfill their covenantal obligations within the community in hope of the expected restoration. Toward the end of the letter, James urges his readers to
be patient until the soon coming of the Lord (Jas 5:7-9). More could be said,
but the point is clear: James not only takes up isolated Jesus traditions here
and there in his letter, but, more importantly, also appropriates Jesus' fundamental vision for the restoration of Israel. James does so by writing the
Jewish Christian communities that are spread abroad in exile and by con-
soling them in their current plight to persevere in the hope of their restoration at the coming of the Lord.

Such considerations have enormous implications for a biblical theology
of the NT. For by examining each NT writing and ascertaining how it may
appropriate Jesus' vision for the restoration of Israel, we begin to see the
extensive tissue that supports and connects the whole body of early Christian thought incorporated in the NT. Thus Paul and James may differ on
matters such as justification by faith and works of the law, but they apparently concur on the more fundamental issue of the future hope for Israel,
through their common dependence on Jesus and the OT/Jewish matrix of
Jesus' eschatological expectation for his people. If this method is carried
out systematically in a thoroughgoing way for the whole NT, following a
more or less chronological order in the process, we may end up with a synthesis that is not only historical and descriptive but also illustrative of the
NT's fundamental unity in diversity. That, of course, needs to be demonstrated.

CONCLUSION

We conclude our considerations with a foray into the question of what all
this means for us today, for a biblical theology of the NT should help to
bridge the chasm between biblical studies and the modern church. As anyone can see, Jesus' vision for the restoration of Israel was not realized in
the first century. Jerusalem was conquered, the temple was destroyed, but
the Lord did not return, the exiles did not return, and Jerusalem did not

become the highest mountain. Meanwhile Gentiles kept joining the new movement, which, perhaps more than any other factor, eventually led to a break between the Christian movement and its Jewish parent.[38]

Twenty centuries have now elapsed, and the institutionalized church continues to recede at a brisk pace ever further from its Jewish roots, even to the extent now of completely assimilating to the culture of the dominant society. Have we taken Paul's universalistic emphasis but lost sight of its underlying connection to Jesus' vision for Israel's salvation? Admittedly the restoration of Israel never seemed further from our thinking, the *maranatha* cry of the early church never further from our lips. Do the intervening centuries give us license to remake after our imagination the vision of Jesus and Paul and James and the other NT writers? Or do we need to reaffirm our commitment to the historic faith and hope of the early church? Here is the recommendation of Peter Stuhlmacher: "Instead of . . . forsaking all concrete images of hope, it is biblically advisable and spiritually more helpful for Christians to pray the Zion Psalms (esp. Psalms 46, 87, and 122) and thereby learn to realize that it is no mythological 'nonsense,' but rather it is God's comforting permission to be able to expect in faith precisely the concrete redemption that goes out from Zion."[39]

---

[38]On the whole question, see James D. G. Dunn, ed., *Jews and Christians: The Parting of the Ways A.D. 70 to 135*, WUNT 66 (Tübingen: Mohr Siebeck, 1992).

[39]Peter Stuhlmacher, "Die Stellung Jesu und des Paulus zu Jerusalem: Versuch einer Erinnerung," *ZTK* 86 (1989): 156.

10

Diversity and Unity
in the New Testament

Andreas J. Köstenberger

The diversity and unity of the NT is one of the most frequently discussed topics in NT theology.[1] The traditional emphasis on the unity of the NT (at least in conservative circles) has in recent years been all but supplanted by the critical consensus that the NT consists of a variety of theologies that, if not irreconcilable, at least stand in considerable tension with one another.[2] This can largely be attributed to the influence of Walter Bauer, Rudolf Bultmann, Ernst Käsemann and, in Anglo-American scholarship, James Dunn. Even a relatively conservative scholar such as Peter Stuhlmacher maintains that "the Bible contains diverse voices that do not merely complement but also contradict each other."[3] Nevertheless, while many critical scholars are able to retain a degree of unity in the NT only by

---

[1]Cf. Gerhard F. Hasel, "The Nature of Biblical Theology: Recent Trends and Issues," *Andrews University Studies* 32 (1994): 203-15. Note that all translations from the original German in the following essay are the author's.

[2]Cf. Peter Balla, *Challenges to New Testament Theology*, WUNT 95 (Tübingen: Mohr Siebeck, 1997), pp. 177-78.

[3]Peter Stuhlmacher, "Der Kanon und seine Auslegung," in *Jesus Christus als die Mitte der Schrift. Studien zur Hermeneutik des Evangeliums*, ed. Christof Landmesser et al., BZNW 86 (Berlin: Walter de Gruyter, 1997), p. 287: "vielfältige Stimmen, . . . die sich nicht nur gegenseitig ergänzen, sondern auch widersprechen."

eliminating allegedly conflicting or contradictory elements, conservative evangelical interpreters continue to maintain that they do not need to resort to *Sachkritik* to salvage the coherence of the theology of the NT.

In what follows we will first consider several aspects of the NT's diversity that have been cited as possibly contradictory: the relationship between Jesus and Paul; the relationship between the Synoptics and John; the Paul of Acts and the Paul of the epistles; the question of alleged developments in Paul's writings; and the relationship among Paul, James and other NT writers. We will then explore integrative motifs that point to the NT's underlying unity and coherence.

JESUS AND PAUL

As Donald Guthrie contends, "Unquestionably the major problem within the variety of NT theology is the relationship between the theology of Paul and the teaching of Jesus."[4] Our brief discussion will focus on one of the most recent contributions to this question, David Wenham's *Paul: Founder of Christianity or Follower of Jesus?*[5] In a reaction against the predominant sweep of twentieth-century German scholarship, Wenham rejects the characterization of Paul as the founder of Christianity. Instead, according to Wenham, Paul consciously built on the foundation already laid by Jesus. While we judge Wenham's stress on the continuity between Jesus and Paul to be only partially successful—the fact that Paul was not a disciple of the earthly Jesus and that his ministry belonged to a later phase of salvation history would seem to qualify the degree of dependence possible at the outset—he has provided a potent reminder that an undue dichotomization between Jesus and Paul fails to do justice to the underlying unity between their theological thought.[6]

With Wenham, it is granted that Paul did not set himself in contrast to Jesus but operated in essential continuity with him. It is less certain that it best served Paul's purposes in proclaiming the gospel to do so by alluding to or echoing Jesus' teaching. For during Paul's ministry, Jesus' identity as

---

[4]Donald Guthrie, *New Testament Theology* (Downers Grove, Ill.: InterVarsity Press, 1981), p. 51 (see discussion on pp. 51-54). See also Balla, *Challenges to New Testament Theology*, pp. 166-70, who concludes that "the differences are not of the nature that would compel us to conclude that there was a contradiction" between the teachings of Jesus and Paul (p. 170).

[5]David Wenham, *Paul: Founder of Christianity or Follower of Jesus?* (Grand Rapids, Mich.: Eerdmans, 1996).

[6]For a more extensive interaction with Wenham, see my review in *Trinity Journal* 16 n.s. (1995): 259-62.

the OT-promised Messiah still had to be demonstrated. This could be accomplished not by quoting Jesus' words but by furnishing proof that the events in Jesus' life, especially his crucifixion and resurrection, fit the pattern laid out in the OT. Thus the OT, not Jesus, was Paul's primary theological source. This is not to deny that in his instruction of believers Paul occasionally used material that could be traced back to Jesus (see esp. Rom 12—13). The point is rather that a mere reference to Jesus' teaching, unaccompanied by an appeal to the OT, would have been insufficient in the context of Paul's missionary proclamation. For this reason, only in exceptional cases does one find direct references in Paul's writings to the teaching of Jesus (e.g., Acts 20:35; 1 Cor 9:14; 11:23-26?; cf. 7:12, 25; 1 Thess 4:15; see also Phil 2:5; 2 Cor 8:9).

Paul is therefore a somewhat more independent theological thinker than Wenham appears to concede.[7] Without involving Jesus and Paul in actual contradictions, we should lay more stress on the discontinuity between these two pivotal figures, primarily owing to the different stages in salvation history they inhabited and to the different roles they had to fulfill as a result.[8] A few examples must suffice. Jesus rarely talks about the church (cf. Mt 16:18; 18:17); Paul develops the doctrine of the church as the body of Christ in great detail (Rom 12:1-8; 1 Cor 12; Eph 5:25-32), while further revealing the salvation-historical mystery of the inclusion of the Gentiles into the people of God (Rom 16:25-26; Eph 3:2-11; Col 1:25-27). Jesus concentrates his mission on Israel (Mt 10:5-6; 15:24); Paul proclaims the gospel to the ends of the earth (Acts 9:15; Rom 16:26).[9]

Again, this does not mean that Paul's teaching stands in actual conflict with that of Jesus. It does mean that Paul did not limit himself to reiterating the teaching of Jesus but that he formulated his proclamation in light of the antecedent theology of the OT and on the basis of the apostolic gospel as called for by his ministry context.

THE SYNOPTICS AND JOHN

At least since the end of the eighteenth century, critical voices have

---

[7]See esp. Wilhelm Heitmüller, "Zum Problem Paulus und Jesus," ZNW 13 (1912): 320-37, esp. pp. 320, 325, and the helpful summary on p. 321.
[8]See esp. Werner G. Kümmel, *The Theology of the New Testament According to Its Major Witnesses, Jesus—Paul—John*, trans. John E. Steely (Nashville: Abingdon, 1973), pp. 246-48.
[9]Andreas J. Köstenberger and Peter T. O'Brien, *Salvation to the Ends of the Earth: A Biblical Theology of Mission*, NSBT 11 (Downers Grove, Ill.: InterVarsity Press, 2001).

claimed that the Synoptics and John stand in irreconcilable conflict.[10] While Schleiermacher still defended the integrity of John's Gospel, the criticisms of Bretschneider (1820) and D. F. Strauss (1835) had a devastating effect on the scholarly assessment of the reliability of John's Gospel. Only in the last few decades has John been rehabilitated, at least in part.[11] However, just as in his day Tatian used the Fourth Gospel as the basis for his synopsis of the Gospels (the Diatessaron), there is no good reason why John should not be viewed today as a reliable witness to Jesus' earthly ministry. No less a historian than Hengel considers John's Gospel to be an important source for first-century Judaism, crediting its author with an excellent knowledge of Palestinian topography and the Jewish calendar.[12] Hengel also points out that several pieces of information are found in John's Gospel for the first time, such as the Samaritan village named Sychar (Jn 4:5), the name *ta enkainia* as a designation for the Feast of Tabernacles (Jn 10:22), and the characterization of Annas as Caiaphas's father-in-law (Jn 18:13).[13] And John's portrayal of Annas and Caiaphas earns Hengel's highest praise.[14]

Another example of the close relationship between John and the Synoptics is the portrayal of Jesus' passion.[15] Here the major obstacle to an appreciation of the close coherence between the Synoptic and Johannine accounts of the crucifixion is the frequently made claim that the respective narratives differ in their dating of the crucifixion. However, a closer look reveals that this contradiction is only apparent. It can be demonstrated that John and the Synoptics present Jesus as having eaten a final meal with his disciples, a Passover meal, on Thursday night, with the

[10]See Andreas J. Köstenberger, "Early Doubts of the Apostolic Authorship of the Fourth Gospel in the History of Modern Biblical Criticism," in *Studies on John and Gender: A Decade of Scholarship* (New York: Peter Lang, 2001), pp. 17-47.
[11]Cf. Martin Hengel, "Aufgaben der neutestamentlichen Wissenschaft," *NTS* 40 (1994): 321-57. See Andreas J. Köstenberger, "John," in *Zondervan Illustrated Bible Background Commentary*, vol. 2, ed. Clinton E. Arnold (Grand Rapids, Mich.: Zondervan, 2002), and Craig L. Blomberg, *The Historical Reliability of John's Gospel: Issues and Commentary* (Downers Grove, Ill.: InterVarsity Press, 2002).
[12]Martin Hengel, "Das Johannesevangelium als Quelle für die Geschichte des antiken Judentums," in *Judaica, Hellenistica et Christiana: Kleine Schriften II*, WUNT 109 (Tübingen: Mohr Siebeck, 1999), pp. 295, 322.
[13]Ibid., pp. 296, 322 (in general); p. 301 (Sychar), p. 317 (Tabernacles), p. 323 (Annas).
[14]Ibid., pp. 322-33, esp. p. 333.
[15]See D. A. Carson, *The Gospel According to John* (Grand Rapids, Mich.: Eerdmans, 1991), pp. 455-58; Craig L. Blomberg, *The Historical Reliability of the Gospels* (Downers Grove, Ill.: InterVarsity Press, 1987), pp. 175-80; and Andreas J. Köstenberger, *Encountering John* (Grand Rapids, Mich.: Baker, 1999), p. 146.

crucifixion having taken place on Friday afternoon.[16]

The reason many have seen John as placing the Last Supper on Wednesday night with the crucifixion taking place on Thursday afternoon (when the Passover lambs would have been slaughtered in preparation for Passover later that evening) is the reference to "the day of Preparation of Passover Week" in John 19:14 (NIV [throughout the essay]; cf. Jn 18:28). However, the solution to this apparent dilemma lies close at hand. In John 19:31, it is made clear that Jesus' crucifixion took place on "the day of Preparation," with the very next day being a "special Sabbath" (i.e., the sabbath of Passover week). Thus, even in John the crucifixion takes place on Friday, with "the day of Preparation" in John, as in Mark and Luke, referring not to the day of preparation for the Passover but for the sabbath (Mk 15:42; Lk 23:54; cf. Josephus *Antiquities* 16.163-64). Moreover, since Passover lasted a week (in conjunction with the associated Feast of Unleavened Bread; Lk 22:1), it was appropriate to speak of the day of preparation for the sabbath as "the day of Preparation of Passover Week" (though not of the Passover in a more narrow sense; Jn 19:14).

Further apparent discrepancies and John's more extended discourses in comparison with the shorter aphorisms in the Synoptics likewise turn out to represent but differing perspectives that can be harmonized without doing violence to the data.[17] In each case the different mode of presentation need not constitute a discrepancy but reflects a theological transposition of the Synoptic tradition onto a higher scale.[18] The Johannine signs deemphasize the miraculous in Jesus' works in order to focus on their christological symbolism. The Synoptic exorcisms are replaced by repeated references to Satan as Jesus' chief protagonist. Jesus' attendance at several Jewish festivals is shown to fulfill their inherent symbolism. And John's extended discourses provide more thorough expositions of a few selected topics. Finally, there are significant "interlocking traditions" between John and the Synoptics,[19] in particular those instances where John seems to presuppose his readers' familiarity with the Synoptic tradition (if not one or several of the written Gospels; cf. Jn 1:40; 3:24; 4:44; 6:67, 71; 11:1-2).[20] Thus there is good reason to conclude that John and the Synoptics provide mu-

---

[16]See Köstenberger, "John."
[17]Cf. Blomberg, *Historical Reliability*, pp. 153-89; and Carson, *Gospel According to John*, passim.
[18]For a brief survey, see Köstenberger, *Encountering John*, pp. 198-200.
[19]Cf. Carson, *Gospel According to John*, pp. 49-58, esp. pp. 52-55.
[20]Cf. Köstenberger, *Encountering John*, pp. 36-37.

tually complementing theologies characterized by an underlying coherence that is not diminished by their respective theological emphases.

THE PAUL OF ACTS AND THE PAUL OF THE EPISTLES

"Is the Paul of Acts the real Paul?" asked F. F. Bruce in an article published a quarter-century ago.[21] In the wake of F. C. Baur, German scholars especially have frequently argued that the presentation of Paul in the book of Acts is incompatible with the way the apostle portrays himself in his epistles.[22] Luke's Paul, it is contended, is invincible and moves from place to place in a victory procession (Acts 14:19-20; 16:40; 18:9-10; 19:11; 20:10-11; 23:11, 31-34; 26:28-29; 27:43-44; 28:30-31), while Paul portrays himself as weak and confounded (1 Cor 2:1-5; 2 Cor 11:16—12:10). For Luke, Paul is a brilliant, persuasive public speaker (Acts 13:9-11, 16-41; 14:15-17; 17:22-31; 20:18-35; 22:1-21; 24:10-21; 26:2-26); Paul says of himself that he has little room for rhetoric and that others often view him as an inferior preacher (1 Cor 2:1-5; 2 Cor 10:1, 10-11). Stanley E. Porter summarizes three additional reasons that have been advanced against an identification of the Paul of Acts with the Paul of the letters: (1) Luke's apparent unawareness of the Pauline solution to the problem of the law-free mission to the Gentiles; (2) the fact that Paul's claim to apostleship is difficult to substantiate from the book of Acts; and (3) the different portrayals of Jewish-Christian relations in Acts and the Pauline letters. Beyond this, some also detect discrepancies in the areas of Christology and eschatology.

Once again, it can be shown that these apparent conflicts are merely a matter of different perspectives that can be integrated very well into a cohesive overall picture.[23] Luke does not write a biography of Paul. He is in-

---

[21]F. F. Bruce, "Is the Paul of Acts the Real Paul?" *BJRL* 58 (1976): 282-305.

[22]For a general treatment, including a taxonomy of views on the issue, see A. J. Mattill Jr., "The Value of Acts as a Source for the Study of Paul," in *Perspectives on Luke-Acts*, ed. C. H. Talbert (Danville, Va.: Association of Baptist Professors of Religion, 1978), pp. 76-98. The disjunction between the Paul of Acts and the Paul of the letters has been most definitively argued by E. Haenchen, *The Acts of the Apostles*, trans. B. Noble et al. (Philadelphia: Westminster Press, 1971), pp. 112-16, and P. Vielhauer, "On the 'Paulinism' of Acts," in *Studies in Luke-Acts*, ed. L. E. Keck and J. L. Martyn (Philadelphia: Fortress, 1966), pp. 33-50. See the critique in Stanley E. Porter, *The Paul of Acts*, WUNT 115 (Tübingen: Mohr Siebeck, 1999), pp. 187-206.

[23]Cf. David Wenham, "Appendix: Unity and Diversity in the New Testament," in George Eldon Ladd, *A Theology of the New Testament*, 2nd ed. (Grand Rapids, Mich.: Eerdmans, 1993), pp. 687-92. For a constructive critique of these apparent discrepancies, see Porter, *Paul of Acts*, pp. 187-206; see also Bruce, "Real Paul," pp. 282-305; L. T. Johnson, *The Writings of the New Testament* (Minneapolis: Fortress, 1986), pp. 231-38; and Ben Witherington III, *The Acts of the Apostles: A Socio-Rhetorical Commentary* (Grand Rapids, Mich.: Eerdmans, 1998), pp. 430-38.

terested in Paul primarily as the leading proponent of the early Christian mission, and this mission overcomes all obstacles—albeit not on account of Paul's strategizing genius or rhetorical brilliance but through the sovereign power of God. By the same token, Paul frequently stresses in his letters that it is not he but Christ in him who is the driving force behind the Christian mission and that the message of the cross, not his persuasive powers, must take center stage (e.g., Gal 2:20; 1 Cor 2:1-5; Rom 15:18-19).

In addition, Bruce lists a whole series of agreements, some of which are in the category of what he calls "undesigned coincidences." First, in his letters Paul points to his impeccable Jewish credentials (Phil 3:6; cf. Gal 1:14; 2 Cor 11:22), but only in Acts do we learn that Paul had been educated in the school of Gamaliel, one of the most prominent Pharisaic teachers of his generation (Acts 22:3; cf. Acts 5:35; see also Phil 3:5; Acts 23:6; 26:5). Second, Paul's activity as persecutor of the early church is recounted repeatedly in the book of Acts (Acts 8:3; 9:1); in his letters, the apostle regularly acknowledges this ignominious part of his past (Gal 1:13, 22-23; 1 Cor 15:9; Phil 3:6; 1 Tim 1:13). Third, the Pauline conversion narratives of Acts (Acts 9; 22; 26) are paralleled by statements in Paul's letters (Gal 1:15; 1 Cor 9:1; 15:8; 2 Cor 4:6), and the location of Paul's conversion at or near Damascus seems confirmed by Galatians 1:17. Fourth, the Paul of Acts, like the Paul of the letters, is shown to support himself by labor (Acts 20:34; 28:3; 1 Thess 2:9; 2 Thess 3:7-8; 1 Cor 9:18). Fifth, Acts and the letters reveal Paul's pattern of going first to the Jews and then to the Gentiles (Acts 13:46-48; 28:25-28; cf. Rom 1:16; 2:9-10; 10:12; 1 Cor 1:22, 24; 12:13; Gal 3:28; Col 3:11). Sixth, the Paul of Acts who can adapt himself so readily to Jew and Gentile as well as a wide variety of audiences is the Paul who speaks in 1 Corinthians 9:19-23. Seventh, while Luke may be the theologian of salvation history par excellence, salvation history is not an alien concept to Paul, so that he can view the age of law as a parenthesis in salvation history (Gal 3:15-19; Rom 5:20).

No wonder Bruce concludes at the end of his essay that the Paul of Acts is the "real Paul." Porter too believes that "the differences between the Paul of Acts and of the letters regarding his person and work, once analyzed in detail, . . . do not point to significant and sustainable contradictions" and that "the standard arguments marshaled regarding differences in theology . . . are also inconclusive." While there may be differences of emphasis and focus, "the evidence is far from substantiating contradictions."[24]

---

[24]Porter, *Paul of Acts*, pp. 205-6.

ALLEGED DEVELOPMENTS IN PAUL

In certain scholarly circles it has been *en vogue* to postulate a pronounced development, even to the point of self-contradiction, from Paul's earlier correspondence to his later writings.[25] Thus it has been maintained by some that the apostle regressed from an egalitarian (Gal 3:28) to a traditional-conservative gospel[26] or that his expectation of Christ's return changed during the course of his career from an imminent to a more distant one. Others see the apostle as moving, in good Hegelian fashion, from libertinism in Galatians to a kind of "legalism" in 1 Corinthians and as taking a more balanced approach in 2 Corinthians and Romans.[27]

In all this, however, it must be remembered that Paul began his writing career only about fifteen years after his conversion, when he was at least forty years of age, whereby very little information is available regarding the intervening years. By the time Paul composed his first extant letter, he was therefore by no means a novice but one whose thought is characterized by considerable theological maturity. Moreover, the content of Paul's letters depended to a significant extent on his specific missionary circumstances. For these reasons it is imperative to exercise great caution not to assume that the silences in Paul's letters necessarily indicate the nonexistence of a given Pauline category.

The substantiation of the thesis of a development in Paul's thinking is therefore fraught with considerable difficulty.[28] It is clear that a paradigm shift occurred in Paul's thinking right at the beginning of his career at the time of his conversion.[29] But if some development occurred in the apostle's

---

[25]See, e.g. Udo Schnelle, *Wandlungen im paulinischen Denken* (Stuttgart: Katholisches Bibelwerk, 1989) and the literature cited below.

[26]Cf. Hans Dieter Betz, *Galatians*, Hermeneia (Philadelphia: Fortress, 1979), p. 200: "In 1 Corinthians Paul has retracted the Galatian position."

[27]Cf. F. F. Bruce, "'All Things to All Men': Diversity in Unity and Other Pauline Tensions," in *Unity and Diversity in New Testament Theology*, ed. Robert Guelich (Grand Rapids, Mich.: Eerdmans, 1978), pp. 82-83, with reference to John W. Drane, *Paul: Libertine or Legalist?* (London: SPCK, 1975). See C. H. Dodd, "The Mind of Paul: A Psychological Approach," *BJRL* 17 (1933): 91-105, in which Dodd argues for a "change of temper" on Paul's part in his later epistles as a result of a "spiritual crisis" or a "sort of second conversion" (p. 104); "The Mind of Paul: Change and Development," *BJRL* 18 (1934): 69-110, where Dodd seeks to show that Paul transcended the dualism of "this age" and "the age to come" in favor of what he calls a "universalism" that also entailed a revaluation of the natural order (pp. 109-10); and more recently, Heikki Räisänen, *Paul and the Law*, 2nd ed. (Tübingen: Mohr Siebeck, 1987).

[28]Richard N. Longenecker, "On the Concept of Development in Pauline Thought," in *Perspectives on Evangelical Theology*, ed. Kenneth S. Kantzer and Stanley N. Gundry (Grand Rapids, Mich.: Zondervan, 1979), pp. 195-207.

[29]See esp. Seyoon Kim, *The Origin of Paul's Gospel*, WUNT 4 (Tübingen: Mohr Siebeck, 1981).

thought, it probably took place before Paul's epistles were written rather than during the comparatively short period during which Paul wrote his letters.[30] This is not to deny that in the course of Paul's ministry certain issues, which the apostle considered to be of great importance, moved to the forefront. One thinks of the conscious formulation of a theology of the church (1 Corinthians, Romans, Ephesians, Colossians) and instructions regarding its organization (Pastorals) during the latter part of Paul's career. At the same time, other questions retreated into the background, such as the Pauline version of a law-free gospel in controversy with his Jewish-Christian opponents (Galatians, Romans). In the end, Paul's writings must therefore be judged to exhibit a considerable degree of theological coherence and unity in the midst of a certain extent of terminological diversity and thoughtful contextualization.

PAUL AND PETER, JOHN, JAMES AND OTHER VOICES IN THE NEW TESTAMENT

Further points of tension are the relationships among NT authors, especially between Paul and Peter, Paul and John, and Paul and James. While it is beyond the scope of this essay to comment on these questions in detail, we may briefly sketch the issues involved in what is arguably the most frequently discussed alleged contradiction under the present heading, the relationship between faith and works in Paul and James.

The argument goes as follows. Paul stresses that salvation is a gracious gift of God to be received by faith independent of works (Rom 3:21-28; Eph 2:8-9; Phil 3:9). James writes that faith without works is dead (cf. 1:3-4: "the testing of your faith develops perseverance") and that a person is justified by works and not by faith alone (Jas 2:17, 24, 26). These statements appear to stand in blatant formal and material contradiction. In the immediate context of his remarks, however, Paul likewise speaks of works that must accompany faith (Eph 2:10; cf. Rom 2:13 with Jas 1:25), and James refers to the demonstration of one's faith by way of works (Jas 2:18). Elsewhere Paul commends the Thessalonians for their works engendered by faith (1

---

[30]Cf. Martin Hengel and Anna Maria Schwemer, *Paul Between Damascus and Antioch: The Unknown Years* (Louisville, Ky.: Westminster John Knox, 1997), pp. 279-91; Eduard Lohse, "Changes of Thought in Pauline Theology? Some Reflections on Paul's Ethical Teaching in the Context of His Theology," in *Theology and Ethics in Paul and His Interpreters: Essays in Honor of Victor Paul Furnish*, ed. Eugene H. Lovering Jr. and Jerry L. Sumney (Nashville: Abingdon, 1996), pp. 146-60; and Rainer Riesner, *Paul's Early Period: Chronology, Mission Strategy, Theology* (Grand Rapids, Mich.: Eerdmans, 1998).

Thess 1:3; cf. Gal 5:19, 22) and speaks of their "every act" being "prompted by [their] faith" (2 Thess 1:11; cf. Eph 4:12). Moreover, James, like Paul, considers works to be a consequence of faith, albeit a necessary one. Not only are Paul's emphasis on grace and faith and James's insistence on the need for works compatible; it is possible that Paul's law-free gospel was abused in the kind of manner that it required just the type of correction James provides (cf. Rom 6). Even under the present heading, it can therefore be maintained that the NT features not material contradictions but different perspectives as a result of differing sets of circumstances within a larger framework of coherence.

THE CENTER OF THE NEW TESTAMENT

As W. J. Harrington aptly notes, "The task [of NT theology] is done only when we have succeeded in showing the unity of the different 'theologies.'"[31] Negatively, the preceding discussion has shown that none of the alleged contradictions in NT theology can be substantiated. Positively, it remains to explore several possible integrative motifs from within the NT. Perhaps the best way to enter the discussion is the quest for a center of NT theology. In this regard one must first distinguish between the unity of the NT and the question of a center in the NT,[32] since, as Maier aptly notes, the Enlightenment separated the issues of unity and center, so that the "center of Scripture" became the substitute for the lost "unity of Scripture."[33] Moreover, though the unity of the NT may be maintained, the history of scholarship on the quest for a NT center is littered with discarded hypotheses. The quest must thus continue in a process of diligent listening to the various theological perspectives of the NT,[34] so that diversity and unity are given their due. The NT's unity cannot be safeguarded through the projection of a given concept onto the NT as a whole. Furthermore, in the effort of identifying the core tenets of the first Christians, the text of the NT, not speculative, extrabiblical reconstructions, must remain the ultimate point of

---

[31]W. J. Harrington, *The Path of Biblical Theology* (Dublin: Gill & Macmillan, 1973), p. 365; cited in D. A. Carson, "NT Theology," in *Dictionary of the Later New Testament and Its Developments*, ed. R. P. Martin and P. H. Davids (Downers Grove, Ill.: InterVarsity Press, 1998), pp. 808-9.

[32]Gerhard Hasel devotes a chapter to this topic; see Hasel, *New Testament Theology: Basic Issues in the Current Debate* (Grand Rapids, Mich.: Eerdmans, 1978), pp. 140-70.

[33]Gerhard Maier, *Biblical Hermeneutics* (Wheaton, Ill.: Crossway, 1994), p. 202.

[34]See the discussion in Andreas J. Köstenberger, "Translator's Preface," in Adolf Schlatter, *The History of the Christ* (Grand Rapids, Mich.: Baker, 1997), pp. 13-14.

reference.[35] Finally, many scholars have concluded that the quest for a single center of NT theology is misguided and should be replaced with an approach that recognizes several themes as an integrated whole.[36] For example, Maier traces a "center of Scripture" within a triadic framework: a personal center found in the person of Jesus, the Son of God and Messiah; a dynamic-historical center culminating in his redemptive work; and the fact that God speaks to us in the entire Bible.[37] Indeed, following Maier's lead, and with Carson, we too conclude that "the pursuit of a [single] center is chimerical" and that what is most promising is the pursuit of "clusters of broadly common themes."[38] We concur therefore that the search for a single center of the NT should be abandoned. It seems more promising to search for a plurality of integrative NT motifs.

INTEGRATIVE MOTIFS IN THE NEW TESTAMENT

As early as 1936, C. H. Dodd, in his inaugural lecture at the University of Cambridge, called for a reversal in scholarship and urged his NT colleagues to counteract disintegrative tendencies in NT theology by accentuating the commonalities of diverse NT perspectives.[39] Dodd's call is still valid.[40] But for the search for integrative motifs in the NT to be successful, the following criteria must be applied. First, an integrative motif must be found in all the major NT corpora, the Synoptics as well as John, Paul as well as the General Epistles. This, for example, would rule out the kingdom of God, which is found in the Synoptics and Paul but not in John (with one or two exceptions). Second, any such theme must be demonstrated historically to be a shared, foundational belief of Jesus and the early church. In the discussion that follows I will argue that at least three NT motifs fulfill these criteria.

---

[35]So rightly Carson, "NT Theology," p. 807.

[36]Cf. C. H. H. Scobie, "Structure of Biblical Theology," *TynB* 42 (1991): 178-79.

[37]Maier, *Biblical Hermeneutics*, p. 206.

[38]Carson, "NT Theology," p. 810; cf. Scobie, "Structure," pp. 178-79.

[39]C. H. Dodd, "The Present Task in New Testament Studies, an inaugural lecture delivered in the Divinity School, Cambridge on Tuesday, 2 June 1936." See Dodd's magisterial work *The Apostolic Preaching and Its Developments* (London: Hodder & Stoughton, 1936), which appeared in the same year.

[40]Cf. Maier, *Biblical Hermeneutics*, p. 193, and E. E. Lemcio, "The Unifying Kerygma of the New Testament," *JSNT* 33 (1998): 3-17 and 38 (1990): 3-11, with initial reference to Dodd, *Apostolic Preaching*. Lemcio's suggestive essay provides some independent confirmation for the conclusions arrived at in this essay.

THE ONE GOD

Like Judaism, Christianity came to be known for its monotheism.[41] The various NT writers all speak of the same, one God, the God of Abraham and Israel (Mt 15:31; 22:32 par.; Lk 1:68; Acts 3:13; 7:32), who revealed himself through the OT and became the sender of Jesus (Jn, passim). The more than thirteen hundred NT references to *theos* provide a telling testimony to the central significance of this God.[42] Thus Jesus, according to the Synoptics, speaks about the kingdom of God (see also Acts 1:3; 8:12; 14:22; 19:8; 28:23, 31; Rom 14:17; 1 Cor 4:20; 6:9-10; 15:50; Gal 5:21; Col 4:11; 2 Thess 1:5; Rev 12:10). Paul chooses the righteousness of God as a central motif (Rom 1:18; 3:5, 21-22; 10:3; 2 Cor 5:21; Phil 3:9; cf. Jas 1:20; 2 Pet 1:1). Several NT authors refer to the glory of God (Jn 11:4, 40; 12:43; Acts 7:55; Rom 1:23; 3:7, 23; 5:2; 15:7; 1 Pet 4:14; Rev 15:8; 19:1; 21:11, 23), and numerous voices even call the Christian gospel "the gospel of God" (Mk 1:14; Acts 20:24; Rom 1:1; 15:16; 2 Cor 11:7; 1 Thess 2:2, 8-9; 1 Tim 1:11; 1 Pet 4:17). Beyond this one reads about the will of God, the knowledge of God, the power of God, the peace of God, the church of God, the work of God, God the Father, God the Redeemer, the word of God, the judgment of God, the Spirit of God or the grace of God. The entire NT is pervaded by the consciousness of God, of his character and of his salvific work in Christ. God is therefore the foundation not only of the NT but also of the entire Bible.

JESUS THE CHRIST, THE EXALTED LORD

The connection between the one God and Jesus the Christ, the exalted Lord, is nowhere clearer than in the remarkable early confession cited in 1 Corinthians 8:6: "Yet for us there is but one God, the Father, from whom all things came and for whom we live; and there is but one Lord, Jesus Christ, through whom all things came and through whom we

---

[41]See the recent work by Richard Bauckham, *God Crucified: Monotheism and Christology in the New Testament* (Grand Rapids, Mich.: Eerdmans, 1999), who argues that from the very beginning "early Christians included Jesus . . . within the unique identity of the one God of Israel" (p. vii). Cf. Eckhard Schnabel, *Einheit und Vielfalt biblischer Erkenntnisse* (Wiedenest: MBW, 1995), pp. 35-36; and the chapter on the one God in Hans Hübner, *Biblische Theologie des Neuen Testaments*, vol. 1 (Göttingen: Vandenhoeck & Ruprecht, 1990).

[42]Cf. Peter Stuhlmacher, *Biblische Theologie des Neuen Testaments*, 2 vols. (Göttingen: Vandenhoeck & Ruprecht, 1992, 1999), 2:309, who notes that "the major witnesses of the NT jointly witness to the one God, who revealed himself definitively in his one Son, who shares with him the same essence, and who provided in him salvation for the world" and that "the joint testimony to the one God, who revealed himself definitively in and through Christ, [is] tied to the proclamation of the one apostolic gospel of Jesus Christ."

live."[43] In light of this close connection between the one God and the Lord
Jesus Christ drawn by the early church Rudolf Bultmann's famous exclusion of the historical Jesus from NT theology appears too radical.[44] Jesus'
messianic consciousness (see esp. Mk 14:62) and the fact that the Easter
event could not by itself produce messianic faith underscore the close connection between the so-called historical Jesus and the faith of the first
Christians.[45] In fact, the conviction that Jesus is the Christ foretold in the
OT and the exalted Lord unites the OT with the NT and the Gospels with
the gospel of the first Christians, including Paul.[46]

THE GOSPEL

The gospel of Jesus Christ is one of the major integrative glues of Scripture.
The term "to declare the good news" is already found in the OT (e.g., Is
40:9; 52:7). Jesus started out his ministry calling people to repentance and
faith in the "good news" (Mark 1:15 par.). Paul discovered in the gospel
the power for salvation of all who accept it by faith, Jews as well as Greeks
(Rom 1:16; 2:9-10; 10:12; 1 Cor 1:22, 24; Gal 3:28; Col 3:11; cf. Acts 13:46-48;
28:25-28; Lk 2:32). Moreover, the gospel did not merely indicate that the
historical Jesus was to be identified with the resurrected, exalted Lord and
Christ who had been predicted in the OT. It was also a message of forgiveness for sins on account of the substitutionary death of Christ at the cross.[47]

As Paul and his apostolic colleagues read the OT in light of Jesus as the
Christ (cf. Acts 17:2-3; Rom 1:2, 17; 1 Cor 15:3-5), they realized that already
in the OT the Messiah is cast as a suffering and resurrected Messiah, whose

[43]Cf. Bruce, "All Things to All Men," p. 92.
[44]See Rudolf Bultmann, *Theology of the New Testament*, 2 vols. (New York: Scribner, 1951), 1:3;
cf. Balla, *Challenges to NT Theology*, pp. 170-77; Stuhlmacher, *Biblische Theologie*, 1:18: "Jesus'
proclamation is not a mere 'presupposition,' but the historical foundation of NT theology."
Cf. Robert Morgan, "The Historical Jesus and the Theology of the New Testament," *The Glory of Christ in the New Testament: Studies in Christology in Memory of George Bradford Caird*, ed.
L. D. Hurst and N. T. Wright (Oxford: Clarendon, 1987), pp. 187-206.
[45]See Otto Betz, "The Problem of Variety and Unity in the New Testament," *HorBT* 21 (1980):
10-11.
[46]See James D. G. Dunn, *Unity and Diversity in the New Testament*, 2nd ed. (London: SCM Press,
1990), p. 369, and *The Theology of Paul the Apostle* (Grand Rapids, Mich.: Eerdmans, 1998), pp. 722-
29, esp. p. 729: "In short, for Paul Christianity is Christ" (cf. Wenham, "Unity and Diversity," p.
711); and E. P. Sanders, *Paul and Palestinian Judaism* (Minneapolis: Fortress, 1977), pp. 441-42, who
identifies the fact "that Jesus Christ is Lord" and "that in him God has provided for the salvation
of all who believe" as one of two "primary convictions which governed Paul's Christian life."
[47]Contra Dunn, *Unity and Diversity*; see also France, "Review," pp. 30-31. Cf. Stuhlmacher,
Biblische Theologie, 2:310: "The (major) witnesses of the NT teach jointly that Jesus' cross-
death is to be understood as an atoning, divinely commissioned death for 'the many.'"

plight is to take the place of others (e.g., Is 53). The gospel of the first Christians, which in turn is rooted in Jesus' messianic consciousness, therefore has as its content the crucified and risen Messiah and Lord—in conscious application of OT passages to the person and work of Jesus. This conviction surfaces repeatedly in all four Gospels (e.g., Mk 8:31; 9:31; 10:33-34, 45 par.), in Paul (e.g., Rom 3:25; 2 Cor 5:21), as well as in Peter (1 Pet 1:2, 10-12, 18-20), in Hebrews (Heb 1:3; etc.), and in the other NT writings (e.g., 1 Jn 2:2; Rev 5:5-6). Finally, in the book of Acts, the gospel is frequently personified, so that it is not Paul and the first Christians who pursue their mission but the gospel itself that marches irresistibly and victoriously to the ends of the earth (cf. Acts 6:7; 12:24; 19:20).

Perhaps the best summary of the gospel is found in Acts 10:36: "You know the message God sent to the people of Israel, telling the good news of peace through Jesus Christ, who is Lord of all." The expression "the Lord Jesus Christ" (e.g., 1 Thess 5:9; 2 Thess 2:1,14; Gal 6:14; 1 Cor 1:7; 8:6; 15:57; Rom 1:4; 5:1, 11; 6:23; 13:14; Col 2:6; Jas 1:1; 2:1; 1 Tim 1:12; 2 Pet 1:16; Jude 4, 17, 21) likewise sums up the unified Christian conviction of faith. Though there are other common motifs (such as the expectation of Jesus' return, the love command and the understanding that the NT church was the new messianic community in continuity with OT Israel), the NT is thus integrated around the convictions that there is one God, that Jesus is the Christ and the exalted Lord, and that the Christian community has been entrusted with the proclamation of the gospel, the message of salvation in Jesus Christ.

CONCLUSION

The diversity and unity of the NT present the reader with the rich legacy of the faith of the first Christians, in which various perspectives of the same Christ and of the same gospel mutually complemented one another. As Wenham puts it, the NT evidences a "concern for the working out of an orthodoxy (and orthopraxis) defined by the person and teaching of Jesus" and an organic development that can be likened to a tree whose branches have a common origin and are part of a common entity.[48] The first Christians concur that Jesus is the God-sent Christ and the exalted Lord. On the basis of this conviction and the resulting gospel message, the NT authors developed their own theologies, depending on their respective requirements of ministry and their faith experience. While Walter Bauer believed

---

[48]Wenham, "Unity and Diversity," p. 703.

he could detect a movement from diversity to unity within the early church, the first Christians rather developed from unity to diversity. Hence, as G. B. Caird warns us,

> The question we must ask is not whether these books all say the same thing, but whether they all bear witness to the same Jesus and through him to the many splendoured wisdom of the one God. If we are persuaded that the second Moses, the Son of Man, the friend of sinners, the incarnate *logos*, the first-born of all creation, the Apostle and High Priest of our calling, the Chief Shepherd, and the Lamb opening the scroll are the same person in whom the one God has achieved and is achieving his mighty work, we shall neither attempt to press all our witnesses into a single mould nor captiously complain that one seems at some points deficient in comparison with another. What we shall do is rejoice that God has seen fit to establish His gospel at the mouth of so many independent witnesses. The music of the New Testament choir is not written to be sung in unison.[49]

The one God, Jesus Christ, and the gospel—these are the major pillars of NT theology.[50] It remains the task of the interpreter to exegete individual passages in the respective NT writings and to relate the diverse motifs of the different NT documents to each other. Yet this may take place in the confidence that the NT is not a disparate collection of ill-fitting parts, which together result in nothing more than a cacophony of voices, but a well-composed symphony, in which different elements form a harmonious work that echoes into all the world to the glory of God and for the edification of those individuals who respond to the divine revelation in faith.

---

[49]G. B. Caird, *New Testament Theology*, ed. L. D. Hurst (Oxford: Clarendon, 1994), p. 24.
[50]Jesus as Christ and Lord as well as the gospel are also cited by Betz, "Problem of Variety and Unity," pp. 8-9, as establishing the unity of the NT.

11

The New Testament
and New Creation

G. K. Beale

Is the quest for a center for a comprehensive biblical theology so fraught with difficulties that it ought to be abandoned in favor of a multiperspectival approach? Or is the quest still open to a fresh search that builds on previous attempts but avoids some of the pitfalls into which they fell? In an attempt to answer this question, this essay sets out the view that the kingdom of the new creation is a plausible and defensible center for NT theology and that it is a needed refinement of the "inaugurated eschatology" center previously proposed by others.[1]

"ALREADY AND NOT YET": ESCHATOLOGY AS THE STARTING POINT FOR THE NEW PROPOSAL
Over the past few decades NT scholarship has made great strides in increasing our understanding that the beginning of Christian history was perceived by the first Christians as the beginning of the end times. Never-

---

[1]For an expanded version of this essay, see "The Eschatological Conception of New Testament Theology," in *Eschatolology in the Bible and Theology*, ed. K. E. Brower and M. W. Elliott (Downers Grove, Ill.: InterVarsity Press, 1997), pp. 11-52.

theless, the atomistic character of much of NT scholarship has often prevented serious broad theological reflection on the entire NT corpus from this perspective. Along these lines, D. C. Allison complained that the history of NT theology was responsible for influencing scholars to focus specifically on the atoning nature of Christ's death without paying sufficient attention to its eschatological ramifications. He continues by saying, "Christian theology has rarely grappled seriously with the eschatological presuppositions that permeate the New Testament, and although the twentieth century is the century of Albert Schweitzer, contemporary students of the New Testament have yet to explore *fully* the importance of eschatological language for the early followers of Jesus."[2]

The phrase "latter days" (and similar phrases) occurs approximately twenty-seven times in the NT, and only sometimes does it refer exclusively to the very end of history as we typically think of it. The phrase "latter days" and its synonyms are used more often to describe the end times as beginning *already* in the first century. The first observation we can make about these eschatological phrases is that they are alluding to identical or very similar phrases in the Old Testament. In the OT this wording is prophetic and refers to a future time when (1) there will be a tribulation for Israel consisting of oppression (Ezek 38:14-17), persecution, false teaching, deception and apostasy (Dan 10:14-21; 11:27; 12:1-10). (2) After the tribulation Israel will seek the Lord (Hos 3:4-5), they will be delivered (Ezek 38:14-16; Dan 12:1-13) and their enemies will be judged (Ezek 38:14-16; Dan 11:40-45; 12:2). (3) This deliverance and judgment will occur because a leader (Messiah) from Israel will finally conquer all of its Gentile enemies (Gen 49:1, 8-12; Num 24:14-19; Is 2:2-4; Mic 4:1-3; Dan 2:28-45; 10:14—12:10). (4) God will establish a kingdom on the earth and rule over it (Is 2:2-4; Mic 4:1-3; Dan 2:28-45) together with a Davidic king (Hos 3:4-5).

In the NT the meaning of the phrase is identical, except for one difference: in the NT, the end days predicted by the OT are seen as beginning to be fulfilled with Christ's first coming. This means that the OT prophecies of God's deliverance of Israel from oppressors, God's rule over the Gentiles and the establishment of his kingdom have been set in motion by Christ's death and resurrection and the formation of the church (see Acts

---

[2]D. C. Allison, *The End of the Ages Has Come* (Philadelphia: Fortress, 1985), p. 169 (emphasis added).

1:6-8; 2:1-43). On the other hand, the persecution of Jesus and the church indicated the beginning of the final tribulation. What the OT did not foresee so clearly was the ironic reality that the kingdom *and* the tribulation could coexist at the same time (cf., e.g., Rev 1:9). The experience of the church is a reflection of Christ's prior experience, whereby his endurance through trials, climaxed by his death, was a veiled form of reigning in the initial form of the unseen kingdom. Therefore, the latter days do not take place only at some point in the future but occur throughout the whole church age, right up to the present.

The first time the actual wording "last days" appears in the NT canon is Acts 2:17. Here Peter understands that the tongues being spoken at Pentecost are a beginning fulfillment of Joel's end-time prophecy that a day would come when God's Spirit would gift not merely prophets, priests and kings but all of God's people (Acts 2:15-17a; cf. Joel 2:28). In 1 Corinthians 10:11 Paul says that the OT was written to instruct the Corinthian Christians about how to live in the end times, since upon them "the end of the ages has come" (author's translation [throughout the essay]). And in Galatians 4:4 he refers to Jesus' birth as occurring "when the time had fully come" in fulfillment of the messianic prophecies. Likewise, in Ephesians 1:7-10 and Ephesians 1:20-23 "the fullness of time" alludes to when believers were redeemed and Christ began to rule over the earth as a result of his resurrection.

The expressions "the later times" and "last days" in 1 Timothy 4:1-3 and 2 Timothy 3:1-9 refer to the presence of tribulation in the form of false, deceptive teaching. That the latter days in 1 and 2 Timothy is not a reference only to a distant, future time is evident in that the Ephesian church is already experiencing this latter-day tribulation of deceptive teaching and apostasy (see 1 Tim 1:3-4, 6, 7, 19-20; 4:7; 5:13-15; 6:20-21; 2 Tim 1:15; 2:16-19; 2:25-26; 3:2-9). In 2 Peter 3:3, Jude 18 and 1 John 2:18 the phrases "last days" and "last hour" also refer to the beginning of the tribulation in the first century as signaled by the presence of false teachers in the churches.

The author of Hebrews also uses the language of "latter days." He proclaims in his opening two verses that in his own day—"in these last days"—Jesus had begun to fulfill the Psalm 2 prophecy that God's Son would judge the evil kingdoms and receive the earth as an inheritance from his Father (cf. Ps 2:1-12 with Heb 1:2-5). In like manner, in Hebrews 9:26 he says "he [Christ] has appeared once for all at the end of the age to put away sin by the sacrifice of himself." In identical fashion 1 Peter 1:19-

21 says that Christ has died as a sacrificial lamb and been resurrected "at the end of the times." And James 5:1-9 warns readers not to trust in riches because the "last days" have come.

This brief survey demonstrates that the last days predicted by the OT began with Christ's first coming. In addition, even when technical latter-day language is not used, there are many other passages in the Old and New Testaments that contain the concept of eschatology (e.g., see Paul's use of "now" in 2 Cor 6:2; Eph 3:5, 10; etc.). In this initial phase of the end times, Christ and the church begin to fulfill the prophecies concerning Israel's tribulation and end-time kingdom because Christ and the church are seen by the NT as the true Israel (Rom 2:25-29; 9:6, 24-26; Gal 3:29; 6:15-16; Eph 2:16-18; 3:6; 1 Pet 2:9; Rev 1:6; 2:17; 3:9, 12; 5:9-10).

Of course, the NT also speaks of the future consummation of the present latter-day period. There are still many end-time prophecies that will be fulfilled only when Christ returns a second time (e.g., the bodily resurrection of all people, the destruction of the present cosmos, the creation of a completely new heavens and earth and the final judgment). There is therefore what some call an already-and-not-yet dimension of the end times. In this respect, Oscar Cullmann has described Jesus' first coming metaphorically as D-Day, since this was when Satan was decisively defeated. V-Day is the second coming, when Jesus' enemies will totally surrender and bow down to him. As a result, as Cullman puts it, "The hope of the final victory is so much more the vivid because of the unshakably firm conviction that the battle that decides the victory has already taken place."[3] But the crucial point for our present discussion is that the great end-time predictions have already begun the process of fulfillment. T. W. Manson has well said, "When we turn to the New Testament, we pass from the climate of prediction to that of fulfillment. The things which God had foreshadowed by the lips of His holy prophets He has now, in part at least, brought to accomplishment. . . . What had been predicted in Holy Scripture as to happen to Israel or to man in the 'Eschaton' [end time] has happened to and in Jesus. The foundation-stone of the New Creation has come into position."[4]

---

[3]Oscar Cullmann, *Christ and Time* (Philadelphia: Westminster Press, 1964), p. 87.
[4]T. W. Manson, "Eschatology in the New Testament," in *Eschatology, Scottish Journal of Theology* Occasional Papers 2 (Edinburgh: Oliver and Boyd, 1953), p. 6. Though this sounds like "over-realized eschatology," Manson qualifies it by saying, "The End has come! The end has not come!" (p. 7).

THE ESCHATOLOGICAL LENS OF
NEW TESTAMENT THEOLOGY

Thus of fundamental importance for the development of NT theology is the realization that the apostles understood eschatology not merely as futurology but as a redemptive-historical psychology for the present. They understood that they were already living in the end times and that they were to understand their present salvation in Christ to be already an end-time reality. Hence every aspect of their salvation was to be conceived of as eschatological in nature. Just as when one puts on green sunglasses, everything seen is green, so Christ had placed eschatological lenses on his disciples, so that everything they looked at in the Christian faith had an end-time tint. This means that the doctrine of eschatology in NT theology textbooks should not merely be one among many doctrines, purportedly describing only the very end of the world as we know it. Rather, every doctrine should be viewed through a latter-day lens.

But how can our hermeneutical glasses be reground in order to see better the end-time reality of the NT? The concluding part of Manson's quotation above is a good place to start answering this question. He said Christ as "the foundation-stone of the New Creation has come into position."

We must think of Christ's death and resurrection as the central event that launched the latter days. This pivotal event of death and resurrection is eschatological because it launched the beginning of the new creation. Of course, the OT prophesied that the destruction of the first creation and the re-creation of a new heavens and earth were to happen at the very end of time. Christ's work reveals that the end of the world and the coming new creation have already begun in his death and resurrection. According to 2 Corinthians 5:15, 17, Christ "died [and was raised]. . . . Therefore, if any are in Christ, they are a new creation, the old things have passed away; behold, new things have come." Revelation 1:5 refers to Christ as "the first-born of the dead," and then Revelation 3:14 defines "firstborn" as "the beginning of God's [new] creation." Likewise, Colossians 1:18 says that Christ is "the firstborn from the dead" and "the beginning," so that "in everything he might be preeminent." In Galatians 6:14-15 Paul says that his identification with Christ's death means that he is a "new creation." While Christ says that he "will raise up" true believers in the future, "at the last day" (Jn 6:39, 40, 44, 54), he also says that the time of resurrection has been inaugurated: "I am the resurrection and the life" (Jn 11:25).

Indeed, the resurrection was predicted by the OT to occur at the end of

the world as part of the new creation. God would make redeemed humanity a part of the new creation by recreating their bodies through resurrection (cf. Dan 12:1-2). Of course, we still look forward to the time when our
bodies will be raised at Christ's final parousia and we will become part of
the new creation. Christ's resurrection, however, has already placed him in
the new creation. The resurrected Christ is not merely spiritually the inau-
guration of the new cosmos, but he is literally its beginning, since he was
resurrected physically with a newly created body. First Corinthians 15:22-
24 says the resurrection launched in Christ will be consummated when he
returns. He is called the "last [or "eschatological"] Adam" (1 Cor 15:45) because he did what Adam should have done and, in so doing, has launched
the new creation, which will be consummated at a yet future point.

In the light of what we have said so far, this then is the eschatological
lens that colors all of NT theology: Christ's death and resurrection through
the Spirit launched the end-time new creational kingdom for God's glory.
In other words, all other eschatological ideas flow out of the idea that
Christ's death and resurrection through the Spirit launched his end-time
reign over a new creation for God's glory. The focus is not merely on new
creation alone but on the messianic king who reigns over the new creation
and is himself the beginning of that creation. The significant theological
doctrines of the NT gain their fullest meaning within the framework of this
overriding idea.

NEW TESTAMENT THEOLOGY IN ESCHATOLOGICAL FOCUS

Let us turn to a few examples of how this is so and of how the eschatological enrichment of the various doctrines also enhances the practical application of these doctrines to our lives.

Missiology. Recall the commission of Adam, Noah and Israel. They were
all to obey God and go to the ends of the earth and subdue it. Of course,
after Adam's fall, Israel's commission to subdue the earth includes shining
their light in the world's spiritual darkness and judging nations who
refuse to accept their light. However, Adam, Noah and Israel all failed to
carry out their mandate. Christ, on the other hand, the perfect "image of
God," last Adam and true Israel, perfectly obeys, dies and rises not only as
new Israel but also as a new creation. The church, as Christ's risen body,
now carries on the commission of the true Adam and Israel to subdue the
earth for God as his vicegerent. Consequently missions, or going to the
ends of the earth, is to be an intrinsic mark of the true church. This is why

the church receives the Great Commission in Matthew 28:19-20 from Christ, who in granting it bases it on his authority given to him by God as Son of Man (i.e., "Adam"; so Mt 28:18 in allusion to Dan 7:14).

Christology and the nature of Christ's miracles. Seen within the framework of the new creation, Christ's miracles of healing not only inaugurated the end-time kingdom but also signaled the beginning of the new creation, since the healings were a beginning reversal of the curse of the old, fallen world. The miracles were a breaking in of the new creation to come, in which people will be consummately healed. Those he healed, and especially raised from the dead, foreshadowed his resurrection. And Christ's resurrection is the firstfruits of all believers. They, like him, will be raised with perfected, restored bodies at the very end of the age, when the new world is ushered in.

In addition, Christ's ministry of casting out demons was an expression of his beginning, though decisive, defeat of Satan, who had brought creation into captivity through his deception of Adam and Eve. This is the significance of the parable of the binding of the strong man (Mt 12:29). Christ's victory over Satan's temptations in the wilderness was the basis for his subsequent victories over the demons. It is not coincidental that in resisting the devil in the wilderness the Gospel writers depict Christ as doing what Israel should have done in their wilderness wanderings,[5] and even what Adam should have done in Eden.[6] Therefore, when Jesus exorcised demons, he was doing what Adam should have done[7] in the garden by casting out the devil and his forces.

The Holy Spirit. The OT prophesied that the Holy Spirit would be given as a gift at the end of the world and its first benefit would be to raise the saints from the dead. The Spirit raised Christ physically and raises people spiritu-

---

[5]Jesus responds to each of the three temptations by quoting a passage from Deuteronomy that refers to what Israel should have done in the wilderness but did not do.

[6]Jesus' three responses also allude to the temptation of Eve in Eden, which is apparent from considering their themes: the fruit of the tree seemed good for food = the bread temptation; the tree was "a delight to the eyes" = the temptation to jump off the pinnacle of the temple and be delivered by angels before Jerusalem's onlookers; "the tree was desirable to make wise" = the temptation to rule over the earth. See S. C. Glickman, *Knowing Christ* (Chicago: Moody Press, 1980), pp. 56-58. Luke's ending of his genealogy with Jesus' being related to "the son of Adam, the son of God" as that which directly precedes the temptation narrative points further to Jesus as an Adamic figure in the temptation, as does Mark's apparently offhand comment that immediately after the temptation, Jesus "was with the wild beasts," apparently residing in peace with them (Mk 1:13).

[7]D. G. McCartney, "*Ecce Homo*: The Coming of the Kingdom as the Restoration of Human Vicegerency," *WThJ* 56 (1994): 10.

ally now and will do so bodily at the second coming. Indeed, the Holy Spirit links us existentially to the new world to come. As Christians we partake of the blessings of the new world to come through the Holy Spirit.

The fruit of the Spirit in Galatians 5 is therefore probably best seen against the background of repeated prophecies throughout Isaiah that in the new creation there would be abundant fruitfulness, which Isaiah sometimes interprets to be figurative for the godly attributes of righteousness, holiness, faithfulness, joy and peace (cf. Gal 5:22-25 with Gal 6:14-16).

One of the gifts that the OT promised that the Holy Spirit would give to the saints in the new creation was perfect righteousness. As Christians we have received the Spirit and his various gifts, but we will not receive the gift of personal, sinless perfection until Christ returns. Nevertheless the Holy Spirit has come into our hearts to begin to work end-time righteousness in us. Moreover, the Spirit of righteousness in us cannot abide in harmony with indwelling sin. Thus Paul tells the Ephesians that if they sin, they will "grieve the Holy Spirit of God" (Eph 4:30). And if the Spirit is in us, then we should grieve along with him when we sin. If we are not characteristically grieved by and convicted about our sin, can we be confident that the end-time Holy Spirit is really in us?

Regeneration. We usually understand regeneration to mean being "born again" in that people are given a new nature. Now we can see that this regeneration is none other than being transformed into a new, latter-day creation. Again, 2 Corinthians 5:17 says, "If anyone is in Christ, he is a new creation; the old has passed away, behold, the new has come," a direct allusion to the prophecy of a new creation Isaiah 65:17. Just as God sovereignly and irresistibly brought the first creation into being, so he brings irresistibly the new creation into being. The creation of a new humanity in the second creation occurs by God's will and not the human, autonomous will. This is one reason Paul says in 2 Corinthians 4:6, "It is God who said, 'Let light shine out of darkness,' who has shone in our hearts to give the light of the knowledge of the glory of God in the face of Christ."

Sanctification. Sanctification is usually understood as the process of a Christian growing in righteousness, being set apart from sin and set apart to holiness. The Greek word *hagiazō* can mean "set apart." But with the glasses of eschatology we can see that sanctification involves being set apart from the old world characterized by sin and set apart to the new creation.

Practically, this means that if we have been regenerated, we have been transferred spiritually into the new creation. Accordingly Ephesians 2:10

says, "For we are his workmanship, created in Christ Jesus for good works, which God prepared beforehand, that we should walk in them." This demands the practical conclusion that genuine Christians will surely, though perhaps slowly, bear fruits of righteousness. All true believers are part of the new creation over which Christ rules. This means that the struggle within the believer is not a conflict between the old man and the new man in which the old man may win out most of one's Christian life. Christians are new creatures who struggle not with an old man or unbelieving self but with indwelling sin and sinful habits of their old life. Yet their old, sinful self will not ultimately prevail over the ability of their regenerate nature to produce righteousness. Those who profess faith but bear no fruit over time should have no assurance that they are genuine Christians or inhabitants of the new creation with Christ as their king.

Justification. Justification too is a doctrine that pertains to the last judgment concomitant with the destruction of the cosmos. This doctrine can be viewed in purely legal terms, whereby Christ bore the eternal wrath of God as our penal substitute so that we could be declared righteous. When we see justification in the light of inaugurated eschatology, we see that the final judgment that unbelievers will face in the future has been pushed back for believers to the cross in the first century. Believers have already passed through the great last judgment when Christ suffered the eternal last judgment for them on the cross.

Reconciliation. Traditionally the doctrine of reconciliation affirms that because God's hostile wrath has been diverted from us to Christ, we are able to come into a peaceful relationship with God. The end-time color of this doctrine is highlighted by recalling that Isaiah 11:6-12 and Isaiah 65:17, 25 predict that when the new creation comes there will be peace not only between God and humanity but also between hostile humans themselves. The predicted harmony of the animals in both texts from Isaiah serves merely to point to the peace among traditionally hostile people groups, particularly Jew and Gentile. For this reason the rallying cry of the NT is that "there is no distinction between Jew and Greek" (Rom 10:12; Acts 15:9; Eph 2:15-19). The pillars of alienated relationships holding up the old, fallen world were knocked out by Christ. And Christ established a new world, which has only one pillar, and that pillar is Christ Jesus. Thus the mark of genuine belief among those in the new spiritual creation is that of unity because they are part of the one Christ (1 Cor 12:13; Gal 3:27-28). Alienation and division are no longer the rule in the new order. Romans

10:8-13 therefore summarizes the theological unity toward which the church should unswervingly strive: "The word is near you, on your lips and in your heart (that is, the word of faith which we preach); because, if you confess with your lips that Jesus is Lord and believe in your heart that God raised him from the dead, you will be saved. For man believes with his heart and so is justified, and he confesses with his lips and so is saved. The scripture says, 'No one who believes in him will be put to shame.' For there is no distinction between Jew and Greek; the same Lord is Lord of all and bestows his riches upon all who call upon him. For, 'every one who calls upon the name of the Lord will be saved.'"

The law. The NT perspective on the role of the law can best be understood in the light of the beginning destruction of the old creation and the emergence of the renovated creation. For example, some have observed that Paul has apparently contradictory views of the law in Romans and Galatians, sometimes viewing it quite negatively and at other times positively. The fact that the end-time new creation has broken into the old world means that these two worlds overlap and that the old world is already beginning to crumble. Consequently, the law for unbelievers living in the old creation results in enslavement to sin and judgment. This judgment begins during the old age (cf. Rom 1:18; Eph 2:1-3; 1 Jn 2:8, 17) and is consummated at the end of the age, when the old cosmos will be judged by being destroyed and old-age inhabitants will be consigned to the second death because of their violation of the law (Rev 20:12-14). On the other hand, the law is a source of blessing for spiritually resurrected believers living in the new creation because in Christ they have power to fulfill the law in Christ in a way that spiritually dead people do not (2 Cor 5:15-17).[8]

Ecclesiology. Ecclesiology is affected in a variety of ways by the dawning of the new creation. For example, worship on the last day of the week in the OT has now changed to the first day of the week because Christ's resurrection on the first day of the week inaugurated the kingdom and eternal rest promised in the new creation. The continuation of a sabbath, a day of worshipful rest, on Sunday is a sign reminding us that the spiritual rest of the new creation has begun in Christ. Sabbath worship on Sunday reminds us to look forward to the time when our eschatological rest will be

---

[8]I am indebted to C. M. Pate, *The End of the Age Has Come* (Grand Rapids, Mich.: Zondervan, 1995), pp. 123-48, for his excellent discussion of how the overlap of the ages solves the dual Pauline perspective on the law, though he does not relate this to old creation and eschatological new creation.

consummated in the final form of the new creation when Christ returns the final time; this is what Hebrews 3—4 looks forward to as support for the epistle's emphasis on perseverance.

Baptism and the Lord's Supper, which Tom Wright would refer to as the "symbols" associated with the biblical "story,"[9] are also charged with notions of new creation. Baptism connotes the believer's identification with Christ's death and resurrection:[10] the old man (position in Adam) was crucified with Christ, and Christians have risen with him in "newness of life" (e.g., Rom 6:3-11). In addition, two other significant NT discussions of "baptism" compare it with Noah's salvation through water (1 Pet 3:20-21) and Israel's exodus through water (1 Cor 10:1-2), both of which are major parts of the overall story line of "re-creation."[11] Also important in this regard is the description of salvation in Titus 3:5 in terms of baptismal *and* new creation imagery: "by the washing of regeneration *(palingenesia)* and renewal in the Holy Spirit."[12]

Likewise, the Eucharist, as part of the weekly worship service on the first day of the week, evokes new creation imagery.[13] Christ's Last Supper

---

[9]Tom Wright, *The New Testament and the People of God* (Minneapolis: Fortress, 1992), pp. 447-48.

[10]See Oscar Cullmann, *Baptism in the New Testament*, SBT 1 (Naperville, Ill.: A. R. Allenson, 1950), pp. 9-22, for the foundation of baptism being Christ's death and resurrection.

[11]See M. G. Kline, *By Oath Consigned* (Grand Rapids, Mich.: Eerdmans, 1968), pp. 63-83. Against this OT backdrop, baptism can be seen as "a sign of the eschatological ordeal" (p. 79). Subsequently, in support of Kline, Wright has observed that baptism was "the mode of entry into the eschatological people . . . *because* it had to do with Jesus, who had himself brought Israel's history to its appointed destiny, and who as Messiah summed up Israel in himself" (*New Testament and People of God*, p. 447).

[12]Not coincidentally the term *palingenesia* ("regeneration") refers in Philo to the renewal of the earth after the flood and in Josephus to the return of Israel from captivity. Likewise, Wisdom 19:6 describes the exodus event as the time when "the whole creation was again renewed in its own kind anew."

[13]Justin Martyr *Dialogues with Trypho* 138, says that the eight people preserved through water in the ark "were a symbol of the eighth day [Sunday, the first day of the week], wherein Christ appeared when He rose from the dead. . . . For Christ, being the first-born of every creature, became chief of another race regenerated by Himself through water and faith." Accordingly, the Fathers viewed Sunday as "the eighth day going beyond the present 'week' into the future age," so that it is natural that believers could be understood already as tasting "the life of the new creation in the bread and wine of the eucharist." See G. Wainwright, *Eucharist and Eschatology* (New York: Oxford University Press, 1981), p. 77, who also observes the Justin reference in this connection. See too P. G. Cobb, "The History of the Christian Year," in *The Study of Liturgy*, ed. C. Jones et al. (London: SPCK; New York: Oxford University Press, 1992), p. 457: "The earliest reason given for celebrating Sunday is that it is the day of the resurrection (*Ep. of Barnabas*, 15.9)"; and, according to Justin (*Apology* 1 67), Christians also believed they were commemorating the first creation, which was on the first day of the creation week, and the resurrection of Christ, who rose on the first day of the week.

and the eucharistic meal of the early church were overtly linked to Israel's Passover and, hence, the exodus. Jewish tradition associated the Passover with the original creation and the coming future destruction and renovation of the cosmos, when the Messiah would come and God's kingdom would be established.[14] Such an association makes it natural that each of the Synoptic accounts of the Last Supper includes a saying by Jesus with respect to the cup that "I tell you I shall not drink again of this fruit of the vine until that day when I drink it new with you in my Father's kingdom [Luke has, "until the kingdom of God comes]" (Mt 26:29; likewise Mk 14:25; Lk 22:18). This could be a figurative reference, echoing the promised fruitfulness of the coming new creation that would be formally inaugurated by the resurrection.[15] This is further pointed to by the reference that the drinking will take place at the time when the kingdom comes, a further installment of the inaugurated end-time kingdom. This saying of Jesus apparently began to be fulfilled during Jesus' resurrection appearances to his disciples when they ate meals together.

On the other hand, 1 Corinthians 11:21-34 affirms that when partaking at the Lord's table saints either must judge themselves in order to partake worthily or they will be judged by God. Whichever is the case, however, true believers receive their judgment *now* at the Supper in order that they "may not be condemned along with the world" at the last judgment (1 Cor 11:32). Hence the Supper contains in itself a beginning form of the last judgment, which will be consummated at the end of time. Consequently, as G. Wainwright concludes, the Lord's Supper is "a projection, from the future . . . of the coming of the Lord . . . who comes to judge and recreate . . . it includes a present moment of judgment and renewal which is the projection of the cataclysm[16] that will inaugurate the universal and incontestable reign of God."[17]

To give just one more example, the church as the temple of God is yet another image for the new creation, especially when seen against the

---

[14]See *Targum Neofiti* Exodus 12, *Targum Pseudo-Jonathan* Exodus 12; 15:18 and the discussion in Joachim Jeremias, *The Eucharistic Words of Jesus* (New York: Scribner's Sons, 1966), pp. 58-59, 206-7.
[15]The OT and Judaism expected abundant fruitfulness in the coming creation, including fruitful "vineyards" producing "new wine" (e.g., Is 62:8-9; 65:17-22; Hos 14:7-8; Zech 9:17; 10:7).
[16]In this respect, *Didache* 10:6, part of the conclusion to the instructions on the Eucharist began at 9:1, says, "May grace (= Christ) come, and may this world pass away."
[17]Wainwright, *Eucharist and Eschatology*, p. 151; on this judgment theme, see also pp. 80-83. For more thorough elaboration on the "already and not yet eschatological and new creation" nature of the Eucharist, see esp. pp. 37-41, 68-70, 77, 80-83, 106, 147-54.

background of the ancient Near East and OT temples that were designed to symbolize the cosmos. For example, the temple in Revelation 21—22, in fulfillment of Ezekiel 40—48, symbolically represents the entire new cosmos as the goal of God's temple-building process throughout sacred history. Revelation 21—22 is the consummation of the prophetic hope of an end-time, universal temple that is coextensive with a new creation. But Revelation 11 and other NT temple texts portray this end-time temple as already having begun fulfillment and, in the resurrected Christ and his church, advancing to fill the entire earth during the interadvent age.[18]

The present tribulation. The OT predicted that a final tribulation would precede the dawning of the new cosmos. For example, Daniel 12:1-13 prophesies a time of great distress before the climactic resurrection of the righteous and wicked. While Daniel refers to the coming trial as one in which there will be deception within the covenant community and persecution of noncompromisers, other OT and NT texts affirm that the final tribulation will be one in which there will be a breakdown of various parts of the natural order of the cosmos, which will be culminated by complete destruction of the heavens and earth (cf. Mk 13:8; Lk 21:11, 23-26; 2 Pet 3:10-13). Against this background, one can see how the final tribulation is but an inextricable prelude to the eventual destruction and re-creation of the cosmos.

Such literal, physical phenomena of cosmic breakup were initially expressed at Christ's death: "there was darkness over all the land" (Mt 27:45), and "the earth shook, and the rocks were split; the tombs also were opened" (Mt 27:51). And such physical expressions of initial destruction will again occur at the very end of history, when the body of Christ, the church throughout the world, will experience climactic, universal persecution like Christ before them and then resurrection (cf. Rev 11:3-13; 20:7-11). But actual phenomena of cosmic dissolution are not the typical characteristic of the inaugurated phase of the tribulation. Rather, its predominant expressions are false teaching and deception. Along with false teaching and deception, Christian suffering as a result of persecution is also an essential feature of the inaugurated end-time tribulation, a theme struck throughout the Synoptics, Paul, 1 Peter and

---

[18]For an elaboration of this paragraph, see G. K. Beale, "The Final Vision of the Apocalypse and Its Implications for a Biblical Theology of the Temple," in *A Biblical Theology of the Temple*, ed. S. Gathercole and T. D. Alexander (Leicester: Inter-Varsity Press, forthcoming).

Revelation.[19] When saints refuse to compromise with false teaching, they often must face persecution (cf. Dan 11:30-33; Rev 2:8-17). Indeed, every manner of suffering is part of the scheme of the overlap of a fallen world that is passing away in the midst of an inaugurated new world (cf. Rom 8:18-23 with Rom 8:35-39). Thus, although the apparent OT perspective was that deception and persecution were seen to occur at the same general period as the convulsions of nature, the NT understands these to occur in stages, in which persecution and deception predominate throughout the age but then converge with the convulsions of nature at the very end.

The hierarchical structure of the church is therefore best viewed within the context of the latter-day tribulation of false teaching (note the overt references in 1 Tim 4:1 and 2 Tim 3:1 to the end-time trial of deception within the church community). Elders or bishops are needed in order to maintain the doctrinal purity of the covenant community, which is always threatened from the infiltration of fifth-columnist movements. Titus 1:5-16 gives this as the formal reason for the establishment of elders throughout the churches of Crete, and the same rationale is apparent in 1 and 2 Timothy (cf. 1 Tim 1:3-7, 19-20 and 1 Tim 4:1-7 with 1 Tim 3:1-15; 5:17; 6:20-21; cf. 2 Tim 2:14-18, 23-26). Such an ecclesiastical authority structure ensured the Christian community that it was continuing in the truth and life of the kingdom, which would enable it to be strong in accomplishing its mission of witness to the world (this is likely as significant a theme in the Pastorals as the concern about false teaching).[20] This positive element of mission is part of the larger, positive role of the church in its responsibility of carrying out the original Adamic commission to subdue the ends of the earth and Israel's similar commission to be a light of witness to the world. Acts highlights this eschatological light-bearing mission of the new creation more than any other NT book, including within it the role of deacons in Acts 6 and elders in

---

[19]Accordingly, in the Synoptics, suffering is related to following the Son of Man, whose own suffering is rooted in the prophecy of Daniel 7, where the Son of Man, representing true Israel, must suffer persecution (e.g., Mt. 8:18-22); Paul also links the church's sufferings as the "body" of Christ with her identification with "Christ's afflictions" (Col 1:24), as does Hebrews (cf. Heb 1:2 and Heb 9:26 with Heb 12:1-7), James (cf. Jas 1:2-4 with Jas 5:1-11), 1 Peter (cf. 1 Pet 1:5-6 and 1 Pet 1:20 with 1 Pet 2:19-23 and 1 Pet 3:14-5:10) and Revelation (e.g., cf. Rev 1:5-6 with Rev 1:9 and Rev 5:6 with Rev 6:9).
[20]See Royce Gordon Gruenler, "The Mission-Lifestyle Setting of 1 Timothy 2:8-15," *JETS* 41 (1998): 215-38.

Acts 20 (see, e.g., Acts 1:6-8; 2:17-3:26; 13:47; 26:16-18).[21]

CONCLUSION

No doubt some scholars will conclude that to reduce the center of the NT to the notion of a new creational kingdom is simply to add to the many reductionistic NT theologies already proposed and that we must content ourselves with a multithematic approach. Nevertheless, this center is supported by the broad sweep of canonical thought, wherein the Bible begins with an original creation that is then corrupted and continues by recounting the redemptive-historical process that is working toward a restoration of the fallen creation in a new creation under God's kingship. The NT sees these hopes being inaugurated and prophesies a future time of fulfillment in a consummated new creation as portrayed in Revelation 21:1—22:5.

---

[21]For the relationship of the eschatology of Acts to the notion of resurrection and new creation, see G. K. Beale, "Eschatology," in *Dictionary of the Later New Testament and Its Developments,* ed. Ralph P. Martin and Peter H. Davids (Downers Grove, Ill.: InterVarsity Press, 1997), pp. 332-34.

12

My Experience with
Biblical Theology

Peter Stuhlmacher

Throughout my academic career, I have enjoyed a great privilege.[1] I have been able to devote all my time to the study of the NT and the Scriptures as a whole, and therefore I could probe more deeply into the special features of biblical thinking than would have been possible in another profession. For this I am profoundly grateful, just as I am for the incentive given me right up to my last seminar by the many students who attended my courses in Erlangen and Tübingen. Without their interest in biblical texts and themes, it would have been much more difficult to persevere without resignation in academic instruction in view of the many circumstances that hinder it. I also recall with gratitude the assistants and coworkers who helped me over the years to hold lectures and seminars, to administer examinations and to fulfill all my academic duties. Together with my doctoral students, they have given me the opportunity through their questions and exegetical research to penetrate biblical statements and traditions that otherwise would have remained closed to me.

Finally, I cannot adequately express my thanks for the fact that I have

---

[1]This essay was translated by Daniel P. Bailey, Ph.D.

been accompanied for four decades by faithful friends in the church and academy. Pride of place among them belongs to Martin Hengel and Hartmut Gese. Both have been and continue to be for me brotherly teachers and advisors. Exchanges with them have opened insights to me that the secondary literature does not offer, and they have always encouraged me afresh to think my way through the biblical texts. Thanks to them and to the support of other academic companions such as Otfried Hofius and Gert Jeremias, I have been happy to pursue the exegesis of the Scriptures. NT scholarship is often running into dead ends, and the mistakes made have unfortunate consequences for the academy and the church. But the truth claims of the Bible transcend all these scholarly slips. It has been and still is encouraging to me in working with Old and New Testament texts to see that God's gospel concerning Jesus Christ and God's truth is anything but superseded. They remain valid for our time as well, and they open themselves to all those who approach them in the fear of God and with the eyes of the heart (cf. Sir 17:8; Eph 1:17-18).

The term "biblical theology" can be used in different ways. I use it to refer to the overall theological presentation of the biblical witness that arises out of the various traditions in the Bible. As I was working on my dissertation on God's righteousness in Paul in the early 1960s, Hartmut Gese gave me the wise advice not simply to pursue Old and New Testament exegesis together, but to concentrate upon NT research and then where feasible to draw in the assured results of OT criticism. I have followed this advice and have thereby had the opportunity of learning again and again from our sister discipline of OT. It is to Adolf Schlatter and Ernst Käsemann that I owe my insight into the fundamental significance and apocalyptic scope of Paul's doctrine of justification. However, from the standpoint of biblical theology, the more decisive impulses for understanding the NT have come to me from OT scholars: Gerhard von Rad and Walther Zimmerli, Hartmut Gese and Klaus Koch, Brevard S. Childs, Bernd Janowski, and several others. They have shown me that it does NT scholarship no good to isolate itself and to pursue its exegetical task only under its own direction. When it does so—as is still the rule—then it falls almost unavoidably into prejudices, which have grown with the history of research, and it all too quickly follows implicit or explicit dogmatic interests. In view of the fact that the Christian Bible consists of Old and New Testaments, specialist exegesis of the NT does much better to pay attention to the biblical canon and the complex process of biblical traditions that unites the two Testaments. When one interprets the NT texts in terms of this canonical process, then fundamental exegetical insights result, which are also of importance for dogmatics.

THE OLD TESTAMENT AS HOLY SCRIPTURE

The first insight has to do with the significance of the OT. If one starts out with the conventional wisdom of the NT guild, then the OT is only one of the religious-historical presuppositions of the NT, and ancient Judaism is only a part of the broader environment of the NT. But this view is laden with two grave misjudgments that seriously hinder a biblical-theological understanding of the NT texts.

Not only Jesus but also the apostles, above all Peter and Paul, would have resisted vigorously the claim that their Jewish origin and religious convictions were only one phenomenon of their environment, alongside of which Greco-Roman traditions could be equally ranked. For the main witnesses of the NT, ancient Judaism—with all its diversity—was the life world in which they had been placed as a result of divine election. Two holy authorities played a decisive role in Jewish life: the Holy Scriptures and the Jerusalem temple. For the founders of the NT faith, to hear and learn Moses, the Prophets and the Psalms was something categorically different than an encounter and debate with Hellenistic philosophy, mystery religions or the religious claims of Rome. Throughout the first century not only Jews but also the representatives of early Christianity, which grew out of Judaism, read the holy Scriptures in Hebrew and Greek as their Bible. Through the spiritual testimony of these Scriptures, Jews and Christians heard the one God speaking to them. For Christians, this one God was and remains the Father of Jesus, the Christ.

All the main books of the NT originated under the influence of Christian interaction with the *graphai hagiai*, and throughout the first century there was still no canonical NT. Under these circumstances, it is historically wrong and hermeneutically misleading for NT exegesis to demote the OT to the level of a Jewish testimony collection. Biblical theology suggests another way of proceeding. As there was not yet a distinct OT over against the NT, and Christians read the holy Scriptures as their Bible, NT statements must be interpreted first and foremost in the light of the OT and the faith world of ancient Judaism. Here it should be remembered that by the first century, the OT had already undergone a centuries-long canonical process and had been translated for the most part into Greek, although on its fringes the OT canon was still not yet closed. In pursuing a biblical-theological exposition of the NT, we must therefore seek to encounter Jesus, the apostles and their pupils by recognizing their Jewish origin and their high regard for the OT as inspired holy Scripture.

JESUS AS GOD'S MESSIAH

It is the right and the duty of NT exegetes always to ask afresh who Jesus of Nazareth was and what he taught. But this question has been hindered for a long time by two deep-seated critical prejudices. The first is the habit of viewing the formation and growth of the Synoptic tradition as a process that was determined above all by the post-Easter needs of early Christianity and that incorporated only splinters of pre-Easter tradition. This picture of the Synoptic tradition stands behind a second critical conviction, namely, that the earthly Jesus was by no means to be identified with that messianic Son of Man and Son of God whom the Synoptics present him to be. Because the Synoptic witness to Christ is supposedly of post-Easter origin, scholars think they ought to replace this witness by more accurate historical reconstructions. According to this view, the earthly Jesus was (only) a Jewish rabbi or a prophetic, charismatic wandering teacher who lived as "the parable of God," as Eduard Schweizer has put it (following Eberhard Jüngel).[2] He became known in the early Christian church as Messiah, Son of God, and the exalted Lord at God's right hand (see Ps 110:1) only after his crucifixion by the Romans and his resurrection, which was attested only by his followers.

Against this double interpretive grid two objections may be raised from the standpoint of biblical theology. The first has to do with the origin and transmission of the Synoptic tradition. When we approach Jesus and the Synoptics with the historical presuppositions of early Judaism and Jewish Christianity, then it creates a problem for the form-critical picture of the formation of the Synoptic tradition, which is informed by the origins and transmission of popular or folk literature.[3] This is still the main model followed by scholarship today. But the prophetic and Jewish wisdom schools

---

[2]Eduard Schweizer, *Jesus the Parable of God,* Princeton Theological Monograph Series 37 (Allison Park, Penn.: Pickwick Publications, 1994).

[3]Cf. Karl Ludwig Schmidt, "Die Stellung der Evangelien innerhalb der allgemeinen Literaturgeschichte," *Eucharisterion für Hermann Gunkel,* 2 vols. (Göttingen: Vandenhoeck & Ruprecht, 1923), 2:50-134; Rudolf Bultmann, *Die Erforschung der synoptischen Evangelien,* 3rd ed. (Berlin: Verlag Alfred Töpelmann, 1960), pp. 17-21.

of the OT, as well as the later rabbinic culture concerning tradition, point
in another direction. This has long since been demonstrated by NT scholars such as Birger Gerhardsson,[4] Heinz Schürmann,[5] Ben F. Meyer,[6] Martin
Hengel[7] and Rainer Riesner.[8] At the beginning of the formation of ancient
sapiental tradition, there always stood the head of a school, whose teachings, deeds and destiny were carefully preserved by his pupils (mathētai)
and passed on, at first orally and later in writing. If we take this into account and pay due attention to Jesus' role as a teacher (kathēgētēs; cf. Mt
23:10), then it is very probable that the Synoptic tradition too started to be
formed in the pre-Easter circle of Jesus' disciples. This circle preserved
Jesus' teaching, behavior and fate, since Jesus' chosen mathētai saw him as
the "messianic teacher of wisdom"[9] and even as the Messiah himself. After
Easter, this circle's view of Jesus and knowledge of his teaching were incorporated into the "teaching of the apostles" (Acts 2:42, author's translation [throughout the essay, unless otherwise noted]) and so became part of
the tradition of early Christianity. In other words, we are not dealing here
only with a personal continuum between Jesus' followers and the members of the early Jerusalem church formed by Peter, the sons of Zebedee,
the other apostles and the family of Jesus. Rather, this circle of persons also
guarantees the continuity of the Jesus tradition from the pre-Easter into
the post-Easter period. The tradition of the Gospels must therefore be
treated with historical respect. It is not ipso facto secondary, but amazingly
reliable, right down to the traditions about the passion and Easter.

If one takes this view of the Synoptic tradition as a basis, then Jesus
could very well have lived and taught as the Synoptics report, including
the fact that people began to part company already over the earthly Jesus.
Jesus and his followers and opponents were Jews. Jesus' claim to be the Son
of the living God and to minister with divine authority led his disciples to
confess, "You are the Christ" (cf. Mk 8:29 par.). But other Jews saw Jesus as
a religious deceiver who blasphemously arrogated to himself divine au-

[4]Birger Gerhardsson, Memory and Manuscript and Tradition and Transmission in Early Christianity, The Biblical Resource Series (Grand Rapids, Mich.: Eerdmans, 1998).
[5]Heinz Schürmann, Jesus—Gestalt und Geheimnis, ed. Klaus Scholtissek (Paderborn: Bonifa-
tius, 1994).
[6]Ben F. Meyer, The Aims of Jesus (London: SCM Press, 1979), pp. 69-94.
[7]Martin Hengel, "Jesus as Messianic Teacher of Wisdom and the Beginning of Christology,"
in Studies in Early Christianity (Edinburgh: T & T Clark, 1995), pp. 73-117.
[8]Rainer Riesner, Jesus als Lehrer, WUNT 7, 3rd ed. (Tübingen: Mohr Siebeck, 1988).
[9]Hengel, "Jesus as Messianic Teacher."

thority (cf. Mt 27:63, 64; Jn 5:18; 7:12, 47; 10:33; 19:7).[10] Indeed, Jesus' claim to authority became absolutely unacceptable when Jesus in his cleansing of the temple made messianic claims upon the Lord's house.[11] In his subsequent trial before the high priests, he not only affirmed this messianic claim but also proceeded to inform the highest Jewish court that it would soon be confronted with him as the heavenly Son of Man and judge of the world (cf. Mk 14:61-62 par.). The *titulus* that the Romans placed on the cross shows that the Jewish leaders accused Jesus before the Roman prefect Pilate for precisely these statements and that he was executed by him for being a messianic pretender. The story of Jesus and his way from Galilee to Jerusalem breaks down into isolated episodes when one gives no priority to the question of his messiahship. But they gain profile and coherence when one understands them as determined by precisely this question.[12]

In the light of Deuteronomy 21:23 the Jewish rulers could understand Jesus' death on the cross as a divine curse upon him (cf. Acts 5:30; Gal 3:13). But over against this the disciples, newly encouraged by the Easter appearances, proclaimed that "God has made him both Lord and Messiah, this Jesus whom you crucified" (Acts 2:36 NRSV; cf. Ps 110:1). Moreover, the early church formed and upheld the confession that "Christ died for our sins in accordance with the scriptures, and that he was buried, and that he was raised on the third day in accordance with the scriptures, and that he appeared to Cephas, then to the twelve" (1 Cor 15:3b-5 NRSV). In this bold interpretation of Jesus' crucifixion and resurrection against the background of Isaiah 53:9-12 and Hosea 6:2, Peter, John and James were following Jesus' teaching regarding the meaning and goal of his vicarious death and of his resurrection (cf. Mk 9:31 par.; Mk 10:45 par.; Mk 14:22-25 par.).

In sum, by viewing these matters from the standpoint of biblical theology, we gain a plausible and coherent picture of the Jesus tradition, the preaching of Jesus and the formation of early Christian tradition.

THE SYNOPTICS

The question about the origin and mutual relationship of the Synoptic Gospels has occupied Christianity for centuries and will not cease to do so

---

[10]Cf. August Strobel, *Die Stunde der Wahrheit*, WUNT 21 (Tübingen: Mohr Siebeck, 1980), pp. 77-94.

[11]Cf. Jostein Ådna, *Jesu Stellung zum Tempel*, WUNT 119 (Tübingen: Mohr Siebeck, 2000).

[12]Cf. Martin Hengel, "Jesus, the Messiah of Israel," in *Authenticating the Activities of Jesus*, ed. Bruce D. Chilton and Craig A. Evans (Leiden: E. J. Brill, 1999), 2:323-49.

in the future. For biblical theology, the following characteristics of Mark, Matthew and Luke are especially important.

1. The three Synoptic Gospels tell the story of Jesus, which elicits faith in him. However, this is not done by free composition but on the basis of Jesus tradition preserved by the apostles and brought up to date for teaching in the churches. Cast in the form of kerygmatic biographies, the three Gospels convey the message that God in his love sent his only begotten Son into the world and delivered him unto death for Jews and Gentiles while they were still unbelieving, weak and sinful (cf. Rom 5:6-8). These three narratives of Jesus' life have the same significance for the end-time people of God that the exodus story had for Israel. They are therefore rightly placed at the beginning of the NT.

2. All three Synoptics convey in their own way that the story of Jesus was an event of messianic fulfillment (L. Goppelt). In Jesus' mission, teaching and destiny, the messianic promises are fulfilled. As a result, first the Jews and then also the Gentiles can learn to see in Jesus of Nazareth the promised messianic representative of God's kingdom. In turn, they can learn to follow him and to confess him as Savior and Lord, because for their sake he went to the cross and was raised by God. In addition, this event of messianic fulfillment is filled with further promises of its own, because the resurrection of Jesus marks the beginning of the period of world mission that ends with the parousia (cf. Mt 28:16-20 with Mt 24:14 par.). With his end-time appearance from heaven, the *kyrios Iēsous Christos* will begin to establish the *basileia* promised to Israel (cf. Lk 12:31-32; 22:28-30; Acts 1:6; 3:20 with Is 9:1-7 [8:23—9:6 Heb]; Dan 2:44; 7:14, 27).

3. The Synoptics offer differently organized, variously long and individually accented narratives of the story of Jesus. All of them received their final edited form and were published only after the great apostles Peter, James and Paul, together with James the Lord's brother, had suffered a martyr's death and the early church in Jerusalem had gone into exile in Pella, east of the Jordan. Hence the Synoptic Gospels preserved the apostolic Jesus tradition for the coming generations. As right and exciting as it is to investigate the Synoptics by means of tradition and redaction history, these documents do not deserve to be treated with wholesale historical skepticism, because it is entirely possible to extend the continuity of the Jesus tradition mentioned above right into the Gospels. Thus, as long as one does not simply brush aside the ancient Church's reports about the authors of the Synoptics, the lines of tradition can

with ample reason be sketched as follows. In the Gospel of Mark, we find the Jesus tradition bound up with the name of Peter. In Matthew we find the teaching tradition preserved by the pillar apostles in Jerusalem, while in Luke, Paul's companion, we gain a glimpse of the Jesus tradition upheld in Antioch. In all three cases the tradition has certainly been supplemented, brought up to date and freshly edited over against its original version. Nevertheless, throughout this process it was subjected neither to serious distortion nor to departures from history. Rather, Peter (and his agent John Mark), the disciple Matthew (and in his steps the Jerusalem teachers), and the founders of the mission church in Antioch who came from the circle of the Hellenists (cf. Acts 11:19-24) carefully passed on the Jesus tradition entrusted to them. As long as the original church in Jerusalem existed and the great apostles were still alive, they stayed in contact with each other, taught in mutual agreement who Jesus was and is and warned their audiences against false prophecy (cf. Mk 13:21-23 par.). The presentations of Matthew, Mark and Luke therefore deserve historical respect and theological attention. In spite of their obviously different presentation of the Jesus tradition they all agree not only concerning the conviction that Jesus was the messianic Son of God, but also concerning the description of his journey from Galilee to Jerusalem, his proclamation of the *basileia*, his vicarious death on the cross of Golgotha and his resurrection of the dead three days after the crucifixion.

THE TEACHING OF PAUL

The book of Acts and the Pauline Epistles both document that the special apostolic commission that Paul received on the road to Damascus is to be seen in the light of Isaiah 42:1-16, Isaiah 49:1 and Isaiah 66:18-21. Paul understood himself to be chosen by the exalted Christ to take the light of the gospel to the Gentiles (cf. 2 Cor 4:5-6 with Is 49:6). Hence at the apostolic council Paul agreed with the pillar apostles from Jerusalem about the missionary task: the pillars should go with the gospel to the Jews but Barnabas and Paul to the Gentiles (cf. Gal 2:1-10). A few years later Paul assured the Corinthians that the gospel he taught was none other than the one preached and taught by the apostles called before him (cf. 1 Cor 15:1-11). In his missionary activities Paul worked, just as they did, toward the parousia and the establishment of the *basileia tou theou* by Jesus Christ that would follow (cf. Mt 24:14 par.; Mt 28:16-20 with 2 Thess 2:3-12; Rom

11:13-14, 28; 1 Cor 15:20-28). His gospel had a global scope. Paul's special joy was that by means of the Gentile mission entrusted to him he could help hasten the day when "all Israel" will be saved by the Christ-Deliverer who will appear from Zion. Furthermore, when the "full number of the Gentiles" (Rom 11:25 NRSV) have entered into the *basileia* of Christ and "all Israel" has acknowledged Christ to be the messianic Deliverer from the judgment of God's wrath (cf. Rom 11:26 with 1 Thess 1:10), then the curse of futility upon the (nonhuman) creation, which has weighed upon it since Adam's fall, will also be taken away. In God's future kingdom, which Jesus Christ will establish, there is no more death, nothing cursed and no suffering. Instead, Gentiles and Jews, delivered from their sins by the atoning death of Jesus, will be gathered before God in the midst of a renewed creation for the purpose of praising God eternally (cf. 1 Cor 15:25-28; Rom 8:18-21 with Rev 21:1-22:5). If one wishes to understand Paul and his gospel, one must therefore see it in the broad eschatological framework in which it stands.[13] This framework is provided by the Jewish and Jewish Christian expectation of the end-time "Zion-*basileia*" (Gese).[14] Jesus strengthened this expectation among his disciples when he taught them to pray in the Father's name, "Thy kingdom come, thy will be done, on earth as it is in heaven" (Mt 6:9-10).

Despite the contribution of Ernst Käsemann,[15] the main representatives of the so-called new perspective on Paul (Krister Stendahl,[16] E. P. Sanders[17] and James D. G. Dunn[18]) have not taken the apocalyptic framework and the end-time scope of Paul's doctrine of justification very seriously.[19] Stendahl, Sanders and Dunn trace the apostle's statements about justification back only to his missionary interest in the soteriological equality of

---

[13]See Peter Stuhlmacher, "Matthew 28:16-20 and the Course of Mission in the Apostolic and Postapostolic Age," in *The Mission of the Early Church to Jews and Gentiles*, ed. Jostein Ådna and Hans Kvalbein, WUNT 127 (Tübingen: Mohr Siebeck, 2000), pp. 17-43.

[14]Cf. Is 2:2ff.; Mic 4:1ff.; Zech 9:9-10 with Mt 8:11-12 par.; Mt 21:1-9 par.; 1 Cor 15:20-28; Rev 19:6-8.

[15]Ernst Käsemann, *Perspectives on Paul* (Philadelphia: Fortress, 1971), pp. 60-78.

[16]Krister Stendahl, *Paul among Jews and Gentiles* (Philadelphia: Fortress, 1976).

[17]E. P. Sanders, *Paul and Palestinian Judaism* (Philadelphia: Fortress, 1977); *Paul, the Law and the Jewish People* (Philadelphia: Fortress, 1983); "Jesus, Paul and Judaism," in *Aufstieg und Niedergang der römischen Welt*, ed. Hildegard Temporini and Wolfgang Hase, vol. 25/1 (Berlin: Walter de Gruyter, 1982), pp. 390-450.

[18]James D. G. Dunn, "The New Perspective on Paul," in *Jesus, Paul and the Law* (Louisville, Ky.: Westminster John Knox, 1990), pp. 183-214; *The Theology of Paul the Apostle* (Grand Rapids, Mich.: Eerdmans, 1998), pp. 335-40.

[19]Cf. Peter Stuhlmacher, "Eschatology and Hope in Paul," *EvQ* 72 (2000): 315-33.

Gentiles and Jews.[20] Sanders even affirms the old view of William Wrede[21] and Albert Schweitzer,[22] which located the main theme of Paul's doctrine not in justification but in the (mystical and spiritual) participation of believers in Christ and his resurrection glory.[23] But from a biblical-theological perspective on the Pauline texts, all these contentions appear to be questionable, especially in Romans, where the apostle presents and defends in summary form the doctrine he preached.

In Romans 1:1-7, 16-17 it is immediately clear that the main content of the Pauline gospel is Christ and justification. In Romans 1:18—3:20 he demonstrates with admirable clarity that no one can stand in the final judgment that looms over the Gentiles but that also will soon come upon the Jews. They are all fatally guilty before God. According to Romans 3:21-31, there is salvation for them only because God in and through Christ has effected their deliverance. On Golgatha God made his Christ to be the *hilastērion*, that is, the supreme "mercy seat" or "place of atonement" for sin[24] (cf. also the NRSV margin at Rom 3:25). This corresponds to the old *kapporet* or "mercy seat" in the Holy of Holies of the desert tabernacle and the Jerusalem temple (cf. esp. Ex 25:17-22; Lev 16:2; Num 7:89), which Israel lost along with the ark of the covenant during the Babylonian exile (cf. Jer 3:16; 2 Macc 2:4-8). By installing Jesus as the new mercy seat, God demonstrated the power of his righteousness to create salvation and forgiveness. He justifies every person who believes in Jesus Christ, and he does so apart from the works of the law.

In Romans 3:21-31 the ecumenical roots of the Pauline doctrine of justification are clearly visible. If one follows the suggestions of Michael

---

[20]Cf., e.g., Stendahl's contention: "Paul's arguments concerning justification by faith have *not* grown out of his 'struggle with the Judaistic interpretation of the law,' and are *not* 'a fighting doctrine, directed against Judaism' [as Käsemann thought]. Its place and function, especially in Romans, are not primarily polemic, but apologetic as he defends the right of the Gentile converts to be full members of the people of God." *Paul Among Jews and Gentiles*, p. 130.

[21]William Wrede, *Paulus*, Religionsgeschichtliche Volksbücher I 5/6 (Tübingen: Mohr Siebeck, 1907), pp. 56-88; ET *Paul* (London: Philip Green, 1907), pp. 122-47.

[22]Albert Schweitzer, *Die Mystik des Apostels Paulus*, 2nd ed. (Tübingen: Mohr Siebeck, 1954), pp. 214-21; ET *The Mysticism of Paul the Apostle* (New York: Henry Holt, 1931), pp. 219-26.

[23]Cf., e.g., E. P. Sanders, *Paul* (Oxford: Oxford University Press, 1991), p. 74: "The deeper levels of Paul's thought are not found in the judicial categories, but in those which express the participation of the faithful in Christ or in the Spirit, a participation which produces a real change."

[24]Cf. Daniel P. Bailey, "Jesus as the Mercy Seat: The Semantics and Theology of Paul's Use of *Hilastērion* in Romans 3:25" (Ph.D. dissertation, University of Cambridge, 1999; forthcoming in WUNT, Tübingen: Mohr Siebeck). See also the summary of this dissertation in *TynB* 51 (2000): 155-58.

Theobald[25] and Christoph Burchard,[26] then the end-time instructional sentences that Paul presents in Romans 3:20, 28 originate from Antiochene tradition (cf. Gal 2:16). It may even be possible to trace them back to the Stephen circle in Jerusalem. I believe that this holds as well for the sentence quoted in Romans 3:25-26 concerning Christ as the place of atonement for believers that makes the temple cult obsolete.[27] Right alongside Romans 3:25 may be set the old christological formula in Romans 4:25, which builds not only on the Greek text of Isaiah 53:10-12 but also on the Hebrew: Jesus our Lord suffered the fate of Isaiah's Suffering Servant. He "was put to death for our trespasses and raised for our justification" (Rom 4:25, author's translation; cf. Is 53:11 NIV). Paul ties all these christological traditions together into a new whole. For him the risen Christ, by means of his intercession, has been effecting the justification of believers ever since his exaltation. This is how he makes his vicarious, atoning death on behalf of sinners effective before God, and according to Romans 8:34 this extends right into the final judgment. The share that believers have in the reign of Jesus Christ and their participation in his death and resurrection glory, as spoken of in Romans 5—6, also have their basis in the event of justification. As and because they participate in the atoning death of Christ (cf. 2 Cor 5:21), believers enter anew into fellowship with God and sanctification. In this situation they no longer serve sin but the *kyrios Christos*. Consequently they may be filled with the twofold certainty that the sufferings in which they still live are of little consequence compared with the resurrection glory about to be revealed to them and that nothing will any longer be able to separate them from the love of God in Christ (Rom 8:18, 38-39).

Finally, if we take Romans 9—11 into account and notice that these three chapters are about God's people and God's righteousness, then the notion mentioned above that Paul's statements about justification were only or principally about the soteriological equality of Gentiles and Jews disappears by itself. According to Romans 9—11, God's work of salvation on behalf of

[25]Michael Theobald, "Der Kanon von der Rechtfertigung (Gal 2:16; Röm 3:28)—Eigentum des Paulus oder Gemeingut der Kirche?" in *Worum geht es in der Rechtfertigungslehre?* ed. Thomas Söding, Quaestiones Disputatae 180 (Freiburg: Herder, 1999), pp. 131-92.
[26]Christoph Burchard, "Nicht aus Werken des Gesetzes gerecht, sondern aus Glauben an Jesus Christus—seit wann?" in *Geschichte—Tradition—Reflexion, Festschrift für Martin Hengel zum 70. Geburtstag*, vol. 3, *Frühes Christentum*, ed. Hermann Lichtenberger (Tübingen: Mohr Siebeck, 1996), pp. 405-15.
[27]Cf. Peter Stuhlmacher, "Recent Exegesis on Romans 3:24-26," in *Reconciliation, Law and Righteousness: Essays in Biblical Theology* (Philadelphia: Fortress, 1986), pp. 94-109.

the Gentiles is embedded in his inscrutable ways with Israel. Paul believed that the people of God had already been chosen in Abraham for justification by Christ. Therefore God's ways with humanity can and will come to an end only when, in addition to those few Jewish Christians who already believe in Christ, "all Israel" has acknowledged Christ as the end-time Deliverer and has received through him the forgiveness of sins. This, then, is the principle of justification and election that God applies in his dealings with Jews and Gentiles: "God has consigned all men in disobedience, that he may have mercy upon all [in Christ]" (Rom 11:32, author's translation).

As Otfried Hofius has shown,[28] this principle is not far from the message of the prophets. They too viewed the one God as the God whose zeal against sin and unholiness is tempered by his grace and mercy; he positively must have mercy on Israel, because he is God and not man (cf. Hos 11:7-9). Paul's gospel of justification is about the saving righteousness and kingdom of the one God, who has mercy on godless sinners in and through Christ and grants them access to his *basileia*. The risen Christ shall establish this *basileia*, and in his missionary activity Paul was working toward his parousia.

THE SCHOOL OF JOHN

The interpretation of the Johannine writings—the Revelation of John, the Johannine Epistles and the Fourth Gospel—is unusually difficult, even when the texts are viewed from the standpoint of biblical theology. Nevertheless, this point of view does open up essential elements of the Johannine tradition.

1. Even if one leaves open the details of how the five Johannine writings are related to each other, what stands out is the vast breadth of the Johannine tradition that opens up when one counts the Apocalypse of John as part of the Johannine corpus. This breadth can all the better be appreciated the more one recalls the Jewish and naturally also Jewish Christian ability to view a subject simultaneously from several different angles or to change one's point of view suddenly in the midst of a train of thought—a style of perception that, according to Hengel, in dependence upon Emma Brunner-Traut, is best described as "*aspective*."[29]

---

[28]Otfried Hofius, "'Rechtfertigung des Gottlosen' als Thema biblischer Theologie," in *Paulusstudien*, WUNT 51 (Tübingen: Mohr Siebeck, 1989), pp. 121-47.

[29]Friedrich Avemarie, "Erwählung und Vergeltung," *NTS* 45 (1999): 113; Avemarie refers to Emma Brunner-Traut, *Frühformen des Erkennens: Aspektive im Alten Ägypten*, 3rd ed. (Darmstadt: Wissenschaftliche Buchgesellschaft, 1996), pp. 173-74, where she cites from a letter by Martin Hengel.

If one takes this "multi-faceted perception"[30] into account, it is entirely within the realm of possibility that the Johannine school spoke simultaneously of future apocalyptic and of realized eschatology, of the *basileia* of God and of his Christ yet to be established and of the universal claim to authority of the *Christus praesens* (cf. Jn 3:13; 16:33). When we compare the vivid representation of the "new Jerusalem" in Qumran[31] with John 14:2 on the one hand and Revelation 21 on the other, it is clear that we are dealing not with diametrically opposed but with related traditions.

2. The surprising affinity of the christological "I am" sayings in Revelation 1:17; 2:23; 21:6; 22:13, 16 to similar sayings in the Fourth Gospel has been noticed again and again. In both books the reader or listener is shown that the Johannine Christ operates in a unity of action with his heavenly Father and is indeed one with him (cf. Rev 21:6 with Rev 22:13 and Jn 10:30). Of course, behind the "I am" predications and John 10:30 stand Exodus 3:14 and Deuteronomy 6:4. But this also meant that the boundary for fellowship between the Jewish congregation and the Johannine school had been crossed. The identification of Jesus with the one God had to appear blasphemous to the Jewish contemporaries of the Johannine school. According to the Fourth Gospel, this identification was the decisive reason for the persecution and execution of Jesus by the Jewish authorities (cf. Jn 5:18; 10:33, 36; 19:7). It was also the cause for the expulsion of the pupils of Jesus (that is, the Johannine circle) from the synagogue (cf. Jn 9:22; 12:42; 16:2). Even this circle's appeal to the holy Scriptures (cf. Jn 5:39; 10:35) could no longer repair the breach. On the contrary, John's school utilized the OT and Jewish wisdom tradition in a consistently christological fashion. It not only saw the risen and returning Christ as the word of God in person but also confessed Christ to be the incarnate Logos par excellence, who is the Creator, Redeemer and Perfecter of the world all in one (cf. 1 Jn 1:1-4; Jn 1:1-18). According to John 14:6, apart from him and his teaching there is no valid relationship with God. The title *Logos* and the statement of John 14:6 must therefore have been deeply offensive to the Jewish contemporaries of the school of John.

3. The christological boldness of the Johannine tradition is also seen in

---

[30]Avemarie, "Erwählung," p. 113.
[31]See the various Aramaic "New Jerusalem" texts: 1Q32; 2Q24; 4Q454-455; 5Q15; 11Q18.

the way in which John and his pupils thoroughly recast the Jesus tradition handed down to them in the "ideolect" of the Johannine circle. In Matthew 11:25-30 we receive some idea of how Jesus could have spoken about himself, his teaching and its reception within his most intimate circle of disciples, and it is no accident that these six verses are marked by wisdom tradition through and through (cf. Is 55:1-3; Sir 51:23-27). In the Fourth Gospel all the teaching of Jesus is cast in this sapiential style of language. Moreover, if we compare the Johannine tradition with the Synoptic and notice that the latter tradition is not only presented differently in John's Gospel but also partly corrected, then we must speak of a self-conscious reformulation and supplementation of the synoptic Jesus tradition by the Johannine circle. Inspired by the Paraclete, the school of John probed more deeply into the truth of the Jesus tradition than did the Synoptics (cf. Jn 14:25-26; 16:13). This school also had in part different and better historical data for its presentation than the Synoptics. But at the same time the Johannine circle developed considerable esoteric tendencies: Jesus' command to love one's enemies is no longer mentioned in the Johannine writings. The concrete questions of church ethics remain entirely in the background in the Johannine Epistles. Moreover, when it appears theologically necessary, John even rewrites the Synoptic story of Jesus. Examples include the free handling of the Lord's Supper tradition (cf. Jn 13:1-20 with Jn 6:51-58), the reports of the trials of Jesus before Annas and Pilate (Jn 18:12-40), the scenes of Jesus' bearing his cross without assistance (Jn 19:17) and the account of his perfect burial (Jn 19:38-42). In such cases, I do not think that it is enough simply to point to the "aspective" nature of John over against the Synoptics. We must learn to see that the Fourth Gospel cultivates a (typically Jewish) idealized type of memory concerning Jesus. The Johannine witness therefore needs to be consistently realigned with the Synoptics, the Pauline corpus and the OT, so that faith in Jesus Christ does not lose its historical roots or evaporate into an esoteric teaching about the true meaning of Christ.

THE CANON AND THE CENTER OF THE SCRIPTURES

We cannot enter here into the complex problems of the canonization of the Scriptures. It is necessary only to stress that the decision of the ancient church not to see the NT writings as a replacement for the holy Scriptures but to canonize them along with the Septuagint was completely appropriate to the gospel of Christ.[32] The Christian Bible consists not of the NT alone but of Old and New Testaments. The NT witness may be detached from that of the Old only at the risk of its falsification.

The ancient church understood its cherished *kanōn tēs pisteōs* or *regula fidei* to be grounded in the two-part Bible, and with good reason. The OT witness concerning the reality and activity of the one God is taken up in the NT and made more precise christologically. The one God is the Father of Jesus Christ, and Jesus the Christ is the Son of the living God, who will serve as the representative of God's *basileia* until he establishes it completely through his parousia and the world judgment entrusted to him. At the center of the Christian Bible stands the person of the living Christ as the Son of God.

But corresponding to his person there has also always been from the very beginning a particular "form of teaching" (Rom 6:17 NRSV) which was and is authoritative for the faith of the church. Indeed, because from the early days of the Jerusalem church onwards the apostles not only preached the gospel publicly but also gave religious instruction, the apostolic letters preserve for us a whole series of teaching formulas. These formulas make it possible to recognize the central teaching of the NT. For example, if one considers the ecumenical roots of the Pauline gospel (see above), then there are good grounds for seeing the old Jerusalem "gospel" that Paul cites in 1 Corinthians 15:3b-5 as the crystallization point for the central biblical teaching about salvation. If we orient ourselves from this text to the rest of the Pauline letters, as well as to 1 Peter, Hebrews, the Synoptics and the Johannine writings, we can summarize the central teaching of the Christian Bible as follows: *The one God, who created the world and chose Israel to be his own people, has provided once for all for the end-time salvation of Jews and Gentiles and for the welfare of the world through the mission, work and vicarious, atoning death and exaltation of his only begotten Son, Jesus the Messiah. A share in this divine work of salvation is kept for all who believe in Jesus Christ and find themselves enlisted by him in the service of righteousness, which is God's will.*

The special capacity of biblical theology is that it not only can support these statements from the Scriptures but also can comprehend their con-

---

[32]Martin Hengel (in cooperation with Roland Deines), "Die Septuaginta als 'christliche Schriftensammlung,' ihre Vorgeschichte und das Problem ihres Kanons," in *Die Septuaginta zwischen Judentum und Christentum*, ed. Martin Hengel and Anna Maria Schwemer, WUNT 72 (Tübingen: Mohr Siebeck, 1994), pp. 182-284; ET *The Septuagint as Christian Scripture: Its Prehistory and the Problem of Its Canon* (Edinburgh: T & T Clark, forthcoming).

tents. It can do this all the better, the more carefully it follows the basic rules of historical criticism and tries with these rules to do justice to the Bible's special character. The texts of the Holy Scriptures are best interpreted as they themselves ask to be interpreted,[33] namely, with humble respect for their statements, with historical sensitivity and, moreover, with an appreciation for the ecclesiastical tradition of faith which is based on these texts. Material criticism of the content of Scripture is possible, but it is appropriate only when the truth of the gospel is at stake and when statements of Scripture contradict one another so fundamentally that the clarity of the gospel is called into question.

LIMITS AND OPPOSITION

To a report of personal experience belongs not only the positive balance but also some indication of the limits and opposition encountered by biblical theology as I have practiced and will continue (Lord willing) to practice it. For the sake of biblical theology, I have had to distance myself from many exegetical judgments and prejudices, which I learned in my youth, because they were not well enough founded exegetically or historically.[34] Yet these very judgments, whether concerning the OT and the so-called background of the NT, Jesus and Christology, the Synoptic tradition and the writing of the Gospels, or Pauline and Johannine theology, are not only upheld but also staunchly defended by not a few exegetes today. These exegetes see no compelling reason and are also unprepared to leave the beaten paths and usual questions of a NT scholarship that stands only upon itself. They therefore ignore the Tübingen model of biblical theology or even oppose it vigorously. The novel perspectives and questions with which Gese has enriched Old and New Testament research attract no attention, and Hengel's outstanding exegetical and historical studies are dismissed or overlooked as too conservative. My own biblical-theological contributions, which build upon Hengel and Gese, encounter a strangely

---

[33]Hartmut Gese, "Hermeneutische Grundsätze der Exegese biblischer Texte," in *Alttestamentliche Studien* (Tübingen: Mohr Siebeck, 1991), p. 249: "A text is to be so understood as it desires to be understood, i.e., as it understands itself."

[34]Hengel summarizes the current situation correctly: "By now the historical foundations of Bultmann's picture of primitive Christianity which led to his radical verdicts . . . have collapsed. The sharp opposition between 'Palestinian' und 'Hellenistic' community cannot be maintained any more than the complete splintering of the tradition, as if there had been neither eye-witnesses nor real memory, and the fundamental anonymity of the tradition and writing of the Gospels." *The Four Gospels and the One Gospel of Jesus Christ* (London: SCM Press, 2000), p. 294 n. 570.

stereotypical criticism.[35] It begins with the curious charge that Gese and I refuse to give the OT as such enough weight over against the NT tradition.[36] It then continues—in quite the opposite direction—with the reproach that if one takes the OT as strongly into account as I do in my biblical theology, then the theological *proprium* of the NT is obscured or even eliminated. The criticism guards itself with unusual bitterness against the view that we can know historically how Jesus himself understood his death and how the apostles, dependent upon Jesus, interpreted this death in terms of atonement theology. It objects to the apocalyptic interpretation of the Pauline concept of mission and doctrine of justification. Finally, the criticism climaxes in the accusation of an inadmissible harmonizing of the biblical traditions and of a typically evangelical avoidance of radical historical and material criticism.

However, what I find even more painful than this academic opposition to my biblical theology is the fact that it also encounters skepticism and rejection by many in the Lutheran church to which I belong. To be sure, there is a sizable minority that gladly and earnestly orients itself to the Bible, including bishops whom I count as my personal friends. But the general impression is a different one: the Lutheran church in my country today is interested in the word of Scripture only in certain exceptional cases. In the course of its history in the nineteenth and twentieth centuries, this church distanced itself so far from the original sense of the biblical traditions and opened itself up so thoroughly to the pluralism of an inclusive church of all and for all, that it no longer has any spiritual power left for a reorientation back to the Bible.

Even though it deeply damages the missionary credibility of the church, all the important themes of faith and of Christian ethics are watered down until two mutually opposed things are held to be true at once. Jesus was the preexistent son of God, was born of the virgin Mary and claimed to be the Messiah, and yet he certainly was not. He went to the cross on a mission from God for the sins of the many, and yet his own understanding of his death remains historically in the dark. Jesus rose from the dead on the third day and was exalted to the right hand of God, and

---

[35]I have dealt in detail with this criticism in *Biblische Theologie des Neuen Testaments*, Band 2, *Von der Paulusschule bis zur Johannesoffenbarung* (Göttingen: Vandenhoeck & Ruprecht, 1999), pp. 336-49.

[36]Christopher R. Seitz repeated this criticism during the conference at Wheaton; see his essay in this volume, "Two Testaments and the Failure of One Tradition History."

yet the entire Easter tradition is only a projection of Christian faith. Christ is the Lord, Savior and Judge, whose message and ministry are necessary for the salvation of Jews and Gentiles, and yet there are considerable concessions to be made today regarding the sole claims of Christ, while the contemporary missionary witness to Christ among Jews and Gentiles must be conceived entirely differently from how it was in NT times. Christ is coming to judge the living and the dead, and yet he will no longer come after two thousand years of church history, and Christianity can do without the whole notion of a final judgment. Jesus and the apostles called the church to sanctification, and their commands are to be obeyed, and yet the ethical standards laid down in the NT are hardly specifically Christian and are so antiquated that today's church must learn to exercise tolerance toward all possible lifestyles and behaviors of Christians and non-Christians alike. Finally—bringing the whole dreadful state of affairs to a head and posing a grave danger to the Protestant church as a whole—the Holy Scripture is the only rule and guiding principle for faith, doctrine and the life of the church, and yet it is about time to free ourselves from this outmoded and authoritarian Scripture principle.

The Protestant church(es) in my country is (are) in the grips of a deep structural and identity crisis, and it is by no means clear how or indeed whether it can be overcome. With biblical-theological argumentation alone one can no longer combat this crisis. It can only be conquered by a God-sent spiritual turnaround to the truth of the gospel by which the church stands or falls. We can and should ask God to make such a turnaround possible, but we will not be able to bring it about by academic means.

What remains? I summarize my experience with biblical theology in the words of Peter, in his answer to Jesus' question as to whether he and the rest of the twelve wished to leave Jesus: "Lord, to whom shall we go? You have the words of eternal life; and we have believed, and have come to know, that you are the Holy One of God" (Jn 6:68-69). Throughout all these years it has been an unparalleled encouragement that I never stood alone in this experience in the circle of my students, friends and faculty colleagues in NT in Tübingen. And so I dare to say: In its great moments it was and is granted to biblical theology to encounter the living word of God in and through the Holy Scriptures. In my opinion, therefore, biblical theology is a rewarding activity, and it should not hesitate to make the most of its opportunities in the years to come.

PART THREE

THE UNITY OF
THE BIBLE

*The Challenge
of Biblical Theology*

13

Two Testaments and the Failure of One Tradition History

Christopher R. Seitz

In an essay prepared for a volume on biblical theology,[1] I examined the tradition-historical method of Gerhard von Rad, especially his attempt to extend this modern approach into the realm of typological exegesis and biblical theology. I argued that von Rad's approach was flawed. Three matters seemed insufficiently addressed. First, in what sense could his approach depend on the historicality that it was the purpose of modern critical approaches to commend, when the traditioning process he was identifying and valorizing as theologically significant was manifestly misdrawing the historical legacy bequeathed to it? In the name of extruding what von Rad called the *doxa* of the tradition's sense of the events, the events were "manifestly misdrawn." The historical fundament was what von Rad sought to uncover, under the rubric of "Israel's own statements about YHWH," as that which constituted the crude matter, or "basic stuff," of a genuinely theological inquiry into Israel's testimony in the OT. And yet the traditioning process both carried forward and vetoed this historical legacy at the same time.[2]

---

[1]Christopher R. Seitz, "The Historical-Critical Endeavor as Theology: The Legacy of Gerhard von Rad," in *Word Without End* (Grand Rapids, Mich.: Eerdmans, 1998), pp. 28-40.
[2]Ibid., pp. 34-38.

Second, had von Rad not isolated a tradition history or streams of tradition that, in the nature of the thing, were to be differentiated from the final form of the theological witness of the canon and that existed in forms nowhere on offer for a NT reflection said to be about the business of continuing the OT's tradition process? Does the NT kerygma find its orientation vis-à-vis tradition history (say, in its most contemporaneous phase) or vis-à-vis a stable textualized Scripture? To put it another way, if the tradition history of the OT identified by von Rad ran so straightforwardly into the NT kerygma, with which it was to be likened in an evolutionary process model, why were there two Testaments and not a continuous tradition history in literary form, with a certain theological self-evidence to be acknowledged by all, concerning its necessary direction toward Christian confession?

Third was the restlessness of the traditioning process not a Christian back projection? After all, certain obvious arrangements of the literature of the canon pointed not to a driving forward of restless traditions but to an opposite tendency: the establishment of the past (especially Sinai) as foundational and stable and constitutive. One thinks above all of the relationship between Law and Prophets as the major theological categories of the present Tanak. The Torah is not seeking some fulfillment beyond itself. If anything, it contains its own seconding and dynamic voice, in the book of Deuteronomy, and this witness looks backward and forward at once, with no restlessness or eschatological pressure for completion by later traditions.

Von Rad's approach to theologizing a reconstructed tradition history belongs, of course, within its own tradition history of twentieth-century biblical scholarship. In this essay, I want to examine the tradition-historical efforts to do biblical theology represented by Hartmut Gese and Peter Stuhlmacher, as these pick up where von Rad has left off.[3] They have put their special signatures on the methodology of tradition history and biblical theology. The indebtedness of Stuhlmacher to von Rad is made especially clear in volume 2 of his biblical theology.[4]

The second part of the essay examines the problem of introducing a con-

---

[3]Hartmut Gese, "Tradition and Biblical Theology," in *Tradition and Theology in the Old Testament*, ed. Douglas A. Knight (London: SPCK, 1977), pp. 301-26; Peter Stulmacher, *Historical Criticism and Theological Interpretation of Scripture: Toward a Hermeneutics of Consent* (Philadelphia: Fortress, 1977), and *Biblische Theologie des Neuen Testament*, Band 2, *Von der Paulusschule bis zur Johannesoffenbarung* (Göttingen: Vandenhoeck & Ruprecht, 1999).

[4]See the discussion of Brevard S. Childs and Gerhard von Rad in Stuhlmacher, *Biblische Theologie*, pp. 342-45.

cept like tradition history to link the Testaments theologically, when, on material grounds, the NT does not relate itself to traditions but to a stable canon. My objection to von Rad's approach was largely substantive in character (having to do with the relationship among history, tradition and the final form of the canonical OT witness). My analysis of Gese and Stuhlmacher focuses more on material objections, stemming from their attenuated conception of the OT canon (a conception not shared by von Rad). Especially in Stuhlmacher's 1972 study, one gets the sense that critical study of the Bible is inaugurated and finds its essential endorsement in the NT itself, with its critical handling of the OT traditions. But I will argue that Stuhlmacher has confused the way the OT functions authoritatively in the formation of the NT and that this confusion is based in part on a faulty understanding of the material form of the canon. The consequence of this confusion is that modern critical approaches to the Bible at large are conflated with very different approaches, involving the appropriation of the OT as canonical Scripture in the NT.

The third section of the essay puts forth an alternative understanding of the authority of the Scriptures of Israel, as Christian Scripture, within the NT and then in subsequent postscriptural use. The hope is that an alternative model to the tradition-historical emerges that better reflects the state of affairs in the earliest Christian usage and that can be safely differentiated from virtually all modern critical treatments, even those that claim to be an improvement because of a special piety (hermeneutics of consent) or a special deployment of so-called Reformation principles (justification by faith and the like).[5]

TRADITION HISTORY: HARTMUT GESE'S APPROACH

"Revelation comes in the form of truth experienced in Israel's life processes" ("Tradition," p. 310). By this, Gese means approximately what von Rad meant when he sought to isolate "Israel's own explicit assertions about Jahweh." The final literary form of biblical books, the internal canonical arrangements and ordering of diverse traditions into a final literary statement, or similar arrangements of books and larger divisions in the canon are essentially meaningless theologically. Gese speaks of the "lived life" of Israel's tradition process as "immeasurably diverse and even seemingly contradictory" (p. 310). The end form of the biblical text is without meaning on a tra-

---

[5]See above all Stuhlmacher's discussion, "Historical Criticism and the Protestant Principle," in *Historical Criticism*, pp. 63-75.

dition-historical understanding, except as an organic, vibrant depository of diverse and "even contradictory" traditions once the process stopped—which it did not do because traditioning cannot stop; traditions continue to "speak over the head" of any final literary statement. What is important is therefore the beginning of the process and the process, this latter emphasis being what differentiates a mature tradition-historical approach from nineteenth-century historicism. "The biblical text thus begins in the life process of Israel. And only the tradition-historical approach can constitute the method for tracing this dimension of a text back into the lived life of Israel" (p. 310). The proximity to the concerns of von Rad should be obvious here.[6]

Why does traditioning take place? Because past statements are meant to be seen, retrospectively, as providing a "point of orientation for present-understanding" (p. 312). Here we have the dynamic dimension of von Rad, and the priority of the process over the original *credenda* as static and authoritative, because self-understanding is always in flux. The "actualization of the text . . . opens it up to a totally new theological perception" (p. 313). The earlier statements have not been suppressed, or else we would struggle to valorize the modifications and transformations and contradictory adaptations of them, not knowing the earlier traditions against which they speak. No, according to tradition history, the entire history of development is there, and what it bears witness to is endless pressure to change and adapt.

It is an empirical fact that the OT is more than growing traditions and endless refabrication, or else it would forever resist literary fixation in deference to movement and change and life processes. We would have no container holding the diversity we seek to valorize, with a fixed form and a delimited scope, if diversity and growth were ends unto themselves.

It is at this point critical to emphasize the necessary direction Gese's approach will take in respect of the canon. After he sets out his tradition-historical conception and traces the processes of growth and adaptation, he concludes with a discussion of the canon. One could well ask, why is there any final, stable form to the OT? Why indeed can we speak of a threefold (or fourfold) canon of the OT literature in the basic sense of the word, if it bears witness to an ongoing process of tradition extending into the NT without interruption? The answer Gese gives is that there is no such stable

---

[6]See Gerhard von Rad, *Old Testament Theology*, 2 vols. (Louisville, Ky.: Westminster John Knox, 2001), 1:105.

form. The canon is open. The end is not closed. The NT relates to traditions in motion, not to a closed canonical literature with a given form. There is no given form that "speaks over the head" of intertestamental traditions, and so there is also no given form within the law and prophets that "speaks over the head" of a reconstructed tradition history of "explicit statements about YHWH" extracted from the canon's form.

It should be emphasized that the movement to a discussion of the canon is critical to Gese's treatment in a way that goes beyond von Rad's approach. (Stuhlmacher quotes Trebolle Barrera in defense of von Rad vis-à-vis Brevard Childs, but it is genuinely unclear to me if von Rad would have lined up with Childs on the question of the material form of the canon or with Barrera; it is striking that von Rad's tradition-historical method did not depend on a wider or open canon for its logic in coordination with the NT kerygma).[7] Gese asserts that the NT is "familiar only with the law and the prophets" (p. 321) as canonical literature, "a third part of the canon was in the process of being formed in the period of the New Testament" (p. 321), and "without Sirach 24 logos-Christology is cut off from older wisdom theology" (p. 325). This is because for Gese, "we can really speak of only one single tradition process at the end and goal of which the New Testament appears" (p. 322). To state it differently, for Gese, the NT ushers in a critical period when the limits of the OT canon are under negotiation. As such, one could not speak about a stable Scripture speaking a word over the tradition process, not even in the case of parts one and two (Law and Prophets).[8] Christian tradition handles the traditions of the OT in a critical manner, and the open canon is the warrant for its approach to the evaluation of Scripture's word. So, it is appropriate to adapt our title in radical ways if we wish to appreciate Gese's approach: "One Tradition History and the Failure of Two Testaments."

In Stuhlmacher's 1972 treatment, this larger picture of Gese (and, less so, von Rad) appears to be in place without comment. "In the same measure as Jesus' appearances and behavior were violently disputed in his lifetime," Stuhlmacher writes, "he unfailingly leads his disciples into a process of crit-

---

[7]J. Trebolle Barrera, *The Jewish Bible and the Christian Bible* (Leiden: E. J. Brill; Grand Rapids, Mich.: Eerdmans, 1998).

[8]Stephen B. Chapman, *The Law and the Prophets: A Study in Old Testament Canon Formation*, FAT 27 (Tübingen: Mohr Siebeck, 2000). Chapman conceives of a process of mutual development and reciprocity, which rules out a simple "law then prophets" formation of the canon. In this he develops, inter alia, the suggestions of Ronald E. Clements and others.

ical Scripture exposition" (p. 23). The "beginning of critical exposition,"
Stuhlmacher states, has to do with the existence of an OT needing to be
sorted out and critically evaluated. Far from speaking a direct word as
Christian Scripture, through its per se voice, we must look to Jesus and the
NT for interpretative moves over against the inherited traditions that "in
essence determine the origin, formulation and unfolding of the gospel of
Jesus as the Christ of God" (p. 22). Stuhlmacher points to the antitheses of
the Sermon on the Mount as evidence of Jesus as "Messianic interpreter"
and in this critical mode a harbinger of "a process of critical Scripture exposition . . . which has not ceased to this day and may not be interrupted as
long as the churches are oriented to Scripture so as to preserve their identity" (p. 23). This identity-preserving function of Scripture is congruent with
Gese's tradition-historical conceptuality but in Stuhlmacher finds further
support in what he calls the "Protestant principle." Quoting Ernst
Käsemann, "Historical criticism promises and guarantees proximity to reality" and "theologically, the right of historical criticism lies in its breaking
through the Docetism which dominates the community" (p. 64). This use of
the term *docetism* is a bold transfer of a conceptuality regarding the earthly
and human character of Jesus, over against claims for his divinity, into the
realm of historical research and claims for positivity in a history made prox-
imate by a method that gets below the traditions to "reality."[9]

This essay's purpose is not to analyze the appeal to a "Protestant principle," either along the lines of Käsemann or of the "justification by faith" ra-
tionality of Rudolf Bultmann or Kurt Ebeling, except to say that, its
rhetorical force notwithstanding, the imprecision regarding docetism is telling. This begs the question, for example, of whether appeal to the canonical
portrait of Jesus is any more or less an appeal to reality than a historically
recovered real Jesus. It is by no means clear how historical-critical retrieval
of reality or of traditions brokering such a reality can be valorized over
against the canonical portrayal, on theological or pneumatological grounds.
More confusing still is how Jesus and the NT can be appealed to for a justification of the historical-critical endeavor (even undertaken with proper respect) based on (1) the role of the OT in the formation of Christian kerygma

---

[9]A particularly insightful essay on this topic was read at the 2000 SEAD conference by Kath-
ryn Greene-McCreight, "The Hermeneutics of Suspicion and a Doctrine of Scripture." She
was responding to an exchange between me and Richard Hays and others at an annual SBL
meeting, where we discussed a "hermeneutics of consent." My contribution appears in *Word
Without End*, pp. 41-50.

and (2) the eventual extension of the "critical exposition" to include the NT, whose plain sense is said to testify to its logic and necessity.

The material form of the Old Testament. I have argued that, for Gese's approach, there must be a close and significant linkage of tradition history as a theological process and considerations of the form of the canon. This linkage is not incidental for Gese. As he sees it (and Stuhlmacher follows him here), for tradition history to function as the bridge linking the witness of two Testaments, the intervening period of tradition processing must be given equal weighting, or else we would misunderstand and wrongly emphasize the role of the canon and the impact of the OT as Scripture, not tradition, in the formation of the NT. When Gese says the traditions are still expanding, he means the OT has no fixed form until Christians (or Jews) give it one. The OT's status as Scripture is a Christian bestowal.[10] Stuhlmacher makes the same point in his own way.[11]

With this larger conception and rationale in place, it is relatively easy to file objections to Gese's understanding of the material form of the canon.

Law and Prophets. For Gese and Stuhlmacher, this twofold and open designation serves the purpose of establishing a contrast with a threefold and closed designation, which the NT does not yet contemplate. The isolated phrase "Moses, the prophets, and the psalms" (Lk 24:44 NRSV [throughout the essay]) does not alter but confirms the inchoate and unfinished character of part three. This is Gese's first main point.

The objections to this view can be quickly rehearsed.

1. The designation *writings (ketubim)* is a subsequent refinement of non-Mosaic books, and so says nothing about the extent of the canon at the time of the NT. David (Psalms) is prophetic, as are Solomon (Proverbs) and Daniel.[12]

---

[10]Brevard S. Childs, *Biblical Theology of the Old and New Testaments: Theological Reflection on the Christian Bible* (Minneapolis: Fortress, 1992), p. 65, sees the implications of this clearly when he writes, "If the New Testament used such freedom in respect to its Jewish heritage, does not the Christian church have a similar right to develop its own form of Scripture in a manner different from that of the synagogue?" To this, Stuhlmacher, *Biblische Theologie*, p. 343, responds accordingly, "Angesichts der enormen Bedeutung der Septuaginta für das neutestamentliche Christuszeugnis muss der Neutestamentler kanongeschichtlich anders urteilen als Childs und von *einem* veilschichtigen kanonischen Traditionsprozess denken, *dem die Hebräische Bibel einerseits und der zweiteilige christliche Kanon andererseits entstammen*" (this last emphasis added).

[11]Stuhlmacher, *Biblische Theologie*, p. 343.

[12]Childs, *Biblical Theology*, p. 56, summarizes the conclusion of T. Swanson as follows: "the third section of the Hebrew canon, the Writings, may have been a secondary canonical subdivision which was effected long after the scope of the non-Mosaic books had been fixed within the comprehensive category of the 'Prophets.'" See T. Swanson, "The Clos-

2. Negatively, no book outside the traditional Hebrew canon (what Origen and others refer to as "the twenty-two") is cited as Scripture in the NT (which points to the very issue at stake, Sirach functioning on a different level, in the nature of the thing, than, e.g., Proverbs or Ruth or Chronicles [from "the writings"] in the NT's world of reference).[13]

3. R. Beckwith has argued that the reference to slain prophets ("Abel to Zechariah") in Luke 11:51 presupposes an order Genesis to 2 Chronicles, or one not unlike the tripartite and closed canon of the later Masoretic Text.[14]

4. Stuhlmacher speaks of the NT's quoting from Torah, Prophets and Psalms, and he gives the figures for this.[15] Yet other books from the *ketubim* are obviously presupposed in the NT, including Ruth, Chronicles, Proverbs and Song of Songs.[16] This makes his use of "psalms" as a single referent misleading (as if Luke 24:44, following Sirach, knows of a truncated and open third section of a threefold canon). Moreover, it is

---

ing of the Collection of Holy Scripture: A Study in the History of the Canonization of the Old Testament" (Ph.D. dissertation, Vanderbilt University; Ann Arbor, Mich.: University Microfilms, 1970). See also the discussions of Roger T. Beckwith, *The Old Testament Canon of the New Testament Church and Its Background in Early Judaism* (Grand Rapids, Mich.: Eerdmans, 1985), and J. Barton, *Oracles of God* (London: Darton, Longman & Todd, 1986).

[13]Note the extreme difference in formulation between Childs and Stuhlmacher. The latter, *Biblische Theologie*, p. 293, states that the NT and church fathers do not shy from quoting Apocryphal and Pseudepigraphic writings from the LXX, and he gives as evidence James 1:19 ("quoting" Sir 5:11) and Mark 10:19 ("quoting" Sir 4:1). Childs, *Biblical Theology*, p. 62, states, "The early controversies with the Jews reflected in the New Testament turned on the proper interpretation of the sacred Scriptures (*hē graphē*) which Christians assumed in common with the synagogue. Although there is evidence that other books were known and used, it is a striking fact that the NT does not *cite as Scripture* any book of the Apocrypha or Pseudepigrapha. (The reference to Enoch in Jude 14-15 is not an exception.) The use of the OT by 1 Clement and by Justin Martyr is further confirmation of the assumption of a common Scripture between the synagogue and the church, even if in fact a slight variation had begun to appear."

[14]Beckwith, *The Old Testament Canon*, pp. 212-22. Qumran (4Q MMT) likewise witnesses a reference to the canon that begins with Moses and ends with "the words of the days" (Chronicles). See the discussion of E. Qimron and J. Strugnell, "An Unpublished Halachic Letter from Qumran," *IEJ* 4 (spring 1985): 9-12.

[15]Stuhlmacher, *Biblishce Theologie*, p. 293: Eighty citations from Torah, eighty from the Prophets, and fifty-five from Psalms; he quickly adds that this cannot mean that the NT (as with Qumran) is unaware of other books. This latter reservation is fine as far as it goes, but it lacks genuine evaluation and, moreover, the general sense of this is not lost on Childs (see n. 13 above).

[16]See Markus Bockmuehl, "'The Form of God' (Phil 2:6) and Variations on a Theme of Jewish Mysticism," *JTS* 48 (1997): 22: "The typlogical interpretation of the Song of Songs appears to go back at least to the first century, as the rabbinic and early Patristic evidence suggests; it may also be attested in what has been tenuously identified as a commentary at Qumran (4Q240, still unpublished). NT hints at such an interpretation include Revelation 3:20 and perhaps 19:7 about the marriage of the lamb (cf. Cant. 5.2; see also John 7:38 with Cant. 4.15)."

false to say that Sirach is quoted in Mark and James (which it is not), and then represent the "writings" by the rubric "psalms" only. The effort to make Sirach and the *ketubim* equivalent is demanded by his and Gese's conception of tradition history, but it lacks confirmation in the NT's literal sense. An argument that places subtle allusion to the Apocrypha on an equal footing with massive and highly intentional citation of the OT as Scripture lacks proper proportion.

GESE'S SECOND MAIN POINT

The OT of the NT's traditioning process is a wider Greek canon, including books indispensable (Sirach) for NT confession. The correlate of an open canon is the longer non-Hebrew list of books, if not also the priority of the "Septuagint" for a genuinely Christian biblical theology.

The objections to this view can again be simply listed.

1. The NT cites OT passages from various languages, presumed orders and listings; there is no single Septuagint to be contrasted with a single Hebrew exemplar, which is given priority in the NT on grounds of anything but convention and/or accommodation, as well as for reasons of specific, local theological argument.[17]

2. This finding also rules out a language-to-scope argument, as though the NT's use of Greek renderings of an original Hebrew said anything definitive about the scope of the canon as wider or open or fuller in terms of available traditions (e.g., Sirach's indispensability for Christology).

3. Richard Bauckham and others have demonstrated the NT's use of Hebrew text types alongside Greek text types, the implication being that some early Christian communities were bilingual and used available text types for reasons having nothing to do with recourse (or not) to a sole, favored tradition.[18]

4. E. Ellis has shown that lists of OT books in the early church tend toward

---

[17]See Richard Bauckham's essay on Acts 15 in *The Book of Acts in Its Palestinian Setting* (Grand Rapids, Mich.: Eerdmans, 1995).

[18]Bauckham, "James and the Jerusalem Church," *Book of Acts*, pp. 452-62; Ben Witherington III, *The Acts of the Apostles: A Socio-Rhetorical Commentary* (Grand Rapids, Mich.: Eerdmans, 1998), pp. 457-58; Richard Bauckham, "Jude's Exegesis," in *Jude and the Relatives of Jesus in the Early Church* (Edinburgh: T & T Clark, 1990), pp. 225-33. Stuhlmacher also sees this issue but draws different conclusions from it. The NT authors had no closed list. They relate instead to a "kanonisch noch unabgeschlossene Sammlung des Heiligen Schriften in hebraischer und griechischer Sprache" (*Biblische Theologie*, p. 292).

conservatism, even when non-Hebrew OT books are cited in the respective source's exegesis.[19]

5. Ellis has also shown that the lists frustrate any simple parent-to-off-
spring logic; namely, there were not two choices vying for ascendancy,
one threefold and proto-Masoretic, one fourfold and septuagintal.[20]
The orderings are too varied and demonstrate the lack of major theological significance assigned either to a "wider Greek" or "narrower
Hebrew" option, in respect of internal order *grosso modo*.

6. F. M. Cross and others have shown, with the aid of the Dead Sea discov-
eries, early pressure toward constraining textual pluraformity in the direction of the proto-Masoretic Hebrew text type. The later decision of
Jerome (*pace* Augustine) to defend the Hebrew textual tradition over
the traditional Greek ecclesial usage, in matters of establishing the
church's Scripture, has its precedent in the *kaige* and proto-Lucian
Greek recensions.[21]

7. Stuhlmacher speaks of Childs's attenuated treatment of Qumran and
the history of the Septuagint as damaging his canonical approach.[22]
Yet Ellis makes important note of an unpublished Qumran text that
refers to "the book of Moses [and in the words of the pro]phets and

---

[19]E. Earle Ellis, *The Old Testament in the Early Church*, WUNT 54 (Tübingen: Mohr Siebeck, 1991), pp. 10-36. Melito's list represents the canon of the OT on terms consistent with *Baba Bathra;* Epiphanius, Origen, Jerome, Augustine and Athanasius are also examined. When asked to list books, they clearly distinguish between canonical and others and give the conservative listing as constituting genuine, undisputed canonical authority.

[20]Ibid., pp. 3-36.

[21]F. M. Cross, "The Evolution of a Theory of Local Texts," in *Qumran and the History of the Biblical Text,* ed. F. M. Cross and S. Talmon (Cambridge, Mass.: Harvard University Press, 1975), pp. 306-20; Emanuel Tov, *Textual Criticism of the Hebrew Bible* (Minneapolis: Fortress, 1992), and "The History and Significance of a Standard Text of the Hebrew Bible," in *Hebrew Bible/ Old Testament: The History of Its Interpretation* 1, ed. M. Saebo (Göttingen: Vandenhoeck & Ruprecht, 1996), pp. 49-66. According to Tov, "History and Significance of a Standard Text," p. 57, "The earliest Qumran finds dating from the third pre-Christian century bear evidence, among other things, of a tradition of exact copying of texts belonging to the Masoretic family, that is, the proto-Masoretic texts." Tov, *Textual Criticism,* believes that 60 percent of all texts at Qumran are "proto-Masoretic" while only 5 percent are "pre-Samaritan" and "those approximating the LXX." So too Childs, *Biblical Theology,* p. 60, states, "The strongest evidence for a fixed Hebrew canon derives from the history of the stabilization of the Masoretic text. . . . The text of a book would not have been corrected and stabilized if the book had not already received some sort of canonical status." And Stuhlmacher, *Biblische Theologie,* p. 291, does concede that "recensional activity at Murabba'at (e.g., the 12 Minor Prophets Scroll) is only possible and logical if the Hebrew possessed some priority over the Greek."

[22]"Die Childs leitende Sicht der Kanongeschichte ist ein Konstruction, bei der weder den Textfunden von Qumran noch der Geschichte der Septuaginta gebuhrende Aufmerksamkeit geschenkt wird" (Stuhlmacher, *Biblische Theologie,* p. 343).

in Davi[d and in the words of the days . . .]"—this latter reference
being to Chronicles. Here is a finding confirming that of Beckwith in
his assessment of the "Abel to Zechariah" delimitation of Luke (Lk
11:51). Ellis likewise sees Philo and Josephus in agreement about a
"Holy Scriptures" distinguishable from "the ancestral philosophy"
of the Therapeutae (for Philo) or "writings not deemed worthy of
equal credit" (for Josephus).[23] The contrast with Stuhlmacher's evaluation is obvious.

In other words, the material form of the canon cannot support the
moves of Gese or Stuhlmacher in the direction of valorizing a single tradition history over a two-Testament form of Scripture as critical to its inner
logic, theologically. The Bible is not one continuous tradition history, like
a novel with a beginning, a middle and an end. Something stops, and a history of effects is set in motion that testifies to the form of the original canon
and the differentiation of traditions, of various sorts, from it.[24] Indeed, it
has been argued that Sirach is itself a witness to its subsidiary status, over
against "law and prophets and other books."

Childs and others have noted that the roots of this perspective, whereby
traditions appear to reckon with a formal literary authority to which they
give testimony, is found within the OT.[25] Zechariah speaks of the words of
former prophets "overtaking" generations after them, after their death; Ecclesiastes speaks of the testimony of Qoheleth as limiting the scope of pro-
verbial sentences and of correlating wisdom and law; Deuteronomy seeks
to correlate law and prophecy; and Malachi sets a limit to prophetic textual
authority beyond Zechariah.

Other understandings of the relationship between the Testaments and
a proper conception of the theological form of Christian Scripture can likewise be ruled out.

First, Christian Scripture is not a Christianizing of an original Hebrew
canon, by means of glosses, literary explanations, *vaticina ex eventu* and

---

[23]Ellis and Childs agree that Ben Sira and Qumran confirm rather than challenge Josephus,
Philo and *Baba Bathra*. The so-called Council of Jabneh belongs to the rubbish bin of the history of ideas.

[24]Even James Barr, *Old and New in Interpretation* (New York: Harper and Row, 1966), p. 156,
notes: "It is theologically meaningful that we do not pass without substantial temporal in-
terval from the main body of the Old Testament into the New. There is, on the contrary, a
time of ripening, as it were, in which the Old Testament is able to develop its effects historically within the life, history and thought of a historical people."

[25]See now the work of Chapman, *The Law and the Prophets*. Compare Gerald T. Sheppard, *Wisdom as a Hermeneutical Construct*, BZAW 151 (Berlin: Walter de Gruyter, 1980).

erasure of the original languages (Hebrew and Aramaic).[26] This would have amounted to the production of a single testamental deposit, declaring therewith (consistent with the logic of Barnabas and Justin) one book for one people, the Jews having forfeited any claims to copyright.

Neither is the relationship properly to be understood as between a single delimited Scripture ("inspired by God and useful for instruction"; "oracles of God entrusted to the Jews"; "Law and Prophets") with a title retained from the NT's conventional language, to which has been appended a secondary literary elaboration, in the form of haggadah, pesher, midrash, halakah and the like. Old is to New Testament not as Tanak is to Talmud. Instead, the concept of a literary canon, based upon a covenantal relationship, is extended to a secondary, literarily distinctive deposit whose formation and rationale are developed on analogy to the first, with a new covenantal relationship at its heart.[27] The Testaments are, of course, different, and they bear witness to the one subject matter of them both, in different ways. "Tanak to Talmud" may actually be more akin to what Gese means by "tradition history," strictly speaking. When Stuhlmacher reckons with two tradition-historical choices, one ending in Hebrew Bible and another in Christian Scripture, he fails to see how OT and Hebrew Bible were competing concepts from the very beginning in the early church's use of the Scriptures of the synagogue, "the oracles of God entrusted to the Jews." It remains meaningful that the terms "Old Testament" and "Tanak" are *both* postbiblical terms. Both require a commitment to a subsequent theological literature. Neither goes straightforwardly back to the Scriptures of Israel without argument and defense.[28]

Finally, the relationship is also not merely germ to full flower, as could be implied by a tradition-historical or "Jesus as first critical expositor" model of development (so Stuhlmacher in the 1972 essay). The first Testament is in the first instance a scriptural, authoritative witness and not a bundle of religious possibilities whose logic is not disclosed until an external agent is brought to bear on it. Here is my disagreement with Francis Watson's recent

---

[26]Justin's claim that the Jews had falsified the texts was proven wrong. Still, it would be a mistake to believe that his debate with Trypho was essentially hedged about by misinformation at a text-critical level. It is sufficient to conclude that Justin was wrong without concluding that he witnesses to a live theological debate over the status of the LXX for the early church over against the (proto-)Masoretic Hebrew tradition.

[27]See Seitz, *Word Without End*, pp. 49-50.

[28]See Seitz, *Pro Ecclesia* 5 (1996):292-303, reprinted in *Word Without End* as "Old Testament or Hebrew Bible?"

effort at christological reading.[29] Jesus sees the witness of the OT to God and to himself in clear terms, from within the per se voice of the Scriptures and not from the application of some external rationale or criteriology unknown or foreign to the witness. "If they do not hear Moses and the prophets, neither will they be convinced if one should rise from the dead" (Lk 16:31). Luke is saying more here about the sufficiency and perspicuity of God's word spoken to Israel than about the challenge of resuscitation.

Watson also wrongly interprets 1 Peter 1:10 as saying the prophets had not the vaguest notion about what they were speaking, christologically considered. In similar fashion, he reads Luke 24 as if Jesus is showing the OT to be about himself in ways that are foreign to its warp and woof. He has, to my mind, also misunderstood the debate at issue in Justin. Justin is not working with a Jewish Scripture and arguing for its genuine, though misperceived, christological correlatability. He is arguing that the Scriptures of Israel preach Christ in their plain sense and that because Judaism (constituted for the first time in this sense) does not see or acknowledge this truth, the church is now the true Israel and the only intended referent of the Scriptures' testimony to its only subject matter: God in Christ Jesus.

THE OLD TESTAMENT AS CHRISTIAN SCRIPTURE

The preceding section has established the main points of disagreement between the approach of Stuhlmacher and Gese and a canonical approach. I have written elsewhere in detail on the implications of a canonical approach for a Christian handling of the OT and will not cover all that ground here. My approach approximates that of Childs at many points, as the reviewers note. If anything, I have tried to underscore, perhaps more than Childs, the deference of the developing Christian kerygma to a scriptural (OT) witness it assumes will continue to sound forth alongside it as the NT writings develop and take their own canonical form. I have rejected the position of H. Hübner[30] (the OT *in Novo receptum*) in favor of an approach that has Christian confession, especially in the realm of eschatology, returning to the OT to learn from its plain sense voice (so, e.g., 1 Cor

---

[29]Francis Watson, "Christological Interpretation of Texts and Trinitarian Claims to Truth" and "The Old Testament as Christian Scripture: A Response to Professor Seitz," *SJT* 52 (1999): 209-32.

[30]H. Hübner, "Vetus Testamentum und Vetus Testamentum in Novo receptum: Die Frage nach dem Kanon des Alten Testaments aus neutestamentlicher Sicht," *Jahrbuch für biblische Theologie* 3 (1988): 147-62.

15; Rom 9—11). Also, in the realm of ethics, I have argued that the decision of Acts 15 is rooted in a subtle handling of the plain sense of Leviticus and Amos (in its Greek and Hebrew text forms), whereby the law of Moses has a perlocutionary force for Gentiles, who find themselves in the "midst of the house of Israel," and for Jews who confess Christ.[31]

It is striking, and worthy of our present reflection, how such a radically different view of the evidence for a stable OT canon is presented in the tradition-historical conception of Gese and Stuhlmacher. It is as though scholars are working with an entirely different set of governing assumptions, which would in turn require confirmation of what would have to be completely different data. Or is it the case that the governing assumptions are themselves preempting a clear look at the relevant evidence? What would the explanation for that be?

One strong possibility is that a theological form of modalism has created a set of false choices for assessing the data regarding the material form of the canon; that is, a predilection for a certain understanding of the theological normativity of the Jesus kerygma, over against all other God talk (even if rooted in the Scriptures of Israel), has forced the conclusion that it is not possible to talk about God in any normative or abiding sense without immediate correction and correlation with talk about Jesus or Jesus' own (distinctive, different, unprecedented) talk about God. This latter talk must be regarded, in the nature of the thing, as different from what the canonical OT brokers in its given form as Scripture.

Stuhlmacher sees to the heart of the issue when he quotes disapprovingly from Childs on the problem with a tradition-historical approach, as follows, "The Old Testament has become a horizontal stream of tradition from the past whose witness has been limited to its effect on subsequent writers. The OT has thus lost its vertical, existential dimension which as scripture of the church continues to bear its own witness within the context of the Christian Bible."[32] Stuhlmacher finds this assessment from Childs of himself and Gese "very disconcerting" ("hochst befremdlich") but he fails to show how it is a misjudgment on theological grounds of the tradition-historical approach. To say, as he does, that Gese sought to uncover genuine revelation through tradition-historical inquiry does not alter the objection that what Gese found was something other than the

---

[31]I follow here the treatment of Bauckham, *Book of Acts.*
[32]The quote (in Stuhlmacher, *Biblische Theologie,* p. 344) is taken from Childs's *Biblical Theology,* p. 77.

theological witness of the OT in its form as Scripture, a form everywhere presupposed by the NT. To call this historically retrieved tradition process "revelatory" begs an entire range of questions as to what is meant by revelation in the first instance (Hans Frei's *The Eclipse of Biblical Narrative* is not cited by Stuhlmacher, and he seems largely unaffected by its thesis). Stuhlmacher appears to object to a portrayal of the OT having a voice only when, as he puts it, it is "baptized" by the New, but the question remains: just how does that per se voice function for him in any normative Christian theological—indeed trinitarian—sense?

To conclude, let me suggest several ways in which the OT's per se voice functions normatively for Christian theological construction.

First of all, let us consider the antitheses of the Sermon on the Mount, where Stuhlmacher finds a critical instinct whose legacy survives, as he has it, in proper deployments of historical criticism by the Christian community, following Jesus' lead.

It is made clear in Matthew 19:4 and Matthew 22:29 that Jesus accepts the OT as a divine word and not as human traditions. In the Sermon on the Mount, Jesus is contrasting his manner of teaching the OT and the teaching of the OT as received ("you have heard that it was said" is not a typical way of quoting Scripture as such). "Jesus never understands Scripture," Ellis notes, "as words of the Bible in the abstract but as the message in its true meaning and application."[33] We see the same distinction at work in Mark 7:13, "thus making void the word of God through your tradition that you have handed on." What is at stake in Mark 7 and the Sermon on the Mount is the effort to perceive in God's word a general principle and then extrapolate this into the area of washing pots or Corban. A high view of the authority of Scripture declares such logic vain and self-justifying, in distinction to true Torah obedience.

This point is further clarified in the antithesis concerning hating one's enemy—a text not found in Leviticus, though its supposed antithesis ("you shall love your neighbor as yourself") is. An interpretation of the Bible in support of hating one's neighbor has been found at Qumran (1QS 1:3-4), thus showing the actual logic of the antithesis teaching of Jesus.

And finally, the canonical shape of the Sermon emphasizes the authority of the law and prophets for Jesus in such a way as to constrain the reader against drawing false conclusions about his teaching authority ("Do not

---

[33]Ellis, *The Old Testament in the Early Church*, p. 128.

think that I have come to abolish the law or the prophets," Mt 5:17).

In sum, the Christian judgment to hear the Decalogue as Christian moral teaching, from the per se witness of the OT, is grounded in a decision about the authority of God's word to Israel and the confirmation of that perspective within the NT's plain-sense portrayal. To put it another way, it is Jesus' acceptance of the authority of the OT that guides the church, not his declaration of its authority in the name of creating a new Christian tradition theretofore without warrant.

A second example: In Romans 9—11, Paul constructs an elaborate theological program involving God's work in Israel, in Christ and in the church, using images of natural and unnatural branches. One could have imagined the narrative logic of Romans moving from creation, to justification, to sanctification, to the new law for Christian life. The only explanation for such a detailed treatment of the eschatological tableau necessitated by the rejection by Jews of Christ in Romans 9—11 is the plain-sense voice of the OT, in which irrevocable promises to Israel were made. That is, Christian teaching about the relationship between the church and an emerging Judaism does not take its bearings from christological teaching or from a developing tradition beyond the plain sense of the OT. Rather, Paul returns to the OT to hear its theocentric and irrevocable word as interpreting the kerygma in Christ. The OT as Scripture guides the church's Christian confession in ways that cannot be adequately captured in a tradition-historical approach.

So too Adolf von Harnack helpfully showed the way the OT first functioned as the sole Christian Scripture, as a venerable and privileged possession used by Christians against paganism, nationalism, idolatry and mythologies of various sorts.[34] It took time for a rival testament to gain anything like the same stature and high purpose for Christian apologetic and defense. Hans Von Campenhausen's much-quoted dictum is consistent with this perspective.[35] The problem for the early church was not what to do with the OT. Rather, in the light of a Scripture whose authority and privileged status were everywhere acknowledged, what was one to make of a crucified messiah and a parting of the ways? It is this dimen-

---

[34] Adolf von Harnack, *Die Mission und Ausbreitung des Christentums: in den ersten drei Jahrhunderten* (Leipzig: J. C. Hinrichs, 1902).
[35] See the discussion in Hans Von Campenhausen, *The Formation of the Christian Bible* (Philadelphia: Fortress, 1972) and in Seitz, "In Accordance with the Scriptures: Creed, Scripture and 'Historical Jesus,'" in *Word Without End,* chap. 5, pp. 51-60.

sion of early Christian use of the OT that is attenuated in tradition-historical approaches of the Gese-Stuhlmacher variety. At stake is nothing less than an adequate Christian doctrine of God. In the early church the struggle was not so much with a low Christology of adoptionist stripes (which might be gleaned from a NT read apart from the Old) as with a high doctrine of God everywhere assumed, either on account of the witness of the OT to YHWH, "the maker of heaven and earth," or on account of Greek metaphysical reflections of the period.[36]

The witness of the OT as Christian Scripture is fundamentally a witness to the One who raised Israel from the dead and who in turn raised Jesus from the dead. He thereby dramatically recalibrated reigning eschatological and pneumatological expectations, still in accordance with those selfsame Scriptures. The challenge of our day is not how to find in Jesus a model of critical exposition of the historical-critical type; those instincts are already well honed in modernity and late modernity. The challenge of our day is how to see in Jesus' death and raising actions truly in accordance with the Scriptures of Israel. For that, we shall need to return to typological and figural senses once more keenly available in the church's handling of the literal sense, before such a sense was conflated with the historical sense. To the degree tradition-historical approaches attempt, as von Rad valiantly sought, to link historical recovery of the real with some larger governing universe of types, they will fail for reasons apparent, on the one side, to a Bultmann and, on another, to those who disparaged Leonard Goppelt in his day. Only when the literal sense is reencountered in our time, apart from a valorizing of "proximity to the real," in history or in tradition, will the way forward be found again for a Christian handling of Old and New Testaments as Scripture for the church and world. This is what I am seeking under the rubric of a canonical approach to biblical theology.

---

[36]On the debate between Athanasius and Arius, and especially their appeal to Scripture, see the brilliant analysis of Frances Young, *Biblical Exegesis and the Formation of Christian Culture* (Cambridge: Cambridge University Press, 1997).

14

Dialogic Conceptions of Language and the Problem of Biblical Unity

Nicholas Perrin

From the first half of the twentieth century until the present, the question of the unity of the two Testaments has been a bedeviled one. Yet even for those who uphold the unity of the Bible, the precise nature of the relationship between the two Testaments has remained a contested matter.

Some scholars have argued that the unity between the OT and NT is essentially a historical one. In this view, the Testaments are linked in their mutual attempt to recount the history of God's relationship with humanity. This notion takes on its most developed form in the salvation-history theologies, typically associated with Gerhard Von Rad and Oscar Cullmann; within Roman Catholic thought, Karl Rahner and Joseph Ratzinger; and within evangelicalism, Geerhardus Vos and George Eldon Ladd.[1] In the past four decades the salvation-historical model has come under fire

---

[1]Gerhard Von Rad, *Old Testament Theology*, 2 vols. (Edinburgh: Oliver & Boyd, 1965), 2:319-429; Oscar Cullman, *Christus und die Zeit: Die urchristliche Zeit- und Geschichtsauffassung* (Zollikon-Zürich: Evangelische, 1946); Karl Rahner, *Theological Investigations* (New York: Seabury, 1979), pp. 97-114; Joseph Ratzinger, *Principles of Catholic Theology* (San Francisco: Ignatius, 1982), pp. 153-90; Geerhardus Vos, *Biblical Theology* (Grand Rapids, Mich.: Eerdmans, 1948); and George Eldon Ladd, *A Theology of the New Testament* (Grand Rapids, Mich., Eerdmans, 1974).

from critics like Franz Hesse, who sees an uneasy relationship between kerygmatic history and the current results of historical criticism.[2] Philosophical and hermeneutical objections have been raised as well. Whereas some have taken issue with the category of salvation history given the specific concerns of postmodernity, others, like Petr Pokorny, have insisted that at bottom such an approach is strictly confessional: "the Christ-event, witnessed in the NT, is not a direct historical continuation or development of the OT event"; it is only faith that makes it so.[3]

There are other models for biblical unity as well. Roland E. Murphy and Claus Westermann are among theologians who see the two Testaments as being connected by a promise-fulfillment schema: that which is promised in the Old receives fulfillment (even if tentatively) in the New.[4] Similar to this is the typological approach, which, despite its critics, has attracted its own following, especially in Roman Catholic circles. According to this view, whose ablest defenders include Leonard Goppelt and Walther Eichrodt, the OT and NT may be correlated by type and antitype, a structural parallelism that comes to expression in the biblical accounting of history.[5] The most vocal opponents of this outlook object that such typological readings of Scripture are artificial and hermeneutically outmoded.[6]

Yet another approach has been to emphasize that the NT and OT voices share a "unity of perspective."[7] Along similar lines are attempts to show the similarities in vocabulary between the Testaments, or similar themes.[8] Finally, there is what one might term the intertextual connection. Unity between the Testaments is implicit in the fact that the NT writers regularly

[2]Franz Hesse, "Kerygma oder Geschichtliche Wirklichkeit?" *ZTK* 57 (1960): 17-26.
[3]Petr Pokorny, "Probleme biblischer Theologie," *Theologische Literaturzeitung* 106 (1981): 4. See too Bradford E. Hinze, "The End of Salvation History," *Horizons* 18, no. 2 (1991): 227-45.
[4]Roland E. Murphy, "The Relationship Between the Testaments," *CBQ* 26 (1964): 349-59; and Claus Westermann, *The Old Testament and Jesus Christ* (Minneapolis: Augsburg, 1970).
[5]Leonard Goppelt, *Typos: Die typologische Deutung des Alten Testaments* (Darmstadt: Wissenschaftliche, 1966); Walther Eichrodt, "Is Typological Exegesis an Appropriate Method?" in *Essays on Old Testament Hermeneutics*, ed. Claus Westermann (Richmond, Va.: John Knox Press, 1963), pp. 224-45.
[6]See Friedrich Baumgärtel, *Theologische Literaturzeitung* 86 (1961): 901-6; James Barr, *Old and New in Interpretation* (London: SCM Press, 1982), pp. 103-48.
[7]That, for example, the eschatological perspective was shared by the NT and OT writers is highlighted by Th. C. Vriezen, *An Outline of Old Testament Theology* (Oxford: Blackwell, 1958), p. 123.
[8]See, e.g., F. F. Bruce, *New Testament Development of Old Testament Themes* (Grand Rapids, Mich.: Eerdmans, 1969); G. van Groningen, *Messianic Revelation in the Old Testament* (Grand Rapids, Mich.: Baker, 1990).

appropriated OT texts and concepts.[9] The question in this connection is whether conceptual or verbal agreement between the texts is constitutive of unity.

This catalogue of proposals is not intended to be exhaustive but rather illustrative of a central concern within contemporary biblical theology for the unity of the Testaments. In view of the diversity of proposals being offered, the state of the question today seems not to be whether there is an organic connection between the OT and NT but whether that connection can be described from within any single category. Although something may be said for many, if not all, of the aforementioned models, the most substantive questions are those regarding the adequacy of each in and of itself. Against the rich, variegated nature of the canon, the individual approaches may be open to the charge of either oversimplifying the biblical message or imposing a kind of framework whereby inordinate weight is attached to certain materials over and against others, leaving behind a canon within a canon. Following his overview of proposals toward a unifying biblical framework, it is with some justice that Gerhard F. Hasel remarks, "No single category, concept, or scheme can be expected to exhaust the varieties of interrelationships between the testaments."[10] Yet if this is the case, how is it possible to stake the claim for biblical unity?

Toward offering a fresh approach to the problem, I would suggest beginning not with a consideration of events or theological developments that may be said to bind the two canons but with a consideration of the biblical authors as they stand in relationship to one another. Of particular importance is the relationship effected between the cadre of NT writers and their OT counterparts. Attending to this relationship is appropriate not only because of certain assumptions within ancient Judaism regarding the nature of language but also because of the inner necessity within biblical theology of speaking to the biblical text and to biblical history.

THEOLOGY *AND* HISTORY

Representing biblical content in a way that is faithful to the theological and historical dimensions of the text has proved to be one of the basic conun-

---

[9]The classic treatment is still C. H. Dodd, *According to the Scriptures: The Substructure of New Testament Theology* (London: Fontana, 1952). See now Peter Stuhlmacher, *Biblische Theologie des Neuen Testaments,* 2 vols. (Göttingen: Vandenhoeck & Ruprecht, 1992, 1999).

[10]Gerhard F. Hasel, *New Testament Theology: Basic Issues in the Current Debate* (Grand Rapids, Mich.: Eerdmans, 1978), p. 201.

drums of biblical theology. How is it possible to study Scripture as a unified, coherent corpus without doing injustice to either the theological/literary characteristics of the documents or the historical events to which the documents attest? What hermeneutic permits material or theological issues (that which is in the text) to be treated on the same level as historical issues (that which is behind the text)? In overemphasizing the former there is a danger of losing the dynamic aspect of revelation. Yet in overemphasizing the Bible as history, it is all too easy to overlook the content of Scripture. Virtually from its inception as a discipline, biblical theology has never decisively resolved the issue as to how these two aspects of the biblical text are to be related. Nevertheless, to the extent that the Bible is a text, and a historical text at that, the biblical theologian cannot neglect discussing what the text means and the historical processes that gave rise to it. Any attempt to correlate the OT and NT, if it is to be a convincing paradigm, must take into even account matters of history and matters of theology. A robust vision of the two Testaments that honors the text equally as immanent sociohistorical reality and as transcendent revelation would, so it seems, require no less. This is not only an a priori assumption; it is apparent from the practice of the past.

In some respects, it is arguable that salvation-historical (and the related typological and promise-fulfillment) models of biblical theology do effectively combine history and theology. After all, are not such approaches concerned with matters behind the text as well as theological content in the text? Undoubtedly this is true, but only in a limited way. In all such treatments it is inevitable that one aspect take precedence over the other. As Bradford E. Hinze asks, "Does salvation history refer to the stories of Israel, Jesus of Nazareth, and emergent Christianity as an ordered set of facts and *events* reconstructed by historians? Or does salvation history refer to the *literatures* in the Old and New Testaments which portray the history of Israel and emergent Christianity in terms of God's saving activity in history?"[11]

In response to the question so posed, it may be said that salvation history and similar models refer to the events and the literatures involved. But from a methodological perspective, Hinze's point is well taken. If the study of Scripture requires attention to the historical and theological aspects of the text, how is it possible to attend to these twin concerns in an evenhanded manner?

---

[11]Hinze, "The End of Salvation History," p. 233 (emphasis added).

THE NEW TESTAMENT AS THE ADDRESSEES
OF THE OLD TESTAMENT

It is at this point that Hans Robert Jauss's theory of *Rezeptionsaesthetik* may
be of some use. In *Toward an Aesthetic of Reception* Jauss speaks to a certain
tension in the field of literary criticism, one that bears analogy to the methodological dilemma under discussion. At issue in Jauss's case was "the
challenge of literary studies which was left unresolved in the dispute between Marxist and Formalist methods," namely, whether literature should
be read as literature on material or formal grounds.[12] If, according to Jauss,
the Marxist critics were preoccupied with the history that lay behind the
text, the Formalists were equally guilty in their narrow philological focus.
In short, the shared failure of both schools was that they lacked "the reader
in his genuine role, a role as unalterable for aesthetic as for historical
knowledge: as the addressee for whom the literary work is primarily destined."[13] Toward resolving the Marxist-Formalist debate Jauss calls for a
hermeneutic that emphasizes not simply the text per se or simply the historical situation that gave rise to the text. Instead, Jauss calls attention to
the original receptors, the addressees, in their historically conditioned horizon of experience. Only in this way, so Jauss argued, was it possible to
formulate a theory of literature that was at once aesthetic and sensitive to
the dynamism of history.

It is my contention that Jauss's focus on the addressee (i.e., the one "for
whom the literary work is primarily destined") is pertinent to the concerns
of biblical theology: to the problematic disjunction between history and
theology in biblical theology as well as to the fundamental nature of biblical unity. Toward making the case for biblical unity, the most basic connection between the Testaments lies not in any material correspondences in
the text or in a certain historical trajectory behind the text (although such
correspondences and trajectories do exist), but rather in the relationship
established between the apostolic writers as recipients of OT revelation
(the addressees of the OT) and the OT authors. The undergirding connection between the two Testaments is, in other words, a dialogical one.

Such a method commends itself because such an understanding of the
two Testaments affords an account of Scripture that is at once theological

---

[12]Jans Robert Jauss, *Toward an Aesthetic of Reception,* trans. Timothy Bahti (Minneapolis: University of Minnesota Press, 1970), pp. 18-19.
[13]Ibid., p. 19.

and historical. An examination of the apostles as historically situated interlocutors with the Law and the Prophets would require attendance not only to the historical background of the apostles' reading of Torah, especially as occasioned by their experience of Christ, but also to the positive theological content that might have been generated out of such reading. In the nature of the case, any investigation of the apostolic writers as addressees would be simultaneously a literary and historical undertaking. By calling attention to the literature's original historical reception, Jauss sought to close the gap between the text as literature and the text as history. If Jauss's solution of focusing on the addressees is a sound one, this opens up new avenues of inquiry for biblical theology as well.

Indeed, the NT writers seem to have been acutely aware of their role as addressees. The apostles were together of the conviction that in Jesus Christ they had witnessed the eschatological in-breaking of the last days, announced by the Law and the Prophets (Acts 2:14-41; Rom 13:11-12). Bound up with this insight was the realization that theirs was the unique task to record and interpret the person, ministry, death and resurrection of Christ. Inasmuch as the NT writers took on their role as privileged interpreters of OT revelation, it can be said—and indeed it was said—that the OT texts were addressed to them. This is not to say that the OT had no relevance to the early church or, for that matter, to Christians today. What the apostolic office does imply, however, is that the truths of the OT can be properly and fully understood only as refracted through the lens of the apostolic *kerygma*. In this sense, the truths of the OT and indeed the truths of all Scripture do not come to the believing community apart from the mediation of the apostles (Eph 2:20; 3:5).

This addressitive quality of Scripture entails a rather broad understanding of audience. Even if the biblical books were occasioned by specific historical concerns, this does not detract from the fact that the original audience was not the only audience or, in the larger scope of things, the primary audience. Whatever promises of comfort or doom were made to the OT prophets' first hearers, the inscripturated voice of the prophets in succeeding centuries would take on a life and authority of its own. This becomes apparent, for example, through even a cursory reading of the Qumran *Habakkuk Pesher*. Although undoubtedly aware that the historical figure Habakkuk had been writing to his situation, the Essene community nonetheless believed that the text of Habakkuk was for them, and more precisely, for the Teacher of Righteousness who was its true interpreter.

Without hesitation the covenanters had come to view the Teacher of Right-eousness as standing in a kind of dialogue with the prophet of old. A sim-ilar understanding obtained for the apostolic church, upon whom the fullness of time had come.

For the NT and Qumran writers alike, such dialogue with the past was possible simply because they, along with the believing communities they represented, envisioned themselves as sharing a common, theological ex-perience and eschatologically driven history as the covenant people of God. Nor is there any indication that this communion was offset by the distance of time that separated one biblical writer from another. In this re-spect, the ancients knew nothing of the modern tendency to see the subject as being circumscribed by the constraints of culture or time, that is, one's sociohistorical situatedness. The very ability to attach typological signifi-cance to events, on the part of OT and NT writers alike, presupposes that one's frame of reference was determined not so much by one's location within time or space but by one's position within the covenant of God.[14] Ancient Jewish interpreters of the OT recognized for themselves an elec-tive status whereby they stood in immediate relationship to God and, de-spite the passage of time, in immediate relationship with those authoritative voices who had gone before.

It is important to underscore that the way in which the NT writers po-sitioned themselves vis-à-vis the OT writers was not a distinctively Chris-tian posture. To be sure, the claims of the Christian gospel were unique, as well as some of its terminology. But there is good reason to believe that this view of Scripture, which I am describing as dialogic, was inherent to all an-cient Jewish understanding of language. If the biblical writings may be characterized as having a forward-looking, addressive aspect and a backward-looking responsive aspect, this is due to the fact that ancient Jewish discourse in general shows marks of being eminently concerned with the speaker, the addressee (responder) and the interaction between the two. To conceive of the NT writers as inspired interlocutors with the past is not only to accord them a role they presumed for themselves; it is to recognize the very structure of ancient Jewish utterance.

---

[14]Along these lines Erich Auerbach, *Mimesis: The Representation of Reality in Western Literature* (New York: Doubleday, 1957), p. 14, sees typology as having a paradoxical quality: "the greater the separateness and horizontal disconnection of the stories and groups of stories in relation to one another . . . the stronger is their general vertical connection, which holds them all together."

This becomes evident when examining the deeper, governing principles of midrash. However one chooses to define midrash, the heart of midrash always assumes the possibility and importance of dialogue. According to Renée Bloch's well-known definition, midrash "designates an edifying genre and an explanatory narrowing attached to Scripture, in which part of the amplification is real but secondary and remains always subordinated to some essentially religious goal, which grants fuller significance to . . . the Word of God."[15] Bloch refines this definition further by citing five characteristics of midrash: (1) it takes Scripture as its point of departure; (2) it has a homiletic aim; (3) it is attentive to the details of the *Vorlage*; (4) it reinterprets the text to fit the present situation; and (5) it is of two kinds: haggadah and halakah. The fourth cited characteristic (how midrash serves to reinterpret texts) and the general definition (how midrash grants fuller significance to the prior text) make a complementary point. For the ancient Jewish exegetes the significance of a Scripture text could not be exhausted, simply because the possibilities for rereading the text were, within certain parameters, virtually infinite. The rabbis were not averse to bringing Scripture to bear quite specifically upon situations in their communities. So reading Scripture through the contingencies of history gave rise to new applications and fuller expression of that which was contained *in nuce* in the text. In this process of relating Torah to the text of history it was inevitable that the voice of Scripture would be transmuted. Steven D. Fraade summarizes the point: "Ancient scriptural commentaries . . . are always about the *whole*. By this I mean that they not only seek for the text to be held in high regard by its interpretive community, but for the interpretive community to regard itself in relation to that text as mediated by its commentary. In other words, such a commentary is not simply a series of declarative assertions about the meanings of words or clusters of words in a text, but an attempt to effect a relationship between that text overall and those for whom it is 'scripture.'"[16]

It is precisely this concern for what Fraade calls "the whole" that betrays the radically social quality of Jewish discourse. In this light, one might rightly speak of the NT record as the apostles' "attempt to effect a relationship" between the Israel of the OT and the community who had put their faith in Christ. Not only within the context of the NT, but indeed

---

[15]Renée Bloch, "Midrash," *Supplement au Dictionnaire de la Bible* 5, col. 1263-81.
[16]Steven D. Fraade, *From Tradition to Commentary: Torah and Its Interpretation in the Midrash Sifre to Deuteronomy* (Albany: State University of New York Press, 1991), p. 13.

for ancient Judaism in general, meaningful discourse about God could not occur in a sociohistorical vacuum. All such discourse was intrinsically communal, intrinsically dialogical.

THE DIALOGICAL NATURE OF LANGUAGE

It is of considerable interest in this connection that this socially embedded and dialogic view of language, so basic to ancient Jewish writings, also finds modern parallel in the thought of Mikhail Bakhtin. A number of scholars, including Fraade, have already pointed out the dialogical element of ancient Jewish commentary and parallels with modern dialogic theories.[17] Of course, when comparing modern literary theories to ancient Jewish texts, there is some danger of anachronism or framing the comparisons in such a way so as to be historically misleading. Nonetheless, in drawing upon modern construals of language, such as that of Bakhtin, it is possible to grant new plausibility to that which is often incomprehensible in modern Western eyes. In this case, Bakhtin's theory of language may be useful toward understanding what the Jews believed to be true as well.

There is perhaps no more concise expression of the theory of language espoused by Bakhtin and his circle than that given (purportedly) by V. N. Voloshinov in "Discourse in Life and Discourse in Art": "any locution actually said or written down for intelligible communication (that is, anything but words merely reposing in the dictionary) is the expression and product of the social interaction of these participants: the speaker (author), the listener (reader), and the topic (the who or what) of speech."[18]

Bakhtin's emphasis on language as a social phenomena came partially in reaction to what he perceived as the abstractions of Russian Formalism. In contrast to Formalism, which stressed meaning as arising from the interrelationship between linguistic markers, Bakhtin and his circle held that meaning was ultimately generated through a social grammar. Communication could be properly understood only in light of the social context attending the act of speech or writing.

This emphasis on language's social context entailed not only those who were immediately present in any given dialogue (written or spoken) but

---

[17]See, e.g., Daniel Boyarin, *Intertextuality and the Reading of Midrash* (Bloomington: Indiana University Press, 1990), pp. 12-13, 23.

[18]V. N. Voloshinov, "Discourse in Life, Discourse in Art," in *Freudianism: A Critical Sketch* (New York: Literary Press, 1976), p. 105. There is some reason to suspect that this essay, while published under the same of Voloshinov, was Bakhtin's work.

all previous users of language. For Bakhtin the words (*slovo*) that made up language were not neutral, transparent signs but "living beings," which possessed their own social and ideological accentuation. Behind each word lay a matrix of meanings derived from all prior interactions between that word and prior speakers. Every word incorporates "a relationship to someone else's utterance as the indispensable element."[19] Every word is "shot through with intentions and accents" and "tastes of the context and contexts in which it has lived its socially charged life; all words and terms are populated by intentions."[20] With the exception of the primeval Adam, all speakers unavoidably appropriate "alien discourses, discourses which are themselves bound up with an array of secondary associations and contextual meanings."[21] Insofar as utterance is derivative, the product of multiple consciousnesses, the act of utterance was for Bakhtin a responsive act. All discourse and thought (the internal discourse of the mind) draw upon and respond to the texts of the past. However a speaker may choose to use a given word in a given context, there is no eradicating immanent reference to other prior contexts and the network of connotations the word invokes. Speaking no less for humanity than for himself, Bakhtin declares, "I live in the words of others."[22] Words always "belong to someone else."[23] Due to the radical sociohistoric quality of language, to use language was for Bakhtin to undertake a dialogue with the past.

It is not too difficult to show that Bakhtin's view of language is similar to that which was taken for granted by the ancients, among them the NT writers. If Bakhtin in his day (not far removed from our own) needed to take pains to point out that we "live in the words of others," for the ancient Jews such an idea was self-evident. This is demonstrable not only from the fact that the Talmud and NT alike are fraught with OT allusion. The manner in which the ancient Jews cited Torah indicates that Torah study involved learning the words of Torah as discrete, context-laden entities. And so when in Galatians 3 Paul speaks of the "seed" (not "seeds") he is referring not just to a promise made in Genesis but to a whole trajectory of us-

---

[19]Mikhail Mikhailovich Bakhtin, *Problems of Dostoevsky's Poetics*, Theory and History of Literature Series 8 (Minneapolis: University of Minnesota Press, 1963), p. 184.

[20]Mikhail Mikhailovich Bakhtin, *The Dialogic Imagination: Four Essays* (Austin: University of Texas Press, 1990), p. 253.

[21]Ibid., p. 279.

[22]Mikhail Mikhailovich Bakhtin, *Speech Genres and Other Late Essays* (Austin: University of Texas Press, 1984), p. 143.

[23]Bakhtin, *Dialogic Imagination*, p. 293.

ages and associations, including the word as it is used in the Song of the Suffering Servant. He would expect his readers to recognize no less. Or, again, in John 8:58 when Jesus says, "Before Abraham was, I am" (NRSV [throughout the essay]), there is absolutely no question as to what these two seemingly innocent words meant. For this reason, it is not going far enough to say that the terminology and conceptuality of the NT are deeply rooted in Torah. More to the point is the fact that when the NT writers appropriate the texts of Torah, they were self-consciously responding to and closing out a conversation that had begun in generations past.

THE FUTURE ORIENTATION OF
OLD TESTAMENT LANGUAGE

For Bakhtin, and for the ancients as well, language has not only a retrospective aspect but also a prospective, addressitive face. At the close of his treatment on Dostoevsky's character, the Underground Man, the Russian thinker writes:

> To speak [for the Underground Man] means to address someone, to speak about himself means to address his own self with his own discourse, to speak about another person means to address that other person; to speak about the world means to address the world. But while speaking with himself, with another, with the world, he simultaneously addresses a third party as well: he squints his eyes to the side, toward the listener, the witness, the judge.[24]

As for the Underground Man, so too for humanity. Bakhtin maintains that all discourse is colored by an awareness of the addressee. "Addressivity, the quality of turning to someone, is a constitutive feature of the utterance; without it the utterance does not and cannot exist."[25] Whatever the nature of communication, even in soliloquy, the speaker cannot elude an awareness of the third party. The speaker cannot help but "squint his eyes to the side."

This "squinting to the side," or more precisely, "squinting to the future," is highly characteristic of the OT. The words of the Law were not simply addressed to Moses' generation. They were to be passed down to succeeding generations (Deut 4:9; 29:14-15). In their writing of history the OT biblical writers were not merely attempting to galvanize the faith of

---

[24]Bakhtin, *Dostoevsky's Poetics*, p. 237.
[25]Bakhtin, *Speech Genres*, p. 99.

their generation. History was ideological, but history was also a testament to the future (Ps 78:4-7). There is in all Jewish religious writings, but especially so in the OT, an inextricable orientation to the future. Unfortunately, historical-critical investigations of Scripture tend to overlook such concerns with the future, largely because the methodology tends to view the text as conditioned strictly by the immediate historical situation. In this respect, historical criticism tells us more about the assumptions of Western post-Enlightenment culture than about the ideologies of ancient Israel.

This addressive aspect of the Hebrew Scriptures is not only bound up in the fabric of the OT but also taken for granted by Jews and Christians in later antiquity. The rationale by which rabbinic Judaism justified its interpretations of the Mosaic tradition lay in the claim that at Sinai God had delivered not just Torah but Mishnah, Talmud and Haggadah as well.[26] In short, the words spoken at Sinai were addressed not only to the wandering Israelites but also to the sages of succeeding generations of Jews to come. The oral law was addressed to them.

The apostles made a similar claim. For the NT writers the Christ event not only signaled the fulfillment of important OT texts; it served to define the proper recipients of the Scriptures. For example, in affirming the apostles' rights to financial support Paul writes the Corinthians, "Do I say this on human authority? Does not the law also say the same? For it is written in the law of Moses: 'You shall not muzzle an ox while it is treading out the grain.' Is it for oxen that God is concerned? Does he not speak entirely for our sake? It was indeed written for our sake, for whoever plows should plow in hope and whoever threshes should thresh in hope of a share in the crop" (1 Cor 9:8-10 NRSV).

Likewise, Paul states that the aftermath of the Moabite rebellion was not merely an unfortunate event by which the church should be warned. Instead, the events of Moab were purposed for the church's sake: "Now these things are warnings for us, not to desire evil as they did" (1 Cor 10:6, author's translation). History and Scripture together were written for us, for the apostles and, *mutatis mutandis*, for members of the believing community who also found themselves living in the last days. From Paul's perspective and from the perspective of the whole NT, whatever was recorded in Torah was recorded with an eye toward the future heirs of the covenant.

Inasmuch as the OT writers anticipated points in the future when God

---

[26]See, e.g., *Exod. Rab.* 47.1.

would reveal himself in new ways, this implied that the OT authors considered their tradition as complete and unified only in a provisional sense. Whatever marks of unity (historical or literary) the OT might bear, its authors were fully of the view that, though they had fulfilled their individual callings, the true Speaker was not done speaking. If neither early Judaism nor rabbinic Judaism nor Christianity saw the Hebrew Bible as being utterly self-contained or, in the words of James Sanders, "standing on its own feet,"[27] then it must be asked whether the assumption against biblical unity is in fact merely a modern one.

CONCLUSION

In applying Jauss's literary theory to the biblical theological task, it is possible to formulate an approach to Scripture that, while embracing the concerns of theology and history, emphasizes the unity of dialogue between the Testaments. The appropriateness of such a dialogic model is further validated when, in drawing from the linguistic theory of Bakhtin, it can be demonstrated that the ancient Jews saw discourse as a social, dialogical phenomena. By viewing the NT writers as conversation partners with the OT tradition, one is essentially recognizing a role that the NT writers recognized for themselves and the OT writers anticipated. A conversational relationship between the writers of the two Testaments is entirely in keeping with the implicit assumption of biblical discourse. Toward a better understanding of this conversation, making recourse to dialogicists like Jauss and Bakhtin may be just the start.

---

[27]James A. Sanders, "Habakkuk in Qumran, Paul and the Old Testament," in *Paul and the Scriptures of Israel*, ed. James A. Sanders and Craig A. Evans (Sheffield: JSOT, 1993), p. 102.

15

The Conceptual Structure
of New Testament Theology

Stephen E. Fowl

There is an obvious rashness in presuming to speak on the conceptual structure of biblical theology. First, it presumes an ability to define the subject in a way that will convince many, if not a majority, of one's audience. Second, no matter how one defines biblical theology, it is going to be too complex a phenomenon to have a conceptual structure (another obscure term) that one could lay out in an essay of this length. I want to avoid this rashness. At the same time, I do not want to get so bogged down in battles over the definition of biblical theology that this essay becomes an exercise in clearing one's throat without ever speaking.

To avoid these problems I am going to look at what I, and many others, take to be the dominant academic strain or tradition of NT theology, a strain that runs from J. P. Gabler through William Wrede and down to Krister Stendahl and Heikki Räisänen and many others. While those within this tradition, including those I just named, differ from each other in many respects, they seem to share some basic assumptions about NT theology. I want to examine some of these assumptions in this essay. Further, I want to contrast these assumptions with those assumptions necessary for the theological interpretation of Scripture. My point in doing so is to suggest that while NT theology can be made to be a more or less internally coherent academic discipline, this coherence will render biblical theology to be of only ad hoc usefulness to those interested in reading Scripture theologically. Hence, for those interested in bridging the chasms that now exist between biblical scholars and theologians, the dominant strain of NT theology will be of only limited importance. Moreover, given the ends toward which Christians are called to interpret and embody Scripture, this tradition of NT theology will be of only limited and ad hoc use.

I realize that by identifying a dominant strain of doing NT theology, I risk obscuring the fact that there have been and are dissenters from this way of doing things. I will try to be attentive to such dissent when and where I can. I would, however, argue that for the most part these characters are dissenters because they dissent from the results of the dominant way of doing things, not because they fundamentally diverge from the conceptual and practical habits that mark the dominant strain of NT theology.

WREDE'S LEGACY: NEW TESTAMENT THEOLOGY AS THE HISTORY OF RELIGION

It is common to claim that biblical theology as a mode of academic discourse was born with Gabler's *Antrittsrede* in 1787.[1] I think, however, that Ben Ollenburger has rightly indicated that Gabler's position was very quickly abandoned, despite rhetorical claims to the contrary, in favor of positions more clearly influenced by Kantian concerns. This culminated in Wrede's essay, "The Tasks and Methods of 'New Testament Theology.'"[2]

Gabler's "pure biblical theology" was a two- or perhaps three-staged affair that would ultimately have allowed for a blurring of the disciplinary distinctions between theology and philosophy.[3] He proposed this at

---

[1]As Gerhard Ebeling argues, prior to the Enlightenment, the term "biblical theology" was used to refer to a pietistic attempt to reform scholastic dogmatics. See "The Meaning of 'Biblical Theology,'" in *Word and Faith* (Philadelphia: Fortress, 1960), pp. 79-97.

[2]See Ben Ollenburger, "Biblical Theology: Situating the Discipline," in *Understanding the Word*, ed. J. T. Butler, E. Conrad and B. Ollenburger (Sheffield: JSOT, 1985), pp. 37-62.

[3]See L. T. Stuckenbruck, "Johann Philipp Gabler and the Delineation of Biblical Theology," *SJT* 52 (1999): 139-57. The confusion between two and three stages of biblical theology has to do with the fact that Gabler's views are not precise here and they seem to change in his later writing.

just the time that Kant was arguing for more rigid disciplinary boundaries within the emerging modern university's division of academic labors. In this respect one could say that Kant's views won the day. Alternatively, although they disagreed on how this was to be done, Kant and Gabler were struggling to demarcate a space for biblical theology as a discipline within the modern university, a discipline that would interact with other newly disciplined modes of inquiry but would also retain its integrity.[4] It was Wrede's essay that most thoroughly exemplified this quest for disciplinary autonomy.

Wrede's argument is a tour de force whereby the disciplinary integrity of NT theology is retained at the expense of both terms. The most famous lines from the essay come from its conclusion: "Nevertheless, the name New Testament Theology is wrong in both its terms. The New Testament is not concerned merely with theology, but is in fact far more concerned with religion. . . . The appropriate name for the subject matter is: early Christian history of religion, or rather: the history of early Christian religion and theology."[5]

Wrede's proposals amounted to a call for a historical report on the religion of the first Christians. This meant that the scope of inquiry could not be confined to the NT. Further, his distinction between religion and theology, along with his demand that NT theology be strictly historical, effectively excluded all constructive theological work from this discipline. "Biblical theology has to investigate something from given documents—if not an external thing, still something intellectual. It tries to grasp it as objectively, correctly and sharply as possible. That is all. How the systematic theologian gets on with its results and deals with them—that is his own affair. Like every other science, New Testament theology has its goal simply in itself, and is totally indifferent to all dogma and systematic theology."[6]

Despite, or perhaps because, of the fact that Wrede's proposals fit quite

---

[4]See Ollenburger, "Situating the Discipline," pp. 44-46.

[5]William Wrede, "The Tasks and Methods of 'New Testament Theology,'" in Robert Morgan's *The Nature of New Testament Theology* (London: SCM Press, 1973), p. 116. The pervasiveness of Wrede's influence can be seen in the fact that James Barr effectively opts for an account of biblical theology very much like Wrede's without devoting much attention to a discussion of Wrede's work. See Barr's *The Concept of Biblical Theology* (Minneapolis: Fortress, 1999).

[6]See Wrede, "Tasks," p. 69. As Andrew Adam nicely points out, however, though Wrede saw NT theology as radically separate from dogmatics, he also argued that dogmatics was utterly dependent on the findings of NT theology. See Adam's *Making Sense of New Testament Theology* (Macon, Ga.: Mercer University Press, 1995), pp. 72-73.

well with his liberal Protestant views about theology,[7] they seemed to win
the day. This is true even though Wrede's untimely death meant that he
never fulfilled his agenda set out in this essay. Wrede's proposals, particularly his concerns with disciplinary autonomy, profoundly shaped the discipline even when scholars reject Wrede's results. The success of Wrede's
attempts to establish a space for an academic discipline of biblical theology, however, has tied biblical theology to a series of theologically unfortunate practices.

As a result of the success of Wrede's proposals, the discipline of biblical
(both OT and NT) theology found itself caught up in two separate but related processes of fragmentation that have their roots in modernity. First,
there is the fragmentation of theology into a set of discrete activities: biblical studies, systematics, historical theology, practical theology, and so on.
I do not mean to say that prior to the rise of modernity people would not
have recognized rough-and-ready distinctions between various theological tasks. Augustine, Aquinas, Luther and their contemporaries all would
have recognized that writing a biblical commentary was not the same sort
of task as writing *The City of God,* the *Summa* or "On the Bondage of the
Will." But Thomas, to take just one example, would have been deeply puzzled by the notion that in writing his commentary on John he was acting
as a biblical scholar and in writing the *Summa* he was working as a systematic theologian. Instead, these tasks were all seen as a part of a more or less
unified theological program of articulating, shaping and embodying convictions about God, humanity and the world.

The fact that theology becomes fragmented in the ways we now know
has a great deal to do with the manner in which Christian theology confronted the challenges of modernity. It may be only now, when more and
sharper questions are raised about the coherence and sustainability of
the intellectual projects of modernity, that we are able to see the ways in
which theology substantially altered (and perhaps deformed) its identity
as it faced the challenges of modernity. I will not go into the details of
these deformations. Rather, I will direct you to John Milbank's magiste-

---

[7]See Morgan's comments in *Nature of New Testament Theology,* p. 22. In a later essay Morgan
argues that Wrede and others did not seek such a sharp separation between NT theology
and previous theological interpretation. What Morgan fails to reckon with is that this result
was already deeply embedded in Wrede's presumptions and presuppositions about theology and epistemology, presumptions and presuppositions Morgan largely shares. See
Robert Morgan, "Can Critical Study of Scripture Provide a Doctrinal Norm?" *Journal of Religion* 76 (1996): 206-32.

rial work *Theology and Social Theory.*[8] Clearly Milbank's argument needs correction in many of its details, but I have yet to find a substantial refutation of his basic theses. While most of my criticisms are directed at the ways in which biblical theology sought and still seeks to distance itself from theological considerations, I note here that, following Milbank, the blame for this lies as much with theology and theologians as it does with biblical scholars.

Second, the fragmentation of theology had an institutional form. This occurred when theology's various parts became professional disciplines within the structure of the modern university.[9] This institutional fragmentation is accomplished as spheres of knowledge are more and more narrowly defined and disciplined. At its best, this economy was designed to produce knowledge more efficiently. Instead, in its most advanced North American forms, each discipline struggles to maintain its integrity and the integrity of its sphere of discourse. To be counted as a professional within each of these disciplines, one has to master such a detailed body of knowledge particular to each field that it is rare to find a scholar in one field whose work is read and used by those in another.

Professionalization institutionalized the separation between biblical studies and theology. Because there is a strong temptation in most universities to treat the work of professional scholars as commodities that can be exchanged for various professional rewards (e.g., tenure, promotion and the like), there is little incentive to take the time needed to engage seriously with the work of those outside one's field. In fact, the commodification of scholarship works to specialize and fragment disciplines further rather than to encourage the breaking down of disciplinary boundaries.

Indeed, from Wrede's explicit disregard for constructive theology to Stendahl's drawing a line between what a text meant and what it means, to Räisänen's desire to move beyond NT theology, the discipline seems inordinately concerned with images of boundaries and separations designed to keep constructive theological concerns at bay until some more properly historical work can be done by the NT theologian. In this light James Barr is correct to note that "'biblical theology' is essentially a *contrastive* notion."[10] The case is more extreme with OT theology because of the

---

[8]John Milbank, *Theology and Social Theory* (Oxford: Blackwell, 1990).
[9]For a stimulating discussion of the effects of professionalization in American higher education, see Burton Bledstein, *The Culture of Professionalism* (New York: Norton, 1976).
[10]Barr, *Concept of Biblical Theology*, p. 5.

added concern to maintain the "discrete voice" of the OT.[11] As long as this set of concerns continues to characterize the dominant strain of NT and biblical theology, the most conceptually clear accounts of the aims and procedures of the discipline will be those who argue that biblical theology should be merely a historical report on the various theological convictions and practices of biblical Israel and the first Christians.

THE PERSISTENCE OF NEW TESTAMENT THEOLOGY

Theologically speaking, this is not particularly satisfying. Biblical theology conducted along these lines will not be much use in generating or regulating accounts of the crucified and risen Christ that might serve as the point around which all things, including our thoughts, might be ordered. Neither will it provide Christians with a way of reading and embodying the Scriptures in ways that will enhance their ends of ever-deeper communion with the triune God and others.

Thus, while Wrede's aim of systematically establishing biblical theology as a separate discipline came to be widely shared, in practice many biblical theologians have never been comfortable making biblical theology simply a report on the religion of the Israelites or the first Christians. Ironically this is the same point Wrede made of biblical theologies from Gabler to his time. Continuing this irony, Räisänen has recently made a similar claim about biblical theologies from Wrede to the present.[12] Wrede and then Räisänen make this claim as part of a complaint about biblical theology and its failure to be thoroughly divorced from theology. I, alternatively, see it as a sign of hope that, for example, NT theologies are for the most part not satisfied with simply accounting for the diverse theological perspectives represented in the NT.

The most common way for NT theologies to move beyond the theologically austere program laid out by Wrede and his heirs is by attempting to manage issues related to the unity and diversity of the theological perspectives one can identify in the NT. That is, one of the results of what is taken to be a thoroughly historical approach to NT theology is the recognition

---

[11]The emphasis on the OT's "discrete voice" comes from Brevard S. Childs, "Toward Recovering Theological Exegesis," *Pro Ecclesia* 6 (1997): 16-26. I discuss the theological and conceptual problems with this way of thinking in *Engaging Scripture* (Oxford: Blackwell, 1998), pp. 25-28.

[12]See Heikki Räisänen, *Beyond New Testament Theology: A Story and a Program* (London: SCM Press, 1990), pp. xi-xviii.

that the NT presents diverse theological views. Therefore, in negotiating issues of the unity and diversity of the NT, NT theologies manifest their theological concerns.[13] Nevertheless, NT theologies operating within this dominant mold tend to exhibit similar tendencies. These tendencies become evident as soon as a NT theologian posits that one or another theological view is the controlling concept that shapes and holds together all others. Such a move tends to generate several sorts of responses. One is to argue that the controlling concept is not biblical, meaning that it is a theological or philosophical construct imposed on the text from outside. Within the strictures of NT theology, this criticism, if persuasive, is usually enough to undermine a proposal. Another tendency is to argue that some other perspective or concept provides the lenses that best unify the theological perspectives found in the NT.

Asserting that any single concept, perspective or theme works to unify the NT often leads others to claim that to give one perspective priority over the others establishes a canon within the canon, thus failing to treat the entire NT with equal seriousness. In the light of this charge, it is not unusual for some to claim that there is no way to unify the differing theological perspectives in the NT, much less the entire Bible, without doing a disservice to some of these other perspectives. In response to this, NT theologians tend to move back toward a practice of cataloging the diverse theologies of Scripture.[14]

There are two important things to note regarding these typical responses of NT theologians to issues of the NT's unity and diversity. First, the recognition of Scripture's diversity is not a particularly modern phenomenon. It may well be the case that the collocation of critical methods that come to be rather clumsily lumped together under the name "historical criticism" along with more recent critical practices point out this diversity in new ways. But as early as the second century, Christians and their opponents recognized the great diversity of perspectives within Scripture. Indeed, Irenaeus's *Against Heresies* makes

---

[13]Räisänen and I agree on our diagnosis of how theological concerns are made manifest in biblical theologies. We disagree quite sharply on how to evaluate this phenomenon.

[14]Perhaps the best variation on this model to date is G. B. Caird's use of the image of an apostolic conference. "[T]o write a New Testament theology is to preside at a conference of faith and order. Around the table sit the authors of the New Testament, and it is the presider's task to engage them in a colloquium about theological matters which they themselves have placed on the agenda." From *New Testament Theology*, ed. L. D. Hurst (Oxford: Clarendon, 1994), p. 19.

clear that a common recognition of the extraordinary diversity of Scripture is the point at which Irenaeus and his foes begin, even if they move in different directions.

Second, and more significantly, by following the dominant mode of doing NT theology typified by Wrede and his heirs, NT theologians have seemingly cut themselves off from the theological and philosophical resources they need to manage the diversity of Scripture. The presumption of NT theologies in this dominant mode is that the NT, understood in very particular historical-critical ways, must provide whatever unity there may be amid the diversity of the NT. Of course, if it is the NT itself, understood in very particular historical critical ways, that has generated the picture of diversity that is the problem for NT theologies, it is not likely that the NT will provide the solution to this problem.[15]

A WAY FORWARD: THE RULE OF FAITH

Again the situation of Irenaeus can be instructive for addressing this situation. Irenaeus and his foes began from the diversity of Scripture. Their strategies for managing the diversity, however, were quite different. As Irenaeus sees it, the Valentinians, for example, order Scripture's diversity by imposing on it a philosophical cosmology. While this provides a sort of order to Scripture, it commits one to adopting a set of views that require so much revision of essential Christian claims about God and the world that the result is not recognizably Christian.

This, in theory, is not a problem for Wrede and his heirs. If biblical theology should render Christian theology unintelligible, so much the worse for Christian theology. Wrede and his followers rule out the Valentinian strategy of ordering Scripture's diversity by means of some philosophical/cosmological principle not because it results in heterodox Christianity but because it makes recourse to something outside of the NT read in a particular historical way. Irenaeus, however, argues that ordering biblical texts within a framework provided by a Valentinian cosmology results in a twisted version of the biblical story. Irenaeus likens this procedure to someone who constructed a story from Homeric verse. It is possible to take some texts from the *Odyssey*, in no particular order, and intersperse them with texts from the *Iliad*, again, in no particular order, and thus create a sto-

---

[15]Even Robert Morgan, who sees himself to some degree as an heir of Wrede, notes that one needs "some theory of their [the Scriptures'] unity to set against the diversity." "Critical Study," p. 212.

ry. This story would contain Homeric language; it would contain Homeric characters. Moreover, it could therefore easily convince the uneducated that it was a true Homeric story. Nevertheless, its connections to Homer would be only superfluous and its assertions and narrative would not be Homeric (*Against Heresies* 1.9.4).[16]

Irenaeus's brilliant alternative is the so-called rule of faith.[17] Irenaeus develops an account of God's economy of salvation that has its definitive and climactic moment in the incarnation, death and resurrection of the Word. By clarifying the economy of salvation in the light of the crucified and risen Lord, Irenaeus can give a coherent account of the various movements of God's economy. This summary account of the whole of God's economy is what he calls the apostolic faith, a faith that is formally represented in the creed. This then provides the framework within which the diversity of Scripture can be rightly ordered so that it can be directed toward advancing the apostolic faith in the life, teaching and worship of the church, a life teaching and worship that is acknowledged throughout the world (*Against Heresies* 1.10.1-3). What is so striking about Irenaeus's account of the divine economy and the rule of faith is that it is so clearly derived from Scripture.

There is a circular movement here. The diversity of the NT poses a problem that is solved by ordering that diversity in the light of the apostolic faith. Only in the light of the NT, however, does that apostolic faith receive its definitive formulations. As Rowan Greer puts it:

> We could say that the quest that Irenaeus accomplishes is basically the discovery of a principle of interpretation in the apostolic Rule of faith. At the same time, . . . it is in another sense Scripture itself that supplies the categories in which the principle is expressed. Text and interpretation are like twin brothers; one can scarcely tell the one from the other.[18]

---

[16]In *Against Heresies* 1.8.1, Irenaeus uses the image of mixing up the stones in a mosaic to come up with an alternative picture. Further, as Paul Blowers notes, "The *Regula Fidei* and the Narrative Character of Early Christian Faith," *Pro Ecclesia* 6 (1996): 211, "Herein the struggle with the Gnostics is not just a battle of straightforward or atomized doctrinal propositions, which presumably Irenaeus could have tendered in the debate. It is more fundamentally a contention of 'our story versus theirs,' a collision of metanarratives, one Christian and one (or more) not."

[17]For a good contemporary reflection on the rule of faith, see R. Wall, "Reading the Bible from Within Our Traditions: The 'Rule of Faith' in Theological Hermeneutics," in *Between Two Horizons*, ed. Joel Green and Max Turner (Grand Rapids, Mich.: Eerdmans, 2000), pp. 88-108.

[18]See J. Kugel and R. Greer, *Early Biblical Interpretation* (Philadelphia: Westminster Press, 1986), p. 157.

This circularity is not vicious as long as one recognizes that theological considerations and church tradition are intimately and complexly connected to Christian interpretation of Scripture. At the same time, the rich history of biblical interpretation following in the wake of Ireneaus indicates that interpreting within the rule of faith does not demand an erasure of Scripture's diversity. It simply orders it harmoniously rather than agonistically. Nevertheless, from the perspective of Wrede and his followers, Irenaeus's solution would represent another incursion of theology into the autonomous domain of biblical theology.

What is striking about the heirs of Wrede is that in theory they allow neither the ordering power of an external philosophical or sociological scheme nor the ordering power of Christian theology when it comes to addressing issues of the unity and diversity of Scripture. This is despite the fact that these appear to be the only two options for unifying the diverse perspectives of Scripture. In fact, they are much more welcoming of those who bring nontheological schema to bear on this issue. This is as true for the philosophically sophisticated frameworks of those like Friedrich Schleiermacher and Rudolf Bultmann as well as for the vapid and facile liberalism of Räisänen.

Having said this, I suspect that one might argue that a Lutheran devotion to the external *claritas* of Scripture and a commitment to *sola Scriptura* might well provide theological justification for a form of biblical theology that is much closer to Wrede than Irenaeus. At least some Luther scholars, however, have been arguing that Luther has much more in common with patristic and medieval interpretive practices than he does with modern ones. They argue that for Luther, Scripture's external clarity is not a property of the text in itself but is "located in the ministry of the word," that is, in the network of ecclesial communicative practice within which text and interpreter are situated. This is further explicated in the distinction between the *verba* of Scripture (its wording) and Scripture's *res* (its subject matter). Because Christ, the subject matter of Scripture, has been revealed, it is possible to read Scripture rightly even if particular words and phrases remain obscure. "Scripture is 'outwardly' clear, therefore, not because there is no obscurity in its words, but because we know what Scripture is *about*, to what *res* it pertains." Obviously this *res* is textually mediated, but for Luther it is textually mediated as Christians read and embody Scripture in the contexts of teaching, preaching, catechesis and liturgical celebration in which Christ is in manifold ways set before the Christian community.[19]

To the extent to which these scholars are correct about Luther, he stands fully in the camp of Irenaeus and would have been puzzled at the dominant tradition of NT theology and its persistent refusal to engage either ecclesial tradition or constructive theology. This would further indicate that the Reformers stand much more in the tradition of patristic and medieval theology and interpretive practice than one might think.

Finally, if my arguments about the limited resources the dominant mode of NT theology can bring to issues of unity and diversity in the NT are on target, I think they can also be applied to a more general matter for biblical theology, the relationships between OT and NT. This issue, however, is further complicated by the worry on the part of OT scholars that the OT will be overshadowed or its distinct voice will be lost in relationship to the NT. While NT theology has consistently defined itself against theology, OT theology tends to define itself against theology and NT theology. If it is the case that from the perspective of the ends and purposes for which Christians seek to interpret and embody Scripture that Christian theology provides the resources needed for dealing with issues of the unity and diversity of NT witnesses, then I would suggest that these will be the same resources that need to be brought to bear on issues about the relationships between the Testaments.

CONCLUSION

In the light of my arguments about the dominant form of NT theology, the time may be right for a reevaluation of the project known as NT theology. One option may be to grant that Wrede is basically correct; the name "NT theology" is wrong in both its terms. If that is so, then let us abandon NT theology in favor of one of two alternatives. One alternative would focus merely on historical work covering the early Christian period. In fact, such work goes on all the time. The second alternative, however, would be a reinvigoration of theological interpretation of Scripture. Rather than fostering a NT interpretation that struggles to keep theological concerns at bay,

---

[19]For two excellent examples of this way of reading Luther, see Bruce Marshall, "Faith and Reason Reconsidered: Aquinas and Luther on Deciding What is True," *The Thomist* 63 (1999): 1-48, and David Yeago, "The Spirit, the Church and the Scriptures: Biblical Inspiration and Interpretation Revisited," in *Knowing the Triune God: The Work of the Spirit in the Practices of the Church*, ed. James J. Buckley and David S. Yeago (Grand Rapids, Mich.: Eerdmans, 2001), pp. 49-93.

let there be space in the academy for theologically interested reading of Scripture.

Perhaps one of the great opportunities arising from the decline of modernity is that all of the Enlightenment arguments against such theological interpretation are now suspect. This is not to say that the academy is any more welcoming to Christian theology than it has been in the past. Rather, the intellectual arguments against such opposition no longer compel the assent they once might have. This would indicate that within at least some academic institutions there is the possibility of reviving a theological interpretation of Scripture. If this is the case, then it will require biblical scholars and theologians to conceive of the theological enterprise in terms that will be much more in line with premodern conceptions of theology. At the same time, we will need to reinvigorate and recast premodern habits of interpretation for our contemporary contexts.

16

Progressive Dispensationalism and the Law/Gospel Contrast

A Case Study in Biblical Theology

Daniel P. Fuller

Professor Peter Stuhlmacher ended his essay expressing the need for the Lutheran Church in Germany to be corrected by heeding, through the Holy Spirit, the teachings of biblical theology. This essay wants to show how biblical theology could also correct the thinking of some evangelical groups in North America that have been influenced by dispensationalism, so widespread during much of the twentieth century. Dispensationalism went beyond Reformed theology in trying to salvage a unity of the Bible from the alleged law/gospel contrast. It divided the Bible into two parts: one teaching salvation by meritorious works for Israel, and a smaller part—mostly Paul—teaching salvation by grace for the church.

This teaching originated with John Nelson Darby in England around 1830. During the next thirty years, Darby launched Plymouth Brethren societies in England, France and Switzerland. He viewed the church as God's heavenly people, who have no connection with Israel, God's earthly people. In an 1840 essay he declared that during this church age Christ is Messiah only for the church and not for the Jews and that "it is for want of taking hold of this exhilarating truth, that the Church has become so weak."[1] Darby also wanted believers to grasp that in being united with the risen Christ, who is seated at God's right hand, they were members of his body and thus an "organism" rather than an organization. So for public worship believers would meet in assemblies small enough to encourage each to make some edifying contribution. Then one would give an extended Bible reading of several passages with little accompanying exposition.

Darby developed these views after trying for several years to evangelize rural people in Ireland as an ordained priest in the Church of England. In a letter written thirty years later to August Tholuck, professor at Halle, Germany, he related how he then came to view himself as so united with Christ that "it is no longer a question with God of this wretched 'I,' which had wearied me during six or seven years, in the presence of the requirements of the law."[2] Instead, God's grace prevailed for true believers, the church, while the law remained for Israel, God's earthly people.

Darby spread his teachings to North America during seven trips to the United States, starting in 1862. There were no state churches in the United States, and so he found little interest among Presbyterians and Baptists to leave their congregations and attach themselves to Plymouth Brethren assemblies. But many were attracted to Darby's teachings about God's unconditional grace and the secret rapture of the church before the great tribulation.

Darby's most lasting influence in America was on James Brookes, a prominent Presbyterian minister in St. Louis. He promoted Darby's prophetic views and teachings on grace through books and his periodical *The Truth*. Starting in 1877, for three years Brookes mentored a young lawyer named C. I. Scofield in most of Darby's teachings, known by then as dispensationalism. In 1885 Scofield published a booklet entitled *Rightly Dividing the Word of Truth*. In it he expressed the basic premise of dispensationalism:

> The most obvious and striking division of the word of truth is that between Law and Grace. Indeed, these contrasting principles *characterize* the two most important distinctions—Jewish and Christian . . . Scripture never, in *any* dispensation, mingles these two principles. Law always has a place and

---

[1] J. N. Darby, "The Hopes of the Church of God," in *The Collected Writings of J. N. Darby*, ed. William Kelley, 34 vols. (London: Morrish, 1867-c. 1900), 2:571-72.

[2] *Letters of J. N. Darby*, 3 vols. (Kingston on Thames, England: Stow Hill Bible and Tract Depot, n.d.), 2:210.

work distinct and wholly diverse from that of grace. Law is God prohibiting and requiring; grace is God beseeching and bestowing.[3]

Twenty years later some Plymouth Brethren businessmen in New York City bankrolled Scofield so he could devote several years to editing a reference Bible. It would contain notes on key biblical passages and chain references for tracing various biblical themes through the Bible.

The Oxford University Press published Scofield's Bible in 1909, and it quickly achieved great popularity. Its foreword talked of input for its notes from a number of leading Christian scholars without saying anything about Darby's primary influence on them. Thus freed from any notion of its Plymouth Brethren origin, it became a mainstay for a broad spectrum of evangelicals during the fundamentalist-liberal controversies in America from 1920 until about 1960. By 1946 it had sold two million copies and become so influential that loyalty to its teachings was sometimes the test of one's orthodoxy. Historian George Marsden observed that

> dispensationalists were developing [in the United States] a major infrastructure of institutions, especially Bible institutes, Bible conferences, evangelistic agencies, mission societies, and publication agencies. These institutions formed the base for what was in effect an informal dispensationalist denomination, superimposed on various traditional denominations but usually not entirely separate from them. The new dispensationalist seminary [founded in 1924] in Dallas did not demand ecclesiastical separation of its staff.[4]

Dispensationalism's root idea was that for the church to enjoy God's grace, it must be viewed as completely separated from Israel, with whom God dealt in a legalistic manner. Thus John Walvoord, the second president of Dallas Seminary (1952-1985), spoke of how Romanism persisted in the amillennialism of covenant theology where "the great contrast between legalism as found in the Mosaic dispensation, and grace as revealed in the present age [to the church] is usually ignored. The effect is often the repetition of the Galatian error."[5] To quarantine the church from Galatianism it must stay with "church truth," found mostly in Paul, and understand the rest of the Bible as teaching salvation for Israel by the merit of complying with the law.

---

[3]C. I. Scofield, *Rightly Dividing the Word of Truth* (n.p., 1883), p. 34.
[4]George Marsden, *Reforming Fundamentalism* (Grand Rapids, Mich.: Eerdmans, 1987), p. 37.
[5]John F. Walvoord, *The Millennial Kingdom* (Findlay, Ohio: Dunham, 1959), p. 81.

DISPENSATIONALISM'S THEOLOGICAL HERMENEUTICS[6]

Walvoord's handling of Romans 11:1-6 is an example of how dispensation-alism keeps the church separate from Israel. In the middle of this para-graph Paul spoke of the Israelite remnant, which consisted of seven thousand in Elijah's time. But before and after mentioning them Paul also spoke of contemporary Jewish believers to prove that God had not rejected his people (Rom 11:1). His disregard for any chronological sequence in go-ing back from currently believing Jews to those seven centuries earlier and then back to the present implies an unbroken continuity in the Jewish rem-nant from OT to NT times.

But Walvoord, despite such data, insisted on drawing a sharp distinc-tion between the OT remnant and the believing Jews of Paul's day. The earlier Jews are "the Israelites who believed in God and kept the law and met the [legalistic] conditions for present enjoyment of the [earthly] bless-ings of the [Abrahamic] covenant." Nevertheless, "there is a godly Israel in the Church [now] consisting of Israelites who [along with Gentiles] are believers in Jesus Christ."[7] This is an instance where Walvoord's theologi-cal convictions, rooted in Darby, prevailed over conclusions based on bib-lical data in immediate contexts.

In his olive-tree analogy of Romans 11:17-24, Paul spoke of Gentile be-lievers being grafted for the first time as branches into a tree previously consisting only of the small Jewish remnant. Nourishment for these new Gentile branches and for the Jewish ones comes from the tree's roots, the Jewish patriarchs. Addressing a single Gentile believer Paul said, "You have been *grafted in among (en autois) the other [previously existing Jewish branches]* and now share in the nourishing sap from the olive root" (Rom 11:17, author's translation).

This intertwining of previously existing Jews with newly engrafted Gentile branches teaches that the whole tree represents God's one people. But Dallas Seminary's theological concern prevails over the "in among" (Rom 11:17) and affirms instead in Article 13 of its doctrinal statement a "complete separation" between Israel and the church. To be sure, Wal-

---

[6]Louis Berkhof explained "theological interpretation" in *Principles of Biblical Interpretation,* 2nd ed. (Grand Rapids, Mich.: Baker, 1952), pp. 133-66. "Analogy of faith" is the term Ber-nard Ramm used for this hermeneutic in *Protestant Biblical Interpretation,* 2nd ed. (Boston: W. A. Wilde, 1956), pp. 125-28. Unlike a "hermeneutic of biblical theology," a "theological hermeneutic" encourages the expositor to find ways that a text's data can plausibly conform to a theological tradition.
[7] Walvoord, *Millennial Kingdom,* pp. 145, 164.

voord insisted that dispensationalists adhere to "the application of the literal method [of interpretation]." But a few pages later he added, "Theological reasons [sometimes] make it clear that the [ordinary grammatical and historical meaning] was not intended by the [biblical] writer."[8] This is the talk of theological hermeneutics but not of biblical theology.

THE BIBLICAL THEOLOGY OF PROGRESSIVE DISPENSATIONALISM

Progressive Dispensationalism, coauthored by Craig Blaising and Darrell Bock, appeared in 1993. Blaising said, "In 1952 George Ladd, working with the methods of biblical theology, strongly criticized classical dispensationalism's [understanding of the kingdom of God]." As a consequence, "Many revised dispensationalists [thereafter] began to find a way to speak of a spiritual kingdom in the present dispensation." "[This revised dispensationalism], through its modifications and the problems it was dealing with, prepared the way for the eventual development of progressive dispensationalism."[9]

And Darrell Bock recently remarked, "[George E. Ladd was clear] . . . in articulating that there was one redemptive program and people of God in this plan. [Ladd] correctly appealed to Romans 11 for this emphasis on unity. One plant [Paul's olive tree] is in view that starts with Israelites, grafts in Gentiles, and looks forward to the day of Israel's return."[10]

So progressive dispensationalism has reconnected remnant Israel with the church and in so doing erased traditional dispensationalism's most distinctive feature. Charles Ryrie, a leading spokesperson for traditional dispensationalism, therefore views "progressive dispensationalism" as an "aberration from what has been considered normative dispensationalism."[11] But the progressives still call themselves dispensationalists, because, unlike the amillennialism often found in covenant theology, they speak of Israel as part of God's one people but retaining the name *Israel* during the future millennium to distinguish itself from the other thou-

---

[8] Ibid., pp 124, 128.

[9] Craig Blaising, "The Extent and Varieties of Dispensationalism," in Craig A. Blaising and Darrell L. Bock, *Progressive Dispensationalism* (Wheaton, Ill.: Victor, 1993), pp. 39, 46.

[10] Darrell L. Bock, "Why I Am a Dispensationalist with a Small 'd,'" *JETS* 41 (1998): 380, citing George Eldon Ladd's *Gospel of the Kingdom* (Grand Rapids, Mich.: Eerdmans, 1959), pp. 117-19.

[11] Charles C. Ryrie, "Update on Dispensationalism," *Issues in Dispensationalism*, ed. W. R. Willis, John R. Master and C. C. Ryrie (Chicago: Moody Press, 1994), p. 20.

sands of earth's peoples, alongside whom it will dwell.

Thus the progressives accomplished the first agenda item Blaising had suggested for the movement soon after it was officially organized in 1985. As for the second item Blaising said, "The relationship of law and grace needs to be articulated. This will involve a reexamination of dispensational teaching on sanctification."[12] But so far the progressives seem disinclined to address this subject.

GOSPEL AND LAW IN PROGRESSIVE DISPENSATIONALISM

Indeed, far from reexamining the law/gospel contrast, in a section entitled "The Crucial Issue," Robert L. Saucy spoke of gospel and law as one of the "resolved issues" and implied that progressive dispensationalism should bypass this subject and work in more promising areas. "The contention over the issue of law and grace has been rendered passé,"[13] he said. He was referring to the clash between covenant theology and classical dispensationalism that lasted for twenty years starting in 1936 with O. T. Allis's articles on the unity of the Bible and the law/gospel contrast.[14]

And progressive dispensationalism seems to agree with Saucy's desire to bypass Blaising's second agenda item. This is surprising, because traditional dispensationalism thought the only solution to the apparent law/gospel contrast was to cut the Bible in two so grace could be for the church and law for Israel. How then can progressive dispensationalism, after reconnecting the church and Israel, be indifferent to gospel and law? It is sincerely hoped that the progressives will stay exclusively with biblical theology and not be eclectic in availing themselves of theological hermeneutics for settling problems rising from the alleged law/gospel contrast. The following suggests how a biblical theology could negotiate six corners—there are others—in working on this subject.

THE SIX CORNERS

The *first corner* involves coming to terms with "faith" in Galatians 5:6:

---

[12]Craig A. Blaising, "Development of Dispensationalism by Contemporary Dispensationalists," *BibSac* 145 (1988): 279-80.

[13]Robert L. Saucy, *The Case for Progressive Dispensationalism* (Grand Rapids, Mich.: Zondervan, 1993), p. 15.

[14]O. T. Allis, "Modern Dispensationalism and the Doctrine of the Unity of Scripture," *EvQ* 8 (1936): 22-35, and "Modern Dispensationalism and the Law of God," *EvQ* 8 (1936): 272-90.

"*Faith*, working itself out in love, avails everything" (author's translation). It would be arbitrary to say that this faith, which "avails everything," nevertheless does not justify. But John Calvin had a theological premise for saying precisely this. "[Justifying] faith properly begins with the promise, rests in it, and ends in it. For in God [justifying] faith seeks . . . a life that is not found in commandments or declarations of penalties, but in the promise of mercy, and only in a freely given promise. For a conditional promise that sends us back to our own works does not promise life" (*Institutes of the Christian Religion* 3.2.29). So while "faith and good works must cleave together [but not fuse], we still lodge justification in faith, not in good works" (*Institutes* 3.16.1). A century later the Westminster Confession echoed this in saying, "[Justifying faith] is not alone in the person justified, but is ever *accompanied with* all other saving graces, and [so] is no dead faith, but works by love" (11.2, emphasis added).

Paul, however, spoke of going through life by faith in "the Son of God, who loved me and gave himself for me" (Gal 2:20 NRSV). This wording shows that the faith, which moved Paul through each day to do good works, involved banking one's confidence for the future exclusively on the continuing love of the risen Jesus. And it also involved believing in Jesus' finished work on the cross, for one cannot expect God's love for one's future if one is still at enmity with him. So the justification coming from this faith opens up the promise of the continued love of the risen Son of God. Then the desire to enjoy the prized blessings of this love strongly urges one to obey all God's commands summed up in "love your neighbor as yourself" (Gal 5:14 NRSV).

The *second corner* involves coming to terms with the meaning of the phrase "works of the law," which appears three times in Galatians 2:16. There, speaking to Peter, Paul said, "We know that a person is justified not by the *works of the law* but through faith in Jesus Christ. And we have believed in Christ Jesus, in order that we might be justified by faith in Christ and not by the *works of the law*, because no one will be justified by the *works of the law*" (author's translation). In his commentary on Galatians Calvin said, "The [larger] context [of Galatians] shows clearly that the moral law is *also* comprehended in [*works of law*], for almost everything Paul adds [after Gal 2:16] relates to the moral rather than the ceremonial law." With this "also" Calvin acknowledged that "works of the law" in Galatians 2:16 refers most directly to circumcision (Gal 2:1-10), kosher eating (Gal 2:11-14) and to other symbolic things Jews did to distinguish themselves from Gentile "sinners" (Gal 2:15).[15]

Why then was Calvin so intent on getting the moral law "*also*" into the "works of the law"? For centuries the church had properly viewed the "works of the law" in Galatians 2:16 as the ceremonial laws. But it had put the moral law on the opposite side from these laws and made it integral with believing in Jesus. This led to the false teaching that faith in Christ justifies only as people earn it by doing the good works commanded by the law. Calvin got rid of this false teaching by joining the moral law with the "works of the law" and viewing both as opposite from believing in Jesus. Nothing, however, in the fifteen verses of the context preceding Galatians 2:16 makes any reference to the moral law. So Calvin resorted to an artificial theological hermeneutic to argue that "works of the law" refers to the moral law.

But Calvin could have easily rid an exposition of Galatians 2:16 of this false teaching had he grasped from Romans 9:32 that the moral law is a "law of faith" and not "the law of works" existing only in the imagination of unbelieving Jews. Then, for example, the faith of committing one's future to the loving Son of God (Gal 2:20) for justification will also want to honor God's promise, "Vengeance is mine; 'I will repay'" (Deut 32:35, author's translation), and obey its resulting command not to be vengeful but benevolent to a wrongdoer (Rom 12:19-20). Moreover, this obedience in complying with a law of faith (Rom 9:32) excludes all boasting (Rom 3:27).

But Calvin felt that Galatians 3:12 is the passage, along with Romans 10:5-8 and Galatians 3:18, that "most clearly" views the law as being "utterly separated" from the faith that responds to the gospel (*Institutes* 3.11.17-18). It says, "The law is not based on faith, but on the contrary, 'the one who does these things shall live in them'" (quoting Lev 18:5, author's translation).

Therefore coming to terms with the meaning of "law" in Galatians 3:12 is a *third corner* to be turned. Nothing indicates that "law" here has a different meaning from "law" in Galatians 3:11. Paul views "law" there also as opposite from faith. And he contrasts the "works of the law" in Galatians 3:10, which bring a curse, from faith in Galatians 3:9, which brings a blessing. So "law" in Galatians 3:11-12 is shorthand for the "works of the law"

[15]John Calvin, *Calvin's New Testament Commentaries: Galatians*, 22 vols., ed. D. W. Torrance and T. F. Torrance (Grand Rapids, Mich.: Eerdmans, 1965), 11:38.

in Galatians 3:10 as the opposite of faith, as it was in Galatians 2:16. Consequently "law" in Galatians 3:12 refers to symbols for displaying one's allegedly superior piety before outsiders, such as Gentile "sinners"[16] (Gal 2:15; cf. Lk 15:2). Such a "law" encourages pride and leaves no room for faith.

An objection against construing "law" in Galatians 3:12 this way is that Paul used wording from Leviticus 18:5 to support his statement that "the law is not of faith." But the Leviticus 18:5 wording frequently appears in the noncanonical Jewish literature of Paul's day. Hundreds of instances of Leviticus 18:5 wording appear in the rabbinical literature, the Apocrypha, the Pseudepigrapha and the Qumran scrolls. One example from the *Psalms of Solomon* suffices: "Faithful is the Lord . . . to them that walk . . . in the law which He commanded that we might live" (*Pss. Sol.* 14:1-2). The meaning given these words comes from the great majority of nonremnant Jews (Rom 11:25). But their meaning is not Moses' intended meaning for Leviticus 18:5. No one welcomes that meaning until the veil that covers the heart is removed in regeneration by the Holy Spirit (2 Cor 3:15-17). Then, for the first time, one makes contact with the revelatory "law of faith [instead of the fictitious] law of works" (Rom 9:32). So Paul's use of the Leviticus 18:5 wording in Galatians 3:12 applies only to that fictitious view of the law "as a law of works" ruled out in Romans 9:32. That wording is irrelevant to Paul's thesis that the revelatory law is a law of faith.

A *fourth corner* to turn in developing a biblical theology of law comes from Exodus 20:6, in the middle of the Decalogue, which says that God "shows mercy *(hesed)* to thousands of those who love him and keep his commandments" (Ex 20:6, author's translation). Commandments that bring mercy to those obeying them—these are laws of faith. They are the sort found in doctors' prescriptions rather than in job descriptions. The mercy of improved health coming from following a doctor's health regimen is not something earned, though it certainly can be spurned by the disobedience of unbelief.

A job description, on the other hand, stipulates the duties of a care provider in meeting a client's needs. Care providers justifiably exult in their abilities to comply with the stipulations of their job descriptions. But cli-

---

[16]James D. G. Dunn, *The Epistle to the Galatians,* Black's New Testament Commentary (Peabody, Mass.: Hendrickson, 1993), p. 137. This meaning of "works of the law" also appears in "Some of the Deeds of the Law" (4QMMT), finally published in 1991. There the phrase stands for specific rules distinguishing one Jewish sect at Qumran from another sect whose members were regarded as "sinners" in the Galatians 2:15 sense.

ents exult in their care providers' skills rather than in how they complied with their instructions.

All God's commandments, therefore, are like a doctor's prescription rather than a job description. God is the care provider for the people whom he has created. So the commandments he gives will always be laws of faith essential for enjoying his blessings of grace. God could never give a job-description law to us who are nothing "but dust and ashes" (Gen 18:27). He is not "served by human hands, as though he needed anything, since he himself gives to all mortals life and breath and all things" (Acts 17:25 NRSV). So none of God's commandments, explicit or implied, are ever laws of works. Instead, they are all laws of faith.

But people in their sinful pride love job-description laws, because with them one can view oneself as a care provider. With a law of faith, however, one must humbly view oneself as a needy client suing for mercy, and the ego abhors such laws. In several places the OT speaks of the great majority of Israel as unwilling to submit to God's laws in being "stiff-necked" and having "uncircumcised hearts of stone" (e.g., Deut 10:16; Ezek 36:26). Paul himself was like this until he was regenerated on the Damascus Road and received a heart of flesh.

So the *fifth corner* to turn is to fit Paul's references to his experiences with the law into a time line. In his preconversion days he had a carnal mind that was "hostile to God and unable to submit to God's law" (Rom 8:7, author's translation). His parents, speaking the Aramaic of the Hebrew language tradition (Phil 3:5), immersed him in the teachings of the law from his earliest moments. Then during his rabbinical training in Jerusalem he was "advancing in Judaism beyond many Jews of my own age, and was extremely zealous for the traditions of my fathers" (Gal 1:14, author's translation). But in looking back on all these years he saw them as a time when he was "apart from the law" (Rom 7:9). During these years "sin, seizing an opportunity in the commandment, deceived [him]" (Rom 7:11, author's translation) into viewing God's commands as parts of an ego-gratifying job description rather than of a humbling doctor's prescription.

But when God removed the veil from his heart in regeneration (2 Cor 3:15-16), Paul was humbled to the point where he regarded himself as "the foremost of sinners" (1 Tim 1:15) in having persecuted the church. When "the commandment came [on the Damascus Road], sin revived, and I died" (Rom 7:9b, 10, 11). Sin first came to life in deceiving him into thinking of himself as working for God. Then sin "*re*vived" as the newly unveiled law of faith convicted Paul of being "sinful beyond measure" (Rom 7:13) in the blasphemy of his role reversal of once thinking of himself as God's care provider instead of his client. But God forgave him all this sin and reckoned him as righteous—justified. From then on Paul sought to live by faith in the continuing love of the Son of God (Gal 2:20). Through persevering in an obedience of faith (Rom 1:5) he would "take hold of [the actual righteousness] for which Christ took hold of him [in justification]" (Phil 3:12, author's translations).

A *sixth corner* to turn in these beginnings of a biblical theology of gospel and law reconsiders the nature of the Galatian heresy. The Galatians had commenced the Christian life by receiving the Holy Spirit through faith (Gal 3:2). Then people came who tried to persuade them that in order to be full-fledged Christians they had to identify themselves as Jews by submitting to circumcision (Gal 5:2). Paul scoffed at the folly in thinking that faith, initiated and maintained supernaturally in the heart by the Holy Spirit, could accomplish maturity only if supplemented by a fleshly, Jewish identity marker (Gal 3:3)! If the Galatians started wearing such an emblem, they would start boasting in this distinctive instead of in "the Son of God, who loved [them] and gave himself for [them]" (Gal 2:20 NRSV). So Paul said, "May I never boast except in the cross of our Lord Jesus Christ, through whom the world has been crucified to me and I to the world" (Gal 6:14, author's translation). Any teaching that supplemented the cross of Christ either for justification or for developing a godly character was anathema to Paul (Gal 1:8-10).

Avoiding the Galatian heresy means staying with the dynamics inherent in justifying faith as we go on to spiritual maturity (Gal 3:3; 4:19). The love demonstrated by Jesus in Gethsemane—"very God of very God" (Nicea)—guarantees the brightest future. Jesus rose from the dead, and so his love for us is just as strong now as it was two millennia ago in Gethsemane (Heb 13:8). So those living by faith in this love (Gal 2:20) will always rejoice in the Lord (Phil 3:1), in great anticipation of his blessings streaming toward them in the near and distant future (Rom 12:12).

This joy dispels the evil attitudes of unbelief: self-adulation, anxiety, covetousness, bitterness, regret, impatience, jealousy, envy and despondency. A heart rejoicing in such confident hope is free from the "deceitfulness of sin" (Heb 3:12-13) that unbelief always produces. Only then is one able to walk circumspectly and avoid doing foolish things that so often hurt others and oneself. "The hope and a future" (Jer 29:11) guaranteed by

Jesus' Gethsemane love strongly urges one to remain in its bright prospects by keeping his commandments (Jn 15:10; Jude 21). The faith that justifies, therefore, is the faith that also works itself out in keeping Jesus' commandments (Gal 5:6).

But Calvin saw it differently. He said the task of faith "ends" in receiving justification (*Institutes* 3.2.29). Then what he called "repentance" (*Institutes* 3.3) commences, developing maturity by leaving justifying faith be and attending instead to the law of works. "However eagerly [the saints] may in accordance with the Spirit strive toward God's righteousness, the listless flesh always burdens them that they do not proceed with due readiness. [So] the law is to the flesh like a whip to an idle and balky ass, to arouse it to work" (*Institutes* 2.7.12). In other words, the "faith working itself out in love" (Gal 5:6) consists of "other graces" that come alongside justifying faith to make it a living faith that obeys the law by considering its threats and promises (Westminster Confession 11.2; 14.2).

Like many others, I want to be like the Bereans of Acts 17:11 and test the validity of various teachings against the biblical data. As of this writing I conclude that Calvin's view of sanctification as coming from the law instead of from faith is an instance of the Galatian heresy. I welcome help from others in calling my attention to data I may have overlooked and in making me aware of some unconscious prejudice that may have skewed my handling of the biblical data. Oscar Cullman said that we must "find out first of all by means of the philological, historical method what the text has to say to us that is new and perhaps completely foreign."[17]

Some expositors, however, believe that "systematics takes the whole of revelation and seeks to weave an inherent unity between the parts."[18] But Cullmann, an Alsatian Lutheran who honored church tradition, "wanted to say a word against even this *Vorverständnis* [of church tradition] on behalf of a deliberate effort at impartiality [in exegesis]."[19]

An example of an exegesis inclined to affirm dogma would seem to be T. David Gordon's exegesis of Romans 9:32.[20] Lacking here is Cullmann's Berean attitude "that my Church's faith [may not always be] that of the

[17]Oscar Cullmann, *Salvation in History* (New York: Harper & Row, 1967), p. 71.
[18]Darrell L. Bock, *A Biblical Theology of the New Testament*, ed. Roy B. Zuck (Chicago: Moody Press, 1994), pp. 12-13.
[19]Cullmann, *Salvation in History*, p. 68 n. 2.
[20]T. David Gordon, "Why Israel Did Not Obtain Torah-Righteousness: A Translation of Romans 9:32," *WJTh* 54 (1992): 163-66.

writers of the New Testament."[21] So to explain why Israel failed to attain the law, Gordon looks not to the linguistic data in the text but brings in the irrelevant Reformed dogma that "the Torah demands perfect obedience" (p. 165). Had Gordon, however, supplied the ellipses in Romans 9:32 in the normal way, from the parallel in Romans 9:31, then "Israel pursued" would be the predication of the causal clause explaining Israel's failure to attain the law. Then his construction of Romans 9:32 would follow most translations in saying this failure occurred because Israel responded impertinently to the law of faith by imagining it to be a law of works instead.

These objections against Gordon's exposition of Romans 9:32 provide some indication of how an exegesis based on biblical theology wants to proceed. Biblical theology, for more than a century now and with ever-increasing momentum, has protested against expositions inclined to uphold some theological tradition. Gordon's arbitrary refusal to supply an ellipsis from the immediately preceding parallelism in Romans 9:31 and his silence about the "as" in Romans 9:32 are crucial to his effort to expound this verse as upholding Reformed theology's view of the law. Wearying with such expositions, biblical theology wants only to get at the intended meanings of the authors or redactors of biblical texts.

It is hoped that these few suggestions for getting at a biblical theology of the alleged law/gospel contrast will stir progressive dispensationalism to move quickly in this direction. Contrary to Saucy, the subject matter of law/gospel is not passé.

---

[21]Cullmann, *Salvation in History*, p. 68.

17

The Future of
Biblical Theology

Ted M. Dorman

The purpose of this essay is not to predict the future of biblical theology but to propose an agenda for biblical theology. In order to look ahead, however, we must first establish from whence we have come and where things stand presently in the discipline of biblical theology. To this end we shall begin by focusing on two important proponents of biblical theology, one past and one present, as case studies of what it means to do biblical theology.

We shall first set forth the hermeneutical perspective of one of twentieth-century biblical theology's pioneers, the late Oscar Cullmann, in whose shadow many of us fulfill our vocations. We shall examine his concepts of eschatology and revelation, two critical issues in the early decades of twentieth-century theology, and how his approach to these issues separated him from the two most influential theologians of his day, Karl Barth and Rudolf Bultmann.

Next we shall evaluate Francis Watson's recent proposal to redefine biblical theology, as set forth in *Text and Truth*.[1] Watson believes that biblical

---

[1]Francis Watson, *Text and Truth: Redefining Biblical Theology* (Grand Rapids, Mich.: Eerdmans, 1997). I have reviewed *Text and Truth* in *JETS* 43 (2000): 162-64.

theology is endangered by modern biblical scholarship's division into "three autonomous communities": Old Testament studies, New Testament studies and systematic theology. He views this threefold division not merely as methodological but also as an "ideologically motivated" enterprise that results in an overall falsification of what the Bible is all about. He therefore "seeks to dismantle the barriers that at present separate biblical scholarship from Christian theology."

Finally, we shall propose an agenda for the future of biblical theology that seeks to bridge (at least up to a point) the traditional confessional stances that have separated Christians over the past several hundred years. Two issues will be addressed: the relationship between the law and the gospel and the doctrine of justification by faith.

OSCAR CULLMANN: A HERMENEUTICS OF *HEILSGESCHICHTE*

The problem of New Testament eschatology. Perhaps the most distinguishing feature of Cullmann's perspective on NT theology is his well-known thesis that the NT writers view the kingdom of God as both a present and a future reality. The kingdom has already arrived in history in the person and work of Jesus Christ and continues to make its power known through the Holy Spirit in Christ's church. At the same time, the kingdom is not yet realized within history in all of its fullness. The kingdom has been inaugurated but not yet consummated.[2]

American evangelical scholars are so familiar with Cullmann's perspective that they seldom delve into the issues that led him to adopt a hermeneutics of *Heilsgeschichte* (the history of salvation). Many of Cullmann's European counterparts, by contrast, have viewed his efforts as a revival of the nineteenth-century Erlangen school in Germany, due in large part to the term *Heilsgeschichte* that is common to Cullmann and the Erlangen school.[3]

Cullmann owes his salvation-historical insights not to the nineteenth-century theological landscape, however, but to twentieth-century theological and hermeneutical issues embodied in the writings of men such as Albert Schweitzer, C. H. Dodd, Karl Barth and Rudolf Bultmann. Schweitzer and Dodd, among others, influenced Cullmann's attempts to articulate the

---

[2]Oscar Cullmann, *Christ and Time*, rev. ed. (Philadelphia: Westminster Press, 1964), pp. 82-84.
[3]See, e.g., K. G. Steck, *Die Idee der Heilsgeschichte: Hofmann-Schlatter-Cullmann* (Zollikon: Evangelischer Verlag, 1959), chap. 1, and Peter Stuhlmacher, *Vom Verstehen des Neuen Testaments* (Göttingen: Vandenhoeck & Ruprecht, 1979), pp. 145-46.

shape of NT eschatology, while Barth and Bultmann caused Cullmann to rethink the hermeneutical assumptions behind the so-called dialectical theology of the third and fourth decades of the twentieth century.

With regard to eschatology, Cullmann recounted in 1988 how the polarities represented by Schweitzer ("thoroughgoing" eschatology) and Dodd ("realized" eschatology) became catalysts for a most significant insight that came to him quite suddenly in 1932:

> It is unforgettable to me how as a young professor in my hometown of Strasbourg, as I was preparing a New Testament exegetical lecture, the solution to a problem which had concerned me for a long time became clear: a future Kingdom of God, which my countryman Albert Schweitzer had interpreted as "thoroughgoing [eschatology]" or a present [Kingdom], as was later referred to by C. H. Dodd as "realized eschatology." It was now clear to me that it was not one or the other, but both: already realized but yet still future. With Christ, the event that accomplished my salvation has occurred, but the completion of it has yet to occur. *Already and not yet.* This "tension" determines the situation in which we, along with the New Testament, find ourselves.[4]

Fourteen years later this already/not yet tension in NT eschatology became the centerpiece of Cullmann's most famous work, *Christ and Time.* During the 1950s and 1960s Cullmann was the theologian of choice for many North American biblical theologians, even as his views were rejected in Europe by those who followed Barth and Bultmann in their attempts to reinterpret NT eschatology in nontemporal (*ungeschichtlich*) terms.[5]

Behind this difference of eschatological perspective between Cullmann on the one hand and Barth and Bultmann on the other lay an even more fundamental hermeneutical issue that must be clarified before one can understand why Cullmann rejected their nontemporal reinterpretations of biblical eschatology.

The concept of revelation in the New Testament.[6] The crisis that rocked continental theology following the First World War was fundamentally one of

---

[4]Cullmann, "Vorwort von Oscar Cullmann," in Karl-Heinz Schlaudraff, *"Heil als Geschichte"? Die Frage nach dem heilsgeschichtlichen Denken, dargestellt anhand der Konzeption Oscar Cullmanns* (Tübingen: Mohr Siebeck, 1988), p. xvi.

[5]Oscar Cullmann, "Le Pensée Eschatologique d'après un Livre Recent," *Revue d'Histoire et de Philosophie Religieuse* 18 (1938): 350-51.

[6]For a more detailed discussion of the concept of revelation in twentieth-century theology, see Theodore Martin Dorman, *The Hermeneutics of Oscar Cullmann* (San Francisco: Mellen Research University Press, 1991), pp. 4-15; Ted M. Dorman, "Oscar Cullmann," in *Historical Handbook of Major Biblical Interpreters* (Downers Grove, Ill.: InterVarsity Press, 1998), pp. 467-71.

the concept of divine revelation. Prior to 1914 theological liberalism had reigned supreme in the German universities for almost a century, due primarily to the influence of Friedrich Schleiermacher. Specifically, Schleiermacher had sought to make peace with the Enlightenment's antisupernaturalist critique of the biblical record by redefining Christianity as a faith that had nothing to do with history as such but rather with the inward religious consciousness of the biblical writers and of Jesus. This in turn meant that biblical interpretation had as its subject matter the inward psychology of the biblical writers. If by reading the Bible one could understand the religious feelings of Jesus and the disciples, that person would gain further insight into his or her own religious experience.

Barth rebelled against Schleiermacher's notion that the Bible is a book about the writers' subjective religious experiences. For Barth, the Bible was a book about God, not about the history of people's feelings about God. At the same time, Barth accepted the results of liberal historical-critical scholarship, which viewed the Bible as a book filled with historical inaccuracies. For Barth and for Bultmann, this was not important, however. Both viewed the subject matter of the Bible not as historical events or the interpretations of those events by the biblical writers but as the suprahistorical Spirit of God, who dwells outside the bounds of history and human contingencies. This emphasis on the fundamental discontinuity between God and humanity (as opposed to liberalism's view of humanity's basic harmony with God via inward religious feeling) became the basis for the so-called dialectical theology movement following World War I.

In 1928[7] Cullmann endorsed Barth's notion that the Spirit of Christ, and not a so-called historical Jesus of modern scholarship, is the subject matter of the NT. At the same time, Cullmann believed that Barth's hermeneutical perspective left too little room for historical control because Barth viewed biblical exegesis as merely a "preliminary" step to the more important task of "theological interpretation," that is, reflecting upon one's encounter with the "object" (*die Sache*) of faith: the risen Christ. Cullmann believed that the Christian exegete's theological interpretations not only must be elicited by the text of Scripture but must also be *controlled* by the text.

The reason Barth would not subject his "theological exegesis" to historical control, noted Cullmann, was that he was operating with a "neo-Kan-

[7]Oscar Cullmann, "Les Problemes posés par la Méthode exégetique de l'École de Karl Barth," *Revue d'Histoire et de Philosophie religieuse* 8 (1928): 70-83.

tian" dualism that places divine revelation completely outside of the bounds of history. Barth, along with Bultmann and other advocates of dialectical theology, had reacted against the historicism of liberal hermeneutics by redefining revelation in ahistorical, noncognitive terms. That is, they refused to define revelation either as divinely bestowed information or as God's activity within the flow of history. Instead, dialectical theologians viewed revelation as a personal encounter between the Spirit of Christ and human beings. Barth stressed the divine Giver of revelation, while Bultmann spoke of revelation from the standpoint of the individual who is addressed by God (an emphasis that, ironically, led Bultmann to focus on the faith experience of the individual, much as Schleiermacher had done).

Cullmann's view of revelation attempted to stress both the Giver of revelation (Christ) and the receivers (the church). In addition, Cullmann saw cognitive knowledge of God as possible because divine revelation, while coming to us from outside of ourselves, has entered into the framework of history and language. Thus Cullmann saw historical exegesis as being able to exercise a positive role in the theological task.

It is therefore not surprising that Cullmann soon backed away from his 1928 endorsement of Barth's notion that the suprahistorical Spirit of Christ was the subject matter of the NT and that the NT exegete must therefore have a prior encounter with the risen Christ before historical investigation can begin. Instead, Cullmann's emphasis on the historical nature of divine revelation eventually led him to view the subject matter of the NT as the events and interpretations surrounding the life, death and resurrection of Jesus as experienced by the earliest Christians. This meant that the subject matter of the NT must be understood only in light of the text of the NT, rather than the text being understood in light of a previously understood subject matter (such as Barth's "Spirit of Christ" or Bultmann's "self-understanding").[8]

Cullmann's emphasis on the definitive status of the NT witness to Christ, as over against postapostolic dogmatic formulas which for him are of secondary authority, led him to state: "I deliberately abstain from *subjecting the texts of the New Testament to questions raised by later dogmas.*"[9] This in turn gives rise to another question. If salvation history did not end with the close of the biblical canon, but also includes a not-yet element,

---

[8]Dorman, *Hermeneutics of Oscar Cullmann*, pp. 33-34; Dorman, "Oscar Cullmann," p. 469.
[9]Oscar Cullmann, *The Christology of the New Testament*, 2nd ed. (Philadelphia: Westminster Press, 1963), p. 42.

why has Cullmann excluded postapostolic witnesses to Christ from his definition of authoritative interpretations of the Christ event? To put it another way: What is the relationship between the NT canon and the rest of redemptive history?

The New Testament canon and salvation history. Cullmann's desire to keep NT exegesis separate from later dogmatic concerns has little if anything to do with Protestantism's principle of *sola Scriptura*. It is instead linked to his view of the NT's relationship to the rest of redemptive history.

Specifically, the NT belongs to that period of *Heilsgeschichte* wherein the Spirit-inspired interpreters of the Christ event were eyewitnesses to the events they recorded and interpreted or were close associates of such apostolic eyewitnesses.[10] The NT tradition therefore differs from postapostolic traditions by virtue of its eyewitness quality and thus belongs with Christ himself at the midpoint of salvation history.

This midpoint of God's *Heilsgeschichte* is what Cullmann refers to as the *Offenbarungsgeschichte*, or "history of revelation," since it serves as the norm for all previous and subsequent events of salvation history. For while the Holy Spirit does continue to reveal himself in the postapostolic church, whether or not it is he who speaks in any instance must be determined in light of the literary deposit of the *Offenbarungsgeschichte:* the NT canon. This qualitative differentiation between apostolic and postapostolic tradition separates Cullmann not only from his Roman Catholic counterparts but also from Barth's notion that revelation is identical with our encounters with the Spirit of the risen Jesus,[11] and that Scripture is a secondary witness we read in order to determine "whether and to what extent" the apostolic writings "reflect and echo" the Word of God that encounters us via the Spirit of the risen Jesus.[12]

The definitive nature of the "history of revelation" thus entails that biblical theology is beholden neither to dogmatic formulas nor to purported "encounters" with the "Spirit of Christ." This does not mean, however, that biblical theology should be isolated from other branches of the theological enterprise. Cullmann stated that a dogmatics or ethics of salvation history "ought to be written someday."[13]

---

[10]Oscar Cullmann, "The Tradition," in *The Early Church,* ed. A. J. B. Higgens (Philadelphia: Westminster Press, 1953), pp. 60-72.

[11]Karl Barth, *Church Dogmatics* 1.2 (Edinburgh: T & T Clark, 1955), p. 118.

[12]Karl Barth, *Evangelical Theology: An Introduction* (Garden City, N.Y.: Anchor, 1964), p. 29.

[13]Oscar Cullmann, *Salvation in History* (New York: Harper & Row, 1967), p. 329.

Nevertheless the twentieth century has witnessed increasing specialization among biblical scholars and theologians, which in turn has led to biblical studies being separated from theological studies and divided into subsets of OT and NT studies. The fact that biblical theology as practiced by Cullmann and his followers has at times been labeled as merely a "descriptive" discipline may have contributed to such separation.[14]

Such lack of interaction between biblical studies and the overall theological enterprise has caused some modern biblical scholars to rethink the relationship between biblical theology and other theological disciplines. Prominent among such scholars is the biblical theologian Francis Watson. His concern, that biblical theology be related positively to other theological disciplines, is the subject of the next section.

FRANCIS WATSON: TEXT AND TRUTH

The theological priority. Watson begins his polemic against modern "barriers that . . . separate biblical scholarship from Christian theology" by defining biblical theology as "a theological, hermeneutical and exegetical discipline" whose "hermeneutical and exegetical dimensions are placed at the disposal of its overriding theological function" (p. vii).[15] To divorce biblical studies from theological concerns, as does much modern academic biblical interpretation, is to deny what the Bible claims itself to be: *theou logos*, theology.

There are several reasons for this divorce between Bible and theology, including a strong belief among many academicians that "theological concerns have an inevitable tendency to distort the autonomous processes of biblical exegesis." This is not merely the result of a secular bias toward matters theological, Watson adds. To the contrary, there also exists an evangelical Protestant mentality that "perversely" uses the Protestant *sola Scriptura* in such a way that "the Bible is typically read with scant regard for the long and intricate dialogue with the Bible that is the history of Christian theology" (p. 4).

At the same time, however, Watson's regard for the history of Christian doctrine does not lead him to view Scripture as a series of prooftexts for

---

[14]See, e.g., George Eldon Ladd, *A Theology of the New Testament,* rev. ed. (Grand Rapids, Mich.: Eerdmans, 1993), p. xi; Donald A. Hagner, "Biblical Theology and Preaching," *Expository Times* 96 (1985): 137.

[15]Page references to Francis Watson's *Text and Truth* in this section are included in parentheses within the text.

later dogmas. This is borne out by his rejection of radical deconstructive hermeneutics in favor of what he terms "unfashionable concepts" such as "literal sense," "authorial intention" and "objective interpretation." Yet even as he affirms what may be called traditional or general hermeneutics, Watson does so primarily for theological reasons, as opposed to linguistic reasons. Specifically, current deconstructive dogmas should be rejected not merely for reasons of incoherence but *"because they conflict with the dogmas held to be foundational to orthodox Christian faith, and because in the light of that conflict, certain inherent problems and implausibilities rapidly come to light"* (p. 97, emphasis in the original).

Here we find an intriguing combination of hermeneutical continuity and contrast between Watson and Cullmann. On the one hand, Watson shares Cullmann's concern that the text of Scripture is understood in terms of the verbal meanings the original authors intended to communicate. On the other hand, whereas Cullmann sought to separate his exegesis from later dogmas, Watson affirms his hermeneutical principles on the basis of theology. A question therefore arises. For Watson, which is the final hermeneutical arbiter: the biblical text or the subject matter to which it points, Jesus Christ?

The sovereign subject matter. While brief summaries of complex issues are dangerous, Watson's perspective on the relationship between "text" and "Truth" appears closer to Barth's christocentric hermeneutics than to Cullmann's grammatical-historical emphasis.[16] That is to say, for Watson hermeneutical sovereignty resides not in the text but in the subject matter to which it points. Evidences for this admittedly provisional conclusion include the following three considerations.

First, Watson's statement that "the Old Testament comes to us with Jesus and from Jesus, and can never be understood in abstraction from him" appears more in line with what Wolfhart Pannenberg has called Barth's Christology "from above"[17] (theological exegesis) than with Cullmann's Christology "from below," which places christological reflections at the end of exegesis rather than the beginning.[18] Such statements also tell

---

[16]See, e.g. Cullmann, "The Necessity and Function of Higher Criticism," in *The Early Church,* p. 16 n. 2, where Cullmann states that the responsibility of the exegete is "simply to confine himself to his own limited task," so that historical philological exegesis can control theological interpretations without becoming subservient to them.

[17]Wolfhart Pannenberg, *Jesus—God and Man,* 2nd ed. (Philadelphia: Westminster Press, 1977).

[18]See Dorman, *Hermeneutics of Oscar Cullmann,* pp. 119-22.

us nothing about whether the verbal meanings of the various biblical writers can be brought together into an overall unity of verbal meaning, or whether there is merely a diversity of meanings that, while ultimately beyond verbal coherence, revolve around the same subject matter, Jesus Christ. But if the latter is the case, then how can we know the meaning and significance of that subject matter?

Second, Watson's exposition of "Creation in the Beginning" (chap. 6) shows the same antipathy toward virtually all forms of "natural theology" that Barth had. James Barr comes in for specific criticism here, as does the traditional Reformed view that Paul's Areopagus sermon (Acts 17) presupposes a rudimentary "natural theology" even among pagans. Watson, to the contrary, views Paul's quotations of pagan poets on Mars Hill as merely "linguistic landmarks" familiar to the Athenians (p. 249), as opposed to any genuine knowledge of God. The altar to an unknown God "serves as a point of contact between Paul and his audience, but not in such a way as to establish a common ground on which both parties can agree" (p. 252). Indeed, Paul's goal is not so much to establish common ground as it is "to identify an internal inconsistency within Greek religious belief and practice" (p. 255).

Third, some of Watson's statements display affinities to Barth's insistence that historical exegesis is only "preliminary" to theological exegesis, since Jesus Christ is the sovereign subject matter of the entire Christian canon.[19] For example, at times Watson appears to run roughshod over historical claims of the biblical text in favor of viewing such stories as "fictive" elements of a narrative that is fundamentally historical but also contains elements that, to be blunt, did not happen as portrayed by the biblical writers (see, e.g., pp. 82-88, where Watson views the transfiguration as merely an interpretation rather than an event in history).

A question for Watson. This third instance of Barthian tendencies in Watson gives rise to the following question: Why not on this basis also dismiss as mere interpretations elements that are clearly portrayed in Scripture as suprahistorical facts, such as the objective existence of the devil? Barth specifically denied the existence of a personal devil, even while affirming that God has sovereignly chosen to communicate his revelation in Christ through the medium of a Bible that does portray a per-

---

[19]For a discussion of Cullmann's critique of Barth's "preliminary" use of exegesis, see Dorman, *Hermeneutics of Oscar Cullmann*, pp. 28-31.

sonal devil![20] In like manner, Watson affirms that "for Christian theology, truth is textually mediated" (p. 1). The potential ambiguity of the words "textually mediated," open as they are to Barth's concept of revelation, indicates that Watson would do well to go one step further and insist, as did Cullmann more than forty years ago, that the biblical text not only mediates truth but also controls our interpretations of theological truth via grammatical-historical exegesis.[21]

Armed with a hermeneutic that, while aware of the riches of the post-apostolic Christian tradition, nevertheless begins and ends with biblical exegesis, let us look to the future and briefly outline how we might address two of the most pressing theological debates of our day: the relationship between the law of Moses and the gospel of Jesus Christ, and the meaning of justification by faith. In so doing we shall unavoidably touch on the question of whether we can meaningfully articulate a unity of the Bible.

AN AGENDA FOR THE ONSET OF THE TWENTY-FIRST CENTURY

Gospel and law: Contrast or continuum? The seemingly endless flow of scholarly studies on the relationship between the law of Moses and the gospel of Christ testifies to the importance of this problem and the lack of scholarly consensus achieved thus far. The central issue is clear, however. Are the law and the gospel fundamentally different in their essential meanings, or do they share a common meaning that teaches salvation by grace through faith?

The two principal paradigms of modern evangelicalism, dispensationalism and covenant theology, both teach the former, though in different ways. John Calvin, for example, described the contrast between the law and the gospel as follows: "the gospel promises are free and dependent solely upon God's mercy, while the promises of the law depend upon the condition of works" (*Institutes of the Christian Religion* 3.11.17). Passages such as Galatians 3:12 ("the law does not rest on faith," NRSV [throughout the essay]) and Romans 10:4 ("Christ is the end of the law") convinced

---

[20]See, e.g., an account of Barth's denying the existence of the devil in "Barth in Chicago," John Warwick Montgomery, *The Suicide of Christian Theology* (Minneapolis: Bethany Hosue, 1971), pp. 192-93.
[21]See Cullmann, "The Tradition" in *The Early Church*, p. 87, and Cullmann, "Andacht zur Eröffnung der S.N.T.S. am 30 August 1965 in Heidelberg," *NTS* 12 (1965-1966): 142. See also the discussion in Dorman, *Hermeneutics of Oscar Cullmann*, pp. 136-38.

Calvin and his Reformed successors that the gospel of Christ is fundamentally contrary to the message of the Mosaic law. Classical dispensationalism went a step further and taught that the Old and New Covenants embodied two different sets of ground rules directed toward two distinct peoples of God: Israel, God's earthly people, and the church, God's heavenly people. More recently those who label themselves progressive dispensationalists have adopted covenant theology's view that there is one overarching redemptive covenant within the history of salvation,[22] while some in the Reformed camp are clearly not comfortable with the notion of a prelapsarian "covenant of works."[23] Yet dispensationalism and covenant theology continue to view the fundamental ethos of the Mosaic law as legal and conditional, as opposed to the nonlegal and unconditional nature of the gospel.

At the same time, this law/gospel contrast within the Reformed and dispensational traditions has not gone unchallenged, due in great part to the findings of Pauline exegetical studies over the past four decades. Most worthy of mention in this regard is the work of C. E. B. Cranfield, who in 1964 distinguished between *nomos* as God's will revealed in the law of Moses and *nomos* as an attitude of "legalism" toward the law's commands.[24] Cranfield's findings challenged Calvin's dichotomy between the law of Moses and the gospel of Christ, a point Cranfield later made more explicit in his exegesis of Romans 9:32, wherein he described the law of Moses as a law that commanded Israel to exercise faith in God.[25] Also noteworthy is Robert Badenas's monograph covering the history of the exegesis of Romans 10:4, which reveals that Reformed theology's teaching that Christ is the *telos nomou* in the sense of "termination of the law" lacks support in the first millennium of the church's interpretation of that crucial Pauline text.[26]

Considerations such as these have led Daniel P. Fuller to insist that the law of Moses commands essentially the same thing as the gospel of Christ:

---

[22]See, e.g., Craig Blaising and Darrell Bock, *Progressive Dispensationalism* (Wheaton, Ill.: Victor, 1993).

[23]For example, O. Palmer Robertson prefers to speak of a "covenant of creation" and a "covenant of redemption" rather than a "covenant of works" and a "covenant of grace." See O. Palmer Robertson, *The Christ of the Covenants* (Grand Rapids, Mich.: Baker, 1980).

[24]C. E. B. Cranfield, "St. Paul and the Law," *SJT* 17 (1964): 43-68.

[25]C. E. B. Cranfield, *A Critical and Exegetical Commentary on the Epistle to the Romans*, 2 vols. (Edinburgh: T & T Clark, 1979), vol. 2.

[26]Robert Badenas, *Christ the End of the Law: Romans 10:4 in Pauline Perspective* (Sheffield: JSOT, 1985); see esp. pp. 38-80.

that we must bank all of our hope for an eternity of happy tomorrows on God's "precious and very great promises" (2 Pet 1:4). Contemporary Pauline scholars generally have not accepted Fuller's thesis.[27] In some cases opposition to the Fuller proposal appears to be grounded more in allegiance to the Reformed tradition than to the biblical text.[28] On the other hand, some who are sympathetic with Fuller's aims nevertheless differ with him on exegetical details.[29]

Perhaps the greatest NT exegetical obstacle to Fuller's thesis remains Galatians 3:12, which for many seals the case for a law/gospel contrast, Romans 9:32 notwithstanding. The recent discovery of the Pauline expression "works of law" in the Qumran document 4QMMT has added new light to the law/gospel debate. Martin Abegg, for example, sees 4QMMT's reference to "works of law" as evidence that Paul was using this expression to refer not to the law of Moses per se but to a legalistic interpretation of Moses that ran counter to the law's original intent.[30]

James Dunn has jumped on board Abegg's bandwagon,[31] though N. T. Wright is somewhat skeptical.[32] The very existence of a Dunn/Wright point/counterpoint over 4QMMT virtually assures that this debate over the significance of 4QMMT, and the larger debate over the relationship between the law and the gospel, will remain on the front burner of biblical theology for some time to come. And so it should.

The doctrine of justification. Whether or not the law and the gospel both teach "salvation by grace through faith" has implications for the doctrine of justification. In addition, the question of how Scripture defines key terms such as "justification," "sanctification," "works," "grace" and "faith" demands that as biblical theologians we follow closely and contribute to the recent dialogues between Protestants and Catholics sur-

---

[27]In contrast to Fuller see Stephen Westerholm, *Israel's Law and the Church's Faith: Paul and His Major Interpreters* (Grand Rapids, Mich.: Eerdmans, 1988).

[28]For example, after *Westminster Theological Journal* (38, 1975) published Fuller's article "Paul and 'The Works of the Law,'" all responses to Fuller's article in subsequent issues of *WThJ* were critical of Fuller's thesis that the law and the gospel stand in essential continuity, not contrast, with one another.

[29]For example, Thomas R. Schreiner agrees with Fuller that the law of Moses is a law of faith but disagrees with Fuller's exegesis of Galatians 3:10 and Romans 10:4. See Thomas R. Schreiner, *The Law and Its Fulfillment: A Pauline Theology of Law* (Grand Rapids, Mich.: Baker, 1993).

[30]Martin Abegg, "Paul, 'Works of the Law' and MMT," *Biblical Archaeological Review* 20, no. 6 (November/December 1994): 52-55.

[31]James D. G. Dunn, "4QMMT and Galatians," *NTS* 43 (1997): 147-53.

[32]N. T. Wright, "Paul and Qumran," *Bible Review* (October 1998): 18, 54.

rounding the doctrine of justification.[33]

Consider, for example, the issue of how to define the term *justification*. Does Scripture bear witness to a rather specific concept of justification as God's declaration that sinners are not guilty in God's sight by virtue of the imputed righteousness of Christ? Or does justification in the NT include not merely a forensic element of imputed righteousness but also an ethical element of infused righteousness?

Protestant exegetes in general not only argue but often assume that "justification" refers solely to imputed righteousness, which ushers in forgiveness of sins. Alister McGrath's survey of the history of the doctrine of justification, however, reveals that the Reformers' definition of justification as imputed righteousness "marks a complete break with the [Western church] tradition up to this point." That is to say, the Reformers introduced a "notional distinction" between justification (imputed righteousness) and sanctification (infused righteousness) where none had previously existed.[34]

Here biblical theologians must take up Watson's challenge to move out of their comfort zones of OT and NT exegesis and address issues of historical and systematic theology. For example, what is one to make of the fact that prior to 1530 Martin Luther held to a view of justification that included what McGrath calls a "sanative" element that incorporated both forgiveness of sins and healing from sin?[35] In addition, Luther's contemporary Reformer Martin Bucer spoke of a "double justification" that included imputed and imparted righteousness.[36] In short, the early Luther and Bucer defined justification in ways similar (though not identical) to that found in the most recent edition of the Roman Catholic catechism. These and other historical data deserve more attention in the current debates over justification, as do details of the proceedings at Regensburg (Ratisbone) in 1541, when Reformed Protestant and Roman Catholic theologians reached a tentative accord on justification, only to have their consensus rejected by Luther on the one hand and the pope on the other.

---

[33]See, e.g., "The Gift of Salvation," *First Things* 79 (January 1998): 20-23, and the Catholic-Lutheran *Joint Declaration on the Doctrine of Justification*, which may be found online at a number of sites, including <www.elca.org/ea/jddj>.

[34]Alister McGrath, *Iustitia Dei: A History of the Christian Doctrine of Justification*, 2 vols. (Cambridge: Cambridge University Press, 1986), 2:2.

[35]See McGrath, *Iustitia Dei*, 2:12-13, and Martin Luther's 1515-1516 lectures on Romans in *Luther's Works*, 55 vols. (St. Louis, Mo.: Concordia, 1963), 25:260. See also Ted M. Dorman, "The Catholic Luther," *First Things* 98 (December 1999): 49-53.

[36]Martin Bucer, *Common Places of Martin Bucer*, ed. D. F. Wright (Berkshire, N.Y.: The Sutton Courteny Press, 1972), pp. 159-69.

CONCLUSION: A HERMENEUTICS OF *HEILSGESCHICHTE*

With respect to the doctrine of justification, as well as all other matters of Christian faith and conduct, biblical theology must insist that exegesis have the final say, since the canon is definitive as the church's written deposit of God's history of revelation, that portion of redemptive history Cullmann labels the *Offenbarungsgeschichte*. But the fact that for almost fifteen hundred years a doctrinal consensus existed that knew little if anything of Reformed theology's "notional distinction" between justification and sanctification should cause us to question, at least provisionally, some of our cherished theological assumptions. For even if a hermeneutics of *Heilsgeschichte* places Scripture at the center of redemptive history, it also recognizes the ongoing "hidden" work of the Holy Spirit in redemptive history,[37] manifesting itself in various ways throughout the historic Christian tradition. Such a *heilsgeschichtliche Hermeneutik* will therefore not limit itself to examining the biblical documents in their historical context but will also attempt to discern to what extent a diachronic survey of historical theology offers us fresh biblical insights from the Holy Spirit, who has been at work throughout the history of the postapostolic church.[38]

---

[37]Cullmann, *Salvation in History*, pp. 299-300.
[38]For further discussion of what I call a "diachronic survey of historical theology," see Ted M. Dorman, "The Case Against Calvinistic Hermeneutics," *Philosophia Christi* 19 (1996): 39-55, and especially Ted M. Dorman, "Holy Spirit, History, Hermeneutics and Theology: Toward an Evangelical/Catholic Consensus," *JETS* 41 (1998): 427-38.

PART FOUR

BIBLICAL
THEOLOGY

Prospect

18

Biblical Theology and the Wholeness of Scripture

Steps Toward a Program for the Future

Paul R. House

The premise for the 2000 Wheaton Theology Conference was exciting. The notion that scholars holding various theological commitments should come together to ponder how, not if, biblical theology ought to proceed indicates that the work of our predecessors has not been in vain. Frankly, it also offers the hope that our work is not without significant purpose. But this excitement must not lead to complacency, for much remains to be done if gains are to be made in the next several years. Still, without question it is a good time to note valuable work that has appeared and to determine how sound, effective theology may be written in the future. Specifically, we are to develop what Elmer Martens defines as

> that approach to Scripture which attempts to see Biblical material holistically and to describe this wholeness or synthesis in Biblical categories. Biblical theology attempts to embrace the message of the Bible and to arrive at an intelligible coherence of the whole despite the great diversity of the parts. Or, put another way: Biblical theology investigates the themes presented in Scripture and defines their inter-relationships. Biblical theology is an attempt to get to the theological heart of the Bible.[1]

---

[1]Elmer A. Martens, "Tackling Old Testament Theology," *JETS* 20 (1977): 123.

Underlying Principles for Biblical Theology

One's presuppositions inevitably drive one's writing. Of course, by presuppositions I mean studied foundational conclusions or underlying principles, not uninformed opinions. It is important for interpreters to reveal their presuppositions so that the myth of neutrality will not be perpetuated. That is not to say that there is no way to know whose presuppositions are true or false. It is to state that those who assess scholarship have as much right to dispute an author's foundational principles as they do to dispute an author's conclusions. Through twenty years of academic study (in literature and theology), teaching and writing I have come to certain conclusions about literature, the canon, interpretation and the practical work of producing theological prose. It is only fair and right to reveal some of them that affect my approach to biblical theology.

First, based on the study of secular texts (a strict designation many of my literature teachers would not accept) I am convinced of the importance of the text being the main focus of interpretation.[2] John H. Sailhamer makes the same point in his *Introduction to Old Testament Theology*,[3] but I first became convinced of this fact while studying literary theory. An interpreter should know as much as possible about historical settings, the author's life, reading audiences, and so forth, but the text is the interpreter's ultimate concern. I also have learned the importance of grasping how authors and written works influence subsequent authors and works. Simply stated, I have realized the importance of intertextuality. Intertextuality means that authors and texts influence one another directly through a later writer reading the works of his or her predecessor. Further, it means that authors and texts influence one another by creating common literary types, devices, themes and schools of thought. Finally, it means that authors and texts influence one another by how they deal with specific societal or literary problems. This type of influence is related to the first, yet is significant enough to merit separate mention, since it demonstrates, for example, how a twentieth-century author may attack a perceived evil in the same manner that a nineteenth-century author might.

---

[2]See Cleanth Brooks and Robert Penn Warren, *Understanding Poetry*, 4th ed. (New York: Holt, Rinehart and Winston, 1976); Cleanth Brooks, *The Well-Wrought Urn: Studies in the Structure of Poetry* (New York: Harcourt Brace and Company, 1975); and Cleanth Brooks, *Community, Religion and Literature: Essays by Cleanth Brooks* (Columbia: University of Missouri Press, 1995).
[3]John H. Sailhamer, *Introduction to Old Testament Theology: A Canonical Approach* (Grand Rapids, Mich.: Zondervan, 1995), pp. 36-85.

Second, from the reading of Scripture I have become convinced that the Bible's main (though not sole) concern is to reveal the character of God. It does so by describing the works of God and by making clear propositional statements about the Lord. As it does so, a distinct portrait of the triune God emerges. Moreover, given the challenges of a pluralistic, polytheistic world, it is not too simplistic a point to make to recall that the Scriptures stress the uniqueness of the one living God of the Bible. Today's global village reminds us that our situation is more like the prophets' and Paul's than it has ever been.

Third, from the reading of sacred texts I am convinced that the Bible is a connected, canonical, theological whole. This emphasis on canonical wholeness leads me to believe that it is possible to use the shape of the canon as a structuring device for biblical theology.[4] My *Old Testament Theology* is an example of how one could use the Law, Prophets and Writings as a natural outline for theological reflection.[5] Certainly other legitimate structuring devices may be discerned and employed, but the canonical order of books is a particularly attractive option because it can be viewed as an inherent part of the text.

Fourth, from reading secular and sacred texts I am convinced that it makes a good bit of difference in what order one reads and studies the Scriptures. It remakes students' minds to read Joshua, Judges, Samuel and Kings as the Former Prophets rather than as the Historical Books. It alters one's perception of Ruth if one reads Ruth as the successor to Proverbs or Judges. Reading strategies do matter.[6]

Fifth, from spending some years teaching and writing about the Scriptures I am convinced that theology and exegesis must be as closely wed as possible. Walter Kaiser was right a generation ago to stress exegetical theology, and he remains correct today.[7] Biblical theology ought to arise from careful analysis of the Hebrew and Greek texts. It ought to utilize the best results of historical research. At the same time, it must not be captive to reconstructed histories of how theology emerged in Israel and

---

[4]On the necessity for a structure for biblical theology see Charles H. H. Scobie, "The Structure of Biblical Theology," *TynB* 42 (1991): 163-94.

[5]Paul R. House, *Old Testament Theology* (Downers Grove, Ill.: InterVarsity Press, 1998).

[6]Cf. Sailhamer, *Introduction to Old Testament Theology*, p. 213, and Richard Schultz, "Integrating Old Testament Theology and Exegesis: Literary, Thematic and Canonical Issues," in Willem A. VanGemeren, ed., *NIDOTTE 1* (Grand Rapids, Mich.: Zondervan, 1997), p. 199.

[7]Walter C. Kaiser Jr., *Toward an Exegetical Theology: Biblical Exegesis for Preaching and Teaching* (Grand Rapids, Mich.: Baker, 1981).

the early church. History must support theology, not the other way around. Exegesis should keep biblical theology biblical in the sense that it will keep scholars from imposing theological systems on texts that cannot bear their weight.

Sixth, from reading ecumenical creeds, denominational confessions of faith and theological works based on sacred texts I have become convinced that a biblical theologian must be committed to interpreting the Bible as a coherent whole because it is the word of an inherently coherent God. As Carl F. H. Henry writes, "The very fact of disclosure by the one living God assures the comprehensive unity of divine revelation."[8] In other words, unitary biblical theology is possible because a united Trinity has breathed out these texts (2 Tim 3:16-17).

Seventh, from positive collaboration with biblical, dogmatic, philosophical and practical scholars I am convinced that unitary biblical theology is the best venue for experts in these fields to share their best insights with one another.[9] Without question, my academic and pastoral work has convinced me that fragmented readings of Scripture, whether practiced by conservatives, moderates or liberals, do not offer the best interpretation of the Bible and therefore cannot lead to the best obedience to biblical teaching. By contrast, I have discovered that when scholars from different fields work together keen insights can develop. A competitive, combative, turf-oriented approach to scholarship honors neither the unity of Christ in the bond of love nor the practical goals of Christian scholarship.

Given these presuppositions, I think the future of biblical theology lies in unitary reading that will lead to canonical interpretation that will reveal a doctrine of God that will guide systematic theology that will inform and empower church doctrine and practice. This approach will be largely thematic, yet it will not cast off history, archaeology, linguistics, or other related disciplines. Instead, it will use these legitimate academic exercises as ways to inform, correct, enlarge and shape thematic analysis. This approach will refuse to pit the OT against the NT, or biblical theology against systematic theology, or the academy against the church. Steps will be taken so that in the future scholars will not be tempted to define biblical theology over against other disciplines but will stress its

---

[8]Carl F. H. Henry, *God, Revelation and Authority*, 6 vols. (Waco, Tex.: Word, 1976), 2:69.
[9]See Paul R. House and Gregory A. Thornbury, eds., *Who Will Be Saved? Defending the Biblical Understanding of God, Salvation and Evangelism* (Wheaton, Ill.: Crossway, 2000).

positive, unifying function.[10] At the same time, this method will not gloss over sharp edges in the biblical material. This approach will always be a work in progress, since we will never expound the nature of God and God's revelation fully.[11] Still, the attempt must be made if we are to be faithful to the faithful God who gave us a faithful revelation.

UNITARY READING FOR CANONICAL BIBLICAL THEOLOGY

First, canonical biblical theology requires a unitary reading strategy that is based on the main sections of the OT and NT canons. As is well known, there was a time when the unity of the Bible was a viable academic topic in nonevangelical circles. Scholars such as H. H. Rowley, Millar Burrows, G. Ernest Wright, and many others wrote openly about ways that the Scriptures might be construed as a historical, thematic whole.[12] As is equally well known, the so-called biblical theology movement decreased in popularity in the 1970s.[13] It seemed clear to most interpreters that the biblical theology movement had failed to reach broad consensus on the most vital unifying themes in Scripture, on the correlation between history and Scripture, or on the relationship between the academic study of Scripture and the use of the Bible in the church.

Though biblical theology did fall on hard times among mainline authors, the situation was somewhat different among evangelicals during the 1970s and 1980s. Walter C. Kaiser Jr., Elmer Martens, William J. Dumbrell, and others wrote OT theological works.[14] George Eldon Ladd, F. F. Bruce, Donald Guthrie, and others penned volumes on NT theology.[15] Numerous scholarly articles devoted to the subject appeared. Despite all

---

[10]See the contrastive definitions of biblical theology in James Barr, *The Concept of Biblical Theology: An Old Testament Perspective* (Minneapolis: Fortress, 1999), pp. 5-17.

[11]On the limits of human knowledge of God, see Henry, *God, Revelation and Authority*, 2:47-68.

[12]In particular, see H. H. Rowley, *The Faith of Israel: Aspects of Old Testament Thought* (Philadelphia: Westminster Press, 1956); Millar Burrows, *An Outline of Biblical Theology* (Philadelphia: Westminster Press, 1946); and G. Ernest Wright, *God Who Acts: Biblical Theology as Recital* (London: SCM Press, 1952).

[13]For a chronicle of its deficiencies and his resultant call for canonical criticism, see Brevard S. Childs, *Biblical Theology in Crisis* (Philadelphia: Westminster Press, 1970).

[14]See Kaiser, *Exegetical Theology*; Elmer A. Martens, *God's Design: A Focus on Old Testament Theology* (Grand Rapids, Mich.: Baker, 1981); and William J. Dumbrell, *Covenant and Creation: A Theology of Old Testament Covenants* (Nashville: Thomas Nelson, 1984).

[15]See George Eldon Ladd, *A Theology of the New Testament* (Grand Rapids, Mich.: Eerdmans, 1974); F. F. Bruce, *New Testament Development of Old Testament Themes* (Grand Rapids, Mich.: Eerdmans, 1968); and Donald Guthrie, *New Testament Theology: A Thematic Study* (Downers Grove, Ill.: InterVarsity Press, 1981).

this productive activity, however, it is fair to say that none of these scholars produced a thorough volume on biblical theology that paid close, sustained attention to the wholeness of Scripture as it unfolds in all the books of the Bible. They did not do so because they shared many of the same goals and methods as their nonevangelical colleagues. Thus they shared many of the same frustrations.

It is important to note that the biblical theology movement and evangelical scholars were correct to seek the unity of the Scriptures as a means of uniting theology, academy and the church. Though they sought proper goals, however, they did not always use methodologies that would allow them to succeed. They rightly believed that vital themes would emerge from an honest reading of the entire Bible, yet they did not always recommend a particular order in which to read and interpret the text. Thus their theories of unity often came unraveled when new historical approaches to the primary sources arose or when vital themes were added to their discussions.

As was discussed throughout the conference, in Luke 24:44 Jesus mentions a three-part canon that includes the Law, Prophets and Psalms. In Matthew 23:29-36 he reflects a Genesis—Chronicles canonical frame of reference when accusing the Pharisees of participating in the tradition of killing the prophets. In Matthew 19:1-7 he follows canonical order when discussing divorce. Though some scholars dispute the significance of these references, and although Jesus often utilizes a variety of Scriptures from a number of places when he speaks, it remains a matter of note that in the small number of texts where he addresses a matter of biblical theology he tends to follow the canonical order found in Palestinian Judaism. Paul reflects the same type of exegesis when dealing with justification by faith in Romans 4, as does the author of Hebrews when discussing faith in Hebrews 11. Though it is impossible to determine with certainty the exact order of the books in the NT writers' canon, it is hard to dispute that they inherited and interpreted a tripartite list of books.[16] Of course, NT writers use the OT in a variety of ways, depending on the context of their argu-

---

[16]For a thorough analysis of this issue, see Roger T. Beckwith, *The Old Testament Canon of the New Testament Church and Its Background in Early Judaism* (Grand Rapids, Mich.: Eerdmans, 1985). For my conclusions on the propriety of using the Palestinian canon as a base for OT theology, see Paul R. House, "Canon of the Old Testament," in *Foundations for Biblical Interpretation: A Complete Library of Tools and Resources*, ed. David S. Dockery, Kenneth A. Mathews and Robert B. Sloan (Nashville: Broadman, 1994), pp. 134-55.

ments. Still, they conceived of the Bible as the Law, Prophets and other books, as the book of Sirach indicates had been the case for some time.

Theological, practical and exegetical statements in the NT should therefore be interpreted in light of its authors' basic reading orientation. We must enter their canonical world if we are to think their thoughts after them. This strategy is as appropriate as trying to understand Paul in light of Palestinian or rabbinic Judaism[17] or attempting to understand Jesus in light of his historical setting.[18] Reading the OT the way the NT writers did is but one more important link to the ancient world of the biblical writers. Moreover, interpreters seeking to understand how NT writers used OT texts to construct their own theology may wish to read and conceive of the canon as they did. This reading strategy does not cast off historical analysis. It recognizes the importance of insights gained from legitimate historical research, yet at the same time refuses to accept theories built on a series of unsustainable hypotheses. At the very least it follows the broad historical framework that the OT portrays.

Without question, it is easier to discern a reading strategy for the OT canon than it is to assert one for the NT. After all, the basic shape of the OT canon that I have suggested is attested in the OT, the Apocrypha, the Dead Sea Scrolls, extrabiblical texts, the NT and rabbinical writings.[19] The NT, however, has no subsequent canonical segment to state its contents or order. Still, the church has long accepted the twenty-seven books of the NT as Scripture, and although there remains disagreement on the contents of the OT, there is no marked disagreement among the major Christian traditions on the contents of the NT canon.[20] It is also true that there is wide agreement on the shape of the NT canon. Virtually all Christians believe the NT consists of Gospels and Acts, Pauline epistles, the Catholic Epistles and Revelation. Thus there is an accepted threefold NT canon that complements the threefold OT canon.

What I have just outlined could be deemed simplistic in several ways. Perhaps the most glaring problem is the fact that many scholars question

---

[17]See E. P. Sanders, *Paul and Palestinian Judaism: A Comparison of Patterns of Religion* (Philadelphia: Fortress, 1977), and W. D. Davies, *Paul and Rabbinic Judaism: Some Rabbinic Elements in Pauline Theology,* 4th ed. (Philadelphia: Fortress, 1980).

[18]See N. T. Wright, *Jesus and the Victory of God: Christian Origins and the Question of God,* vol. 2 (Philadelphia: Fortress, 1996).

[19]Beckwith, *The Old Testament Canon,* pp. 16-62.

[20]For an introductory discussion of these issues see F. F. Bruce, *The Canon of Scripture* (Downers Grove, Ill: InterVarsity Press, 1988).

the authorship and date of some of the Pauline material. I would argue that those who dispute Pauline authorship still write about the books as being somehow Pauline, so the canonical designation still stands. Another problem is whether to read Acts as part of the Gospels or as part of the Pauline material. I opt for the former possibility because Luke-Acts seems to be a two-part book (Acts 1:1). Yet another difficulty is where to place Revelation in this scheme. Since the book addresses specific congregations, I do not think it impossible to interpret it alongside the Catholic Epistles. A final problem is the order of the NT books. At this point in time I would leave room for discussion of reading strategies within the three large blocks of material. Variations on this three-part scheme are possible, but without some means of specific thematic-historical reading there is little chance of producing a thorough whole-Bible theology.

This reading strategy could allow biblical theologians to pursue biblical theology by working carefully and systematically through the whole canon: Law, Prophets, Writings, Gospels, Pauline Epistles, and Catholic Epistles. The effect of this plan will be that the Bible will be treated as a book of Scripture, not as a group of texts that have some unifying principles. Christ will now be the literary and theological center of the book. The history of Israel and of redemption will move from earlier to later times as the exegete works forward. Connections between texts can be better noted, and one-of-a-kind contributions to theology rescued from oblivion.

BOOK-BY-BOOK EXEGESIS FOR CANONICAL THEOLOGY

Second, this unitary reading should proceed on a book-by-book exegetical basis so that each book's discrete message will be recognized.[21] Unitary canonical biblical theology must be built through the sustained testimony of successive books; it must not be constructed at the expense of any part of Scripture. Difficulties have arisen in biblical theology in the past because some parts of the canon have not yet fit into authors' chosen patterns of analysis. In some ways this result is inevitable, but the goal must be to combat this problem. Perhaps the most evident example of books being neglected is the omission of the Writings in some OT theologies and biblical theologies. Many of the psalms, Job, Proverbs and Esther are not al-

---

[21]For a discussion of the importance of each book and each Testament having its own separate (discrete) witness, see Brevard S. Childs, *Biblical Theology of the Old and New Testaments: Theological Reflection on the Christian Bible* (Philadelphia: Fortress, 1992), pp. 70-79, and House, *Old Testament Theology*, pp. 53-54.

ways included because they do not overtly address salvation history, covenant, or some other legitimate centering theme. The same could be said of some NT books, particularly portions of the Catholic Epistles.[22] The result is the unfortunate loss of vibrant discussions of how these biblical books fit into the Bible's overall theology.

A related but quite different problem is the smoothing over of sharp edges in biblical theology. When seeking unity one can fail to deal with differing perspectives within the canon on the same issue. My work has been justly criticized at times for not dealing with such sharp edges. Perhaps subsequent scholars can learn from the example of Rolf Rendtorff, who projects two volumes on OT theology, one that states all the OT themes, regardless of how well he thinks they mesh immediately, and one that sketches unifying themes.[23]

CENTERING THEMES FOR CANONICAL THEOLOGY

Third, this canonical book-by-book analysis will need to identify and collect vital centering themes so that a synthesis of data can be possible and so that the study can have order. Many of the best OT and NT theologies of the past have utilized central or centering themes to carry out their program. One thinks of Walther Eichrodt's stressing of covenant,[24] George Eldon Ladd's emphasis on the kingdom,[25] Geerhardus Vos's commitment to revelation,[26] G. B. Caird's tracing of salvation,[27] Samuel Terrien's focus on the presence of God,[28] Peter Stuhlmacher's highlighting of reconciliation and righteousness,[29] and the list could be extended. Elmer Martens effec-

---

[22]See, e.g., the neglect of 2 Peter (along with 1 Peter and James), as outlined by Robert W. Wall, "The Canonical Function of 2 Peter," *Biblical Interpretation* 9 (2001): 64-81.

[23]The first of these volumes has been published. See Rolf Rendtorff, *Theologie des Alten Testaments: Ein kanonischer Entwurf*, Band 1, *Kanonische Grundlegung* (Neukirchen-Vluyn: Neukirchener, 1999). Note also his methodological statements in *Canon and Theology: Overtures to an Old Testament Theology* (Minneapolis: Fortress, 1993).

[24]Walther Eichrodt, *Theology of the Old Testament*, 2 vols., OTL (Philadelphia: Westminster Press, 1961-1967).

[25]Ladd, *A Theology of the New Testament.*

[26]Geerhardus Vos, *Biblical Theology: Old and New Testaments* (Grand Rapids, Mich.: Eerdmans, 1948).

[27]G. B. Caird, *New Testament Theology*, ed. L. D. Hurst (Oxford: Clarendon, 1994).

[28]Samuel Terrien, *The Elusive Presence, The Heart of Biblical Theology* (San Francisco: Harper & Row, 1978).

[29]Peter Stuhlmacher, *Reconciliation, Law and Righteousness: Essays in Biblical Theology* (Philadelphia: Fortress, 1986) and his two-volume work *Biblische Theologie des Neuen Testaments*, Band 1, *Grundlegung Von Jesus zu Paulus*, Band 2, *Von der Paulusschule bis zur Johannesoffenbarung* (Göttingen: Vandenhoeck & Ruprecht, 1992, 1999).

tively utilizes a cluster of themes in his OT theology.[30] Most of the themes these writers have chosen have been gleaned from the biblical texts, not from an external system used to explicate the texts, though biblical scholars such as Donald Guthrie have utilized categories drawn from dogmatics with good effect.[31]

Biblical theologians can agree on a lengthy enough list of major themes to do justice to the theological breadth of the Bible, yet short enough to give the discipline some recognizable continuity. We should give up arguing that one theme and one theme only is the central theme of the Bible and highlight major themes that allow other ideas as subpoints. Of course, we should never fail to assert that God the Father, God the Son and God the Holy Spirit are at the center of any unitary biblical theology. Nor should we ever fail to assert that the Bible unfolds God's redemptive history, and the necessity of human response to God's gracious acts.

At the same time, we must acknowledge that salvation history, covenant, creation and messiah are necessarily broad themes that require elaboration and schematization. *Any* theme that links much of the Bible must be broad and must not be rejected for being broad. A broad theme is not the canon's only theme; it is a centering theme. As long as the major theme is clearly discernible in several parts of the canon, as long as it is charted alongside other major themes, as long as it is treated as an important part of a whole instead of being the whole, then it should be welcomed, used and critiqued.

INTERTEXTUALITY AND CANONICAL THEOLOGY

Fourth, for canonical, book-by-book, thematically sensitive, collection-minded analysis to occur it must be committed to intertextuality. D. A. Carson asserts that

> ideally *biblical theology will not only work inductively in each of the biblical corpora but will seek to make clear the connections among the corpora.* In other words, it is committed to intertextual study, not simply because as an accident of history some texts depend on others and it is worth sorting out those dependencies, but because *biblical* theology, at its most coherent, is a theology of the *Bible.*[32]

---

[30]Martens, *God's Design,* pp. 11-24.
[31]Guthrie, *New Testament Theology.*
[32]D. A. Carson, "Current Issues in Biblical Theology: A New Testament Perspective," *Bulletin for Biblical Research* 5 (1995): 30.

Richard Schultz adds that "if canon is the context for OT theology, one can legitimately compare a theological theme, such as creation, with analogous presentations *anywhere* in the canonical OT Scriptures, not simply in what one considers to be chronologically *antecedent* texts."[33] Certainly the NT does not always take texts in chronological order when making theological arguments, and the OT canon, indeed several books within the canon (e.g., Jeremiah, Psalms), does not always proceed in strict chronological order. The canon produces a theologically united portrait within history, and for that and scores of other reasons history is vital to biblical theology, yet the canon was not ordered to give later readers a detailed report on the exact historical order in which the theology arose. Thus, as important as historical analysis is, it cannot dominate every facet of biblical theology. It must be a vital part of making theology relevant and understandable.

Intertextuality means several things in biblical theology. It means that later texts cite or allude to earlier texts. It means that themes develop as the books and major sections of the Bible unfold. It means that the canon presents some material that was likely written later than subsequent portions of the canon but that the later material serves as an introduction or theological foundation for what follows. The ways in which 1-2 Kings prepare readers for themes and events found in the Latter Prophets illustrates this principle. It also means that biblical theologians may legitimately collect data from the canon as a whole without always offering a reconstructed history of revelation. On the other hand, following the canonical order suggested above will help interpreters avoid theological hopscotching and illegitimate sorts of prooftexting.

CANONICAL SYNTHESIS AND CANONICAL THEOLOGY

Fifth, unitary canonical biblical theology should include canonical syntheses of major themes. After intertextual exegetical work has been done in book-by-book canonical order for the purpose of identifying and utilizing major themes it is necessary to produce clear treatments of major biblical themes as they emerge from the whole of Scripture. A systematic theology of the canonical Scriptures will result. This systematic theology will follow the themes of the Bible as they appear in Scripture, and it will trace those themes throughout the whole of the Scriptures. For example, such a theology would begin with creation, examining this theme as it proceeds, for

---

[33]Schultz, "Integrating Old Testament Theology and Exegesis," p. 199.

example, from Genesis 1—2, to Deuteronomy 4, to Isaiah 40—55, to Psalms 95—99, to Proverbs 8, to John 1, to Colossians 1, to Revelation 21. Then the next major theme should be pursued in the same manner. This procedure has been done in the past on specific themes or on a smaller scale, but many thorough treatments of successive themes are sorely needed.

MINISTRY AND CANONICAL THEOLOGY

Sixth, biblical theology ought to have as its goal the presentation of the whole counsel of God in ministry settings. There must always be a place for the scholarly monograph, the thorough commentary and the specific journal article. Still, the goal of biblical theology must be not only to "reflect structure, storyline, corpus theology, and the like; it must also capture this existential element and thereby call a new generation to personal knowledge of the living God."[34] In other words, biblical theology needs to be at the forefront of preaching, church renewal, advancement and mission. If biblical theology becomes integral to the thinking of students and pastors, if it becomes the heart of pastoral theology, if it becomes the basis for discussions on worship, if it becomes the basis for doctrinal debates, then the church will be a better place for the next generation than it was for many of us.

CONCLUSION

This shamelessly exhortatory essay has sought to delineate a unitary canonical approach to biblical theology. It has proposed that the canon be used as a structuring device, that themes be identified and utilized as cohering centering devices and that the explication of the Bible's presentation of the triune God's personality and saving acts in history be adopted as the goal of the whole theological enterprise. This essay has attempted to outline a method broad enough to include many biblical theologians and celebrate their creativity, yet specific enough to keep discussions among likeminded persons from losing necessary focus. In many ways the paper has tried to bring together ideas already expressed by effective biblical theologians.

No doubt any essay of this sort can only partially succeed. It is unlikely that everyone will now ask, "What *did* we do before House wrote this essay?" Still, the essay will have succeeded if it facilitates further discussions

---

[34]Carson, "Current Issues in Biblical Theology," p. 31.

about how to pursue biblical theology in a coherent way that will leave a solid, doctrinally sound body of work for subsequent generations. It will have succeeded if it spurs us on to do the enormous amount of work involved in producing unitary canonical biblical theology. It will have succeeded if in some small way it helps to build our confidence that our prospects are as bright as our heritage, or even more so.

19

Biblical Theology as the
Heartbeat of Effective Ministry

Graeme L. Goldsworthy

In 1894, Geerhardus Vos gave his inaugural lecture as professor of biblical theology at Princeton Seminary. After expounding the nature of biblical theology he went on to say, "I have not forgotten, however, that you have called me to teach this science for the eminently practical purpose of training young men for the ministry of the Gospel."[1]

In his mind, there was no doubt that biblical theology was to serve the work of ministry in the local churches. Indeed, biblical theology should be a core subject in all ministerial training, and it needs to be the heart of our preaching and of all Christian education in the local church. Yet it would seem that much academic theology has come to be self-serving, and its function to build up the church of God has been largely lost.

BIBLICAL THEOLOGY AND THE
INTEGRATION OF THEOLOGICAL STUDIES

Biblical theology is principally concerned with the broad theological message of the whole Bible. It seeks to understand the parts in relation to the

---

[1]Geerhardus Vos, "The Idea of Biblical Theology as a Science and as a Theological Discipline," in *Redemptive History and Biblical Interpretation: The Shorter Writings of Geerhardus Vos*, ed. Richard B. Gaffin (Phillipsburg, N.J.: Presbyterian & Reformed, 1980), p. 21.

whole, and to achieve this it must work with the mutual interaction of the literary, historical and theological dimensions of the various corpora and with the interrelationships of the corpora within the whole canon of Scripture.[2] Only in this way do we take proper account of the fact that God has spoken to us in Scripture, which thus has both divine and human dimensions. As such, biblical theology is central to the determination of the meaning of the biblical text and of its application to the members of the local congregation of believers. The fact that we must distinguish it from other theological disciplines, such as systematics, historical theology, apologetics and practical theology, does not mean that it is totally independent of them. The relationship is one of interdependence, since the biblical text is not the exclusive property of any of these disciplines. Nor should there be an imperialistic domination of the one discipline over all others. Indeed, the integration of the theological disciplines, without ignoring either their distinctives or their complementarity, is essential in pastoral practice.

Biblical theology, then, when practiced consistently within the presuppositional parameters of the Bible, is a prime force for the reintegration of theology. Francis Watson's plea for the reintegration of the disciplines based on the pursuit of biblical theology together with dogmatics is therefore timely.[3] Biblical studies and dogmatics belong together. If the pastor needs to be a good theologian, then to be such, he or she must be self-consciously engaged in biblical and systematic theology. Especially for those who believe that the Bible is the inspired Word of God and the final authority for doctrine and practice, biblical theology becomes essential for working this out in practice.

At the same time, while it is true that dogmatic presuppositions shape our approach to biblical theology by determining in advance our attitude to Scripture,[4] it is also true that the relationship of the two disciplines in-

---

[2] For an outline of my basic position, following the work of Donald Robinson, concerning the threefold structure of the epochs of biblical revelation that forms the heart of biblical theology (i.e., the kingdom of God revealed in Israel's history, the kingdom revealed in prophetic eschatology, and the kingdom revealed and fulfilled in Christ), see Graeme Goldsworthy, "Is Biblical Theology Viable?" in *Interpreting God's Plan: Biblical Theology and the Pastor*, ed. R. J. Gibson, Explorations 11 (Carlisle, U.K.: Paternoster, 1997), pp. 18-46, and its fuller presentation in Graeme Goldsworthy, *Gospel and Kingdom: a Christian Interpretation of the Old Testament* (Exeter, U.K.: Paternoster, 1981), *The Gospel in Revelation* (Exeter, U.K.: Paternoster, 1984), and *According to Plan* (Leicester, U.K.: Inter-Varsity Press, 1991).
[3] Francis Watson, *Text and Truth* (Grand Rapids, Mich.: Eerdmans, 1997), pp. 1-29.
[4] See Graeme Goldsworthy, "'Thus Says the Lord': The Dogmatic Basis of Biblical Theology," in *God Who Is Rich in Mercy: Essays Presented to Dr. D. B. Knox*, ed. P. T. O'Brien and D. G. Peterson (Grand Rapids, Mich.: Baker, 1986), pp. 25-40.

volves us in a hermeneutical spiral. There is no absolute priority of one over the other, except that we start with the biblical text. Biblical theology promotes the integration of the various theological disciplines by providing the metanarrative of the biblical story. The coherence of this metanarrative is reinforced by the dogmatics of the gospel, including the testimony to Jesus' attitude to Scripture and the formulation of some satisfactory way of dealing with the incarnation of God. The unity and consequent authority of Scripture are therefore exegetical conclusions and dogmatic presuppositions.

Thus, regardless of our theological framework, we cannot escape the question of theological presuppositions. I state my convictions from the position of a conservative evangelical and Reformed Christian. In dealing with the Bible as Robinson suggested, "in its own terms to discover what it is all about,"[5] I am convinced that we discover a coherent and self-consistent set of presuppositions about God and his dealings with humankind. Carl Henry has proposed these presuppositions of Christian theism to be uniquely self-consistent and to contain superior explanatory power in comparison to the alternatives that have been produced by the Enlightenment.[6] In this he follows a similar path as that taken by John Calvin in the early chapters of his *Institutes of the Christian Religion,* in which he demolishes the presuppositions of medieval scholastic theology and establishes the basis of Christian theism in its Protestant and Reformed dress. However, pastoral models are valid only insofar as they reflect the biblical realities understood from the perspective of biblical theology. Christian education is one example of this inextricable interplay between biblical and dogmatic theology.[7]

BIBLICAL THEOLOGY AS FOUNDATIONAL TO CHRISTIAN EDUCATION[8]

Behind a church-based Christian education program are several theological assumptions that inform and flow from the gospel. These include, first,

---

[5]Donald Robinson, "Origins and Unresolved Tensions," in Goldsworthy, *Interpreting God's Plan,* p. 7.

[6]Carl F. H. Henry, *Toward a Recovery of Christian Belief* (Wheaton, Ill.: Crossway, 1990).

[7]For an application of biblical theology to preaching, see Graeme Goldsworthy, *Preaching the Whole Bible as Christian Scripture: The Practical Application of Biblical Theology to Preaching* (Grand Rapids, Mich.: Eerdmans, 2000).

[8]My ministry as an Anglican clergyman in Australia has been almost equally divided between pastoral ministry and full-time seminary teaching. My last position before returning to the Moore College faculty in 1995 was as minister for Christian education in an Anglican church in Brisbane for fourteen years.

the privilege of all Christians to express their membership in the body of Christ in the fellowship of the local congregation. Second, there is the recognition that God gives to every member gifts for the benefit of the whole body. Third, there is the place of deliberate and intentional training for the use of spiritual gifts and ministries.

The nature of the gospel thus establishes certain priorities in Christian education. The person and work of Jesus of Nazareth are theologically and existentially the center and starting point for Christian formation. That is, the life of faith is established on the basis of who and what Jesus was for us in his life, death, and resurrection. Existentially, we start our spiritual journey by being reconciled to God through Christ. But in submitting to the Christ of the gospel we find ourselves submitting to the authoritative interpretation of Scripture that is implied in the gospel as well. Jesus makes it clear that he has come as the one who gives final meaning and fulfillment to the OT Scriptures.

A biblical theology cannot avoid the claim of the gospel event to be considered the center of the biblical message. Here the interaction with dogmatic categories, even as they occur in the NT, is crucial. For example, Paul's categories of justification, sanctification and glorification demand careful scrutiny concerning their nature and relationships. The perspective the NT gives is that the believer is justified by faith in the gospel event (for us) and that what was done for us in Jesus is now being formed in us by his Spirit. This will reach its consummation at the return of Christ. The point is that the gospel gets us started, keeps us going and will bring us to the consummation.

When it comes to Christian education, the gospel must be equally central in the life of the believer and must be perceived to be central. Biblical theology, because it deals with the sweep of salvation history, encompasses all future history up to the end of the age and the new heaven and earth. It does not do this by providing historical details and clues to where in the scale of time we are but by showing the theological relationship of our present spiritual status, and of the present time in which we all live, to the past event of the gospel and the future event of the consummation. One of the main goals of Christian education is to establish such a self-understanding, based firmly on the gospel, within believers.

So often Christian education in the local church is presented as a good but optional opportunity that some people might perhaps like to take advantage of. Various types of activities are provided, and it is left to individuals to decide what, if anything, they will taste from the smorgasbord that is offered. The situation that results is one in which all kinds of teaching ministries to children, youth and adults are carried out by people who may be keen and spiritually mature but who unfortunately do not have any formal training in the matter of how to understand the text of the Bible. Often the inexperienced are called upon to implement a moralistic curriculum, imposed from some denominational department, that fails to integrate the good news of the grace of God with matters of faith, life and behavior.

This is not an elitist sentiment that forgets the great Protestant teaching on the clarity of Scripture. It simply recognizes that unhealthy traditions regarding the way to read and apply the Bible can be easily handed down without questioning from one generation to another. And because the present age does not breed concern for right distinctions, experiential concerns can often override clear theological analysis. An evangelical pietism that declares itself uninterested in theology is a good example of this rejection of the necessity of biblical and doctrinal clarity.

In contrast, the nature of the gospel within the broad sweep of Scripture suggests an educational strategy in which the serious and informed teaching of biblical theology is essential to the life of the church, like the hub of a wheel. The hub of the church and of the life of the believer is Jesus Christ, the crucified and risen Lord. He is not only the hermeneutical center of the whole Bible, but, according to the biblical testimony, he gives ultimate meaning to every fact in the universe. He is thus the hermeneutical principle of all reality. Since the whole Bible testifies to this Christ, biblical theology is by its nature the study that is most closely and directly governed by the nature of the gospel of Christ. In turn, this gospel leaves us no option but to pursue a biblical theology by which we grasp the rich texture of the whole Bible's testimony to the person and work of Christ. Consequently, biblical theology should be the mainstay of all Christian education. It will be the means by which christological perspectives on all aspects of spiritual formation are promoted. From it will radiate, like spokes in a wheel, all the various concerns of the church, providing the center that holds it all together.

BIBLICAL THEOLOGY AS ESSENTIAL TO THE LIFE OF THE CHURCH

There is probably not a church or denomination in existence that does not claim to be Bible-based and Christ-centered. This, I suggest, indicates an instinct for the truth that may or may not be realized in practice. But what does it mean to be Bible-based? At the very least it should mean that biblical theology, conducted from the conviction that the canon of Scripture accurately mediates the truth that comes from a communicating God, becomes essential for promoting congregational ministry practice and spiritual growth.[9]

In the first place, an emphasis on biblical theology in the church has the salutary effect of enthusing Christians for the study of the Bible by presenting a coherent theological perspective on the whole range of biblical literature. It makes sense of what is a large and daunting body of literature.

Second, biblical theology is a major means of preventing a superficial Jesus piety. Christology is vital to Christian faith and its essence lies not in a few prooftexts or doctrinal summaries but in the testimony of the whole Bible to the Christ. The Christ we serve and worship is the Christ revealed in the whole testimony of Scripture.

Third, biblical theology nuances the gospel by anchoring the person and work of Christ in the OT. The linking of the gospel event to the whole range of salvation history is vital. It was the loss of the OT in its historical sense that led to the implicit docetism of allegorical interpretation. It also led to the locating of the saving event in the believer's inner experience and in the infusion of grace in the sacramentalism of the medieval church. These dehistoricizing tendencies were not entirely left behind at the Reformation but reappeared in Friedrich Schleiermacher's liberal theology of feeling and in Rudolf Bultmann's sell-out of the historical gospel to existential self-understanding and decision. The pietism of a modern evangelical Protestantism that has lost its place in salvation history and biblical theology is often closer to Aquinas, Schleiermacher and Bultmann than to Luther, Calvin and Thomas Cranmer.

Fourth, biblical theology, when applied to the understanding of ministry in the church, calls into question the pragmatism of the latest quick-fix, church growth theory. The pastor who is forever looking for the next fad to save his church is probably the pastor who has lost sight of faithfully teaching the Bible and of bringing biblical theology to bear on his expository preaching. Authentic ministry will reflect the nature of the gospel. The big picture of God's work for salvation is a perspective achieved, how-

---

[9]For the impact of biblical theology on the following five aspects of church life, see Graeme Goldsworthy, "The Pastor as Biblical Theologian," in *Interpreting God's Plan*, pp. 110-30. See also Graeme Goldsworthy, "The Pastoral Application of Biblical Theology," in *In the Fullness of Time: Biblical Studies in Honour of Archbishop Donald Robinson*, ed. David Peterson and John Pryor (Homebush West, Australia: Lancer, 1992), pp. 301-17.

ever, only through biblical theology. Once gained, it provides the biblical-theological perspective needed for ministry aspects such as leadership, encouragement, reproof and discipline.

Fifth, biblical theology gives us an antidote to the parochialism that so often overtakes the people of God. Ordinary people in the pews and the home group and youth fellowship need to understand that they are part of the universal church and players in the same cosmic drama as the members of the churches to whom John addressed the Apocalypse. They need to learn to stand firm in the face of the battle that has already reached its outcome in the victory of Christ.

CONCLUSION

Our concern at Moore College in teaching biblical theology is that it not only will be a key factor in the spiritual formation of those training for the ministry, but also that it will bear fruit in the congregations to which they will go to minister. To achieve this, we must convince the students of their need to place biblical theology in the center of an integrated theological mindset and to propagate the same mindset in their congregations. This can be achieved in the local church only if the pastor is prepared to preach and instruct in a way that illustrates the application of biblical theology to the exposition of the text. In addition, there will need to be an intentional teaching of biblical theology to all laypeople who wish to engage in any kind of Bible teaching or pastoral ministry.

Effective ministry cannot happen unless the significance of the gospel is applied consistently to the lives of the people of God. This requires an effective lay involvement in ministry. Unless the leaders, teachers and lay pastors (whether functioning in a formal capacity or as part of the fellowship) have a clear idea of the message of the Bible, where it is coming from and what its goal is, there will not be effective ministry. I would dare to suggest that if the senior pastor is not making sure that all of the teachers and leaders are being trained in biblical theology, he or she is undermining his effectiveness and should make it his or her first priority to rectify the matter. Biblical theology is the key to sound interpretation, the source of a reliable topical analysis of the Scriptures and the heartbeat of effective ministry.

It ought to be the aim of every pastor to bring all the members of his or her congregation to maturity in Christ. But they cannot mature if they do not know the Christ of the Bible, the Christ to whom the whole Bible, Old and New Testaments, gives a unified and inspired testimony.

Subject Index

Abraham, promises to, 71-72

Adam/Second Adam/Israel, 43-44, 61-63, 123-25

biblical theology
  center of, 17, 110, 129-30, 153-54, 157-58, 159, 173, 188, 214, 231, 275-76, 283
  definition of, 175, 226-27, 256, 267, 280-81
  fragmentation of, 228-30
  hermeneutics of, 216-24, 233-35, 240-41, 256-57, 259, 263, 268-72

biblical theology movement, 21, 271-72

canon, LXX, 203-4

canon, structure of, 17-18, 25-27, 32, 34-36, 67-68, 74-77, 79-82, 84, 94, 187-88, 201-7, 269, 272-74

canonization, 27-32, 37, 68, 199, 201-7

covenant, 21, 46, 65, 77, 87, 89, 115-17
  new, 45, 48, 79

covenant theology 19, 242, 259

creation/new creation, 21, 38, 40-41, 43, 45, 47, 51-52, 57, 64, 68-69, 86-87, 115, 120, 124, 162, 163-72, 182

dispensationalism, 19, 237-241, 259
  progressive, 241-42, 260

Eden as temple, 57-61, 65, 69, 79-80

eschatology, inaugurated, 136-37, 139-43, 162-63, 164-72, 251-52

exile, 27-29, 35-36, 42-43, 45, 47, 48, 49, 50, 68, 74, 76-78, 81, 104, 116, 119-20, 121, 137, 141

faith, nature of, 243-44, 245-46, 248

Fall, the, 45, 63-64, 68

gospel tradition, reliability of, 147-48, 177-81

history of redemption/salvation, 16-17, 21, 33, 65, 112, 150, 212-13, 215, 251-52, 255-56, 283

judgment (de-creation), 43, 44, 45, 46, 47, 48, 49, 121

justification, 167-68, 183-85, 247-48, 261-62, 283

kingdom of God, 21, 47, 49, 50-51, 57, 63, 108-9, 133, 134-36, 139-40, 155, 160, 162, 180-82, 185, 186, 251-52, 281

kingship (messianic, Davidic), 44, 45, 46, 47, 48, 49, 50-51, 58, 73-74, 76, 79-81, 104, 106-7, 119-20, 160, 164, 180-82

latter days/last days, 160-62, 171-72

law/gospel contrast, 17, 237, 238, 239, 242, 259-61

Rad, Gerhard von, approach of, 195-96, 197

remnant, 47, 48

restoration (from exile/sin), 78-79, 118, 120, 121, 122, 124, 125, 131, 132-43

revelation, nature of, 20-21, 253-55

sabbath, 54-55

Scripture
  clarity of, 234-35
  diversity of, 15-16, 34-36, 101-3, 109, 145-53, 230-32, 275
  unity of, 16, 19-20, 33-34, 38-39, 41-43, 51, 67-68, 111-13, 153-57, 212-14, 230-31, 233, 271-72, 275-77

Tanak, 25, 32-36, 66-67, 123, 196, 206, 272-74

temple/tabernacle, 45, 46, 47, 48, 50, 57-61, 64-65, 73-75, 79, 80

toledot formula, 39-41, 55, 89, 95, 97

tradition-history, 175-77, 197-201, 205-9

von Rad, approach of, 195-96, 197

wisdom, 49, 50

works of the law, 243-44, 246-47

Scripture Index

Old Testament
Genesis
1, *53, 54, 55, 58, 61, 76, 87,*
    89, 92
1—2, *89, 92, 93, 94, 95, 107,*
    278
1—3, *39, 64, 114, 115, 121,*
    124
1—4, *38, 39, 40, 41, 42, 43,*
    45, 47, 49, 51, 52
1—11, *39, 55, 71, 86, 91, 94,*
    95
1—15, *54, 59*
1:1—2:3, *39, 40, 53, 55, 97*
1:1—2:4, *87, 89*
1:1—4:26, *40*
1:1—5:32, *88*
1:2, *40, 58, 77*
1:26, *56*
1:26-28, *69, 108*
1:28, *115*
1:29-31, *115*
2, *53, 55, 56, 58, 59, 60, 61,*
    62, 64, 65, 92, 94, 108
2—3, *95*
2—11, *97*
2—50, *97*
2:1, *53*
2:1-3, *54, 55*
2:1-17, *53, 55, 57, 59, 61, 63,*
    65
2:2, *54*
2:2-3, *53, 54*
2:3, *53, 54*
2:4, *39, 53, 55, 60, 87, 89, 97*
2:4-25, *55, 92*
2:4—3:24, *63*
2:4—4:26, *39, 40*
2:4—50:26, *97*
2:5-7, *55*
2:6, *58*
2:7, *31*

2:8, *55, 56, 57, 61, 78*
2:8-17, *55*
2:8-25, *55*
2:9-14, *56*
2:9-17, *56, 61*
2:10-14, *58*
2:15, *59, 60*
2:15-17, *56, 60, 61*
2:16-17, *63*
2:19, *31*
2:22, *78*
2:23, *50, 91*
3, *60, 63, 69, 89*
3—4, *95*
3:1—6:4, *95*
3:3, *116*
3:8, *69*
3:14, *71*
3:14-19, *63, 91*
3:15, *44, 45, 46, 60, 69, 70,*
    72, 75, 76, 116
3:17, *64, 71*
3:17-19, *50*
3:21, *124*
3:22, *58*
3:23, *59*
3:24, *56, 60, 69, 75*
4, *40*
4—11, *89, 90*
4:1-16, *70*
4:11, *71*
4:17-24, *70*
4:23, *91*
4:25-26, *70*
5, *40, 41, 80*
5:1, *40, 41*
5:1-32, *41, 70*
5:29, *70, 71*
6:5—8:22, *95*
6:9—9:29, *43*
6:9—11:26, *88*
8—9, *90*
9:1-3, *40*
9:1—11:26, *95*
9:8, *87*
9:25, *71*
11, *80*
11—25, *92*

11—50, *92*
11:4, *97*
11:10-26, *70*
11:26, *70*
11:27—25:10, *88*
11:27—25:11, *98*
11:27—25:12, *43*
12, *51, 68*
12—36, *89*
12—50, *91, 95*
12:1-3, *71, 85, 90, 95, 117*
12:2, *98*
12:3, *71, 75, 124*
13:14-17, *117*
14, *71*
14:18-20, *71*
15, *95*
15:1, *87*
15:1-6, *85*
16:2, *69*
17, *95*
17:2-8, *117*
18:27, *246*
22, *72, 76*
22:1-19, *72*
22:11-12, *76*
22:17, *72*
25:11, *72*
25:19-26, *72*
25:19—35:29, *43, 98*
25:21, *89*
26:5, *91*
28—36, *93*
28:10-15, *72*
29:31—30:24, *72*
29:35, *72*
30:3, *69*
32:28-29, *72*
37—50, *89, 96*
37:2—50:26, *44, 98*
37:5-11, *98*
37:26, *98*
38, *98*
43:3, *98*
43:8, *98*
44:14, *98*
44:16, *98*
44:18, *98*

27:63, *179*
27:64, *179*
28:16-20, *180, 181, 182*
28:18, *165*
28:19-20, *165*

Mark
1:9-11, *134*
1:13, *165*
1:14, *155*
1:14-15, *134, 139*
1:15, *156*
4:26-29, *141*
6:1-6, *135*
7, *209*
7:13, *209*
8:29, *178*
8:31, *157*
9:31, *157, 179*
10:19, *202*
10:33-34, *157*
10:45, *136, 157, 179*
11:9-10, *135*
11:11, *135*
13:8, *171*
13:21-23, *181*
14:22-25, *179*
14:24, *136*
14:25, *136, 170*
14:61-62, *179*
14:62, *156*
15:34, *135*
15:42, *148*

Luke
1:68, *155*
2:32, *156*
4:16-21, *135*
6:20-21, *141*
6:24-25, *141*
7:19-20, *104*
9:1-6, *139*
9:1—19:44, *124*
11:51, *202, 205*
12:31-32, *180*
15:2, *245*
16:19-31, *141*
16:31, *207*

21:11, *171*
21:23-26, *171*
22:1, *148*
22:17-20, *21*
22:18, *170*
22:28-30, *180*
22:30, *133, 135*
23:54, *148*
24, *207*
24:44, *32, 201, 202, 272*

John
1, *278*
1:1-18, *65, 186*
1:40, *148*
3:13, *186*
3:24, *148*
4:5, *147*
4:44, *148*
5:18, *179, 186*
5:39, *186*
6:39, *163*
6:40, *163*
6:44, *163*
6:51-58, *187*
6:54, *163*
6:67, *148*
6:68-69, *191*
6:71, *148*
7:12, *179*
7:38, *202*
7:47, *179*
8:58, *222*
9:22, *186*
10:22, *147*
10:30, *186*
10:33, *179, 186*
10:35, *186*
10:36, *186*
11:1-2, *148*
11:4, *155*
11:25, *163*
11:40, *155*
12:42, *186*
12:43, *155*
13:1-20, *187*
14:2, *186*
14:6, *186*

14:25-26, *187*
15:10, *248*
16:2, *186*
16:13, *187*
16:33, *186*
18:12-40, *187*
18:13, *147*
18:28, *148*
18:36, *109*
19:7, *179, 186*
19:14, *148*
19:17, *187*
19:31, *148*
19:38-42, *187*

Acts
1:1, *274*
1:3, *155*
1:6, *180*
1:6-8, *173*
2, *160*
2:14-41, *217*
2:15-17, *161*
2:17, *161*
2:17—3:26, *173*
2:36, *179*
2:42, *178*
3:13, *155*
3:20, *180*
5:30, *179*
5:35, *150*
6, *172*
6:7, *157*
7:32, *155*
7:55, *155*
8:3, *150*
8:12, *155*
9, *150*
9:1, *150*
9:15, *146*
10:36, *157*
11:19-24, *181*
12:24, *157*
13:9-11, *149*
13:16-41, *149*
13:46-48, *150, 156*
13:47, *173*
14:15-17, *149*

List of Contributors

G. K. Beale is Kenneth T. Wessner Professor of Biblical Studies, Wheaton College and Graduate School.

Stephen G. Dempster is Stuart E. Murray Associate Professor of Religious Studies, Atlantic Baptist University.

Ted M. Dorman is professor of theology, Taylor University.

William J. Dumbrell is former dean of graduate studies and professor of Old Testament and biblical theology, Moore Theological College and Regent College.

Stephen E. Fowl is professor of theology, Loyola College.

Daniel P. Fuller is professor of hermeneutics, emeritus, Fuller Theological Seminary.

Graeme L. Goldsworthy is a former lecturer in Old Testament, biblical theology and hermeneutics at Moore Theological College.

Scott J. Hafemann is Gerald F. Hawthorne Professor of New Testament Greek and Exegesis, Wheaton College and Graduate School.

Paul R. House is professor of Old Testament, Wheaton College and Graduate School.

Andreas J. Köstenberger is professor of New Testament, Southeastern Baptist Theological Seminary.

Nicholas Perrin is a research fellow at Westminster Abbey.

John H. Sailhamer is professor of Old Testament, Southeastern Baptist Theological Seminary.

Richard Schultz is Carl and Hudson T. Armerding Professor of Biblical Studies, Wheaton College.

James M. Scott is professor of New Testament, Trinity Western University.

Christopher R. Seitz is professor of Old Testament, St. Mary's College, University of St. Andrews.

Peter Stuhlmacher is professor of New Testament, emeritus, University of Tübingen.

Brian G. Toews is professor of Old Testament, Philadelphia Biblical University.

M. Jay Wells is an independent scholar in Loma, Colorado.

Gerald H. Wilson is professor of Old Testament, Azusa Pacific University.